Tragic Spirits

Tragic Spirits

Shamanism, Memory, and Gender in Contemporary Mongolia

MANDUHAI BUYANDELGER

The University of Chicago Press
Chicago and London

Manduhai Buyandelger is associate professor of anthropology at the
Massachusetts Institute of Technology.

The University of Chicago Press, Chicago 60637
The University of Chicago Press, Ltd., London
© 2013 by The University of Chicago
All rights reserved. Published 2013.
Printed in the United States of America

22 21 20 19 18 17 16 15 14 13   1 2 3 4 5

ISBN-13: 978-0-226-08655-2 (cloth)
ISBN-13: 978-0-226-08656-9 (paper)
ISBN-13: 978-0-226-01309-1 (e-book)

Library of Congress Cataloging-in-Publication Data

Buyandelger, Manduhai.
  Tragic spirits : shamanism, memory, and gender in contemporary Mongolia /
Manduhai Buyandelger.
    pages ; cm
  Includes bibliographical references and index.
  ISBN 978-0-226-08655-2 (cloth : alkaline paper)—ISBN 978-0-226-
08656-9 (paperback : alkaline paper)—ISBN 978-0-226-01309-1 (e-book)
  1. Shamanism—Mongolia—Baian—Uul Sum—History—20th century.
  2. Shamanism—Russia (Federation)—Buriatiia—History—20th century.
  3. Buriats—Religion—History—20th century.   4. Buriats—Economic
conditions—20th century.   5. Neoliberalism—Mongolia—Religious
aspects.   6. Communism and religion—Mongolia—History.
  7. Communism and religion—Russia (Federation)—Buriatiia—History.
  8. Baian—Uul sum (Mongolia)—Religious life and customs.   9. Baian—Uul
sum (Mongolia)—Economic conditions—20th century.   1. Title.
  GN635.M66B89 2013
  299'.42—dc23

                                                        2013014427

♾ This paper meets the requirements of ANSI/NISO Z39.48-1992
(Permanence of Paper).

For my mother,
Buyandelger Menget,
with love and appreciation

CONTENTS

ACKNOWLEDGMENTS

My deepest gratitude goes to the people of Bayan-Uul and its neighboring districts in Mongolia for sharing stories and meals with me, inviting me to their homes and rituals, and adopting me as their daughter, sister, and cousin. Their generous assistance helped me to learn more about their culture, lives, and shamanic practices than I could ever fully discuss in a single book. I apologize beforehand to anyone who may find that a subject particularly dear to his or her heart is insufficiently represented here. I plan on giving fair treatment to the rest of my field notes in other writings.

In order to protect the privacy of individuals who appear in the book, I have used pseudonyms throughout. Some individuals expressed their wish to appear under their real names. But after much hesitation, I chose to maintain the anonymity of all my sources. Because origin spirits are part of an individual's identity, I have used pseudonyms for them as well.

To my sorrow, several of my older friends who appear in this book passed away within a few years after my departure. The time that I spent in their homes, filled with engaging conversations, laughter, and dramatic rituals, was truly some of the happiest in my life. I am tremendously sorry to have lost them and saddened that they will not see the fruits of their generosity. But I hope that the book will pay homage to them in some ways.

My field research was generously supported by grants from the Wenner-Gren Foundation for Anthropological Research, the IDRF Social Science Research Foundation, the Matsushita Foundation, and grants from Harvard University. For my writing, I received a small grant from the Soros Foundation and several grants from Harvard University, including a resident fellowship at the Center for the Study of World Religions, also known as "God's Motel." I am thankful to Lawrence E. Sullivan, the center's director at the time, for making my stay a truly special experience.

I owe my interest in shamanism to my undergraduate advisor at the National University of Mongolia, Dulam Sendenjav. He encouraged me to pursue opportunities abroad, even looking for a scholarship for me through the German Academic Exchange Service (DAAD) and securing me a spot in a much-coveted German-language program. I am endlessly grateful to him even though I chose to seek my intellectual niche elsewhere. The enthusiasm and help of Shagdarsuren Tsedev and Dagvadorj Choisuren helped me to remain in academia during the years of the country's food rationing without my embarking on "suitcase trading" to make a living.

The Department of Anthropology at Harvard University provided generous and intellectually stimulating guidance and valuable camaraderie. My colleagues, Stanley Tambiah, Mary Steedly, and Rubie Watson, provided me with consistent advice, generous feedback, and much more. Dr. Tambiah tirelessly nourished my brain and appetite with the fine arts of anthropological deliberation and his culinary adventures. Dr. Watson read an earlier draft of the entire manuscript and throughout the writing process made sure that I kept to my deadlines without losing my mind. Dr. Steedly was there for me at all critical moments throughout my writing while consistently teaching me to think creatively about ethnography and writing, pushing the limits of my thinking, and encouraging me to probe what anthropology could aspire to at its best. Engseng Ho is a model scholar and mentor who taught me, among countless other things, how to combine intricate detailed analysis with narratives of a larger scope. Conversations with Smita Lahiri, an exquisite thinker, greatly aided the book and my life beyond it. I extend my gratitude to Michael Herzfeld for his steadfast and kind help, generosity, and much-appreciated humor. I thank Nur Yalman for his exceedingly generous support and nuanced and empathetic teaching. James "Woody" Watson, Arthur Kleinman, Steve Caton, Jennifer Cole, and Byron Good influenced this project in numerous ways and generously extended their valuable advice. My heartfelt thanks go to my dear friends and writing comrades Vanessa Fong, Erica James, Nicole Newendorp, and Sonja Plesset. My colleagues Erica Evasdottir, Saroja Dorairajoo, Haley Duschinski, Aykan Erdemir, Ellen McGill, Young-a Park, Wen-ching Sung, Michelle Tisdel-Flikke, Tahmima Anam, and Irving Chan Johnson read and commented on various parts of the manuscript. Melissa Caldwell read the entire manuscript and suggested the best ways to transform it from a dissertation into a book.

Special thanks go to my editor, David Brent, whose excitement and enthusiasm about this project transformed my life. He has been superbly patient while I worked at the speed of a turtle and failed to meet numerous deadlines for production. I thank Piers Vitebsky for his exceedingly generous suggestions for improving the book, and an anonymous reviewer for nuanced and considered commentary. Priya Nelson's kind and cheerful help were absolutely crucial at the most difficult stages of the manuscript. Many special thanks to Ryo Yamaguchi and Erik Carlson and Yo Barbara Norton for her meticulous copy editing and suggestions.

As an anthropologist specializing in Mongolia and also a native of that country, I owe a special debt to Caroline Humphrey for her exemplary and dedicated research on Buryats and other Mongols. During my visit to Cambridge, England, in 2010 she graciously allowed me to peruse her extensive collection of rare books on Buryats. Without my dear friend and colleague Christopher Kaplonski, a senior anthropologist specializing in Mongolia, this book would have never been written. I need countless rebirths in order to thank him adequately. I benefited from memorable conversations and correspondence with several spectacular anthropologists of Mongolia: Rebecca Empson, Morten Pedersen, and Katherine Swancutt. For his nuanced translation of the important term *shanar*, I am grateful to the Japanese anthropologist Ippei Shimamura, Dr. Khatagin Akim for giving me photos of Khambin Ovoo burials, and Dr. Munhdalain Rinchin for helping with the materials on state violence and rehabilitation. I thank Judith Hangartner and Margery Mandelstam Balzer for giving me valuable suggestions in revising the manuscript.

My colleagues at the Massachusetts Institute of Technology have given me all the support one could ever wish for. Stefan Helmreich's comments helped to deepen my arguments on memory and history, as well as issues of mobility. My department chair, Susan Silbey, has supported my project above and beyond my expectations. I thank her for organizing a daylong conference on my book, and the scholars who devoted their time and energy to the discussion: Pamela Balinger, Julie Hemment, Laurel Kendall, Kim Gutschow, and my colleagues Heather Paxson, Jean Jackson, Erica James, and Graham Jones. Esther Cervantes and Donna La Rue expeditiously edited and proofread various versions of the manuscript. My friend Khishigsuren Yadamsuren in Mongolia gave me a most thoughtful gift: commissioning the book's historic and contemporary maps, for which I had fruitlessly searched the world over. None of the individuals who helped me are responsible for any mistakes and weaknesses of the book. They are entirely my own.

My friends Alimaa and Chaganbaatar and their children have given me unforgettable vacations of laughter, lollipops, and the steamed dumplings known as *buuz* during my loneliest periods of writing. I am forever grateful to my American mother, Melinda Mills Lee, for her all-around kindness and for listening so tirelessly, together with her friend Bill Beans, to my deliberations over different aspects of this project.

Finally, my family has been an integral part of the project. I am grateful to my extended family in Mongolia, especially to my aunt, Dr. Suren Nanjid, and her two sons, my cousins Tulga Byambajav and Gantulga Byambajav, for taking care of our much-beloved late grandmother, Nanjid Magsar. Their caregiving (however expected, in our Mongolian culture of filial piety) gave me a peace of mind that enabled me to concentrate on my doctorate in the United States.

I thank my husband, Jesse Tawney, for his unwavering emotional commitment and consistent support of my work. A trip to Florida's great sunshine during a particularly long and dark New England winter was crucial in allowing me to regain my energy and complete the first full draft. He took care of our daughter Eevee (Evelyn Buyan Tawney) on the countless weekends and weeknights as I made my endless revisions. My mother, Buyandelger Menget, laid out the foundations for this project and made critical contributions to it, about which the reader will learn in the introduction. I dedicate this book to her with love and appreciation for too many things to mention, among them raising my baby, and for giving me a wonderful childhood home that, on a single mother's income, she managed to fill up with books from all over. She is my hero and a model of profound compassion and no end of erudition. Without her sharing with me the works of Hans Christian Andersen, Mikhail Lermontov, Prosper Mérimée, Alexander Pushkin, Chinghiz Aitmatov, and Oscar Wilde, to name just a few, I would never have dreamed of learning new languages—or of embarking on the writing of a book, for that matter.

As one's memory always has many gaps, I am certain there must be individuals whose contributions I have forgotten to acknowledge. For that I beg their forgiveness.

MPRP	Mongolian People's Revolutionary Party
MPR	Mongolian People's Republic
CF	collective farm
SF	state farm
DP	Democratic Party
IMF	International Monetary Fund
ADB	Asian Development Bank
H1	History One
H2	History 2

The great linguistic variations among the people known as Buryats depend on their location, neighboring groups, historical specificity, and ethnic origin. Most Buryats in Mongolia, especially those of the older generation, speak both the Buryat dialect and the official state language, which is the dialect of the Khalkhas, the ethnolinguistic majority in central Mongolia. The Buryat dialect in various parts in Mongolia also tends to vary in its degree of incorporation of Khalkha. In Dornod province, the Buryats of Bayan-Uul district speak a Buryat dialect that has been influenced by the dialect of the Khalkha, sometimes mixing the two, owing to the fact that it borders other Khalkha districts. The Buryat dialect in some other Buryat districts of Dornod province (e.g., Bayan-Dun, Tsagan Ovoo, etc.) has been less strongly influenced by the Khalkha Mongols, even though most people there also speak both dialects.

Since the Bayan-Uul Buryats use both Buryat and Mongolian words, I adhered neither to standard Buryat nor to standard Mongolian transliteration, but have used instead a transliteration of the local vernacular. In theory, when the Khalkhas use *ts, ch*, and *s* (for example, in *tsagan, chuluu, and suu*), the Buryats use *s, sh*, and *h* (*sagan, shuluu,* and *huu*). But in Bayan-Uul this rule is not followed strictly. For instance, many use the Khalkha pronunciation *tsagan* (*sagan* in Buryat) but employ the Buryat pronunciation *degel* (*deel* in Khalkha); the variation can occur from one conversation or even one sentence to the next.

As for Mongolian words, I transliterated them according to modern-day pronunciation. That is because contemporary Mongolia officially uses the Cyrillic alphabet, which does not always catch the specific phonetics of the language (and is not meant to do so), and because transliterations of traditional Mongolian script differ greatly from transcriptions of modern Mongolian speech.

In the glossary I included only those words and terms that are repeated throughout the book; I omitted those that I used rarely, for which I instead provided an explanation, a translation, or both in the text.

Wherever possible I used the English word for clarity and the reader's convenience.

The Return of the Suppressed

Chugging along on an old Soviet motorcycle I had hired for the day, the driver and I leave a rural town called Bayan-Uul (Rich Mountain).[1] We pass through the town's streets, which are bordered by tall wooden fences that separate individual families' plots of land from one another. Through the narrow spaces between the planks one can catch glimpses of *gers* (round felt tents) and log cabins. We pass the ruins of a machine repair center, a defunct power plant, and some odd pieces of tractors and trucks rusting on the outskirts of town. These are the remnants of the state farm, the town's only means of livelihood since the 1950s, which was dismantled in 1993 as a part of the neoliberal policy of "shock therapy" demanded by international monetary institutions in exchange for qualifying Mongolia to receive loans and subsidies. After a few minutes, winter grassland—yellow and dusted with powdery snow—stretches toward the horizon. The dirt road, bumpy in summers, is packed with snow in winters, making the ride smoother. Riding into the cold wind burns our skin, so we wrap our faces with scarves to prevent frostbite from the minus-twenty (Celsius) temperatures.

After four summers of traveling in the nomadic countryside from 1996 to 1999, I am finally spending a full year, 1999–2000, in the Bayan-Uul district of Dornod province in northeastern Mongolia. Following decades of suppression under state socialism, coupled with Soviet domination (1921–1989), public shamanic practices among the Buryats have been proliferating. Almost every family I know has a member who has been initiated as a shaman in order to appease the sudden influx of *ug garval* (origin spirits), the returned souls of deceased shaman ancestors.[2] They have returned, people say, to take revenge for having been largely forgotten during socialism.

I am rushing to meet Luvsan, a shaman, who is holding a ritual of propitiating an origin spirit for a client. Like most spirits abandoned during socialism, this one is impatient in his demands for propitiation. Luvsan's winter home is about thirty-six kilometers from the center of Bayan-Uul, where I stay in between my trips to the countryside. During my motorcycle journey, I pass no people or vehicles: almost the entire country has been deprived of oil, which was usually imported from Russia. We pass *ovoos*—mountain cairns made from piles of rocks that serve as the dwelling places of landscape spirits. We toss crumbs of bread to them as we pass by but stop at the largest one and contribute some rocks to the pile.

Over dirt tracks that, without written signs, merge and split again, we approach Luvsan's valley. From the back seat of the motorcycle, I see the visitors' old Soviet jeep parked next to Luvsan's ger, fences enclosing herds of sheep and cattle, a storage cabin, and Luvsan's only son's log house, where he lives with his wife and children. Luvsan's grandson, a boy of seven dressed in a sheepskin-lined *degel* (traditional robe), wants to wrestle with me whenever I visit. Upon seeing us, he stops playing with the calves and runs to the ger to tell the adults. The door of the ger opens up, and Luvsan's son, a man in his early forties, emerges to keep the barking dogs from attacking the driver and me.

Inside the ger, Luvsan greets me with an exclamation and orders his daughter-in-law to steam *buuz* (dumplings) for me. I take off my grandmother's prized degel, which is insulated with snow leopard fur, and join the daughter-in-law, who is quietly making noodle soup for the visitors. Luvsan's disciple, a tiny woman in her forties named Tsendem, is setting up the ritual offering table with butter candles and sweets for the spirits. A family of seven has arrived from another district to learn the reasons for their misfortunes. They hold their breath while Luvsan divines with his red dice and consults with aged *sutras*—sacred Buddhist books written in Tibetan. Modern biomedicine has not been able to relieve or stop the illnesses and deaths that have been afflicting this family. And despite all their hard work, they are still impoverished. According to Luvsan, this situation indicates that there is an origin spirit who has been abandoned without worship. Since the family has never encountered a spirit before, Luvsan has arranged for Tsendem to be possessed by the newly found origin spirit so that he can converse with it on behalf of the family.

The bittersweet smoke of burning *ganga* (wild thyme)—to attract spirits—indicates the start of a ritual. Tsendem's clear voice, accompanied by the deep rhythms of a drum, is summoning the celestial deities of the Buryat shamanic pantheon, her own origin spirits, and the local landscape spirits to the "banquet table." She then enlivens her paraphernalia—mirrors, headdress, antelope-skin gown, and capes—with her origin spirits, after which Luvsan and his son help her to put them on. Only after armoring her body against the attacks of the malevolent spirits who constantly lurk does Tsendem finally summon the client family's origin spirit. She drums faster, sings louder, gets up off the stool, and begins spinning around. We all stand alongside the beds lining the ger's round walls. Tsendem spins so fast that all the metal-tipped silk straps ("snakes") hanging from her headdress and cape fly out into a big circle around her. She stops spinning but keeps drumming, slowly. She hunches her back, drops her head, and whistles a sad melody. Seeing that she is possessed by a spirit, Luvsan comes closer to her and inquires politely: "*Burhshuul* [This is term of endearment for a spirit!]. Who are you? Where do you come from? Please have a seat on our snow-white lambskin rug." In response to the greetings, a scratchy voice emanating from behind the swinging black tassels of a headdress responds in song—with a curse:

> The stupid puppets of flesh,
> The empty skulls without the traces of the past,
> Cursed by illness, afflicted by misfortunes, with little to eat and drink,
> How *good* have your lives been so far?[3]

Luvsan beckons the eldest man of the visiting family, Dorji, and tells him to bow to the spirit. Dorji, who has never seen a shamanic ritual, is trembling in silence. Luvsan then calmly leads the conversation:

> Burhshuul, please forgive us!
> Times were hard, the state was harsh.
> Your beloved children of later generations
> Have all come to worship you . . .

The spirit interrupts Luvsan and sings angrily, pointing to Dorji with a drumstick:

> Diviners and lamas inquired about a mountain spirit in your lineage
> . . . You hastened to reply "no," without knowing the truth.
> You rejected and abandoned me!
> Without food and drink, eating flesh and drinking blood,
> I wandered in wilderness and mountains,
> Abandoned by my children.

I hovered as a black crow over you, hoping that you would notice me.
I blocked your only daughter's fortunes.
I turned your red brain into dullness and confusion . . .

Dorji sobs. Luvsan pleads with the spirit, explaining that no one could worship the spirit because the state had suppressed all religious practices. The family, he begs, needs help from the spirit to alleviate their misfortunes.

It all began around 1990. The dissolution of the socialist state, the collapse of the economy, and neoliberal changes all took place randomly, chaotically, and without much warning. People who went into small tradesmanship and shopkeeping were extremely lucky if they managed to find their place in a new economic order. But for the majority of Mongolians, even their best efforts and hardest work would bring them very little, if anything at all. Like most in Mongolia, Dorji's family was wrecked by what people called the "storm of the market economy." The collapse of socialism in 1990 and the subsequent implementation of neoliberal reforms, which entailed a dismantling of the state and collective farms, led to the destitution of entire regions. Without jobs, some of Dorji's family members stayed in town, expanded their vegetable garden, opened a little shop, and traded goods from Russia and China. Others stayed in the countryside to increase their livestock, hunt gazelles, and trap marmots. But all to no avail. Subsisting on potatoes and cabbage, children seemed to have stopped growing. Every year a family member fell ill and died. In response to the request for help, the spirit revealed his identity and why he harassed them:

I am Baldan's son Sodnom, a shaman with the title of *zaarin*,
    who died at the age of ninety-six.
I am your ancestor in your father's lineage.
I am the lord of the mountain in the Aga steppes.
You neglected me. Why should I help you?
You never acknowledged my existence.
Why should I accept your offerings? . . . Go away . . .

The spirit turns away from Dorji, who is still sobbing.

Dorji says that he lost his parents as a small child during the political violence of the late 1930s that swept throughout Mongolia (replicating that in the Soviet Union) and thus had no chance to learn about his origins. The family begs the spirit for forgiveness, bows, and promises to worship him forever. After a few minutes of appeasement, a sip of tea, and a gulp of liquor, the spirit begins to calm down. He agrees to look after the family but requests the sacrifice of a sheep the following year. He finally takes off by spinning and beating a distancing rhythm on the drum. Someone throws a handful of ganga on the cinders in the metal plate in order to produce more smoke so that spirit will leave gently, without hurting the shaman. Tsendem drops into a chair, blows her nose, and wipes her face, which is drenched in tears and sweat. Dorji continues to weep; he has lived all his life—he was now in his sixties—unaware of his past. This was the beginning of his family's attempt to grapple with the forces of incipient capitalism on a more metaphysical level, beyond the practical activities of trading, herding, and gardening.

Dorji's family was not alone in dealing with a sudden influx of angry origin spirits following the end of socialism and the arrival of incipient neoliberal capitalism starting in the early 1990s. Families in Bayan-Uul and the neighboring area could not keep up with the origin spirits' requests for propitiations mediated by shamans. But since most people were unfamiliar with shamanism, they constantly verified the spirits' authenticity and the shamans' credibility by soliciting alternative opinions from multiple shamans and staging additional rituals, thus contributing to a proliferation of public shamanic practices. After my initial trip, I kept coming back to these people because I did not want to miss bearing witness to their experiences in encountering their past, and the challenges and frustrations of dealing with the repercussions of erasure and suppression by a totalitarian regime. As I continued to follow the shamans and their clients, I came gradually to realize that the fragmented stories of spirits were beginning to compile themselves into a tragic and shifting history of the Buryats' distant past. Hence, this book tells the story of how these marginalized ethnic Buryats' attempts to deal with their ongoing misfortunes by propitiating their forgotten origin spirits has expanded almost inadvertently into a cultural production of history.

The Buryats about whom this book is written live in northeastern Mongolia, in Dornod province. Of the four Buryat districts—Tsagan Ovoo, Bayan-Dun, Dashbalbar, and Bayan-Uul—the last, with five thousand inhabitants, is the largest. Most Buryats in the area are the descendants of migrants from Russian Buryatiya who came to Mongolia to escape the turmoil of the Russian Civil War in 1905 and the Bolshevik Revolution in 1917. In Mongolia these Buryats were persecuted harshly during the political violence that swept the country in the 1930s. Since then the Buryats had been politically marginalized with respect to the mainstream Khalkhas. At the same time, as a part of the Mongolian state, the Buryats shared the ex-

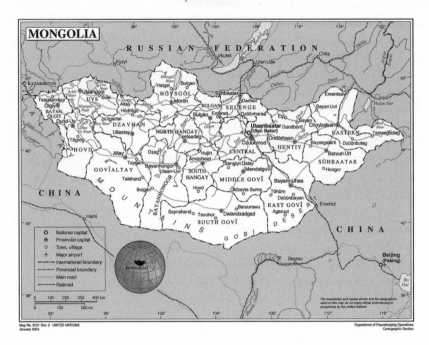

Map 1. Map of Mongolia

periences of other Mongolians: collectivization in the 1930s through the 1950s, cultural campaigns and modernization in the 1960s and 1970s, and, finally, the collapse of socialism and the arrival of neoliberal capitalism in the 1990s.

The book explores the gendered politics, economics, and circumstances of shamanic proliferation as well as the narratives of spirits conveyed by shamans. A gendered lens helped me to explore deeper relations among the state, memory, and shamans' power. I have been especially interested in how gender influences shamans' power and their ability to make and distribute memory. For instance, in chapter 4 I explore why certain kinds of origin spirits are well remembered, while others are remembered only partially or forgotten. And chapter 5 deals with the degree to which the social order, the state, and economic conditions influence the quest for power by male and female shamans. To a limited extent, then, this book also offers a study of the state—its functions, policies, ideologies, presences, and absences in the lives of the people during the eras of both socialism and neoliberal capitalism.

In the 1990s hardly anyone could have imagined what the dissolution of socialism would entail. As far as I know, even among the country's political leadership and international consultants from the International Monetary Fund (IMF), the World Bank, and the Asian Development Bank (ADB), no one predicted (or they chose to remain silent) that a drastic implementation of neoliberal reforms (privatization of state assets, ending government subsidies, and liberalizing prices) would lead to a complete devastation of entire settlements and towns. Former bosses and supervisors almost automatically gained control of the state's resources, while the majority of workers were laid off with nothing but vouchers and bonds that made little sense to them.[4] In 1993, as a part of the neoliberal policy of "shock therapy," Bayan-Uul's state farm—the only source of jobs in the area—was dismantled, and its livestock and machinery were distributed to individual families. Within two months Bayan-Uul had changed from a prosperous state farm town into a ghost town, where the majority of inhabitants suddenly found themselves in the middle of nowhere and without any immediate means of earning a living. They were forced to eat their portion of livestock or exchange it for other necessities. Left to survive on the ruins of their state farm, many Buryats worked hard to find new ways of making a living. Yet, like Dorji's family, most endeavors met with little success, and families were plagued by illnesses and other misfortunes.

The ubiquity, complexity, and continuity of the shamanic rituals in the 1990s signal the depth of people's anxiety and uncertainty about their past and future. After the decades of relative predictability and certainty of socialism, suddenly people were now overwhelmed by a sense of epistemic crisis and total chaos. Most people's lives seemed to be nothing but a string of emergencies: fighting wildfires almost barehanded, saving their loved ones from accidents and illnesses, risking their lives and safety by stopping fistfights in their extended family, or running around the neighborhood trying to find someone with money to lend. People often interpreted their situations as a result of having become the target of some kind of unknown spiritual forces nestled in the bodies and spaces around them.

The suspicion and hostility toward each other that people experienced in Bayan-Uul have many similarities with the contexts of witchcraft in some African countries.[5] Witchcraft signals a condition of acute "spiritual insecurity" (Ashforth 2001) in which "life must be lived in terms of a presumption of malice" (Ashforth 2005:313). A similar kind of unspoken rule operates among the Buryats: neighbors, coworkers, and acquaintances can be potential sources of harm, and shamans' powers can be interpreted in myriad ways, including as the manipulation of people around them.[6] However, if in witchcraft "a meaning of misfortune is sought in the actions of ill-disposed people nearby" (Ashforth 2000:253), the Buryat shamans also interpret misfortune as the result of the forgetting of the past that is rooted in the contexts of oppression and resistance, and in tragic events associated with a loss of ancestral lands, displacement, and violence by more powerful states and empires. By placing misfortune beyond isolated individual accidents, mistakes, and local rivalries, the Buryat shamans limit the further disintegration of local communities. However, as the present book demonstrates, the influence of shamanism on the life of the community—its social relations, gender dynamics, and material life—is complex and diverse. Sometimes shamanism can aggravate existing anxieties or even create new ones.

In this study, shamanic clients and audiences are crucial actors who extend the work of shamans, often in unexpected ways. The book demonstrates how shamanism proliferates not only due to a belief in the supernatural and remembering the past. Forgetting also made additional room for creative imagination. Besides the actual forgetting (the limits of which are impossible to define), the belief in forgetting and erasure is so pervasive that it creates more anxiety about the past.

Yet shamanism is much more than a way of dealing with postsocialist transformation. If it were just that, then most people could most likely get by by soliciting help from Buddhist practices, which offer many services for dealing with misfortune. And unlike the elaborate and expensive shamanic rituals, the Buddhist ones are short, compact, and inexpensive, and they require no sacrifices of sheep or other livestock. While the Buryats do solicit help from Buddhist practitioners, they also inevitably employ shamans. And thus, I explore what Crapanzano (1977) refers to as "the multiple significances" of shamanism by looking at the internal mechanisms, politics, and circumstances of shamanism, and the discourses and cultural practices produced by shamans and their clients.

The book engages with several bodies of anthropological literature, including those on shamanism, the supernatural, neoliberal capitalism, gender, and postsocialism. I discuss the relevant literature at appropriate points throughout the book in order to show individuals' experiences in dealing with an ad hoc mixture of multiple incomplete systems, such as those left over from disintegrating socialism, partial capitalism, and poorly designed neoliberal projects. I discuss the often incongruous, antagonistic, and contradictory elements and practices that come from newly emplaced as well as disintegrating systems. Together they create unique, unsystematic, and fleeting experiences for the people with whom I lived and traveled in Bayan-Uul. One of the most notable features of postsocialism in Mongolia has been the lack of continuity, repetition, and routine in most spheres of life, from the everyday economic supply to government policy. Instead, people live their lives in the midst of constant crises, unpredictability, and making do. I argue that in Mongolia, postsocialism and neoliberal capitalism—both having their constitutive components—are intertwined parts of everyday life, and it would be meaningless to isolate one from the other when discussing people's lives. The kind of postsocialism that has evolved in Mongolia in the twenty-first century cannot be imagined without understanding the impact of neoliberal capitalism on the country, and vice versa. What has emerged in Mongolia is a mixture of leftover (and re-recreated) elements of socialism, an incipient neoliberal capitalism, and some traditional practices.[7] However, it is also necessary to note that the capitalism that came to Mongolia and other postsocialist and post-Soviet areas at the turn of the millennium assumed a more hegemonic stance than did previous versions. At least in Mongolia, people welcomed the capitalist order as a savior, rescuing them from the failed socialist order, and as a system of fair competition and equal opportunity.

Instead of gaining economic and other opportunities to rebuild their lives, most people fell into a life of endemic poverty, uncertainty, and ongoing crisis. This book shows that even though the Buryats have been utilizing their shamanism to deal with the anxieties brought up by such drastic changes, their shamanism does not become a part of capitalism, nor is it subsumed by the new economic system. On the contrary, the Buryats, who are seeking their place during the chaos of postsocialism and incipient capitalism, end up subsumed by shamanism. Owing to the region's isolation and the country's economic instability, on one hand, and to shamanic competition and mutual censorship in a tightly knit community, on the other, shamanism has had little opportunity to develop into what Comaroff and Comaroff call an "identity business" (2009:74)—an organized and sustained "rediscovery" of one's "tradition" and its commodification to produce capital.[8] Instead, my overarching argument is that shamanism uses the freedoms and anxieties of capitalism to generate its own economy, which produces not material profits, but individual memories and communal histories. Shamanism demonstrates that the so-called transition to capitalism is not about "the universalization of capital" (Chakrabarty 2000:71), and that a capitalist economy is only one among many complex and intersecting "life-worlds" (ibid.). The Buryats' pursuit of capitalism neither actualizes it nor makes them into proper capitalists, but it literally and metaphorically feeds the shamans who produce historical narratives. What started as an attempt to deal with anxieties brought on by an economic crisis has transformed into a cultural production of the suppressed past that brings little if any benefits to capitalism or overall economic growth in the area.

The stories of spirits in the ritual arena often contain crucial information and insights for solving clients' problems, but at other times they have none. Regardless of their relevance and instrumentality, the stories remain in the community beyond the ritual and circulate as a part of communal and individual memories.

While the narratives of origin spirits convey the tragedies of war, displacement, and loss of loved ones in the distant past, the stories of contemporary Buryats about their struggles to survive the dissolution of socialism seemed to continue the genealogy of misfortunes from their origin spirits. And therefore, by weaving together the narratives of shamans about the Buryats' distant past during their possession by origin spirits and the contemporary stories of struggle to survive the ongoing crisis, I build a shifting history of the Buryats through colonialism, socialism, and neoliberal capitalism that differs from the colonial and state histories. In that sense, this book is about the politics of shamanic practices in remaking the past after their suppression and the history that shamanism yields, as well as being my own narrative about the Buryats. What follows in the rest of the introduction is an explanation of the main questions about capitalism and shamanism, memory and forgetting, gender and power, and belief and authenticity that reverberate throughout the book. I then discuss my fieldwork, the people, and the circumstances of doing fieldwork among shamans in rural nomadic Mongolia.

Recreating the Past

With the collapse of socialism starting in 1989, Mongolia adopted the principles of democracy and a market economy. The Soviet Union, which had subsidized 30 percent of the Mongolian economy, stopped sending aid, and the country fell into a deep recession. Several Mongolian delegations traveled to the United States and Europe to solicit aid and advice for dealing with the economic crisis. In 1991 the IMF, the ADB, and the World Bank all admitted Mongolia to membership and agreed to make loans to it. In return, they imposed on Mongolia certain programs for macroeconomic reform that included the liberalization of prices, the termination of government subsidies, opening the country to foreign trade, and the rapid privatization of state assets.[9]

But by failing to provide citizens with much-needed knowledge about market economies, adequate infrastructure, legal frameworks, and start-up support, these neoliberal reforms undid their own goal: they failed to turn rural nomads into property owners capable of caring for themselves. Instead of bringing the expected capital, the reforms brought lingering economic devastation to the majority of the population, which the Buryats explain as revenge taken by origin spirits for their having been forgotten.

Many families became engaged in shamanic rituals hoping to find ways to lessen their misfortunes and to engage in and benefit from capitalism. From what I have seen, however, little has improved in people's material lives over the years. Capitalism was a trigger for the Buryats to return to shamanic practices, but shamanism did not bolster capitalism in return. Most devout Buryats expect that once the angry spirits stop harming them, their livelihoods will improve. In the meantime they have had to deal with an uncontrollable flock of spirits and an abundance of stories. Capitalism, with its uncertainty, chaos, and instability, led the Buryats to seek shamanism. But shamanism in turn redirected the people's economic pursuits into a cultural production of the past. Here capitalism serves, but shamanism thrives.

The Buryats' engagement with shamanism is not a willful illusion. For many people, the mere possibility of gaining knowledge that was different from the official state version, a chance to question and to encounter and deal with ambiguity, marked a break from socialism's epistemic constraints and an opening up to something newer and freer. Simple curiosity should not be underestimated, as well as doubt and a desire to experiment and test. And some people, even the ones who disbelieved shamans and found spirits a sheer fantasy, found no harm in attending the rituals and even sponsoring one "just in case."

Such actions, in the aggregate, have resulted in an intriguing situation. On one hand, the Buryats use capitalism's entrepreneurial freedom and the end of state suppression of religion to revive their shamanism and reconstruct their past. On the other, shamanism has not become a part of capitalism and created monetary profit, which is what many people want from their engagement with it, as either shamans or clients. Instead of bringing good fortune and the power to attract money, shamanism enables its adherents to build a mobile history through remembering. Shamanism has its own economy, which is different from that of capitalism. The two do not merge; rather, they are mutually constitutive. The Buryats, like other Mongols, desire for-profit capitalism in order to pursue material enrichment, but they end up participating more in the shamanic production of history than in the capitalist economy.

Many scholars, including Mauss (1967), Bataille (1985, 1989), Godelier (1999), Baudrillard (1975), and Sahlins (1972), have demonstrated that Western capitalism is only one kind of economy, and that many economic activities go on outside and in opposition to it, such as those of gifts, festivals, and rituals. However, as Yang (2000) notes, these authors critiqued capitalism by looking at so-called primitive or precapitalist economies, and they did so also in order to highlight the variety of other economies. Chakrabarty (2000), however, explores the limits of capitalism from the inside, from Western or Westernizing societies, and shows that even in its homeland, capital, which is supposed to generate more capital through the medium of money, cannot encompass the activities that produce nonmaterial goods, such as playing the piano. In this way Chakrabarty shows the multiplicity of economies in the homeland of capitalism. Located in postsocialist Mongolia, this book shows the multiplicity of economies by bringing in a rather different context and economic formation, both outside so-called primitive and Western societies. I show shamanism's interaction with newly arriving capitalism without singling out any of its known characteristics: as a tool for subversion, resistance, or complying with capitalism. Instead, shamanism has its own stand in relation to capitalism.

The fact that shamanism is an alternative to capitalism does not make the two mutually exclusive. Chakrabarty's ideas help to recognize the complex ways in which capitalism influences the Buryats' engagement with shamanism and vice versa. Chakrabarty notes that while in many places people might be aware of the limits of capitalism, and some even live in an alternative system, their thinking is influenced by notions of Marxist epistemology and capitalism. Indeed, in Mongolia capitalism is not seen as a part of multiple life-worlds but is instead envisaged as a totalizing and domineering system that is expected to take over the socialist system. In their quest to reach a capitalist utopia, with material affluence and a modern lifestyle, the Buryats have encountered shamanism and become engaged and entangled in it while in the long run still pursuing the dream of economic abundance.

Gradually, the initial motive that brought these people to the shamans—to end their economic calamities—has shifted into the background, while the search for truthful history continues. The past from which they were once estranged has gradually become familiar and a part of the present. Misfortunes have come and gone, and although many people associate their relief from troubles with the rituals, others ignore them. Regardless of the efficacy that the Buryats attribute to the spirits, the spirits' stories, which represent the past and serve as frameworks for interpreting the present, remain and travel beyond the rituals.

Anthropologists have been keen to document the role of the supernatural during major historical events such as anticolonial resistance (Comaroff 1985, Lan 1985, Taussig 1987, Feeley-Harnik 1991, Steedly 1993) and the spread of capitalism (Ong 1987, Nash 1993). One aspect these studies have in common is that the supernatural forces are attributed multiple agencies to express the hosts' (whether individuals or groups) "internal dialogues, and fragmented subjectivities" (Ahern 2000:13). The supernatural also conveys, at least in the Buryats' case, ambivalences, conflicting subjectivities, and memories that are fragmented, uncertain, and weak owing to voluntary and forced forgetting. All of this indicates multiple and competing forms of history.

According to Chakrabarty (2000), the field of history—the Enlightenment-driven official discipline—omits the role of gods and spirits in human life. He distinguishes History One (H1), the rational-secular narrative of modern capitalism, from History Two (H2), the other history that includes gods, spirits, and other supernatural beings. Anthropologists have been studying locally produced histories that differ from the Enlightenment-driven ones for a long time, albeit under a variety of terminologies. The studies on mythicohistory among Hutu refugees in Tanzania (Malkki 1995), rituals and narratives of spirit possession (Lambek 2002, Steedly 1993, Stoller 1995), and the past being "arrested" (delayed) on its way to becoming widely shared history (McGranahan 2010) contribute to the studies of politics, poetics, and narratives of alternative history. In my view, these are variations of Chakrabarty's H2s that are missing from H1. The reason I mention these unofficial, culturally specific, locally produced histories against Chakrabarty's term is not so much to remind the reader that historians might benefit from the work of anthropologists, but in order to make explicit the Buryats' multiple and conflicting historical and epistemological backgrounds.

So for the Buryats, the history that emerges through shamanism would be H2; the history that is imposed by the socialist state, to use Chakrabarty's terms, would be a version of H1, which can be called H1A; and the history of capitalism that is spreading in Mongolia in the twenty-first century can be called H1B.[10] These distinctions help to shed light on the disparity between the agency of the spirits, as historical beings, and that of the humans in modern times. Specifically, the spirits are an economic burden.

The Buryats refer to their shamans not to revive their past, but to seek help in surviving capitalism. Because shamans explain economic miseries as being related to the forgetting of the past, the past emerges as a necessary element with which Buryats must wrestle as they seek to survive the new economic order.

If the Buryats express their attempt to withstand the market economy in a straightforward way, why do they sneak their past in covertly, through shamanism, and only as a condition for survival? The answer is complex. But in part, the Buryats have been distanced from their past as a result of the suppression of that past (H2) and of Mongolia's appropriation of the secular history of socialism and then capitalism (H1A and H1B).

At the very least, the Buryats' covert way of carrying their past relates to their experiences of state violence. State socialism implemented some brutal measures to ensure the forgetting, homogenizing, and control of knowledge throughout the country; it also strove to eliminate religion. Furthermore, the Buryats have been politically marginalized as outsiders owing to

Figure 1. A shaman in paraphernalia
during a ritual

their status as immigrants from Siberia to Mongolia at the turn of the twentieth century, and they were brutalized more than other ethnic groups were during the state violence of the 1930s. With the collapse of socialism and the arrival of capitalism, the Buryats sought to reconcile H2 and H1A, and they attempted to become a part of H1B—capitalism—while also getting (re)acquainted with H2—their suppressed unwritten history—through their spirits. Should H2 be openly expressed, however, it would lose its identity and validity as the suppressed, rival other to H1. Spirit narratives represent the suppressed, forgotten, subversive, and sometimes secret memories— the outcomes of violence and suppression under state socialism. They also remind us about the different life-worlds and temporalities beyond the secular history of capitalism. Hence, the economy of shamanism is not akin to capitalism, which produces material goods and a homogenizing narrative; instead, it produces particular kinds of stories that convey both suppressed memories and agencies beyond everyday language and awareness.

Remembering and Forgetting

Speaking through the language of poetry and accompanied by drumbeats in the possession rituals, the origin spirits recount stories of their lives in the distant past through a medium of the shamans' bodies, and they often reveal Buryat experiences that are not mentioned in official colonial and state accounts.[11] Every ritual brings in a fragment of the past when shamans, possessed by origin spirits, impersonate men and women from different historical epochs. These spirits may be ordinary people who fell victim to oppression as well as remarkable warriors and magic healers who lost their lives during Catherine the Great's Enlightenment project, shamans who were burned alive by Buddhist missionaries, or people who were shot by socialist revolutionaries in the early twentieth century.[12] Ideally, as the spirits one by one possess a shaman, different components of their narratives map the lost ancestral lands, lengthen and mend genealogies disrupted by socialism, and revive the Buryats' suppressed memories. These spirits constitute a nation-state of spirits as citizens ruled by the celestial court—a hierarchy of communal spirits and deities. In practice, families with a complete spiritual genealogy are rare.

As impoverished Buryats devote their meager resources to their angry origin spirits, they also discover that their lives are plagued by even more vicious beings—the souls of the people who died during political violence and who did not receive proper burials; they turned into demonlike creatures known as *uheer*. The outcasts of the spirit world, they torment the living, but unlike origin spirits who can be contacted and summoned, owing to their identities, belonging, and narratives, the uheer cannot be appeased. They are mute and elusive, and they lack identities and identifications. The book explores how the Buryats' attempts to deal with uheer lead them to search for memories of their violent past as well as to come to terms with the erasures and ruptures that resulted from the state violence in the 1930s (and beyond). Uheer, as empty memories, conceptually coincide with the mass burials of the victims of political violence. Together they constitute metaphors for as well as products of the perpetuation of silence by the new postsocialist neoliberal state and by individual agents who employ the former socialist state policies based on multiple motives for it.

The contrast between the origin spirits, who are brimming with identities, and uheer, who are devoid of identity markers, is akin to that between memory and forgetting. In exploring the remaking of the past, it became necessary to figure out how the state carried out forgetting, as well as the people's experiences of forgetting. What actually happened during the state's suppression of memory, and how do the repercussions of that suppression now affect people's relationship with the past? If state socialism was centered on creating a single, generalized history of the nation, shamanism is about dispersing, diversifying, and personalizing the past. It is about the power of the particular and the importance of distinct identities. Quite coincidentally, shamanic proliferation demonstrates vividly that neoliberal capitalism does not homogenize cultures or obliterate local differences, but can perpetuate existing structures and cultural practices.[13] In Mongolia the neoliberal state is still riding on the momentum that socialism created for the general over the particular—a more convenient and less troublesome way to manage the past. How do people gauge shamans' powers and the authenticity of spirits when disruption of the transmission of shamanic knowledge has robbed them of the knowledge needed to judge those things? For one thing, owing to the disruption in shamanic practice and the forgetting of the past, the Buryats, ridden with doubt and sometimes disbelief, continue to verify the authenticity of the knowledge and reliability of shamans by soliciting additional opinions. In their quest for the most truthful answers, many families further expand the shamanic proliferation and deepen their entanglement with shamanism.

Since much of the audiences and clients question and assess the shamans' authenticity, the latter hustle for recognition. Shamans, as Atkinson (1989), Tsing (1993), and Steedly (1993) properly emphasize, must attract and maintain audiences. Buryat shamans do so by using not only their shamanic knowledge, but also their entrepreneurial skills, domestic and international travel, dramatic performances, and displays of wealth. While shamanic rhetoric promotes gender-neutral rules, the quest for power is gendered, since the road to power for a shaman winds through systems of gender and kinship that are, as Yanagisako and Collier (1987) have argued, mutually constitutive. The shamanic rhetoric frames the road to power as gender-neutral, but in fact a proper shaman must comply with gender norms. Gender performativity—being good at being a man or a woman (Herzfeld 1991)—is an unspoken and informal prerequisite for becoming a shamanic performer and for a shaman to successfully gain his or her powers.[14] The problem is that the neutrality of shamanic rhetoric suits men's worlds—their activities, their forms of socializing, the spaces they occupy, and the relationships they build—but women must modify and extend themselves beyond their usual worlds in order to be shamans. More, in the aftermath of socialism, the rapid transformation in previously established (although contested) official gender norms and the opportunities for remaking gender differences that have been explored by Gal and Kligman (2000), created further challenges for female shamans in their quest for power. Shamans' access to power and rewards do not necessarily correspond to their actual shamanic skills and knowledge. And yet it is the male shamans who gain wider recognition and better opportunities to shape and influence the production of the past and individual and communal memories.

This book argues that shamanism blurs the boundaries between history and memory into a dynamic dispersion of knowledge. While I am aware of the shortcomings in the separation between history and memory in academic discourse, there are some overlapping points between academic terms and those of the Buryats. Hence I keep these terms as tools for analyzing the Buryats' shifting relationship with their past. The word for memory in Buryat is not a noun, but the verb *hanah*—to remember, and also to miss.[15] It indicates that memory is not a static object, but an activity undertaken by an emotionally and cognitively invested individual, and it echoes Nora's (1989) idea that memory retains an emotional connection with the past. For the origin spirits, the Buryats use the word *hundleh*—to respect. To respect is to remember. And respecting is a culturally mediated and emotionally entangled relationship between spirits and people.

The word for history in Buryat is *tuukhe*, which means to gather or collect. It assumes that an individual compiles knowledge from external sources. This idea is similar to Nora's notion that history is written by historians who are external to the group about which they are writing. Yet for Buryats it is not only history but also memory that can be discovered and learned from external sources. Memory is enacted through a shaman possessed by a spirit who is conversing with an audience. Regardless of whether the audience believes in spirits, knowledge of and by a spirit often becomes part of a person's individual knowledge after the excitement of (or disbelief in) the ritual has faded. The ultimate work of shamans in reconstituting the past, however, is not history, but memory—knowledge of the past that is emotionalized, embodied, and attached to an individual. Therefore, I use the word "memory" in this book when I tell stories of individual persons' and families' relationship with their past. But the word "history" is more suitable for indicating the Buryats' past at large, beyond individuals' knowledge of their own origin spirits. The Buryats themselves use *tuukhe* to indicate their group past.[16] Shamans, I argue, use facts and stories and engage simultaneously with multiple audiences to make communal histories and individual memories. By doing so, the shamans obliterate the boundaries between memory and history, which are based on fixed forms and structures. Instead, they help to bring into focus a new notion about the possible distinction between the two categories that is based on the quality and degree of individuals and communities' relationships with their past.

Since the shamans' ability to change individuals' relationship with the past transgresses the boundaries between memory and history, the terms "history" and "memory" can be used interchangeably. That is, the same body of knowledge constitutes memory in the case of personal attachments, but history if a person relates to it indirectly, as a member of an imagined community. In a dialectical and sometimes random way, shamans personalize distanced knowledge and thus make memories; they also disperse the memories of individuals into larger groups, thus making history. Often the same ritual can serve two different audiences: the memories that shamans make for immediate clients (and the descendants of origin spirits) also constitute history for the rest of the audience, even if they are unrelated to the clients.

Shamans claim to retrieve knowledge from a supernatural domain. I make no pronouncements on the veracity of this claim, nor do I think it necessary to do so, since I am not a shaman but rather an observer. I learned that shamans gain much of their knowledge by networking with elders and other shamans, reconnecting with their kin, and traveling through the Buryat ancestral homelands in Russian Buryatia and northern Mongolia. They personalize, adapt, and improvise generic stories of war, escape, loss of loved ones, defeat, betrayal, and abandonment and place these stories in the context of larger events known through official histories. Through highly emotional conversations with clients, shamans turn distanced knowledge about the past into individual memories; and through dramatic performances, they often persuade their skeptical postsocialist clients that spirits exist. The meticulous communal job of sacrificing sheep, which involves slaughtering and dressing the sheep and then cooking and presenting the meat to the spirits, is geared toward making the spirits real through physical and economic investments. Contrary to clients' expectations, however, the sacrifices (along with other gifts) bring nothing material in return—only narratives about the past.

In addition, the requests of the shamans to propitiate their newly found origin spirits at regular intervals of three to five years continue to create contexts for generating additional spirits and, thus, narratives. The spirits became "real" to their once-disbelieving postsocialist descendants, as they were expected to *sanah* (remember) the spirits throughout the day; when they opened a bottle of vodka for a guest or served dinner to their family, the first portion always went to the spirits. For the Buryats, all of these rituals fall into the category of *hundleh* (respect). And by respecting, they demonstrate that they are *sanaj baina* (remembering these spirits). The shamans are crucial in the making of memories. Through channeling of their possession by spirits and the performance of dramatic scenes that move audiences emotionally, they create vivid and lasting memories that the witnesses circulate.

Unlike the official state histories of victorious revolutions and successful modernizations, the history that shamanism recreates is profoundly tragic. Freed from suppression after the collapse of socialism, most spirits are the restless victims of death by violence who came to the world of the living as if to make up for their prematurely ended lives by possessing their descendants. Hierarchies of gender and age and norms of politeness and propriety are transgressed: male and female spirits alike drink alcohol, smoke pipes, sing songs, tell jokes, spit, toss cups, flirt, scold audiences, cry, and enact anger and hurt, experiencing vicariously the pleasures of the life out of which they were too quickly ushered. They tell tragic stories of their lives and receive at least temporary consolation from their descendants' appeasement. Through a shaman's performance, the unseen spirits are made imaginable and potentially memorable.

But many spirits remain tragic because they are not remembered properly, because much of their descendants' knowledge of them was lost during socialism. With the destruction of family genealogies, the names of the spirits vanished, and with the killing of shamans and prohibition of rituals, the "addresses" of the spirits in the celestial realm and their identities in the ancestral landscape were lost. Instead of being able to supply the shaman with necessary knowledge, the clients have to rely on the shaman's ability to trace their origin spirits. When the shaman is unable to find the addresses and identities of forgotten spirits, they remain tragic.

The most extreme form of such tragic spirits is that of uheer—anguished souls trapped in decaying corpses, unable to leave the human world and enter the afterlife. With their murky identities, uheer cannot be evoked out of oblivion by shamans, and their existence is felt only through illness and misfortune. Uheer are the most vicious and harmful spirits; they epitomize forgetting as an outcome of violence.

There are many reasons for the forgetting of spirits. My contribution lies in unpacking the state mechanisms that led to both deliberate and incidental forgetting and the gendered politics through which the Buryats reconstitute their past. I argue that shamanism, as an alternative mobile history, offers a genealogy different from the traditional, linear kind. Buryat genealogy is patrilineal and based on patrilocal residency. However, the stories that the Buryats find include women who had been forgotten and unacknowledged. Gender runs at the core of remembering and forgetting. In turn, shamanism, while shaped to meet men's advancement, at the same time offers room for challenging the patriarchal system.

The book will discuss official and unofficial technologies of forgetting during the state socialism. Intertwined with these moments of forgetting are the politics of gender, which inflect forgetting in their own distinctive way. Unlike displacement and violence, which have specific time frames and tangible technologies and, most important, have been initiated and carried out deliberately and mostly by external forces, gendered politics leads to forgetting from within, and in a more diffuse and ongoing way. Many gaps that the Buryats are desperately trying to fill imply the forgotten origin spirits of female shamans and even non-shaman female ancestors. These days, Buryats enrich and modify their past often by incorporating such spirits into patrilineal genealogies that have also been disrupted by state socialism.

"Nowhere is genealogy simply a straightforward reckoning of lineal descent," writes Ho (2004:152) in his expansive study of the Hadrami diaspora, which originated in Yemen but spread across the Indian Ocean during the past five hundred years. "Genealogy combines with poetry, biography, history, law, novels, and prayers in the diaspora" (XXII). Through travel, hybridization, and burials, among many other social processes, Ho shows how Hadrami genealogies expanded from their elemental linear form and became a "vehicle for narrative" (XXII) in the diasporic literature. That literature forms a canon of hybrid texts that "incorporate contingency, the real-world blending of history, geography, and biography" (XIV).

I find Ho's idea about the expansion of genealogies into a rich narrative to be instrumental for analyzing gaps that the Buryats encounter in their ongoing attempt to recreate their past through shamanism. Official Buryat genealogies consist of the names of male ancestors, including male origin spirits. Female origin spirits are remembered through narratives; their documentation in genealogies is rare and often arbitrary. Unlike the Hadramis, who rely on written tradition, Buryats remember their past through oral narratives and shamans' possession by origin spirits. There is a tension between the genealogy, which is patrilineal, and shamanism, which is gender-neutral. The Buryats' search for the causes of their misfortunes gesture toward the possibility of the existence of forgotten, unknown, and often unknowable female origin spirits whose identities and names are difficult to restore. Instead of knowing clearly the names of origin spirits and identities, which are necessary for appeasing them, the Buryats find fragmented stories of loss, love, forgetting, and neglect. And they encounter stories of separation brought about by displacement, adoption, remarriage, violence, and patriarchal norms. I regard those stories as elements of the genealogies that help to update the names of the ancestors according to the context and prevent the genealogies from acquiring a sacred, monopolistic quality. From a feminist perspective, the Buryats' ascription of their tragedies to the forgetting of their female spirits seems to be a creative way to claim a space for women in the male line. Shamanism complements and conflicts with genealogy through the participation of women, through the inclusion of their stories, and mainly through marking lacunae in the past that were created by the absence of women. As this book will illustrate, filling in that absence proves to be highly productive.

The politics of gender are central to the Buryats' history of tragedy, and the link between forgetting and gender is also strong in contemporary times. Women's participation in shamanism and mediumship throughout the world has been studied in many different ways: as a creative transgression of the patriarchal order (Tsing 1993, 1994); as a temporary shift in identity (Steedly 1993); as resistance to male domination (Lewis 1971, 1989) or to the powers of capitalist exploitation and discipline (Ong 1987); as attempts to exert control over capitalism's volatility (Kendall 1985); and as an assertion of an identity that differs from those available to women in mainstream religion, as well as a reflection on their "ideological subordination in the context of daily life" (Boddy 1989:346). This book attends to issues of gender from the point of view of female shamans, who consider themselves the equals of men. To an outside observer who starts with a preconceived notion of Buryat women's positions as inferior to those of men, many of these female shamans certainly look empowered and successful. But because Buryat female shamans start with a notion of the genders being equal, they hold that rewards, prestige, and empowerments should be equal as well. The glass ceiling that impedes women's empowerment lies beyond shamanic norms, inhering rather within the structures of kinship, state politics, the market economy, and international travel and representation. My exploration of men's and women's gendered quest for power uncovers how women are indirectly discouraged from participating in shamanism and remaking the past. At least some of the gaps in Buryat memories stem from gendered access to resources—travel, kin and social networks, and material resources.

The title of this book refers to various spirits (remembered, partially remembered, and forgotten) who were created through centuries of colonial oppression, Buddhist persecution, and state suppression of religion, memory, and tradition. Tragic spirits are the secret and disowned offspring of official history, sired by a state that implemented its techniques of forgetting in the name of nation-building and state formation. They are also a metaphor for the present-day victims of neoliberal changes, economic violence (both intended and inadvertent), and gender inequality.

Mongolia and the Buryats: A Brief History

The peculiar history that the Buryats create, carry, and care for through their shamanic practices is the hallmark of their identity as Buryats of Mongolia, who are distinct from Buryats in Russia and other Mongols in Mongolia. These Buryats trace their ancestral homeland to the shores of Lake Baikal, the Aga and Duldurga steppes in Russian Buryatia, and lands closer to the Russian-Mongolian border. The Buryats suffered repeated displacements from the time of the Russian incursions into Siberia in the seventeenth century. Their grief and sorrow over the loss of their lands and their nostalgia for their homeland are reflected in their shamanism. Buryat shamanism is distinct from other practices in the region, which are largely animistic— based on the worship of the spirits of wild animals, natural features, and plants, and less on ancestral spirits. Buryat shamanism is based on the worship of the spirits of their ancestors, who are remembered as historical and sometimes mythical individuals. This makes Buryat shamanism a mechanism for creating individual memories, communal history, and group identities. In that sense, Buryats are an important and unique group with respect to issues of memory and forgetting. The rituals during which origin spirits possess shamans and communicate with audiences are not merely problem-solving, utilitarian events. Their meanings, purposes, and outcomes permeate almost every aspect of Buryat lives.

Within the Buryat diasporic groups in Russian Transbaikalia, Mongolia, and northeastern China, these Buryats belong to a group known as Khori Buryats.[17] Here, I use the term "Buryat" unless I discuss additional Buryat groups, in which case I use "Khori Buryats" for the purpose of differentiating among them.[18] The Khori Buryats have a peculiar history of migration, anticolonial struggle, and loss of land that sets them apart from other Buryats as well as other Mongols. Beginning in the sixteenth century, they moved clockwise from the western part of Mongolia up north to the shores of Lake Baikal; they then returned to Mongolia, but to the eastern corner, escaping colonialism and interethnic wars and seeking pastureland.

By moving to Mongolia, they merged their historical faiths, for better or worse, with those of other Mongolians. For most of the twentieth century, Mongolia (also known as Outer Mongolia [1911–1924] and the Mongolian People's Republic [1924–1990]) was a socialist country and a satellite of the Soviet Union. Although it was never formally colonized or settled by the Soviets, they exerted tight control over the region. Because of the fear of Chinese influence, Mongols do not feel as much resentment toward the Soviets as former Eastern European socialist countries have. The Buryats are the only sizable group that joined Mongolia at the turn of the century. Immigration usually ran in the other direction, and both China and Russia claimed parts of Mongolia at different times. Because the Buryats left Russia at the birth of Soviet Union, Stalin considered them enemies of the state. They endured brutal political violence, and their twentieth-century representation in the official Mongolian history is vague and scarce. Yet, although underrepresented in the official history of Mongolia,[19] contemporary Buryats nevertheless "carry" their earlier history and the memory of their ancestral lands in Russia in the form of a shaman adorned in full paraphernalia.

Modern Mongolia's Buryats are scattered all over the country, but they are concentrated in the northern and eastern provinces of Dornod, Khentii, and Selenge, and in the capital, Ulaanbaatar.[20] Like other Mongols in rural areas, they maintain a semipastoral lifestyle, living in felt tents and intimately connected to their land, water, and livestock. Along with shamanism, the Buryats also practice Buddhism. They seek the services of lamas and propitiate the Buddhist gods, who have been personalized by lamas to families and individual family members over the last few generations.

In geopolitical and international contexts, the Buryats pride themselves on being Mongols; but on an interethnic level they complain that their contributions to nation building have not been acknowledged either by the state or by popular sentiment. The Buryats stereotype the dominant Khalkhas as lazy and careless; the Khalkhas consider the Buryats to be shrewd and overachieving. Troubled by their limited mention in the official Mongolian history textbooks, the Buryats strive to prove that they belong to the Mongolian state and point to their presence in Chinggis Khan's thirteenth-century empire. They identify themselves as *oin irged* (the forest people), a group mentioned in *The Secret History of the Mongols*—the chronicle of the Mongol tribes from mythological times to the establishment of Chinggis Khan's empire. At the same time, the Buryats use their migrant identity to differentiate themselves from other Mongols.

In Mongolia, the Buryats are also considered to have a more rigid patriarchal structure than the Khalkhas. The boys are raised with the awareness that they may someday be heads of households, whereas girls are expected to serve and obey their husbands and in-laws. Gender differences are enforced through the division of labor in the household. Women are expected to do almost all of the household chores, whereas men are expected to travel, tend livestock, and carry out the social roles of hosts and community members. Although this type of arrangement is common throughout rural Mongolia, the Buryats observe it rigidly—a topic of charged discussion among many young women in Bayan-Uul.

The Buryats have adopted more Russian ways of life than have other Mongol groups. They build log cabins, grow and preserve vegetables, and make butter and sour cream, as opposed to hard cheese and fermented mare's milk. In their pastoral economy, however, like other Mongols, they raise cattle, horses, sheep, goat, and camels. Unlike Khalkhas, who prize horses more than other type of livestock, the Buryats privilege cattle breeding. The Buryats who have migrated to the capital city of Ulaanbaatar occupy positions in all socioeconomic spheres.[21]

Most of the Buryats I lived with reside in the area's largest district, Bayan-Uul, whose population consists of about five thousand partly sedentarized nomads. During socialism (1924–1990), the people prided themselves on having one of the richest and most modernized state farms in the country, fully subsidized by the state, which was the sole employer in the district. But when, following the end of socialism, the state farm was dismantled in 1993 as part of the process of privatization, the people of the district found themselves with almost no means of subsistence. By embracing the ideology of capitalism—that hard work yields rewards (which did not work during planned and top-down managed socialism)—the Buryats threw themselves into every possible opportunity to earn a living. Yet the more energy they invested, the less they got in return. Disoriented and disconcerted by the absence of any apparent link between their efforts and the anticipated rewards, many sought an explanation for their misfortunes in various sources, including shamanism.

In the late 1990s romantic enthusiasm for building a new democratic society faded, and frustration and anxiety began to dominate the social atmosphere. Unfair market reforms that were pushed too hastily resulted in the massive and ongoing impoverishment of entire settlements, on one hand, and the rapid enrichment of a small segment of society, on the other. Riddled with corruption and internal disagreements and lacking adequate funds, the state struggled to fulfill its basic obligation to provide health care, education, and infrastructure. The presence of both forms of the state, the socialist authoritarian one and the postsocialist neoliberal one, figures in shamanic practice through various rituals, symbols, stories, and metaphors. The state is never a monolithic entity: its image ranges from oppressive ruler to vulnerable protector to incompetent establishment. The

Figure 2. Portrait of a female shaman

Buryats' representation of the state is amazingly well contained, its deeds differentiated and its meanings interpreted. I argue that the Buryats exert control of their past by presenting the state in such a highly dynamic, multifaceted, and nuanced way. They are trying to control both their history and their destiny, and they refuse to be dominated by the state. Because of their migrant past and their political marginalization, they are also able to view and experience the state from various perspectives. Shamanism, as an analytical and interpretive tool, accommodates the Buryats' heterogeneous relationship with the state in a sensitive and flexible way.

Buryat Shamanism: Postsocialism and Beyond

The Mongolian (and Buryat) word for a male shaman is *böö*; the term for a female shaman is *udgan*. The scholarly term for shamanism is *böö mörgöl* (shaman + the act of bowing). I use the terms *shaman, female shaman*, and *shamanism* mainly for the convenience and in order to connect with theoretical contributions by scholars, as well as to speak to popular audiences and their conceptions and imaginations associated with the term. The Buryats are known to have one of the most elaborate practices of shamanism in both the scholarly literature and travelers' accounts. Yet the meanings, uses, and transformations of their shamanism have been little explored. This book is not an account of what shamanism is or supposed to be like. But it tries to shed light on the Buryats' uses and meanings of their shamanism at a particular time and place: during the transition from state socialism to neoliberal capitalism in Mongolia.

Shamanism is an analytical and interpretive tool which the Buryats use to make sense of the world around them through rituals tailored to individuals' specific concerns, backgrounds, and identities. Yet the Buryats do not live exclusively in a world of spirits. State socialism was extremely successful in delivering universal secondary education and providing access to radio and television, although these were dominated by propaganda. After the collapse of socialism, cable television, cell phones, SUVs, and the freedom to travel abroad, among others, were being added to the everyday lives of nomads and connecting them to the rest of the world. Thanks to their windmills, solar panels, and generators, most of them watch Hollywood movies, Latin American soap operas, and Bollywood serials, and via television they learn everything from English to Christian doctrine. If science, as Evans-Pritchard (1976) observed, explains how things happen, then economists, at least in the postsocialist Mongolian context, might reveal at least some of the mechanisms behind the failures of privatization; political leaders might explain why the subsidies from Soviet Union stopped; bankers might trace the foundations of inflation; and media and rumors—though often there is only slight distinction between the two— might explain the darker forces behind those politics. But, going back to Evans-Pritchard, none of these theories and observations sufficiently explains the specific nature of an individual's misfortunes and suggests a tailored plan for actions that an individual could take. In that sense shamanism constitutes and triggers a response to the surrounding world. And because shamanism is a response to the outside world, in particular to the changing politics of the state, to modernity, and especially to different kinds of violence, it is modernity's counterfeiting other, both a response to and a result of modernity.

Yet, despite its shifting nature, shamanism is also a "thing"—a set of time-sensitive epistemologies and rules interpretable and modifiable by its practitioners and users. Shamanism is, in fact, many things: representation; local practice; a useful tool for resisting, healing, diagnosing, and making sense of a particular phenomenon; and a set of epistemologies. Shamanism's ability to order an alternative history and use it to explain the present, along with its mechanisms for making, transmitting, and delivering that history, is the most important aspect of the practice and one that I privilege in this book. To that end, this book dialogues with the study of memory and forgetting in the context of memory's long-term suppression and silencing during socialism and its reawakening in neoliberal times.

This book engages with the studies of shamanism as well as other inspirational practices that are known under other different names (e.g., spirit possession, mediumship, and the like). I based my approach on the resonance of theoretical and ethnographic questions that these studies address, yet without limiting my inquiries to geographical areas or definitions of shamanism with respect to similar practices. In fact, anthropologists have already warned against making a distinction between shamanism and other inspirational practices throughout the world (Atkinson 1992, Humphrey 1996, Thomas and Humphrey 1996), primarily to guard against essentializing a practice that is in constant metamorphosis and that even within a single narrow type is full of variety and riddled with inconsistencies.

But a separation of shamanism from other inspirational practices that involve human interaction with the supernatural persists among wider audiences as well as within the scholarly community. These distinctions have many bases, among them the simple attempt to differentiate among regional variations, technical differences (the shaman's soul travels to the supernatural realm, while the medium becomes possessed), and gender (male practitioners are called shamans because their souls travel, while females are referred to as spirit mediums because their bodies are possessed by outside spirits). In this book I situate Buryat shamanism within the literature on shamanism and spirit mediumship—not only as a way of rejecting essentialism, but also because Buryat shamanism has some characteristics of both.

In this book I argue that although shamanism is associated with the ancient world, shamanism is modernity's disowned creation. The proponents of modernity have either shunned shamanism as the most primitive form of superstition or constructed it as a backward practice in order to highlight their own sophistication and superiority.[22] For example, Buryat shamanism in the eighteenth century became the target of Catherine the Great's Russian Enlightenment.[23] And in the twentieth century, the socialist state constructed shamanism as a "dark belief," or superstition, and the most primitive form of consciousness. The state made almost no distinction between shamans, the insane, and those individuals who had chosen to shun society.

In contrast to these constructions, the Buryats appear to have been much more relaxed and diffuse about delineating and labeling their spiritual practices. The Russian-educated Buryat scholar Dorji Banzarov, writing in 1846, noted that the beliefs of the Buryats and other Mongol groups that were based on mythology and rituals did not have a specific name among Buryats and Mongols (Banzarov 1891). They called them "black beliefs" in order to indicate their primitive character, as opposed to Buddhism (the "yellow belief"), which was considered more sophisticated. In the aftermath of socialism, some assumptions about the backwardness and dangerousness of shamans remained, but owing to the arrival of a market economy that the Mongols consider to be amoral, the shamans are now also cast as charlatans who trick audiences out of their money. They are capitalism's interpretive other.

I do not intend to undo dominant constructions of shamanism in this book or to separate shamanism from spirit possession or even from other inspirational practices. I follow Humphrey (1995), who argues that it is more fruitful to look at the identities of the practitioners, their roles in the community, and the meaning of their practices in a historical context.[24] Fortunately for my purposes, research in various parts of the world on different inspirational practices deconstructs the existing separation. For example, in some African countries, such as Niger and Mali, there are female practitioners whose work is similar to that of shamans, and these "female shamans" can be far more powerful than male ones (Stoller and Olkes

1987, Stoller 1989). The distinctions also arise out of the history of ethnography. In Karoland, Indonesia, as Steedly (1993:38–39) notes, colonial ethnographies and folk tales distinguish between the trained male guru and the inspired female medium. In practice, Steedly argues, the distinctions are blurred, since each taps into the other's wisdom and experiences.

Shamanic trance or possession is the most exoticized and debated aspect of shamanism. With respect to different kinds of possession, Crapanzano (1977) suggests that a distinction needs to be made between cases of spirit possession that aim to cure the possessed by expelling the spirit and those that create a lasting relationship between spirit and practitioner. In postcolonial Niger, possession is not just an occasional public performance but a complex cultural process of establishing an often lifelong bond between spirit and practitioner "that requires . . . constant and faithful nurturing" (Masquelier 2001:107). In Zimbabwe, spirit mediums, both male and female, supported the guerrillas during the movement for independence from the British (1966–1980) and helped the revolutionaries by means of their knowledge and as authorities in their communities (Lan 1985). These are just some examples of the diverse meanings of the practices, their contexts, and the identities of the practitioners. Their variety makes it impossible to isolate any one practice from the rest. There seem to be just as many types of inspirational practices as there are other types of cultural differences.

The practice among Buryat Mongols in the aftermath of the state suppression of religion encompasses the characteristics of shamanism, spirit mediumship, and other spiritual practices. For instance, depending on their powers and personal skills, some shamans become possessed by spirits and claim no consciousness during possession. Others remain perfectly aware of their surroundings while allowing spirits to use their bodies to communicate with audiences. Among different Mongol and Siberian groups, such as the Darkhats and the Evenki, shamans claim to make spiritual journeys to the realm of the supernatural. But the Buryats of northeastern Mongolia during the time of my research were unfamiliar with the notion of the souls of shamans ascending to the supernatural realm. Only spirits travel through landscape, paraphernalia, and the supernatural realm; the shaman's soul stays near his or her body. It is possible that in centuries past Buryat shamans claimed that their souls ascended to the sky; origin spirits may now be more prominent than shamans' souls, since, on account of the disruption of shamanism and the absence of genealogical records, possession is often the only route whereby clients can be convinced of the spirits' existence.

The Buryat Mongol term for possession is *ongon oruulah*, which literally means to guide the spirit to enter the body. In terms of techniques of possession, the ritual most resembles the types of spirit possession found in postcolonial Africa, Indonesia, Sri Lanka, and Thailand. There, when a person is first afflicted by a spirit, he or she falls ill, afterward gradually gaining control over the spirit.[25] Buryat shamanism is not always equivalent to healing, but its efficacy is based on transformation in the subjectivity of a shaman, who learns to live with her illnesses, the burdens of which were shared by her origin spirits, through whom a shaman builds social networks and material wealth. The fact that Buryat shamans become possessed by spirits does not mean that they must necessarily be called spirit mediums.

Suspicious Clients and Persuasive Shamans

One of the main themes of this book is the tension between the Buryats' acceptance of the shamans' claims about the spirit world's being a trigger for their misfortunes and their suspicion about the motives and powers of individual shamans and the truthfulness of the spirits. Owing to the state's disruption of the Buryats' knowledge of religious practice, they have little information about what shamanism is supposed to be like. The country's entry into the free market has also created distrust of the possible motives behind the shamans' practices. Anxious about the possibility of shamans' faking the spirits or attaching random spirits for the sake of maintaining their clients as sources of income, Buryats sponsor additional rituals to acquire the opinions of other shamans. Ironically, the most skeptical clients end up supporting the proliferation of shamans. For every spirit whom the shaman evokes, several others emerge. In the absence of genealogies and adequate knowledge, skeptical and suspicious audiences consult as many shamans as possible and stage rituals of possession in order to tease out a consensual answer regarding the authenticity of each origin spirit. The harder the Buryats attempt to gauge the authenticity of spirits and the truthfulness of shamans, the further they catalyze the very practice that they seek to tame. Creative agents of their culture no less than the shamans, clients test the "realness" of the spirits, weave together the scattered knowledge provided by spirits through the mediating shamans, and compile their lost or disrupted genealogies. However, because the uncertainty, chaos, and instability of a neoliberal economy can bring more losses than gains, misfortunes continue. In the shamanic realm, this can indicate that the families still have more origin spirits to worship (Buyandelgeriyn 2007). And gene-alogies perpetually remain incomplete.

Besides engendering suspicion of the shamans, state-induced forgetting has had a profound effect on individuals' confidence in the dependability of their own knowledge about the past. Even when recalling some details of a family or community past, many people insisted to me that they had been cut off from their past and that theirs was a generation of non-knowledge. Belief in the destruction of the past is so pervasive that some people have discredited their own memories as trustworthy repositories of information about the past. This, and the fear that there might always be more hidden knowledge lurking, led people to imagine their past as lying somewhere between the obscure and the unobtainable. Mistrust in shamans, the separation of memories from individuals, the socioeconomic crisis, and the real and perceived unknowability of the past each in its own way triggered the explosion of shamanism.

While living in Bayan-Uul and becoming closely acquainted with different shamans, whom I observed on a regular basis, I came to realize that the proliferation of shamanism was not just a result of shamans' success-ful manipulation of the populace at a time of politicoeconomic crisis. The shamans I knew were interested in economic fulfillment, but they also cared about their clients. The economic incentives for becoming a shaman are limited, and the road to becoming a fully accomplished shaman is long and expensive. A few well-to-do shamans were already economically secure before they were initiated. This shows that shamanism is not just a ritual of controlling the chaos of transition. For such purposes, the Buryats also have Buddhism, the religion of most Mongols. Compact, cheap, and con-venient, Buddhist rituals address all the anxieties of transition. More than just a way of dealing with calamity, Buryat shamanism makes use of capi-talism to mend the casualties of socialism and to unfold a history that dif-fers from colonial and state accounts. In this book, I expose the production of such histories, set against the grain of disbelief by audiences and the ex-plosion in numbers of shamans attempting to gain recognition and power. As audiences question shamanically delivered knowledge, they sponsor ad-ditional rituals. Shamans, in turn, compete for "devoted and appreciative audiences" (Atkinson 1989:279, 289) through elaborate paraphernalia, skillful performances, and many other tactics of persuasion and astonish-ment. As a result, rituals proliferate. Within this proliferation, truth is a consensus that is commissioned through the shifting structures of power and gendered social networks.

Figure 3. Ritual

Nomadic Fieldwork among Rival Shamans

I met some Buryat shamans through my mother, a journalist working for Mongolian National Broadcaster (MNB), the country's official state-sponsored television station. She initially became acquainted with shamans while working on a documentary for MNB during the Symposium on Central Asian Shamanism, held at Lake Baikal in Russian Buryatia in June 1996. It was the first regional gathering of shamans from Central and Inner Asia and included a three-day-long performance with an audience consisting of international scholars, journalists, and filmmakers. When I came back from my first year of graduate school in anthropology at Harvard, my mother and I visited the shaman Jigjid, who had participated in the symposium and who lived close to the city of Ulaanbaatar. He was a biology teacher at the local high school and practiced bone setting and healing secretly under socialism. Seeing that I was interested in shamanism "from a scientific point of view," as he put it, Jigjid offered to guide us to the district of Bayan-Uul, where he also performed his next *shanar* (initiation ceremony and subsequent degree-elevating ceremonies) guided by his teacher, Luvsan, who also attended the symposium.

After Jigjid completed his rituals in Bayan-Uul and I began my research by taping, interviewing, and asking many seemingly irrelevant (and, in the shamans' view, often trivial) questions, we drove back together in a Soviet jeep and a truck with Jigjid's extended family of thirty packed in the back. After thirty-six hours of driving, we dropped off Jigjid in the former coal-mining town of Nalaikh and arrived home in the city of Ulaanbaatar well after midnight.

After an initial introduction to Bayan-Uul shamans by Jigjid, my mother and I traveled together for four summers (1996–1999) in the nomadic countryside of Bayan-Uul, building networks by living with individual sha-mans' families for several days at a time. We became closely acquainted with the families of several shamans and their friends, relatives, and cli-ents. But because many shamans seemed to be concerned about my taking sides in their power struggles, I needed to find a neutral position. How to study rival shamans?

My mother's experience and wisdom were valuable throughout this time, but her help in finding for me that neutral position as a researcher in a world of competing shamans was essential. During a conversation with an individual shaman, for example, my mother would recognize the exact moment to tell the shaman that it was important for me to learn the "truth" from him. At the same time, she pointed out that I needed to learn from all shamans in order to appreciate the more "established" ones' wealth of knowledge, and that I was not supposed to discriminate against anyone, as I was a novice in this study. In response, some shamans warned that there were fakes out there, but most agreed that for the sake of finding "objective" knowledge, I needed to talk to as many shamans as possible. In a place where age, social status, and occupation were crucial for estab-lishing credibility, my mother was in a better position than I to convince people of my need to maintain scientific disinterestedness. With her help, I was able to study shamanic politics without taking sides or being excluded by some because I had worked with others.[26]

The male shamans in the countryside could not have been better posi-tioned. With families and relatives tending their livestock, their personal and economic lives looked solid. Many were surrounded by both local and long-distance clients who lined up, waiting their turn, for days and weeks at a time, carrying truckloads of food and gifts and camping out with their sheep. Having been informally adopted as an oldest daughter in the fam-ily of the shaman Tömör, I had originally planned on living with Tömör's family for a year while traveling to visit other nomadic families on horse-back for my research. Tömör and his wife, Sunjidma, along with their chil-dren, were gracious and generous hosts, but they constantly worried about my safety and warned me about "pollution" from other people and spirits that I could contract during my travels. I realized that living with the family of a shaman would prevent me from undertaking extensive travel.

After considering many options, I settled upon the sedentary center (town) of Bayan-Uul as a more viable option than the countryside for my living arrangements. In the fall of 1999 my mother helped me rent and then renovate a room in an old schoolhouse in town. After I moved in, she spent a night with me to make sure that the newly built brick stove worked properly; she then left in the jeep we had rented in Ulaanbaatar. I was settled in for a whole year (1999–2000), and my room served as a permanent space where I could store my belongings, write up my notes, and have long conversations with the many people who dropped in for a chat.

To my bewilderment, I quickly discovered that the town was also a center of shamanic practice, but of a kind that differed from that found in the countryside. I met a great number of female shamans, many of whom had completed a number of shanars and offered the same services as the male shamans I previously met in the countryside, and their powers were considered appropriate for their stage of training. But unlike the wealthy, established shamans in the countryside, these women were struggling to make ends meet and gather resources to stage their next shanar. My stay in the sedentary center allowed me to attend closely to the politics of power and gender and to explore the reasons that, despite shamanism's egalitarian norms, the female shamans' skills and achievements did not translate into material or political power equivalent to that of male shamans.

In a place where shamans were scrutinized by clients against a backdrop of disbelief and almost every family had a member who had become a shaman, the competition for power was fierce. Due to a perceived as well as a real lack of knowledge about the past, consensus about truth was largely determined by the shamans' power, obtained through, among other means, public display of paraphernalia, dramatic rituals, and the staging of shanars. These successes were fostered through the gendered realms of power—kinship, networking, travel, and conversations. Because the market economy, even more than socialism, has accentuated the patriarchal structure, truth tends to be dominated by men, even though the female shamans' challenge does play a crucial role in reconstruction of the past.

Life in nomadic rural Mongolia is not structured around time: as with the pastoral Nuer of East Africa (as described by Evans-Pritchard (1969 [1940]), changes in the environment, weather, and livestock demands dictate events. Planning interviews or activities ahead of time was not the most useful method for conducting fieldwork in Bayan-Uul. I made my research intentions and my desire to go to all ceremonies, activities, and rituals, and to meet whoever wanted to become acquainted with me, widely known. I was ready to run to the other end of the village for a ceremony that I would hear about while picking up bread at the local market, or to meet a shaman who had arrived from a neighboring district for the day, or to leave for the countryside with my notebooks and sleeping bag when the jeep driver came in the middle of the night after an emergency trip to the hospital.

By "living through winter" (*övöljih*) in Bayan-Uul, I was accepted as a member of the community, especially in the countryside. I was no longer a transient researcher who came only in the summer with a tent and lived on my own. This time, I slept in nomads' gers, lying with their daughters like so many sardines on a felt mattress spread on the dirt floor. I assumed various kinship roles—daughter, sister, city relative—and performed household chores. That I kept turning up at the nomads' gers at the most unexpected times during winter storms or at night was what brought me close to the local people and convinced them that my interest in their lives was genuine. Most people stopped commenting that I might sell their culture to postcard and photo-album companies upon returning to United States, or write a best-seller adventure story, and tried instead to help me with my research in all possible ways.

Among the numerous individuals who will appear and reappear in various places in the book, the reader will get to know well the female shamans Chimeg and Baigal and the male shamans Tömör, Luvsan, Jigjid, and Molom, among others. Chimeg's most dramatic spirits, Bud and Navaan, represent their historic periods and also are active in contemporary politics. The stories, experiences, and presences of Dolgor, my confidante, and Tegshe, my traveling companion, are threaded throughout the entire book. Genen and Khorlo are the most celebrated origin spirits from the era of socialism, and while almost everyone is related to them by kin or social network, Tsend and Baigal are their respective descendants. Baasan is the shamanic client whose experiences encapsulate the entire range of forgetting and remembering. Her journeys to the above-mentioned shamans accentuate the role of gender in the Buryats' construction of memory and in the contemporary politics of gendered shamanic empowerment.

Chapter Overviews

Chapter 1 is a history that I recreated from shamanic narratives and official histories in Russian and Mongolian. It is an antidote to, and set against the backdrop of, forgetting. It shows that the recent proliferation of shamanism is not just a product of modern-day reaction to the outside world, but is based on their resistance to oppression from the past.

In chapter 2 I discuss forgetting under socialism and its persistence after socialism's collapse. The less obvious technologies of forgetting, which are enmeshed with other forms of oppression, include the routinization of state-sanctioned narratives, undermining the framework of collective remembering by suppression and substitution. I argue that forgetting is a heterogeneous process that has not only altered the content of memories but also impaired confidence in memory.

In chapter 3 I explore the multiple contexts of Bayan-Uul's economic devastation. I argue that the conditions for misfortunes that were imposed from outside by international neoliberal institutions have transformed the local fabric into a source of suffering.

Chapter 4 is about the interrelated politics of gender, power, and memory. It explores why despite the locals' claim about the prominence of powers of two female shamans who practiced secretly during socialism, the memories of one shaman are widespread, while those of the other are silent. I argue that this discrepancy is linked to the politics of power and gender among contemporary descendants and disciples.

Chapter 5 concerns the dilemmas that female shamans face in their quest for power. By exploring the rise and fall of Chimeg, a female shaman, the chapter unpacks the discrepancy between egalitarian rules and hierarchical practice and asks why female shamans' skills as shamanic practitioners bring them almost no political and material empowerment. It argues that shamanism might give women a temporary escape from the tyranny of household patriarchy, but at the price of making them victims of patriarchy in the public sphere.

In chapter 6 I shift to the practices of highly successful male shamans to investigate their strategies, both conventional and creative, for success. The reader will follow shamans to the celestial realm, where they trick the spirits, as well as to earthly destinations such as Parma, Italy, where they attract international audiences.

Chapter 7 takes the reader through the journeys of a shamanic client, Baasan, as she travels to consult with shamans and through them to encounter origin spirits in the hope of alleviating her misfortunes. In bringing together the themes of remembering, forgetting, gender, state violence, and neoliberalism through Baasan's attempt to build her past, it shows how individuals push the limits of remembering and knowing.

My goal in this book is to bring up some of the paradoxical outcomes of socialism's suppression of memory. The main issue is not what and how much has been destroyed, but a fostering of belief in forgetting, which often makes remembering unbelievable and forgetting impossible. Persistent anxiety about vanishing memory and the suppressed past has led to the proliferation of knowledge through shamanism whereby the Buryats have recreated parts of their missing or destroyed genealogies, family histories, stories, and symbols, as well as the names of gods and deities, and have revived their historical consciousness. Yet this past is always incomplete and unsatisfactory. Cynicism is ever-present, and indifference lurks in the background, repercussions of the techniques of forgetting. But because misfortunes continue, spirits and stories proliferate. It is only by situating their present misfortunes (which actually stem from the calamities of the market) within their tragic history of their ancestral past that the Buryats have been able to construct their new identity and their understanding of being in the modern world.

ONE

Mobile Histories

Hoimorin Högshin is a Buryat deity who protects children and families. The Buryats make her figurine, usually about twelve inches high, from copper and dress it in finery described in her evocation:

> A red silk vest and blue degel with mink-trimmed sleeves
> A beaver hat with a mink brim
> And silver earrings frame [your] face
> The great mother of all, please descend . . .

It is then swaddled in layers of white sheep's wool and white cloth, like an infant, and a *khadag* (prayer scarf) is folded around it, as would be done with a sacred object. Cradled in a birchbark case that is then wrapped in felt, the figurine is placed on a family altar.

Of all the deities of the celestial court[1]—a governing body of the spirit world—Hoimorin Högshin is the only one who is represented by a figurine rather than by poetic descriptions and symbols alone. As her name indicates, she is a *högshin* (elder) who resides in the respected *hoimor* (upper part) of a ger.[2] Hoimorin Högshin is accompanied by her granddaughter Chandagat, a white rabbit.[3] Her figurine, made of the fur of a white rabbit, is placed next to that of her grandmother on the altar. They are enlivened with a shaman's poetry and offerings of mutton, milk, and other delicacies.

The only female member of the celestial court, Hoimorin Högshin staves off death and illness and ensures the continuity of a family's lineage. Although she is a shamanic deity, even families who are indifferent to shamanism worship her. There is a generic Hoimorin Högshin for all Buryats, but each family makes and enlivens their own figurine, and sometimes one

Figure 4. Hoimorin Högshin in a felt that her granddaughter
Chandagat made of white rabbit fur

for each child. As caretakers of their families' previous generations (i.e.,
memories in the form of origin spirits) and, possibly, future origin spirits
themselves, children are especially important for maintaining the links between families' past and present.

Like most spirits, Hoimorin Högshin is both a blessing and a burden.
Once a family creates their Hoimorin Högshin, they must pass her down
to successive generations to continue the rituals of respect. She requires the
sacrifice of a sheep as often as every year—a heavy burden for most families. Yet if families fail or delay in staging the rituals, they begin associating illnesses and deaths in their families with her wrath. According to shamanic logic, in order to live, one must remember the past; otherwise, one
joins it. Unlike in cultures where the past is predictably contained within
history books, designated items such as family heirlooms, or architecture,
the Buryats' past emerges almost inadvertently, woven through multiple
media and mediators.

For one thing, in a shamanic realm, remembering is a multisensory
act of carrying and caring for origin spirits. For instance, the acts involved
in maintaining Hoimorin Högshin emulate the care that individuals give
their loved ones throughout all stages of life from infancy to death. She is
swaddled and cradled like an infant, adorned with fur and jewelry like a
beloved daughter or wife, and worshipped like a family origin spirit. She

is also physically transported by family members. I was told that in the past, during disasters and wars, the first thing fleeing Buryats would shove into their *övör* (a chest pouch of the degel) to take with them was their Hoimorin Högshin.

Caring for an infant or an elderly person requires the physical labor of carrying the person in one's arms. It also necessitates the mental effort of remembering and prioritizing their needs and wants throughout one's daily activities. The Buryat (and Mongol) word for "to care" is *hanaa* (*sanaa*) *tavih*, which literally translates as "to put down one's mind to." The phrase "to care for an elderly parent" is best captured by the term *örgöh*, which literally means "to lift" or "to elevate." The noun *hanaa* (*sanaa*), which means "mind," has the same root as the verb *hanah* (*sanah*), which means "to remember and to miss," indicating the close relationship between caring and remembering.

Shamanic rituals expand these everyday and often taken-for-granted mental and physical acts of remembering and caring for one's past in ways that enable audiences and clients to be more mindful of it. When shamans become possessed by individual spirits, accompanied by beating a drum or shaking a bell, they tell stories of the past lives of those spirits—tragic tales of heroic battles on a horseback, fleeing from enemies, the loss of loved ones, and being killed at border crossings. As I continued to attend the rituals and listen to these narratives, they began to come together into a shifting history that spread over the lands of the Buryats' ancestors and filled in the chronology that I had learned mainly from the official history. The stories, which seemed random at the very beginning, began to make sense as connected to one another not only through events, networks, and gossip from the past, but also more concretely, through kinship, genealogy, and places. For the descendants of the origin spirits, these narratives constitute the family's past, while for outsiders they are part of a group history.

Whatever concern initially brought an individual to a shaman—illness, bankruptcy, a legal dispute—might transform, fade away, or be resolved. The narratives, however, tend to take on lives of their own and are remembered and retold among various groups. My focus is these very narratives, the fragmented and detailed accounts of individual experiences. Inevitably interwoven with other representations of the past, such as paraphernalia, genealogy, myth, rituals, specific bodily acts, and individuals' dreams and imagination, they constitute the most detailed memories of the past. In this chapter, by selectively weaving together the narratives of spirits against a background of official histories, I compose a version of the Buryat past in place of the customary history chapter that usually begins most ethnographies. Because the Buryats were split up between Russia and Mongolia in 1729, I attend to the historical events that influenced the faith of Buryats in both countries.

Layered Remembering: Russian Colonialism

The earliest known sources mention that the Khori were part of Chinggis Khan's empire in the thirteenth century.[4] During a period of internal discord among the Mongol princes in the sixteenth century, the Khori Buryats became the subjects of Altan Khan, in western Mongolia. But Altan Khan gave them away as a gift to Buubei Beile as a part of his daughter's dowry. Rejecting their new master, the Khori escaped to the north and settled on the shores of Lake Baikal (part of the territories of the Khalkha Mongols).[5] Most Khori Buryats trace their ancestral homelands to the shores of Lake Baikal, especially Oikhon (Ol'khon) Island and the Aga and Dul'durga steppes. Some contemporary Khori Buryats in Mongolia also claim a pre-Russian homeland in western Mongolia, where their ancestors had lived before fleeing north; but the link to this distant past is weak compared to Buryats' deep nostalgia for their lost homeland in Transbaikalia.

Shortly after these Buryats settled in Transbaikalia, Russians began to

Figure 5. Lake Baikal and a sacred tree on the island of Oikhon

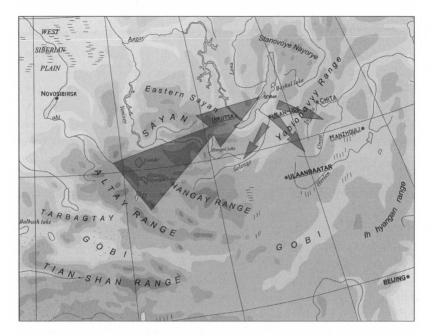

Map 2. Map of Buryats and their movements throughout history

explore the region's economic resources.[6] Around 1625 they built fortresses on the western shore of Lake Baikal and subjugated the local population, forcing them to pay tribute to the czar in the form of mink, fox, and other furs in return for protection from attacks by Buubei Beile, from whom they had escaped (Humphrey 1979). But when the Russians' demand for tribute increased in the 1630s, numerous Buryats, including the Khori, refused to pay and moved, first from the western to the eastern shore of Lake Baikal and then farther east.[7] The Buryats on the western shore of Lake Baikal (western Buryats) were soon subdued (Humphrey 1983). But the Buryats on the eastern shore (eastern Buryats), who had been a part of Chinggis Khan's empire, were skilled in fighting on horseback with bow and arrow, used the natural terrain to carry out ambushes, and waged guerrilla warfare in the forests (Forsyth 1992:87–89).

Given the Buryats' prolonged armed resistance to colonialism, which went on for centuries, it is no coincidence that a Buryat shaman adorned in full paraphernalia resembles a warrior in full armor. Humphrey (1995) calls the shaman "a citadel" (1996:204), "a fortified city" (1995:151), and "a world-conquering time machine" (1996:202). A shaman's paraphernalia mirrors military armament: for instance, the shaman's shield is a mirror;

spiked armor is represented by an *arhali* (short cape), adorned with two giant snakes, that protects the shoulders, back, and arms; and the helmet is an *uulen amitai* (metal headdress covered with representations of snakes and crowned with antlers decorated with antique prayer scarves).

During the seventeenth, eighteenth, and nineteenth centuries, many Buryats moved farther east to Mongolia and Manchuria, in northeastern China, to escape Russian colonialism (Forsyth 1992:92). Small-scale migrations continued sporadically throughout the eighteenth and nineteenth centuries. The most recent notable move took place at the turn of the twentieth century, when many Buryats fled from Russia to Mongolia to escape the turmoil of the Bolshevik Revolution in 1917 and Russian civil war in 1905–1907. Divided between Russia and Mongolia, the history of the Buryats written by these two countries reflects their political interests. The Russian empire considered the Buryats to be their colonial subjects and regarded them as a cultural other. The Soviets brought modernization, gave them the status of an autonomous region, and, in a political move intended to distance the Buryats from other Mongols, declared them a distinct nationality (*natsia*) with its own ethnogenetic roots, one that was unrelated to other Mongols.[8] The Buryats who moved to Mongolia at the turn of the twentieth century ended up receiving little, if any, mention in the homogenizing history of the socialist state.

Although they are underrepresented in the official histories of these states, the Buryats carry their past in shamans adorned in full paraphernalia representing origin spirits, ancestral lands, and the spirit world.[9] Each of the twenty-one separate objects of paraphernalia, from the coral bracelets to the metal headdress and the antelope-skin gown, belongs to a particular spirit and serves as a station for its descent. Since the origin spirits who occupy each piece of paraphernalia also possess the shamans who relay their narratives, the paraphernalia symbolizes an interactive history. Their geographical displacements have made the Buryats' connection with their past fragile. Yet they have developed ways to carry, care for, and keep in touch with their past through their portable and movable shamanism. Origin spirits play a special role in this process. By having settled their lost ancestral lands with their origin spirits when they fled their homelands, the Buryats maintain their memories of their tragic past. Yet the spirits are mobile, so they are able to connect past and present, lost and settled lands, and human and celestial worlds.

The Buryats' displacement and the loss of their lands, combined with their nomadic lifestyle, prevented them from building tombs and cemeteries, maintaining archives and libraries, and erecting statues and mon-

Figure 6. A Buryat shaman in front of his paraphernalia hung on a rope

uments—the usual memorials created by sedentary populations. The shamanic paraphernalia are the tangible and objectified representation of the origin spirits. Each piece of paraphernalia is animated by an origin spirit. In order to summon these spirits, the descendants must remember each one's identity and identification. Each origin spirit has a name, kinship and social identifications, earthly and celestial titles, and *huudal buudal*—"addresses," or places of birth, death, residence, and visitations. These addresses point to multiple locations that mark the life passages of those who have become origin spirits: their birthplace, where they lived and died, and their rites of passage from burial through cremation to *degdeh* (ascent to the celestial world). The spirits also have *buudaltai* (places of descent) and *naadamtai* (places of play), *shungalagtai* (rivers and lakes to bathe in and streams to drink from) and *guideltei* (paths to run along, where they often cause mischief). The origin spirits also have institutional identities, since when they ascend to the celestial court they take on work—for example, serving deities such as Higan Tengri (the deity of warfare), Arin Arvan Gurvan Noyod (the Thirteen Lords of the North), or Darhan Dorlik (the deity of blacksmithing). The most common positions are *haalgachin* (door keeper), *tulhuurchin* (keeper of keys), and *tahilch(in)* (altar attendant). As shamans summon the origin spirits one by one, poetically reiterating the names, geographical locations, and social positions and relations with which they are associated, they recreate lost ancestral lands, fragments of the client's clan genealogy, and (parts of) the celestial world.[10] Remembering the spirits means knowing these identities and addresses so that a shaman can evoke them. Each time a shaman reiterates a spirit's identifications—name, clan name, kinship affiliations—he or she reconstructs a piece of Buryat genealogy; with the reiteration of the huudal buudal (addresses), usually mountains, ravines, steppes, cliffs, rivers, and lakes where each spirit may ascend, descend, play, run, bathe, and drink, the shaman reconstructs the lost ancestral lands; by naming the origin spirits' celestial titles and the deities they serve (such as "key keeper of Burhan Garval"), a shaman reconstructs the Buryat celestial court; by summoning the spirits to descend into and take possession of their designated paraphernalia, a shaman reconstructs his or her full paraphernalia as well. By putting on the paraphernalia, a shaman brings the spirits into intimate association with his or her body, making him- or herself ready to be possessed by spirits. Adorned in spirit-saturated paraphernalia, the shaman appears as a condensation of the past.

There is, however, another important space to which the origin spirits descend, and it needs special mention. The clients and audiences attending the ritual make up the social space to which the spirits come. During the evocation, the shaman must introduce every participant, even visitors, to the spirits (which is why these introductory evocations alone can last an entire day). Every person at the ritual must inform the shaman of his or her name, age, ethnic group, parents' names, names of ancestors three generations back, clan name, and clan's *uraa* (cry). The shaman (or his or her assistant) writes down all that information in a notebook or on a piece of paper; he or she then introduces the participants to the spirits in chant by reiterating multiple times the identifications of each individual.[11] The uraa, as the shaman Tömör puts it, is "parole"—a password used to identify members of the lineage and detect enemies. Each uraa is purposefully counterintuitive. For instance, the Bodonguud (wild boar) lineage has the *shono mergen* (wise wolf) uraa, and the Galzuud (crazy) lineage has the *daagan* (steed) uraa. In the past, during chaos and war, the uraa most likely was kept secret within a clan; today, however, it is a part of one's lineage identification, uttered openly during rituals. The introductions, although meant for the spirits, are actually culturally distinctive public introductions of all participants to one another.

Such introductions lead to another layer of remembering. During the possession of the shaman by origin spirits, audience members are told about their past—which is also the client's past. They then retell those stories to others outside the ritual; I often learned about individual families' origin spirits and their narratives from their acquaintances, neighbors, and friends. It was common for individuals to know about the origin spirits of other members of their community without necessarily getting to know those members themselves. By sharing their past with the larger community at rituals, individuals increased their chances of maintaining their past even if they died or forgot—even though this was almost never the original impetus for sharing. The ritual sharing of one's past adds another layer to ensuring the remembering. In the past, chaos and war made it necessary to deposit one's memory in as many media and mediators as possible, including relatives and clansmen, paraphernalia, and the mediator-shaman—to ensure that a memory would live on even if one of these people, places, or things were killed, destroyed, or lost. Oral histories tell of the displacement of children and a widespread loss of kin. When lineages reunited, especially for the purpose of fighting a common enemy, it was important to be able to distinguish relatives from foes based on the clan's uraa and stories about an individual's past.

Indeed, the stories of spirits indicate that the Buryats had more enemies than friends. The Russians employed Cossacks as well as local Khamnigans to force the Buryats into submission. The Mongol khans were interested in subordinating the Buryats and making them pay taxes, since the khans were themselves forced to pay taxes to the Qing emperor. In the words of Agamben (1998), the Buryats epitomize "bare life"—biopolitical subjects stripped of their identities, land, and basic human rights. Perhaps because they have been threatened with a loss of identity through cultural assimilation and even genocide (threats that have often been carried out to varying degrees), Buryats have invested themselves in protecting, caring for, and carrying their memories. They multiply their memories by infusing them into various spaces, both imagined and physical, such as landmarks, paraphernalia, genealogies, origin spirits, and communities. Also engaged in the act of remembering are their senses, rituals, and physical habits, such as carrying, caring, respecting, imagining, communicating, and—in the case of shamans—being possessed by origin spirits. The resulting memories are layered, distributed, multiplied, and mobile. A shaman adorned in full paraphernalia symbolizes multiple aspects of memory: a piece of genealogy, a homeland, a movable history, the spirit world, a warrior. In addition, the densely symbolic and meticulously detailed articles of paraphernalia and the protective powers of the origin spirits with which they are infused turn a fully adorned shaman into a statement of cultural distinction and immortality. As such, a shaman in the context of colonialism is the opposite of "bare life."

I now turn to the narratives of spirits as a part of this complex system of remembering and resisting.

The Birth of Hoimorin Högshin

In the winter the Buryats would dig holes in the ice of the Ingedei River in order to water their livestock. One morning a herdsman noticed a woman in a blue degel and red vest come out of one of the holes and walk along the shore of the river. A little later another man saw the same woman going back into the hole in the ice. The two men hid and secretly watched how, for several mornings, she came out of and went back into the river. The news about the strange woman spread in the settlement and eventually reached the Mangaduud [Russians]. They also spied on her and saw the woman come out of one of the holes in the Ingedei and that she was accompanied by a little girl. They captured and incarcerated the two. After several days, however, the woman and child disappeared from the prison cell.

For the next three years, the Buryats living on the shores of the Ingedei had no babies. When they staged a communal shamanic ritual and consulted with the spirits to find out why they no longer had children, they were told that the deity of warfare and soldiers, the Higan Tengri, had sent a female deity to the struggling Buryats to support their procreation and well-being under Russian domination. She was offended by her treatment, and that was why the people no longer had children. Since then the Buryats have worshipped Hoimorin Högshin and sought her protection for their children.[12]

In this story, the Buryats anchor a fragment of their past to the deity who, owing to her power to protect children, inhibits forgetting. Her role in Buryat history is as indispensable as that of actual people, as Chakrabarty (2000) would have viewed it. Hoimorin Högshin is a vehicle of historical memory. Because the Ingedei River is known as her birthplace, those who have family members who have drowned in it are told to appease their Hoimorin Högshin, because their misfortune is an indication of the deity's wrath or curse.

The story indicates the presence of oppressors in the vicinity of the Ingedei River, which runs through the far eastern region of Transbaikalia, close to the Mongolian border, and far from Lake Baikal, so at the time it arose the Russian empire must already have established its administration throughout Transbaikalia. The Buryats transformed their resistance accordingly in order to deal with and understand the Russian government and to learn to live with colonizing settlers, rather than carrying out guerilla warfare against the Cossacks and Khamnigans.[13] Therefore, in addition to a deity of war, the Buryats also needed one of procreation to help them overcome the effect on the population of the many deaths that occurred during colonial administration.

The Russian colonial power is represented through the police, and through the surveillance, capture, and imprisonment of the deity. One of the most potent signs of oppression is the jailing of a woman and her child without telling her what she is accused of or giving her a chance to defend herself at trial. Intriguingly, while Hoimorin Högshin is an epitome of resistance to Russians, it is not they but the Buryats who bear the consequences of Hoimorin Högshin's imprisonment. Why, instead of taking revenge on the Russians for mistreating her, does Hoimorin Högshin punish the Buryats?

Here the power to control the Buryats' procreation—and to punish—is attributed to Hoimorin Högshin, not to the Russian empire. That way, the Buryats fold Russian colonial power into Hoimorin Högshin and symbolically transform the Russians' oppressive powers into their own. The Russian colonial power is limited to jails and police; it is not a part of the supernatural.

The Buryats and other Mongols believe that representation contains the power of the represented. Representation can ignite an object's influence and must therefore be controlled in its extent and frequency. By keeping the representation of their colonizers at a minimum, the Buryats prevent their "legitimation and hegemony in the form of a *fetish*" (Mbembe 1992:4), which protects them from internalizing the oppression and making it deeper, more subconscious, and more naturalized. Instead, they describe their oppressors' institutions of power soberly while fetishizing their shamanic deities, such as Hoimorin Högshin, through layers of material and verbal representations: figurines, accessories, clothing, poetic evocations, and actions of swaddling and cradling—and, specific to this discussion, by attributing to her the power to punish. As Taussig (1993:105) discusses through his reading of Cuna chants previously studied by Norman Chapin, a former member of the Peace Corps, to represent something in detail is to display its power and authority.

It is through a detailed representation of their own spiritual world that the Buryats have resisted their oppressors. The harsher the Buryats' experience of oppression, the greater they seem to have made their supernatural entities. This makes sense if we stick to a rational calculation that the Buryats took the powers of their oppressors and attributed them to their own deities, making the latter correspondingly powerful. By attributing the characteristic of a dominant figure to Hoimorin Högshin, they shifted the power of the oppressor to their own supernatural world. Yet the Buryats do not imitate the images, appearance, and language of their oppressors. In fact, they imitate only the exercise of power—nothing else. Everything else remains as distinct from the oppressors as possible. This targeted mimicry, this demonstration of the acquisition of their powers, is entirely different from colonial mimesis, which involves assuming the power of colonizers by imitating them in appearance, action, and gesture, as exemplified by the making of figurines of the colonizers among the Cuna Indians in Panama (Taussig 1993) or by imitating a colonial persona through spirit possession among the Hauka in West African (Stoller 1995). By transferring the specific power of the colonial into their own deity, the Buryats also transform their own relationship with the colonial power. Hoimorin Högshin takes over the role of a brutal punisher, as if she were on the side of the oppressors, albeit temporarily. This temporarily renders the oppressors obsolete. At the same time, the Buryats also make Russian colonialism closer and more familiar. I wonder if this hints at the memories that are excluded from their anticolonial narratives: the acceptance of Russian rule.

Love and War

The narratives of spirits from the time of Russian colonialism depict intensified interethnic rivalries between the Buryats and their neighbors. Because the Russians employed previously conquered western groups to beat their eastern neighbors into submission, as Peter Lyashenko notes (Mote 1998:40), the Buryats clashed with the neighboring Khamnigans in fierce and lasting battles. Even today, the Buryats openly scorn the Khamnigans.

An origin spirit named Chödör has one of the most poignant stories of the Buryats' struggles against the Khamnigans. When the spirit of Chödör possesses his mediator, the female shaman Chimeg, who is known as a great-great-grandniece of Chödör, he laments the battle with the Khamnigans, who, instead of fighting through their shamanic skills, used modern firearms:

> Suppressed by my magic, they turned to firearms;
> Unable to strip off the powers of my ancestors, they attacked my body . . .
> In the face of danger I resisted bravely;
> In battles with a harsh enemy I fought to the death . . .

Chimeg told me a more complete story of Chödör's premature death at the age of thirty-three. Chödör was an exceptionally talented shaman and became a zaarin (a male shaman of the highest rank) before reaching his teens. He remained single until his thirties but eventually fell in love with a woman from a Khamnigan clan. The couple decided to marry despite the rivalry between the Buryats and the Khamnigans. The Khamnigans, who disapproved of the marriage, attempted to kidnap the bride and employed magic and curses to separate the couple. All this having proved unsuccessful, the Khamnigans then raided the Buryat settlement armed with firearms supplied by the Russians. The presence of the couple in the settlement threatened the lives of Chödör's clan members, and the couple fled into the forest. After a few days they were found dead in their log cabin: Chödör had been shot and his bride had been hanged.

Shaman Healers and the Russian Enlightenment

Russia's expansion to the east was also accompanied by imperial projects of enlightenment, modernization, and Europeanization. Starting with Peter the Great (r. 1682–1725) and Empress Elizabeth (r. 1741–1761), Russia gradually became technologically modern, bureaucratically efficient, and culturally similar to Western Europe. These transformations were limited to the nobility, however, and much of the country was left in serfdom until 1861. Catherine the Great (r. 1762–1796) was utterly determined to change Russia's image from Asiatic to European. For her, shamans encapsulated the "antiself of Enlightenment" as J. G. A. Pocock put it (Boekhoven 2011:34). She "damned Russia as a nation confounded by its shamans," whom she tortured and killed. The enlightened empress even wrote a play called *The Siberian Shaman*, staged at St. Petersburg's Hermitage Theater in 1786, in which she attempted to expose shamans as charlatans (Flaherty 1992; Boekhoven 2011:34).

The transformations in scholarly thinking propelled by the scientific revolutions of the sixteenth and seventeenth centuries influenced Catherine's attitude toward shamans and the indigenous population of Siberia. As Tambiah (1990:4–10) discusses, during this time in Europe religion came to be seen as a domain of the cognitive and the intellectual, rather than of the personal and the emotional. At the same time, it became an object of study, and scholars compared the histories of individual religions and even classified them into higher and lower orders, with shamanism often occupying one of the lowest rungs. The distinction made between religion, the domain of God's sovereignty and omnipotence, and magic, a false religion in which practitioners attempt to manipulate the forces of the divine, cast the latter not simply as inferior but as subversive to religion. As for healer-shamans, at that time disease was coming to be considered a natural process rather than a kind of divine punishment. Further revolutions in science, technology, and medicine brought about the decline of folk religion and healing practices. These very specific Enlightenment-era developments led to the further persecution of shamans.

To this day the Buryats tell stories of how the Russian imperial court detained shamans and challenged their powers. For instance, the shaman Luvsan summoned the spirit of an eighteen-year-old female *tulmaashi* (a special type of "white" healer-shaman) named Sagan. While possessing Luvsan, Sagan cried and spoke of being ridiculed and then assassinated at the imperial court of Catherine the Great. Famous for her skills in bone setting, Sagan was taken to the imperial court to demonstrate them. There she was blindfolded and was ordered to identify various animals' ankle bones. The bones were hung on strings and rotated quickly while she tried to touch each of them. When Sagan identified the bones without a mistake, the empress told her that she would spare her life and the lives of her tribesmen if she could cure a member of the royal family who was dying from a mysterious illness. When the cure proceeded well and the patient recovered, the court doctors, jealous of the young tulmaashi's talent, poisoned her.

Buryat territory was essentially a meeting point of Russian and Mongol influences. Russia imposed on the Buryats not just taxes and regulations, but also Christianity and enlightenment. From Mongolia, the Buryats were exposed to Buddhism, specifically the school known as Gelugpa—the reformed Yellow Hat sect of the Dalai Lama. Also known as Lamaism, it flourished during the Qing administration, from the seventeenth century through the nineteenth.[14] Like other Mongols, the Buryats in Mongolia resisted Buddhism. The Buryat shamans in Russia, however, adopted Buddhist elements into their practices and used them to strengthen their shamanism as a foil against Christianity and as a form of resistance to Enlightenment-driven persecution.[15] It may have been because medicine was coming to be considered a profession and disease to be seen as a natural phenomenon that the tulmaashis gained prominence among the Buryats. The tulmaashis integrated Buddhist elements—deities and *dharani* (spells)—into the powers of their origin spirits and were skilled in herbal medicine and the setting of broken bones.

Luvsan evoked Sagan by ringing a large silver bell with "Ekaterina II (1762–1796)" engraved on its rim. Luvsan was convinced that his prized possession had come from the empress, who, impressed with some shaman's power, had decided to make him a gift of a bell with her name on it. The bell also epitomizes how, along with resisting the Russian empire, the Buryats strove to transfer its power to their possession, just as they attempted to fold the oppressive powers of the Russian colonial state into their Hoimorin Högshin.

Earthly and Celestial Negotiations with the Russian Empire

In 1689 the Russian and Manchu administrations signed the Treaty of Nerchinsk, which, along with the Treaty of Kiakhta in 1729, established the border between the Russian-administered Buryats and Qing-occupied Mongolia; it eventually became the modern-day border between Russia and Mongolia.[16] The Buryats and other Mongols, as subordinates, had little influence over the outcomes of the treaties that decided their future national borders. The event made the great majority of Buryats part of Russia. The new border not only decreased the mobility of the groups in the area, but also led to the Buryats' cultural and political alienation from other Mongols. As discussed by Humphrey (1983), during the eighteenth century many Buryats adopted Russian ways of life, and some even chose to adopt Russian citizenship owing to the harsh conditions in Mongolia during Manchu rule: even with its smaller and less fertile pastures, Russia offered better conditions than war-torn Mongolia. Many other Mongols, as Humphrey documents (1998:24), also moved north for the same reason, becoming "Buryats" in the process.

The Buryat resistance to Russian domination went beyond military action and spiritual resistance to include official political negotiations and petitions. A story about a remarkable female shaman named Ereehen Baljir shows that the Buryats, especially the Khori, were politically united, fluent in the language of negotiation, and able to carry out official missions with the imperial court. The shaman Luvsan, who sometimes evokes Ereehen Baljir's spirit, recounted the story to me.

With the increase of Russian settlement in Buryat lands, the latter's livelihood deteriorated. Our Buryats were pushed to infertile lands and were losing their livestock. Russian taxes increased, the army drafted all the able men, and the local administration exploited women and children. The Buryats decided to send a delegation to the Empress Elizabeth to plead for better treatment. The leader of the delegation was a female shaman named Ereehen Baljir. On the way to St. Petersburg, the delegation ran out of food in the Siberian taiga and was in danger of starvation. Ereehen Baljir ordered the delegation to eat her flesh in order to continue their journey to the imperial palace. She then killed herself, ensuring that the delegation had enough provisions. They successfully negotiated favorable treatment from the empress, who or-

dered the colonial administration to reduce taxes on the Buryats, minimize
the military draft, and allow them use of their pastures. Because of that trip,
the Buryats have survived until today.

Among many remarkable aspects of the story is the fact that the leader was
a woman. She is also remembered as a moral exemplar and altruistic leader
rather than as a talented and skillful shaman—possibly an indication that
despite Russian persecution of shamans and brainwashing of the Buryat
population, the shamans continued to act as political leaders in their communities. Paralleling this story, official histories indicate that the Khori
Buryat clans were united in negotiating with the Russian government for
the right to keep their pasturelands against repeated incursions by Russian
settlers.[17] For example, in 1702 the Khori sent a delegation to Czar Peter I
to request official recognition of their pastures. In 1804 they successfully
concluded another negotiation for their pastures, and in 1880 the Buryats
sent more representatives to Moscow to discuss the question of settlers on
their lands.[18] These initiatives and many trips through the inhospitable Siberian taiga are testimony to the Buryats' nostalgia for their lands, demonstrated today through repeated representations of those territories in shamanic paraphernalia and the evocation of spirits.

If stories about shamans speak of struggles against the Buryats' oppressors, some official histories recount the failures of the Buryat leadership.
The Russians bribed local leaders and plied influential locals with liquor
during critical negotiations. The Buryat chiefs gave away the most fertile
lands in exchange for Russian administrative titles, gold and silver medals, and sables. The Russian administration did, however, provide the Buryats with some benefits: starting in 1816 the Russians built schools among
the eastern Buryats, and in 1836 the University of Kazan' accepted the first
Buryat students. The Russians also introduced the Buryats to modern medicine and agriculture.[19]

Nevertheless, Russian-Buryat conflicts over land intensified at the end
of the nineteenth century. The Russian government imposed a system
of land reform whereby all local populations, whether engaged in small
mixed farming or extensive pastoralism, were to have an equal amount of
land per household. As a result, the Buryats lost over half their pastureland,
and their livestock declined. The government also sought to administer the
area on a territorial basis, as opposed to the indirect clan rule to which the
Buryats were accustomed (Humphrey 1979:25; Bulag 1998:81). In addition, at the beginning of the twentieth century, Buryat men were heavily recruited to fight for Russia in World War I and the Buryats' horses and other

livestock confiscated to support the military, leaving the women, children, and elderly little to survive on. During the Bolshevik Revolution, Buryats were robbed, killed, and otherwise exploited by both the Whites (czarists) and the Reds (Bolsheviks). After Mongolia gained its independence from China in 1911, some Russian Buryats sought peace and refuge across the border. These details of the Buryats' land loss, the threatened destruction of their clan system, and the loss of family members to violence help to explain, yet again, the Buryats' preoccupation with remembering their land, maintaining knowledge about their clans, and knowing their kinship origins through shamanic rituals.

So far I have discussed the Buryats' experience during Russian advances into their territories. In the next section discuss the Buryats who remained in Mongolia in the seventeenth through the twentieth centuries.

Buryats in Mongolia in the Seventeenth through the Nineteenth Centuries

Mongolia in the seventeenth century offered little to Buryats seeking freedom and peace. The Mongol princes in the north were fighting armies of Russian Cossacks. The loss of Transbaikalia to Russia—the historical land of the Mongols—coincided with the struggles to keep the Manchu Qing conquest at bay in the remaining parts of the country.[20] Mongolia fell to the Qing dynasty in 1691 and remained its tributary until 1911.[21] The border between Russia and Mongolia was closed but permeable: migration took place in both directions. Sometimes, when the Mongol khans fought against Russian incursions to maintain their power to extract taxes from the neighboring Buryats, the Buryats fought with the Russians against the Mongol incursions, thus cementing their allegiance to the Russian czar.

The Qing conquest of Mongolia took well over a century (1622–1756), for various Mongol khanates (those of Khalkha, Inner Mongolia, and Zungaria) violently resisted. The Manchus, using internal discord and infighting among the khans to their own advantage, conquered one khanate at a time until they finally ruled over all of the Mongols. The shamanic spirits of the Khalkha and the Buryats who remained on the Mongolian side of the border from the time of the Manchu Qing conquest sing army songs, ride horses, and use daggers as well as bows and arrows. They request offerings of such Chinese-style delicacies as Beijing wine, dried dates, and candied fruit, unlike the spirits from the Russian side, who like baked *kartokh* (potatoes) with sour cream, *konfetka* (sweets), and *makhorka* (tobacco).

Most shamanic spirits from Mongolia express bitterness and hostility toward Buddhist practitioners. Many of the spirits who returned after socialist suppression also claim to have been repressed by Buddhism even prior to socialism and thus remained unknown for several generations. Although modern Buryats practice Buddhism and have friendly and reciprocal relationships with local lamas, they also argue that Buddhism weakened Mongolia as much as the Manchu conquest did. It is known that the Manchus supported the Mongols' conversion to Tibetan Buddhism in order, as both scholars and the public argue, to keep the Mongols' identity separate from that of the Chinese, and to prevent the unification of Mongols and Chinese against their common oppressor. They also argue that Buddhism was promoted in order to pacify the warlike Mongols and turn them into contemplative lamas. Many Mongol khans also supported conversion so that they would receive rewards from Tibet and as they competed for expanding their individual powers by unifying the warring tribes under their rule.

Prior to the sixteenth century most Mongols practiced folk religion and shamanism and performed occasional rituals of Red Hat Buddhism, also known as Nyingmapa, a version of tantric Buddhism. In order to implement Buddhism, many Mongol khans forbade, under threat of punishment, the possession of shamanic ritual objects and the performance of blood sacrifices (Heissig 1980:36). The proponents of Buddhism burned shamanic *ongghots* (spirit figures), paraphernalia, and other ritual objects. The shamanic gods were replaced by corresponding deities in the Buddhist pantheon.[22]

Buddhism reached the Buryats—the northernmost Mongols—last, in 1730, after it had been introduced to the tribes of what are now Inner Mongolia and Mongolia. The monastic assembly began persecuting shamans in 1819–1820 in the territory of the Khori Buryats and "destroyed through fire all Ongghot (spirit) figures, instruments and costumes of shamans and shamanesses" (Heissig 1980:38). The contemporary Buryats I know in Bayan-Uul do not make ongghot figures, except for those of Hoimorin Högshin. The spirits who possess the shamans today lament being burned, along with shamanic paraphernalia, by Buddhist missionaries. When Buryats today suffer accidental fires, they explain them as the wrath of spirits who were burned in the form of sacred objects during the Buryats' conversion to Buddhism.

For the most part, Buddhism replaced shamanism among the Khalkhas.[23] The Buryats have practiced both: they have modified and enriched their shamanism and adopted Buddhism on the side.[24] Buryat shamanism consists of "black" spirits (protectors and warriors) and "white" ones (the spirits of healer shamans).[25] The Buryats adopted Buddhist elements into

Figure 7. Buddhist celebration of One Thousand Butter Candles

their white branch while leaving the black ones intact. The incorporation of Buddhism empowered shamanism in a number of ways. Many Buryat men who became Buddhist lamas had originally been destined to become white shamans (within the shamanic realm and outside of Buddhism). After they died, instead of being reincarnated as other Buddhist lamas were, they turned into white origin spirits. Once they returned to their descendants as origin spirits, the new generation of shamans added the powers of Buddhism to their spiritual arsenal. Some Buryat lamas are also believed to have practiced shamanism in disguise, which made them more powerful than ordinary or non-Buryat lamas. In other words, Buryat shamans and lamas alike, owing to their disguised additional identities (lamas were also shamans in disguise, and shamans also acquired some shamanic powers), had more power compared to their non-Buryat counterparts. Contrary to its goal, Buddhism did not suppress or erase the Buryats' shamanism but instead strengthened it. In contemporary times, Buddhist and shamanic practitioners mutually enhance each others' prominence even while competing against one another. The identities of shamans and lamas remain sharply distinct, even if the two types of practitioners might share the same skill or powers of the same deity. Since most clients have multiple religious identities and thus owe offerings and rituals to different kinds of spiritual beings, they require the services of both types of spiritual intercessionaries.

Contesting Magic Powers

Contemporary Buryats tell many stories about contestation between Buryat shamans and Buddhist lamas, especially in controlling and manipulating the world around them, people's minds, nature, and social events. Shamans would fly on drums and escape through the skylights of felt tents, eat fire, and shape-shift into animals and rocks. Lamas would make rain, cure deadly illnesses, and transgress distance. Although only one party wins, either shaman or lama, there are also stories that encompass the complexity of belonging to multiple religions and the tensions that individuals feel over reconciling their beliefs. Such tensions were often resolved by winner's remorse and a belief in punishment's being expressed as accident.

The following is a story about the zaarin Bud, the father of Chödör, who was killed by ethnic Khamnigans, as described above. Upon possessing the shaman Chimeg, Bud often shifted from a happy and entertaining mood to a sad and tearful one, and he cried about having been killed at the age of forty-four following a fight with a Tibetan lama.

> Bud was one of the most powerful shamans in the area. He got into a fight with a high-ranking Tibetan tantric lama with the title Sangasva and defeated him. But the victory brought only worry. Bud's parents accused Bud of picking a fight with Sangasva and arranged a ritual of the sacrifice of a horse, in addition to cattle and sheep, to try to soothe Sangasva's spirit. Unfortunately, the spirit did not accept the sacrifice and took revenge. During the sacrifice ritual, a few young men got into a fight and stabbed each other. Bud ran to stop the fight. He separated the men and carried them away from each other. In the process, their blood—the most potent medium for delivering pollution—was smeared onto his skin and clothes. By the time Bud had a chance to wash off the blood, it was too late—the Sangasva's curse had already materialized. Shortly after this incident, Bud died.

It is not so much the battle between a shaman and a lama, but Bud's parents' remorse over the death of the lama, that draws my attention in this story. The Mongols' conversion to Buddhism took two centuries, and this lengthy process involved both resistance (Heissig 1980), especially by the general population, and willing acceptance (Bawden 1968) by the nobility and khans. The story of Bud shows that even within a kin group, the degree to which members adhered to Buddhism was inconsistent and led to disputes. Bud's story also shows that identity is a process rather than a fixed category, and that it is contested, dynamic, and generative.

Buryats and Their Political Activities
in the Early Twentieth Century

In 1911 the revolution in China overthrew the Qing Dynasty. The new Chinese Republic continued to claim Mongolia as an integral part of the nation but changed its administrative policy toward it. Unlike the Qing government, which carried out a policy of separating Mongolia from China, the Chinese Republic aimed to assimilate Mongolia into China. Thus, the centuries-old decrees separating the Mongols and the Chinese were replaced with policies of resettlement. The Han Chinese had been encouraged to migrate to Mongolia, to intermarry local women, and the new law required the use of the Chinese language all over Mongolia.[26]

This direct colonial policy was also fueled by the Chinese response to the increased military presence of the Russians and Japanese in the Far East. Fearing that these two powers might intervene in Mongolia and Manchuria, China decided to buffer its northern border by establishing a unified Chinese nation that included Inner and Outer Mongolia. Such developments spurred strong anti-Chinese sentiment and led to an independence movement in Mongolia. The Mongolian nobles approved the new provisional government, and on December 1, 1911, they proclaimed Mongolia's independence from China and the establishment of a theocracy ruled by the Bogd Khaan.

Meanwhile, Russia's civil and international wars were draining the local population, including the Buryats. Between 1900 and 1925 many Buryat families, mostly the Khori and Aga, immigrated to Mongolia in the hope of escaping Russia's ongoing wars; they settled in the northeastern Mongolian provinces of Khenti and Dornod. Other Buryats, known as Selenge and Ulan-Ude, settled along the central part of the Russian-Mongolian border, mostly in Selenge province.

These Buryats' hopes to escape the violence in Russia came to a halt, for it spread all over Mongolia. Many Buryats became politically active during this period. (Their activism would be turned against them during Mongolia's state cleansing in the 1930s.) For instance, in 1919 some of the Buryat intelligentsia collaborated with Japanese and anti-Bolshevik Russians to launch a pan-Mongolist movement aimed at establishing a pan-Mongol empire comprising Outer Mongolia, Buryatia, and other Mongols in Russia and China. However, in the 1915 Tripartite Treaty, signed by China, Russia, and Mongolia, the Russians accepted only Outer Mongolian independence under Chinese suzerainty. The Buryats were to remain part of Russia; the Inner Mongols, a part of China. In this context, pan-Mongolism was a threat to Outer Mongolia's independence. Furthermore, the Buryat leaders of the movement "planned to deliver Outer Mongolia to the Soviet Union in return for both more favorable treatment of the Buryats and the advancement of pan-Mongolism" (Murphy 1966:24; Bulag 1998:83). The Outer Mongolians saw the Buryats as traitors, and the Soviets saw them as separatists. The pan-Mongolist movement was put down.

Further events in Mongolia worsened the Buryats' political reputation in the eyes of the Soviet Union and Mongolia. In 1921 the czarist general Baron Roman von Ungern-Sternberg, who had been defeated by the Red Army in Russia, arrived in Mongolia intending to establish a Central Asian empire with the remnants of the White Army under his command (Bulag 1998:82). The Buryats, who had been mistreated by the local Russians, joined Ungern-Sternberg (Battogtoh 1991:44). Many Buryats in Mongolia were also recruited, under threat of arrest, into his army (Galsan 1994).

Ungern-Sternberg's arrival in Mongolia influenced the fate of the country in an unexpected way. Bolshevik Russia at first showed little interest in Mongolia. But when Ungern-Sternberg threatened the Soviets with attack from his stronghold in Mongolia, they chose to defend their revolutionary victory in the Far East and Siberia. The Soviets sent troops to aid the Mongolian army in defeating Ungern-Sternberg and establishing socialism in the country.[27] Ungern-Sternberg was arrested and executed by the Russians in 1921, and three years later Outer Mongolia became the Mongolian People's Republic (MPR), the only independent country of Mongols. It did actually have de facto independence from China, even though the Sino-Soviet Treaty of 1924 recognized Chinese sovereignty over Mongolia. The majority of Buryats remained in Russia, but the ones who fled to Mongolia became targets of Stalin's revenge.

Stalin was enraged by the Buryats' immigration to Mongolia. He was especially bitter about their joining Ungern-Sternberg's army and demanded that they return to Russia. But after Mongol leaders negotiated for dual citizenship for the Buryats, Stalin seems to have relented. On September 5, 1924, Mongolia and the Soviet Union signed an agreement giving Buryats dual citizenship rights (Dondog 1988).[28] Between November 18, 1924, and March 1926, about twenty thousand individuals in 5,243 households became Mongolian citizens. Most of the Buryats of Mongolia live in the northern and northeastern provinces of Selenga, Hentii, and Dornod. The Buryat intelligentsia reside in the city of Ulaanbaatar, and many occupy important decision-making positions. The Bayan-Uul district of Dornod province was formed in 1922, and a branch of the Mongolian People's

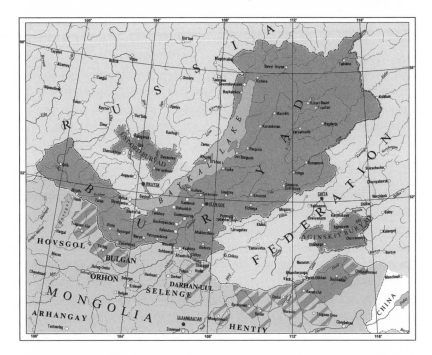

Map 3. Map of the distribution of Buryats in contemporary Russia and Mongolia

Revolutionary Party (MPRP) was established in 1929 to lead political meet-ings and educational activities.

Subsequent political events in northeastern Asia in the early twentieth century favored the Soviet presence in Mongolia, such as the Soviets' dis-pute with Japan over its far eastern border in the 1930s. The 1928 victory of the Chinese Nationalists over the Communists also strengthened Soviet influence in Mongolia. Stalin aimed to prevent Mongolia from being used as a zone of counterrevolutionary activity, whereas Mongolia depended on Soviet support to keep Chinese influence at bay.[29] Though the Soviet Union recognized Mongolia's independence and did not attempt a territo-rial settlement, it dominated Mongolia politically by controlling the ruling elites of the MPRP.

Mongolian leaders of the early twentieth century had a number of deci-sions to make regarding the future of the nation. Although state socialism is known for its atheist politics, at least in the beginning the Mongol lead-ers had no intention of destroying Buddhism. As Rupen (1979) points out, it was not until the Soviets began to exert pressure on the Mongolians to destroy the power of the Buddhist clergy that the new socialist government became convinced of the importance of reducing the power of the clergy and the upper class. The initial measures were nonviolent, such as reeducation, propaganda, and taxation of the lamas, but the government shifted to physical violence in mid-1930s.[30] It affected not only lamas but also the intelligentsia, the upper class, and the Buryats, all of whom were labeled enemies of the people.

Carrying Their History

By now it should be clear that the Buryats' distinctive way of remembering their past through shamanic practices has developed in the context of their experiences of colonialism, displacement, and marginalization. The Buryats carried their history with them in the form of shamans adorned with paraphernalia. That a people are mobile does not automatically make their history movable. Almost everything that constitutes the Buryats' past, one that is brought into being by means of shamanism—including the spirits, their stories, the shamans, their paraphernalia, and the audiences—is movable in its own way. Their mobility was not only mechanical (e.g., in the portability and transferability of the stories that make up the Buryats' history), but also conceptual (e.g., in the agility of the shaman's mind when improvising stories), though the two often overlap and enable each other. The constituent elements of this shamanism-evoked past cover different social terrains, thus ensuring the greatest protection against forgetting.

The origin spirits—the Buryats imagine them as *hii biyet* (air-bodied beings)—travel faster than the imagination. This is why an origin spirit can maintain several residences on earth and in the celestial realm, including its homeland, the place of its death, and the places it visits—huudal buudal. As a shaman pronounces the name of a spirit's residences, he or she reminds the living of the names of their lost ancestral homelands. When possessed by origin spirits, the shamans enact the cultural stereotypes of the time of the spirits through dialect, posture, gesture, and the stories they tell about their lives during that period. Most Buryats in Mongolia rarely traveled to their ancestral homelands in Russia during socialism. Since its demise, foreign travel is no longer controlled by the state, but financial hardships have restricted mobility. And thus origin spirits remain the mobile agents of the memory of the past.

The skills necessary for harnessing the origin spirits are not given automatically, but acquired through travel. The shamans must travel to their teachers for consultation, to blacksmiths and seamstresses to obtain their paraphernalia, and within and outside their communities to build and maintain their networks. They transport their paraphernalia wherever they go. A shaman adorned in full paraphernalia, the components of which are infused by the powers of origin spirits, is a condensed, movable, and interactive history. A shaman's upward mobility depends on the completion of *shanar* (degree ceremonies), eleven for men and seven for women, and is crucial to his or her maintaining power as a practitioner and achieving the highest rank—zaarin for men and *duurisah* for women.

Clients' mobility is equally crucial for maintaining communal and individual pasts through shamanism. For one, clients accumulate and organize the knowledge relayed by various shamans. When a shaman reveals additional spirits who had been suppressed or forgotten, the clients make links among these spirits to build continuity between different generations, stories, and events. That is because, for the most part, a shaman's rituals are intended to communicate with an individual origin spirit, rather than to build a continuous history. Furthermore, because there is no way for clients to judge the truthfulness of either the shamans or the spirits, many sponsor additional rituals to get a number of opinions to compare and choose from, further intensifying the proliferation of shamans. This search for authenticity and credibility contributes to the making of history by the creation and dissemination of new knowledge. The clients are not necessarily aware of their roles, but their actions, the organizing of obtained knowledge and generating new knowledge—which often take place simultaneously—contribute to the making of history.

In the context of shamanism, knowledge is mobile on many levels. It is a product of a shaman's mobile (i.e., thinking) mind, an object that is passed around; and it is mobile from within, because it constantly transforms. Empirically, most knowledge mediated by shamans is the product of careful selection, remembering, and improvisation based on the client's needs. The transmission of knowledge also involves persuasion: the shaman must convince his or her audience that the knowledge conveyed matters to all of them, not just to those individuals who are the "children" of the origin spirits. To accomplish this, shamans must move the audience emotionally. They employ various psychological, linguistic, and performance techniques to transform distant knowledge into the audience's past. Cole (2001:281) notes the importance of the power of emotion among the Betsimisaraka of Madagascar in molding what she calls emotional memories. She states that these memories are not about knowing the past and retaining information; rather, they enable the Betsimisaraka to create and maintain a view of how the world works. Similarly, for the Buryats, remembering also involves the moving of emotions.

A shaman must move the audiences emotionally in order to transform distant history into a more personal memory. The same origin spirit (and his or her stories) may be a personal memory for his or her descendants' family, but a piece of history for the rest of the audience. Importantly, the relationship is dynamic, not fixed: some individuals who have grown distant from their family past treat this knowledge more like history, while others may develop closer emotional attachments to the spirits of their distant relatives and consider them to be part of their memory. In addition, knowing more details about someone's tragic life can spur enough emotion to bring that life closer to the realm of memory.

The knowledge a shaman transmits is multifaceted. It is history to the extent that the shaman produces the story as work for the client, but that history also proves the shaman a specialist in maintaining a link between a community with its past. The distinction between memory and history thus is based on a kind of a relationship between an individual and a past. It does not really indicate the existence of two different categories of unrelated knowledge. What may be memory for one person is history for another. This means that calling something exclusively "history" or "memory" risks presupposing homogeneity in those who hold that knowledge. For instance, Nora (1989) distinguishes memory from history by suggesting that memory presupposes that an event was directly witnessed; history, on the other hand, is a detached and rational work of outsiders based on archives and other materials. While this may be the case in some instances, Buryat shamanic practices also show that the boundary between memory and history is fluid and dynamic. It has to do with relationships between individuals and knowledge and the meanings that individuals attribute to those relationships, both of which are in flux. The general goal of a shaman is to gain as many audiences as possible by creating memory for his or her immediate clients and, simultaneously, history for the wider audience. The shamans, however, are most interested in making memory out of history for as many people as possible, because that brings them clients and not just transient audiences. Thus, delivering knowledge for shamans also means moving the supposed boundaries between history and memory and shaping individuals' relationship to knowledge.

Finally, the content and structure of the narratives carry special weight in making them memorable and broadly relevant. Several of the stories that I related in this chapter contain contradictions that preclude a smooth turn of events and a single meaning for a particular audiences, thus excluding other audiences. Instead, there is always a moment of stepping back, an act of semi-betrayal, and what can be seen as an inclusion of an exclusion into the mainstream narrative. For instance, Hoimorin Högshin is the symbol of resistance to Russian colonialism, but at the same time she turns almost treacherous by halting the birth of babies. As I suggested, she embodies some colonial powers, and transforms them (under the condition that the Buryats worship her) to protect the Buryats. The attribution of colonial powers to the deity could be a way of conveying the acceptance of the Russian way of life by many Buryats. And that is the untold narrative behind this story of resistance.

Another contradiction inheres in the story of a tragic death of Chödör and his fiancée, who came from a warring clan of Khamnigans. What remains unclear is how Chödör, a popular and respected shaman (and presumably highly visible), has developed a relationship with a woman from a warring group. The couple's relationship suggests that while interethnic hatred is the main issue of the story, intermarriage between Buryats and Khamnigans took place prior to colonial war as well as during it.

Bud's story about the fight with the Tibetan lama Sangasva describes another complex situation from which none of the participants has an easy way out. Bud was wrong to defeat the lama; but if he had not, the lama would have killed him. He could not win either way, and his resistance is poignant and tragic. No matter which side the story is viewed from, it is conceptually and ideologically incomplete. On the one hand, it concerns shamanic resistance to Buddhism—but that is not its only point, because Bud's family scolds him, setting limits to resistance. On the other hand, it deals with acceptance of Buddhism—but again, not entirely, because Sangasva dies. The leakages, diversions, and inclusions of exclusions from the mainstream narratives, make these stories attractive to multiple audiences, thus targeting a larger audience. Although the stories of Hoimorin Högshin, Chödör, and Bud depict resistance to injustice and mistreatment, they also imply untold stories of another kind: the Buryats' acceptance of Russian rule, conversion to Buddhism, and marrying Khamnigans. But because they were not chosen to become narrative memories, these other truths are represented through logical slippages: Hoimorin Högshin exhibits the same kind of brutality as the colonial oppressors do; Bud is scolded and instructed by his own family to make a sacrifice for a rival lama; and Chödör falls in love with a woman from a warring clan of the Khamnigans. These slippages are forms of narrative expression that construct not only events, but also "the exclusion of events from the narrative possibility" (Steedly

1993:30). Because social remembering involves deliberate exclusion and selective remembering (Halbwachs [1925] 1992, Cole 2001), the stories are not about the brutality of their oppressors, but emphasize the Buryats' experiences under them.

A final mobility bears mentioning: that of the shaman's mind. The Buryats believe that during possession by origin spirits, the souls of shamans temporarily leave their bodies to accommodate that spirit. To do so, the shamans' souls must already be mobile. Obviously, I cannot attest to that; I can only describe what I have observed. Most shamans I have met are described as having *guilgee uhaan*—literally, a "mind that runs fast." The phrase implies fluidity uninhibited by any obstacles. Coincidentally, there is a somewhat symbolic connection between shamans, who possess the ability to think through obstacles, and the shifting and dynamic history that this ability produces.

TWO

Technologies of Forgetting, State Socialism, and Potential Memories

This chapter is about state-enforced forgetting—its technologies and representations—and the repercussions of forgetting on shamanic practices, different generations, and individual relationships during and after socialism. I trace the ways in which forgetting influenced the local politics and discourses that shape the day-to-day lives of individuals and communities. State-enforced forgetting is different from noninvasive forgetting as a part of the dialectic of remembering and forgetting through which societies sort out their collective memory. Not only does forced forgetting erase parts of the past and prevent their transmission to newer generations; it also creates anxiety about the loss, which weakens individuals' confidence in their own memories. It is this profound sense of loss, a belief in endless oblivion despite the proliferation of memories, that led me to question the state technologies of forgetting.[1] What did the state do to create a sense of endless forgetting in addition to the acts of erasing and suppressing the past?

I concentrate on social forgetting, which I define as techniques and procedures that the state uses in order to undermine social remembering. Social remembering consists of the culturally specific and dynamic systems and practices that communities rely on to keep in touch with their past. It features, for example, group membership (Halbwachs 1992 [1925]), commemorative rituals (Durkheim 2001 [1912]), physical habits (Connerton 1989), and a memoryscape—the spatiotemporal terrain on which memories are distributed, such as landscape, buildings, and roads (Cole 2001). The Mongolian socialist state enforced forgetting through at least three processes: destruction; the erasure and suppression of the memories of that destruction and suppression (the forgetting of forgetting); and, finally, the construction of new memories intended to substitute for those that were eliminated. In practice, these processes were not isolated and categorized.

It is done here in order to highlight the fact that state-enforced forgetting was a systematic and continuous process that extended far beyond the initial destruction and killing. In order to erase the memories of its own violence, the state, for instance, buried purge victims in unmarked mass graves, closed and controlled archives, and silenced individual stories. The new memories and remembering practices it created were meant to distract from, override, and substitute for actual memories. Many of them took the form of grand public rituals designed to compel acceptance of the state's narrative as unquestioned truth.

Of course, I cannot access forgetting (individual and social) that is beyond representation, so I focus on the technologies of forgetting, for they are visible. I forgo examining individuals' memories that remain beyond representation, though not because I wish to isolate individual memories from societal ones. I agree entirely with Bloch (1996) and Cole (2004) that the individual and society shape remembering and forgetting dialectically, and that in some cases individuals are fully dependent on the society for maintaining memory (Halbwachs 1980 [1950]). However, the state's long-term, systematic, forced forgetting altered the dynamic between individual and social memories and created certain gaps and omissions.[2] Given the Buryats' enduring and creative resistance to the state's policies of suppressing the past, it is possible that a great many unarticulated and unshared individual memories lie outside social representations of remembering and are beyond our grasp.[3] Hidden rituals, healing disguised as physical therapy, and the use of "evocative transcripts" (Humphrey 1994:22) that purposely multiply and confuse meanings all indicate that memory was very much alive in certain private and semiprivate domains. We already know from the scholarship on memory in socialist and postsocialist contexts that oppressive regimes never "precluded the active construction and transmission of unofficial pasts" (Watson 1994: 2) and that state socialism was a weak and disorganized institution (Mueggler 2001).[4]

But the secretive nature of the resistance also suggests that confronting the state openly put too much at stake. Of special interest are the techniques and processes used by the state toward the end of socialism, which created anxiety about forgetting and a loss of confidence in individuals' remembering. The concern here is not what has been objectively and quantitatively lost, but the ways in which the technologies of forgetting created among the people specific feelings and convictions about their losses, and how such feelings influence their understanding of the present-day remaking of the past.

Indeed, as Kaplonski (2004) illustrates, anxiety about the past was one impetus behind the democratic movement that came at the end of socialism. Elites and intellectuals expressed an almost nationwide questioning of the past and urged that the suppressed past of the early years of socialism be brought up publicly. The Buryats' angry spirits, who have returned to exact revenge for having been forgotten and abandoned, are a culturally specific part of this unofficial frenzy about the past. The Buryats' attempts to calm these spirits and thus remake their past have exploded into a seemingly endless proliferation of them. On one hand, the Buryats suspect that there are additional memories waiting to be revealed. On the other, weighed down by the extent of the destruction and erasure, they are also skeptical about the possibility of retrieving credible memories. In order to understand these anxieties about the loss of the past and the problems that have arisen while remaking it, we need to understand what it meant to live under a totalitarian regime that suppressed memories and engineered history. For that, we need to examine the state technologies of forgetting and their implementation.

Our analytical tools for the study of forgetting, however, are limited. Despite the proliferation of research on memory at the turn of the millennium, forgetting has received little attention in the social sciences. Only recently have scholars emphasized forgetting as an integral part of memory (Cole 2001, Fabian 2003, Connerton 2009, Vivian 2010). Far from being merely a failure of biology and neurology, forgetting is socially constituted within the contexts of power, agency, and resistance. For instance, in postcolonial Madagascar forgetting is one way communities have dealt with traumatic events (Cole 2001). In the European and American urban world, according to Connerton (2009), forgetting is an inevitable outcome of the postmodernization of architecture and the lack of continuity and connection in public spaces.

Some philosophers have advocated for the potential uses of forgetting for humankind. For instance, Nietzsche regarded forgetting as a moral impulse "in the service of the future and the present" (1983:77), as a remedy for the malady of history, which he said no longer knew how "to employ the past as a nourishing food" (1983:120). Ricoeur (2004) has argued that forgetting is a precursor as well as a result of forgiving. Some scholars suggest that structured forgetting is necessary to maintaining national unity and building democracy after violent conflicts (Misztal 2005, 2009). I see these arguments as critical and humanistic engagements with making history. They advocate omitting violence in making history in order to prevent future hostilities. Yet they do not ask what forgetting entails, what methods and technologies have been used, and what its impact might be on individuals and communities. I raise these questions because forgetting has been the cause and a part of generating violence, establishing domination, and oppressing others. The Mongolian socialist state, for instance, induced forgetting in the Nietzschean sense: to serve the future and present, to maintain national unity, and, as Misztal suggests, to prevent future bloodshed in the form of revenge. The state also strove to achieve "a dramatic and unprecedented break between past and present" (Appadurai 1996:2–3) in order to build a modern socialist state in which all individuals benefited from the progress of modernity. Yet what seemed to be good intentions and correct measures has led to the suffering, to various degrees, of most of the nation and to the consolidation of the totalitarian state.

It is not surprising that historians' attempts to understand the circumstances and power relations that led to the erasure of history led them to attend to the larger ideological contexts of racism, colonialism, slavery, and social evolution. For instance, Brundage (2000) questions the paucity of black historical narratives, and Vidal-Naquet (1992) explores the contexts of Holocaust denial. Trouillot (1995), for instance, argues that the Haitian Revolution of 1790—the first slave revolution—received almost no coverage in Western media and histories because European and American journalism and scholarship were dominated by eighteenth-century racism and invalid ideas about social evolution. Deeply held convictions about the inferiority of black people prevented them from recognizing the Haitian Revolution (Trouillot 1995:72).

I join Brundage, Vidal-Naquet, and Trouillot in exploring the larger ideological, geopolitical, and national circumstances behind forgetting. As an anthropologist, I also examine the state techniques of forgetting and the ways in which some of them became a part of everyday life and acquired values and meanings that invade social and individual memories. I show that in Mongolia, forgetting in general involves three processes. First, there is destruction and killing; the new socialist state in the 1930s destroyed about 8 percent of its population and almost all material objects that were, in the state's view, related to the past. Secondly, the state suppressed memories of its own violence while continuing to suppress the past. And thirdly, the socialist state created new memories to substitute for the ones it had destroyed. The new postsocialist state maintains the past under its control, but in indirect and less visible ways.

Technologies of Forgetting

First, Extermination of the Past

Mongolia's political cleansing began in the late 1920s and peaked in 1937–1940. The socialist state labeled the Buddhist clergy, the intelligentsia, the upper class, wealthy nomads, and the Buryats "enemies of the people" and began prosecuting them. Sources give the number of those killed as being between 50,000 and 100,000—in a country with a population of less than 800,000 at the time. The exact figure will probably never be known, because many records of the period were lost or destroyed.[5] The state also destroyed material objects related to the people it purged and exterminated, among them eight hundred Buddhist monasteries with their libraries, religious objects, and artworks.[6]

The Buryats were one of the state's primary targets. Stalin took revenge upon them for their flight to Mongolia, for joining Ungern-Sternberg, and for their pan-Mongolist aspirations. He labeled them antiproletarians, traitors to the Bolshevik Revolution, and White (czarist) allies. He sent the Mongolian prime minister, Khorloogiin Choibalsan, thirty thousand bullets as a birthday gift, implying his support for the extermination of the Buryats (Kaplonski 2002). The purge was further fueled by suspicions that the Buryats were allies of the Japanese during the 1935–1937 Soviet-Japanese border wars. About fifteen thousand Buryats—half of the adult population—were killed.[7] In some Buryat settlements, all of the able-bodied men were arrested, leaving women and children to fend for themselves; there were no men left, I was told, to slaughter a sheep—strictly a man's job—for provisions. This cleansing was carried out not only in order to secure the country's independence but also out of loyalty to the Soviet Union, because it offered protection from outside intrusion and economic assistance.

In addition to the destruction and killing, the socialist government also used interpretation, through which it altered the meanings of events that took place in the past. The interpretation of history, as Foucault (1977) calls it, is a conspicuous form of domination. One particular Buryat case at the turn of the twentieth century constitutes a vivid example.

In 1920, after being defeated by the Bolsheviks, the czarist general Ungern-Sternberg went to Mongolia. At that time Mongolia was fighting the Chinese, who were trying to annex Mongolia to China. Internally, Mongolia's political leadership was fractured into multiple groups, the most active ones being the new revolutionaries who fought against the theocratic monarchy. Ungern-Sternberg sided with the monarch and fought against the Chinese troops. He recruited many Buryats (voluntarily and by force) to fight the war that was to liberate Mongolia from the Chinese. This was an important victory for Mongolia in its march toward independence.

Until Ungern-Sternberg went to Mongolia and began making military movements, Bolshevik Russia ignored Mongolia and its requests for assistance. But Ungern-Sternberg's proximity to the Siberian and far eastern borders of Russia worried the new Bolshevik government in Moscow. In order to protect its recent victory, it promptly sent Red Army troops to help the Mongol revolutionary forces defeat Ungern-Sternberg's army and establish socialism in Mongolia. The Buryats, who had fought the Chinese with Ungern-Sternberg, were now fighting revolutionary Mongol and Bolshevik forces. The Bolsheviks prevailed and established a socialist government in Mongolia. The Buryats who had joined Ungern-Sternberg and fought against the Chinese, and then against the Bolshevik Russian and revolutionary Mongol troupes, were cast as enemies of the Soviet and Mongolian states. The Buryats' negative image was based on their fight against the Russians and the Mongolians, while their contributions to Mongolia's independence were selectively suppressed until after the purges of the late 1930s.

Silencing Individual Stories

Since the dead do not talk, the stories of those who were arrested and killed were silenced even before they could materialize. Because their deaths went unwitnessed, their last moments remain surrounded by mystery and guesswork. Strangely, the narratives of the living seem to struggle to break free from the silence of the dead. In Bayan-Uul, when I asked people about state violence, their answers were often vague and distant. Most people with whom I spoke were born after the violence. The ones who were alive during the 1930s only witnessed or heard about the arrests, which took place in the dead of night or in pastures, where there were few witnesses. Family members expected those arrested to return home, as did the detainees themselves, convinced of their innocence. Many women waited in vain and died without ever learning the whereabouts of their male relatives.

Most people dwelled on the magnitude and spread of violence, hardly questioning why the state engaged in violence to begin with. The Buryats explained the magnitude of the violence by the fact that once it began, it took on a life of its own, became embedded in local life, and transformed into a self-perpetuating, uncontrollable force. Purges and local denunciations were used as a tool for settling accounts from previous struggles during revolution and collectivization and turned into a chance for have-nots to take revenge on their former dominators. Another reason violence was widespread was because of the quota laid on each perpetrator: failure to meet it resulted in punishment. And "some perpetrators wanted more power and did their job to perfection," while "others used their power to settle existing interpersonal conflicts."

While these remarks gave me a nuanced understanding of the circumstances that led to the proliferation of violence, they also made the state's role in the violence ambiguous, distant, and insignificant.[8] Most of those with whom I spoke refrained from blaming the state, saying such things as, "Once it began, the state had little control over the purging." They also emphasized the impossibility of identifying victims and perpetrators in the state's repeated cycles of violence: "Everyone was a victim at that time. There was no escape. People who carried out the arrests one day became the victims the next morning." It seems that people chose to accept and endure the violence as an uncontrollable force because there were no losers or winners, and because the suffering was communal. Only a few individuals assigned the state any responsibility for the violence. While it is clear that for the Buryats the local politics behind the spread of violence was much more understandable and traceable, it still puzzles me why and how the state got away with little, if any, blame.

For one thing, the state dissipated the notion of victimhood through repeated cycles of purges and rehabilitations. Throughout socialism, Mongolia had at least three cycles of state violence, each followed by rehabilitations of the wrongly accused and purges of the perpetrators.[9] A historian of twentieth-century Mongolia whose acquaintance I made, Munhdalain Rinchin, describes the cycles of state violence and the rehabilitations that immediately followed them—all of which help us to understand the confusion, terror, and uncertainty that people were living under during socialism, especially in the 1930s and 1940s. The violence of the 1930s aimed to eliminate the enemies of the socialist revolution. In the 1940s, during the second cycle, the state targeted remnant antirevolutionaries, especially within the MPRP. The third cycle, in the 1960s, combined internal cleansing with the suppression of intellectuals (Rinchin 2000). Following each cycle of violence, the state acknowledged that there were some aspects that went wrong in the process of eliminating enemies—individual officers' misconduct, internal power struggles, bureaucratic confusion, and the like—and would rehabilitate those whom it found to have been falsely accused. Then it would purge some of the perpetrators on the grounds that they committed crimes during the violence or for some other reason. Thus we can see how the purgings of the perpetrators and the rehabilitations of the accused following each cycle of violence blurred the boundaries between innocent and guilty, and between perpetrators and victims. It turned almost everyone into a victim, either real or imagined, either from the time of the purge or during its aftermath. The repeated cycles of purging and shifting of targets partly explain why the Buryats told me that there was no escape from the violence. It was not always clear what criteria were used to arrest individuals, or how someone who was correct today could be wrong tomorrow. None of the rehabilitations were publicly announced or commemorated, nor did they ever enter local historical lore.

The repeated cycles of persecutions and rehabilitations, as well as the fact that persecutions were publicly known while rehabilitations were handled privately, contributed to the silencing of individual stories. Public accusation gives the victim a public identity as an enemy of the state. But private rehabilitations remove individuals' identities as victims in the private realm without necessarily rehabilitating them publicly. Some people experienced all three cycles of repression and rehabilitation, while others suffered only repeated repressions; yet others were repressed and rehabilitated once, only to be repressed again in the next round and remain a victim. The obliteration of the boundary between perpetrator and victim owing to the repeated cycles of persecution and rehabilitation creates the impression that everyone has been a victim. It is no coincidence that even after the collapse of socialism, the postsocialist state fashions the political violence as a national tragedy, not an individual one: that way, victimhood becomes part of a common experience and a common narrative, and individual memories become secondary. At the local level, remembering violence is often reduced to discussions about the equal distribution of suffering. The memories of individual experiences are often subsumed under a communal narrative, which renders them silent or insignificant.

In the following section I unpack some of the techniques through which the state was able to hide its agency in the violence while perpetuating a positive and benevolent image.

Exploiting the Fear of Outside Domination

The fear of outside domination, especially by China, has the strongest influence on Mongolian nationalism in the twentieth century. When Soviet/ Russian influence diminished in the 1990s, for the first time since the 1920s, and Mongolia was opened to the outside world, many older individuals expressed fear that the country had lost the protection of its "Soviet brothers" from foreign takeover. Fear and hatred of the Chinese in particular spanned generations. The aggressive tactics of the late Qing Dynasty and the new Chinese republic in assimilating Mongolia into China in the late nineteenth century spurred Mongolians to vigilance and lasting nationalism. The state advocated strengthening itself in order to withstand intrusion from without and eliminating enemies, traitors, and perpetrators of violence in order to protect ordinary citizens. Violence for the purpose of protection renders the state's wrath tolerable and justifiable. State violence is perceived as "good" if its goal to protect the innocent and target the enemy. The state devised its own narrative justifying violence as necessary to protect itself from its enemies. In one popular discourse, which was spun off from history textbooks and literature, Stalin was the savior of Mongolia's independence from China. The purges of the clergy, the intelligentsia, the upper class, and the Buryats were depicted as part of the revolutionaries' struggle to defend the nation-state against counterrevolutionaries, reactionaries, and terrorists.

For instance, in films about the 1921 socialist revolution, aristocrats were represented as exploiters and as the allies of Chinese politicians.[10] Buddhist lamas were represented as *eserguu*—terrorists skilled in the most horrific tortures. In a film called *Into Hiding*, a counterrevolutionary head lama nicknamed Dambiijaa pulls the heart from the chest of a captured revolutionary while he is still alive. The camera pans to a hand raising the still-beating heart while blood splashes on a ceremonial banner. The scene, which is accompanied by Buddhist ceremonial music rhythmicized with cymbals and drums, was meant to provoke a visceral reaction of terror and hatred. In the Mongolian Revolutionary Museum the exhibits of the early twentieth century displayed the instruments of torture and illustrations of people being tortured under the orders of Qing officials, Mongol landlords, and clergy. Schoolchildren in the city of Ulaanbaatar from kindergarten on up often made class trips to the museum.

We see here a parallel to Taussig's concept of colonial mimesis. The Mongolian state mimicked the cruelty it attributed to the enemies it yearned to destroy, just as Spanish colonizers in the Americas mirrored in their own behavior the savagery they imputed to the Indians they colonized. In fact, the colonists themselves actually devised the tortures of which they accused the natives (Taussig 1987:134). In Mongolia, the state's representation of its enemies as more cruel than itself was one of the ways in which it justified its own violence against its enemies. In so doing it strengthened its image as a rescuer of the people and vindicated itself of any charges of gratuitous oppression. "The importance . . . of fabulation extends beyond the nightmarish quality of its contents," writes Taussig. "All societies live by fictions taken as real. . . . The epistemological, ontological, and otherwise philosophical problem or representation . . . becomes a high powered medium of domination" (1987:121) that renders the dominators capable of anything (1987:122). Mimicry and storytelling justified the violence of the Mongolian state. Mongolia's revolutionaries themselves raised their enemies' hearts to salute ceremonial banners. A film about the military commander Khatanbaatar Magsarjav represents the ritual not a gruesome and sickening act of bloodthirsty torture, as it was in the hands of the lamas, but as part of a respected leader's victory celebration.

Repression, fear, and uncertainty kept individual memories from being articulated, and the constant repetition of the state's narrative robbed people of confidence in their own memories. "When you repeat something a hundred times, it starts becoming the truth," a friend in Bayan-Uul said of the state's rhetoric. The omnipresence, repetition, and routinization of state narratives through media, party meetings, and political celebrations "creates an uncertain reality out of fiction, giving shape and voice to the formless form of the reality in which an unstable interplay of truth and illusion becomes a phantasmic social force" (Taussig 1987:121).

Unconditional Love and Selective Forgetting

Many Mongol leaders resisted Stalin's despotic plans in the 1930s. Stalin assassinated seven who refused to implement his plans before he finally promoted Choibalsan to head of state, in which role he carried out state-sponsored murders.[11] As Baabar (1999:345) suggests, the remaining leaders were forced to accept direction from Moscow for a number of reasons. For one, the Soviet Union warned Mongol leaders who disagreed with Soviet policies that the Soviets had no obligation to help Mongolia maintain its independence from China. The popular and scholarly discourse continues to emphasize that Stalin was the only leader in the international arena who recognized Mongolian independence, so the violence he imposed had to be carried out lest he follow through on his threat to withdraw essential Soviet support for Mongolia's independence from China.[12] Stalin's violence was seen as the inevitable fate of what the Mongolians called themselves *jijig uls* (a small nation); there was little the Mongolian state could have done to withstand *ih gurnii deerenguy uzel* (the domination of the great empire). Although people are aware of Choibalsan's role in the violence, most view him as a leader who saved Mongolia's independence during its fragile years. He influenced Stalin to continue defending Mongolia's independence against the Chinese. Based on popular narratives, Stalin, as the leader of a powerful empire, wielded more leverage over the Chinese Communist Party and Mao Zedong than did Choibalsan. By the latter half of the twentieth century, Soviet domination was seen as preferable to the possibility of Chinese colonialism. For this independence, as many people told me, some sacrifices might have been necessary. In other words, the memories of state violence were refracted through the prism of nationalism, which was, in turn, shaped by cold war geopolitics.

In addition to building a narrative with a persuasive content, the state strived to disseminate it as widely and deeply as possible, so that it would substitute for and suppress individual narratives. It intended to engrave its narrative in people's minds and to that end utilized various representations, methods, and delivery channels that targeted different areas of cognition and emotion. Starting in 1925, every town or settlement built a ger called the "red corner," and bigger towns built imposing *soyolin tov* (culture centers) for concerts, shows, films, and meetings. These red corners were the houses for the state screens on which were projected to the people the ideals they were to adhere to as they were socialized and entertained. In those spaces, people were subjected to *uzel surtlin ajil* (ideological workings) in ways both subtle and overt. A number of museums, national radio broadcasting stations, newspapers, magazines, and theaters were established during that period.[13] These were the state's nonrepressive, constructive forms of power, meant to entertain and educate the nation. As Foucault wrote, "What makes power hold, what makes it accepted, is simply the fact that it doesn't only weigh on us as a force that says no; it also traverses and produces things, it induces pleasure, forms knowledge, produces discourse" (1994:120).

The propaganda representations were meant to create some very specific states of mind in the populace. The state narrative represented the nation as vulnerable, fragile, and alone in the geopolitical arena, but also stoic in its struggle to keep outside domination at bay. This was intended to generate feelings of altruism in citizens, the impulse to protect the nation, and, if necessary, acceptance and perhaps even forgiveness of the state's violence against its own people. The state claimed a higher priority on the spectrum of love and dedication than people's family members. In one well-known poem, a young soldier announces that he is burning with love for a special someone. Not only are these his first deep emotional stirrings, but this is also the first time he verbalizes his feelings in the words "I love you." And then the audience learns that the soldier "had never yet uttered such words to anyone, including his beloved spouse"; the object of his affection is his country. Socialist poems such as this pledging the speaker's life and unconditional love to the motherland also made the threat of military conquest as real as possible.

The Buryats occupy a complex position in this discourse. They share other Mongolians' feelings of nationalism and desire for national independence. Yet unlike the dominant Khalkhas, the Buryats feel Mongolia's state oppression and their own marginalization more acutely. They dealt with two domineering actors that also opposed each other: the state and the larger geopolitical powers that dominated it. Many Buryats I know privilege belonging to the Mongolian state and resist larger powers' efforts to dominate the country. At the same time, their emotions about their country conflict with the resentment and grief, among other things, that they feel about the violence of the state.

Undermining the Contexts for Remembering

The socialist state strove to make memories of the past irrelevant to the present by undermining their contexts. After the socialist government was established in the 1920s, it began renaming public and historical spaces, streets, rituals, and celebrations were changed to reflect the goals of the present. For instance, the capital city, Da Hüree (Big Monastery), was renamed Ulaanbaatar (Red Hero). The Mongolian Lunar New Year was renamed Herders' day, and its celebrations were basically prohibited. In Ulaanbaatar (and the next-biggest city, Darkhan) the state built wedding palaces, thus making marriages and the establishment of families matters that came under state control. The alphabet, personal names, food, hairstyles, consumer goods, clothing, and fashions also changed due to the revolution. All this meant that the younger generations had little reference in everyday life from which to inquire about the past. When the memories of those belonging to an older generation contradicted the national narrative, there was little chance they would be heard by succeeding generations, whose ideological training and values conflicted with those of the past. "The erasure of socio-political context . . . allowed for the absorption of the particular (memories) into the general" (Steedly 1993:131), and furthered the homogenization of history and the nation. In a homogenizing society, to be a misfit, a reactionary, was not only a source of shame and public alienation, but also invited the threat of state intervention.

Jambal worked as a researcher at the state Academy of Science in the sections on religion and history in the 1970s and 1980s. He was also trained as a Tibetan medical practitioner by his grandfather and secretly practiced for a clientele who found him through underground networks. Once he was riding a crowded city bus at the end of a workday, wearing a Western-style suit and carrying a briefcase, to all appearances a proper white-collar employee of his time. A schoolboy of about ten, however, shouted to the entire bus, "I can smell lama in this man!! This man smells of lama!" Everyone stared at Jambal silently, and he experienced the most unbearable feelings of shame and exclusion. Since then, he made sure always to wash his hands and face and air out his suit after his Tibetan medical practices in order not to provoke remembering in public. He performed forgetting by erasing the marks of his practice in order to enter the public space.

Although the "old" knowledge was remembered, despite its repression, by a young child, this story also points out its lack of context and potential to cause trouble. His memory of the smell is inherently politicized. He is alarmed at the smell of a Tibetan medicine not because of its pungency, but because it was dangerous, deserving of abhorrence and denunciation. The child's memory was the official (and thus politically correct) public memory—and he demonstrated it well. Jambal's was the individual memory that needed to be (and was) repressed.

So far I have discussed some of the state's technologies of forgetting: physical destruction; public repression combined with private rehabilitation, which led to confusion about memory; and the processes of suppression, substitution, repetition, and monopolization of memory. There is also the production of knowledge, manipulation of emotions, exploitation of a fear (i.e., of domination by a foreign power), and the erasure of context by means of the alteration of names and customs. The weakening of existing social frameworks along with the building of new ones, as well as the labeling and denigration of the past—these too were among the technologies of forgetting. The list could go on and on, and each item on it can be expanded upon: forgetting takes multiple guises and sometimes infuses life in the most subtle and taken-for-granted ways. Therefore, forgetting consists not only of markers that indicate the erasure of knowledge, but also the habits, routines, and physical movements that lead one to present and practice detachment and hiding. It includes hiding the outward indicators of one's religion. It is taking care when choosing one's words in public, or even when speaking among family, so that the children will not learn what is supposed to be forgotten. Practicing these habits until they become ingrained and no longer require conscious attention makes forgetting a part of everyday life. The very fact that the state had to pursue a long-term campaign of forgetting implies that remembering persisted. However, even when all the remembering and resistance are taken into account, it is crucial not to underestimate the force of forgetting. In the following section I discuss forgetting across generations and the impact of forgetting on social and kin relations.

Generations of Forgetting and Remembering

Mapping the distribution of forgetting and remembering during socialism across different generations is a conceptually problematic task. For the sake of clarity and convenience, I loosely define at least three generations based on the ways in which people in Bayan-Uul defined them and compared their own knowledge of the past to that of other generations. The first generation lived through the political violence of the 1930s and 1940s. Their personal experiences and memories were directly silenced. The few elders with whom I spoke in Bayan-Uul were meticulous about separating their personal opinions from the official narrative and about distinguishing what they considered to be the state's bad actions from its good ones, with different explanations for each. Members of this generation accommodated a range of contradictory emotions and beliefs.

Those of the next generation were born in the 1940s and 1950s, after most of the political massacres had been carried out. They grew up with socialist propaganda and were removed from the past, owing to the silencing of their parents' memories and the dominance of the state's narrative. The past seeped through to them accidentally, against the will of their parents. Tegshe, a woman in her fifties, remembers that she and others secretly observed a shamanic ritual when they were children, even though their parents had forbidden them to play around the ger where the ritual was taking place. Later the adults caught them imitating the ritual while playing and punished them by making them stand against a wall for a long time with their hands raised. This generation is radically different from the previous one. Their majority constitutes the core of the socialist state, the loyal party cadres, who believed in the state's narrative. Enthusiasm for and belief in the glorious socialist future led members of this generation to pour their energies into building socialism. For many, their family experiences of violence and death do not undermine their belief in state propaganda. After socialism, they were surprised to learn not only their estranged past, but the fact that they knew very little about their family history and kin. When I spoke with them, they usually told me the official narrative first before starting on either their own, rarely articulated memories or the newly learned knowledge of their past.

Members of the generation born in the 1960s and 1970s claim that they grew up with even less knowledge about their past. For them, unlike their parents, belonging to the state is less of an outcome of enthusiasm and propaganda and more a result of being encompassed within its bureaucratic matrix. They see the state as a resource to benefit from rather than an entity that spurred enthusiasm. The circumstances of and motives for the third generation's silence are different from those of earlier generations. The third generation embodies some specific sentiments that could be called ideological fatigue. They were born into the routinized bureaucratic state, as opposed to being part of (or witnessing) large-scale events such as political violence or collectivization. Thus many have taken the socialist state for granted and feel bored with the system overall. Some look outside the state for an identity. Overall, this generation has a strong desire to learn about the past, but individuals often become discouraged by its inaccessibility and the amount of work required to uncover it. Many of those whom I interviewed saw themselves as the last generation that had some connection to the past and told me that if socialism had not collapsed, then without doubt the next generation would have faced the obliteration of their ethnic identity and the end of shamanism and of memories of the past.

As socialism continued, each generation thought of the previous one as having endured a more oppressive regime than they themselves were experiencing. The 1930s are known as a time of arrests, fear, and suspicion, when "one had to be afraid of one's shadow." It was the time of the worst oppression, and memories of it are murky at best. It is possible that the technologies of forgetting became less obvious and less coercive, or that individuals became desensitized. At the same time, each generation thought of themselves as knowing less than the others. In particular, those born in the 1950s and 1960s claim that they were the most tightly controlled and thus knew even less than those who were born later and have better access to their past. Those in the third generation, however, also feel that they are even further removed from their past than their parents. Despite all these differences in remembering and forgetting, the anxiety about the loss of the past and a profound uncertainty about the newly discovered past spans all the generations to differing degrees.

Potential Memories and Uheer

Forgetting is immeasurable: no one can tell what and how much is being lost. There is no end to forgetting, for it is "like an endless abyss" (Ricoeur

2004:414), and there is "no accurate measure to destruction" (Düttman 1993:54). Studying forgetting is tricky because it implies loss and absence. As soon as forgetting is mentioned, it can be considered remembering.[14] If something is really forgotten, then, does that mean that no one knows that it ever existed? While extensive deliberation on these questions is beyond the scope of this chapter, one answer lies in the possibility of representations of forgetting through culturally specific symbols or media. Measuring the amount of memory does not help to determine or represent forgetting. It all becomes remembering. It is not a matter of volume, but of different categories: sets of symbols, entities, representations, and relationships that mark forgetting and distinguish it from remembering. And these forgetting-based categories influence social and cultural practices in ways different from the categories of remembering, which also shows that forgetting is a process, not an event.

As discussed in the previous chapter, to remember is to know the spirits' identities: names, kinship ties, huudal buudal, titles and social networks, and other identifications. Sung as poetic evocations, such descriptions are the origin spirits' verbal memorials. Further, upon possessing a shaman the spirits relay the narratives of the past through his or her body, thus expanding the memory representations of the past among the living.

The Buryats represent forgetting, as opposed to remembering, through incomplete spirits with partial identities, associations, and belonging. Incomplete spirits are partial or even "empty" memories. Depending on the degree to which their identities have been forgotten, they do not make their appearance through possession of a shaman's body to tell stories. The more forgotten they are (and the less people know about them), the less chance the shamans have to summon them. Forgotten and having thus fallen out of touch, such spirits inform the living of their existence by inflicting misfortune. The Buryats associate crimes, premature deaths, repeated illnesses, severed relationships, violence, and impoverishment with the revenge of forgotten spirits.

Because forgetting is a process, it does not produce homogeneous spirits, but infinite kinds from whom various characteristics are missing. The spectrum from almost completely forgotten to partially remembered spirits is wide and ranges from uheer on one end and well-remembered *ongon* and ug garval on the other. For these spirits, the Buryats also use the generic word for spirits, ongon. They are neither fully established ug garval in the celestial world, nor are they uheer—obscure, "empty," angry creatures who roam the earth.[15] Overall, most Buryats describe their ug garval (origins, which is more understandable if imagined as shamanic genealogies) as *du-*

tuu (incomplete). Thus many are in a perpetual mission to *ug garvalaa guit-seekh* (complete their origins), which means that they need to identify every single origin spirit of their lineage and complete the worship of them. Thus the families must reveal their forgotten origin spirits and their identities and huudal buudal. Although forgotten spirits can to some extent be seen as unsettled memories that keep erupting into the present from the past, the Buryats meticulously distinguish remembering from forgetting by varying their representations.

Uheer are the most pervasive representation of forgetting. Although they are not new in the Mongolian spiritual imaginary, the political violence of the 1930s and the state suppression of memory, including shamanic practices, created additional uheer. The mass killings, burials of the dead in secret in unmarked graves, and absence of rituals of mourning caused the souls of the victims of state violence to remain trapped on earth and turn into uheer. One detail that must be provided in order to make a soul into an origin spirit is the place of the person's death. The souls of those who die without witnesses to remember the place of their death and make the necessary evocations do not become origin spirits. As seen through the lens of shamanism, mass executions, secret mass burials, and the erasure of individuals' identities create uheer, not only from the souls of deceased and unremembered shamans, but from the souls of ordinary non-shamans as well.

In a culture where most people live with family members, dying without witnesses and loved ones is seen as especially tragic. Victims of political violence who were arrested and subsequently executed died in a spiritual wilderness, without sympathetic witnesses, and with no one to remember their place of death. Such a death is not only physiological, but also social. The erasure of identity and uncertainty about the time and place of a person's death prevents proper mourning rituals. If the victim was a shaman, the kin and family would have needed the name of the place where he or she died in order to memorialize it in poetic evocations. Not only did the souls of purge victims turn into uheer, but so did the souls of many people who died of natural causes but were not mourned and buried properly. Importantly, and eerily, this abundance of uheer coincides with a lack of official records about the victims of violence. Kaplonski, who studies the purges of the 1930s, indicates that there are almost no traces of violence against Buryats in a number of archives in which he has been working, including the national and historical archives and those of the internal ministry (personal communication, 2008).

Even the souls of some ordinary people who died nonviolent deaths became uheer because they did not receive proper mourning and burial. With the state suppression of religion, the transmission of shamanism became risky, and younger generations had little or no exposure to it before the end of the socialist regime. Throughout socialism the Buryats were unable to create new origin spirits out of the souls of their dead. They also lost touch with most of their existing presocialist origin spirits. Many of the souls of the people who died during socialism and some of the forgotten origin spirits turned into uheer. While some Buryats did sponsor occasional shamanic rituals, as I discuss in chapter 4, they were not public or communal. Sporadic, hidden, and condensed, they were one-to-one consultations effected to appease the spirits, explain to them the harsh state politics, beg them not to come back, and send them off as far away and for as long a time as possible. These rituals were as much about remembering as about forgetting. Owing to the prohibition of shamanic practices, only a few individuals were initiated as shamans.

Uheer constitute the opposite of the Buryats' intention to memorialize deceased shamans in their families and turn them into origin spirits. Only shamans can become origin spirits, and then only if after death their souls have been propitiated through the appropriate rituals. Everyone else is reborn in the Buddhist manner. If something goes wrong, then anyone can become uheer, shamans and ordinary people alike, regardless of their shamanic or Buddhist background.

When I lived in Bayan-Uul, most Buryats searched for the huudal buudal of their origin spirits, who floated along the spectrum of remembering and forgetting. In addition, some people struggled to tame the uheer, who have the smallest chance of becoming origin spirits. The ways in which the Buryats imagine uheer demonstrate the fact that they are indeed empty memories and entities without identities. They exist in stark contrast with the origin spirits, who are made up of layers of identification and encompass history. Uheer are imagined as deformed figures roaming in packs, wearing drab rags, and screaming in their suffering. Most shamans refuse to be associated with them and claim that Buddhist practitioners exorcise them. But Buddhist practitioners are only able to *darah* (suppress) them temporarily. Yet uheer become even more harmful after suppression withers. The older the uheer (that is, the more generations they span), the more potent they are—*hatuursan* (hardened) by their battle with suppression, but also more distant, obscure, and harder to tame. Since their identities are forgotten, they cannot be evoked by shamans and appeased through rituals. At the same time, they cannot be sent into oblivion, because that is done only through a ritual, which in turn requires the same information about the spirits as is needed to evoke them. But once some information about the uheer becomes known, they are no longer uheer, but potential memories.

The only way to destroy uheer is to turn them into origin spirits—an act of turning forgetting into remembering. To do that the shamans must locate the identities, clan and kin affiliations, and huudal buudal of the uheer. Once an uheer begins to turn into an origin spirit, the members of the celestial court need to be contacted and given appropriate gifts and sacrificial livestock so that they will bestow titles on the new origin spirit and allocate him or her a job and place, enabling the new member of the celestial world now to leave the Earth. Shamans and their origin spirits are the main agents who, by contacting and negotiating with the members of their networks in the celestial court, strive to accomplish the process. There is no guarantee, no matter how much time and effort have been invested, that an uheer will turn into an origin spirit and stop harming the living.

Uheer, as empty memories, are conceptually the opposite of origin spirits, who are verbal memorials. The Buryats' representation of forgetting through uheer—mute and elusive spirits who cannot tell narratives about their pasts—neatly captures the intentions behind the state's technologies of forgetting, which were meant to homogenize the populace by stripping away their ethnic and gender identities as well as the networks and kinship affiliations that tied them to their past. One of the state's projects for making a complete break with the past was to destroy or confiscate families' genealogical records; another was to force people to drop their family name and adopt their father's patronymic instead (the mother's name if the child was born out of wedlock). Separated from their families, removed from their genealogies, and stripped of their identities, the uheer join similar entities to create a society that metaphorically mirrors the human world.

Origin spirits, unlike uheer, are brimming with markers of identity as historical personages and are recognized through their social networks in the spiritual realm. State violence created a virtual army of uheer. Yet some impromptu encounters with the mass burials of the victims of political violence from the 1930s led me to see uheer as having a peculiar material representation as well. Dr. Rinchin told me that every province in Mongolia (of which there were eighteen during socialism) has a few unmarked mass burials. Together with his colleagues he excavated several of them in different parts of the country. The piles of thousands of human bones, and sometimes clothing, personal items, and utensils, tell stories of the group, but reveal little about individuals. Individual identifications and identities are hard to establish; without DNA identification it is impossible to assemble individual skeletons of the victims. Beyond the numbers of people in specific burial sites, the methods of killing, and the ages of the individuals, little can be learned.

I see the mass burials as material versions of uheer—not only because they both exist as groups and defy individual recognition, but also because of their highly controversial meaning. Both the mass burials and uheer are sacred and polluting at the same time. They are worshipped and respected, but they are dangerous and frightening, and thus the living try to get rid of them. Buddhist practitioners, who have disproportionately more political and economic power than shamans, ritualize at least some of the burial sites by cremating the bones of the dead, building *stupas*, and performing mourning rituals for the collective deaths. This provides some solace to the survivors but does not help to identify the whereabouts of individual family members. Mass burials make death anonymous and identities unknown. Similarly, Buddhist practice suppresses the uheer and sends them away, and thus they do not replace the origin spirits—the verbal memorials for individuals.

Figure 8. Bones. Photo by Akim Khatagin

Figure 9. Skulls in mass burials. Photo by Akim Khatagin

The uheer symbolize involuntary forgetting—something imposed externally, rather than selective, willed forgetting by a community. They are the remembering of the forgetting—empty memories. Describing a spirit and thus demonstrating intimate knowledge of it is a strategy, as Taussig argues (1993:105–106), for gaining control over the spirit and defending oneself against the harm it can do. This is particularly true of the Buryats, who must know and repeatedly verbalize the spirits' evocations to show that they are remembered. But losing the identities of the spirits means also losing control over them. Moreover, by knowing (and rediscovering) the identities of spirits and articulating them, the Buryats create and retain social personae in the face of physical death. The origin spirits may be disembodied, but culturally and socially they are alive. Forgetting these spirits results in a kind of second death—a social and cultural one. The Buryats try to save their origin spirits from becoming uheer—bleak, forgotten, lost, indistinct, and miserable. The uheer is doubly dead, physically and socially. The spirit world is a mimetic reconstruction, in Taussig's terms (1993), of the Buryat world. Through the rituals of resurrecting their origin spirits and making them tangible, the Buryats remake and reassert their ethnic and group identities after decades of homogenization and suppression during state socialism. Here, the representation of forgetting is a foil against which to reconstruct ethnic and national identity. The uheer are the necessary representation of what not to be. The origin spirits are the positive representations: multiply placed, integrated into relationships, and unique.

Uheer are not new in the Mongolian political imaginary. Their images and powers, however, have changed in response to the political, cultural, and historical characters of different eras. Oral accounts suggest that in pre-socialist times, the uheer resembled naked women, with long, straggly hair and fierce, pale, lifeless faces.[16] Physically invincible, they ran fast, laughed hysterically, and targeted solitary male travelers. As Buddhist lamas recited sutras evoking powerful deities, the uheer lost their power and fell down flat, struggling to lift their heads off the ground while bursting into creepy, hysterical laughter. During the Mongolian Revolutionary Party's campaign against religion in the 1930s, the commissars announced that they had "tamed" (although it is unclear how) thousands of uheer. Socialism, apparently, did bring a significant decline in uheer attacks, largely because people stopped being afraid of them. After the collapse of socialism, the uheer returned, along with other forgotten spirits struggling to become memories. Since uheer are how misfortune is interpreted, their very existence depends on the conditions experienced by individuals in the community or even by the community at large. Thus, at least in this context, they are the uncanny representations of past violence. The uheer are a cultural metaphor for forced forgetting and violence that carry all the negative connotations of suppressed knowledge instantly in a single powerful symbol. While living in Bayan-Uul at the juncture of socialism and incipient capitalism, I came to see the place as a community of unfortunate individuals held together by a past that is "difficult to remember, but impossible to forget" (Mary Steedly, personal communication, 2007).

An Unsatisfactory Past

"To articulate the past historically does not mean to recognize it 'the way it really was' (Ranke)," writes Walter Benjamin (1968:255), citing Leopold von Ranke. He describes the work of memory as "the ceaseless, 'rhapsodic' excavation of vestiges: 'ruins of torsos in a collector's gallery,' fragments broken off from the chain of prior connections so as to stand unassimilated in the 'sober chambers' of retrospection" (Comay 2000:250). According to Benjamin, remembering never leads to an organic closure, for the work of memory is "unearthing what has been buried" (Comay 2000:250); it "dissolves and disintegrates . . . the dismembered, inorganic body, reminder of incurable mutilation" (Comay 2000:251). And "deformity or 'distortion' (Entstellung)—literally, 'misplacement' or 'displacement'—is the essential hallmark of oblivion" (Comay 2000:252).

Benjamin's is an apt description of the repercussions of state violence in Mongolia. It matches almost precisely the ways in which the Buryats characterize the uheer—distorted, displaced, pained, miserable creatures stripped of their identities. It is no surprise that most Buryats are unhappy about the past that they have encountered, one that is incomplete because there is no end to the spirits' demands for rituals. Not only that, but the rituals of appeasement do not bring the help that people expect in dealing with economic calamity. Indeed, for those Buryats who are surviving on the ruins of state farms, the rituals are a burden. The spirits are expected to help economically, but they bring history instead.

Each time we recall something, it is slightly different from the previous time, which explains why our memories change over time.[17] Because of the intensity of the Buryats' forgetting and the length of time their memories have been disrupted, those memories feel out of place, distorted, and unfamiliar. That is why the descendants strive to find explanations for the return of their potential memories and to accommodate and appease the spirits who embody them. But the erasure of context is only part of the issue. The context for the spirits' return—the Buryats themselves and their surroundings—has also changed profoundly. Two important elements in Benjamin's work help to decipher the problems of the Buryats: his concept of the deformity and distortion of the fading past and his critical attempt to separate history from progress through what he calls the "angel" of history. The angel's face is turned toward the past, where "he sees one single catastrophe which keeps piling wreckage upon wreckage. . . . A storm is blowing from Paradise; it got caught in his wings with such violence that the angel can no longer close them. This storm propels him into the future to which his back is turned. . . . This storm is what we call progress" (Benjamin 1968:258). Like the angel of history, the Buryats see their past as a pile of wreckage. During socialism they were forced to move toward "progress" even if their backs were turned to it. Since the destruction of the socialist economy, the angel has used the energy of the storm to sort through the pile of destruction, trying to reconstruct something out of it, but with little success.

State socialism strove to leave the past behind in order to focus on the future (Humphrey 1983; Verdery 1991, 1996; Watson 1994; Kotkin 1995). The present was determined not by the past, but by the future, so people structured their lives and work around creating it. When the collapse of socialism disrupted the present and brought uncertainty about the future, the past was again called upon to explain the present. The spirits remain indifferent to the failure of progress and the disappearance of the future because history and progress travel along two different tracks that do not merge or reconnect. Progress is not a natural continuation of the past.

In the Mongolian political imagination, Dagdangiin Amgalan's paint-

Figure 10. *Bypassing Capitalism*

ing *Bypassing Capitalism* represented the ideals of socialism in the most exemplary way. It was reproduced on the wall of a building on one of the
main streets of Ulaanbaatar, as well as in history textbooks, and shows a
man on horseback leaping from a stripe labeled "feudalism" over a black
stripe labeled "capitalism" to land on a lighter stripe labeled "socialism."
The man wears a traditional Mongolian *deel* (robe) and hat. He is determined, his face is serious but relaxed, and his horse is fast and strong. He is
jumping right onto the track of progress, of socialism, which is the horseman's savior. This was exactly how the revolutionary government imagined
the nation: leaving the past behind, getting on the fast track, compressing
time, leaping over capitalism, and catching up with progress.

What went wrong? How might one imagine the sequel to that painting in the context of the collapse of socialism and the revival of shamanism? In light of my understanding of Benjamin's separation of history from progress and his conception of memory as the work of unearthing something buried, I imagine the sequel this way: During the decades of socialism, the horseman galloped away from the past on the track of progress. The past was left in ruins, in piles of corpses. After almost seventy years of galloping through progress, the people no longer recognize their past (the spirits), for both the past and the people have changed. When "progress" failed and the state collapsed, the borders that separated the socioeconomic tracks (feudalism, capitalism, and socialism) disappeared. As a result, the people and the spirits collapsed onto a single track and met up with each other. They again coexist, but now they cannot recognize and interact with each other. This is where the shamans come in: to mediate between the two.

The Politics of Silence after Socialism

There is no doubt that the democratic changes that went into effect beginning in the 1990s brought an opportunity to reinstate the past, contest state-created history, and propose alternative histories. However, memories of state violence remain under close watch from the state, since they trigger strong responses from the populace. Among the Buryats, the persistence of silence, epitomized by the uheer, is directly related to the postsocialist state's illicit undermining of the dissemination to the public of knowledge about the past even while claiming to initiate the rehabilitation process. Although there are many memories of the distant past, certain silences persist, especially those regarding the details of the violence of the 1930s. Because shamanism is about consolidating and memorializing the identities of personages from the past, it requires not just general information but specific stories. The state, in contrast, is interested in a general narrative that would apply nationwide and in which individual details would play no part. Therefore the memories that the state allows to become public do not help shamanism to deal with absent and partial memories, including the uheer.

To illustrate the perpetuation of silence after the collapse of socialism, I will present some incidents that occurred between 1992 and 2007 that historians of the Research Center for the Rehabilitation of Victims of Political Repression uncovered in their attempts to recreate the history of state violence in the 1930s and 1940s. They concern the discourse and actions that emerged when the historian of the Center discovered some mass burials and made a film about them. The state's and the people's reactions to the historians' work go at least some little way to explain the persistence of uheer—the unrealized memory. Among marginalized Buryats, the uheer persist owing to limits in the dissemination of history, since the new post-socialist state still maintains much control over it.

In the late 1980s the socialist state began another round of rehabilitating the victims of violence. These intensified with the democratic changes of 1990, and the state established various working groups and offices for researching and compiling materials and cases in the archives, the legal system, and other branches of the government.[18] The state also established a Research Center for the Rehabilitation of Political Repression (hereafter referred to as the Rehabilitation Center) to research the backgrounds of the victims of political violence. But the state failed to consider people's possible reactions to potential information about the past, about which the historians of the rehabilitation project expected people would be eager to learn.

In the early 1990s the head of the Rehabilitation Center, Dr. Rinchin, and his group began discovering evidence of numerous mass burials in northern Mongolia. They made a documentary about finding mass burial sites of thousands of Buddhist lamas in northern Mongolia, where the permafrost had preserved many bodies still in their robes. The film received tremendous media attention in the mid-1990s, and it was used by members of the democratic coalition in the 1996 parliamentary election campaigns. By portraying the Mongolian People's Revolutionary Party as the oppressor and perpetrator, the documentary helped the opposition to gain seats, and many in the Democratic Party credited the film for their victory over the much more powerful MPRP. Some members of the Democratic Party suggested that I get a copy of the film to aid in my research.

After making several phone calls to set up a meeting, I went to Dr. Rinchin's office—previously an apartment in an old building in one of the central districts of Ulaanbaatar. It consisted of three tiny rooms (Dr. Rinchin's office, a room for researchers, and a room for an administrator) separated by a hallway. I introduced myself and told Dr. Rinchin about my research. He welcomed me graciously and warmly, and our conversation flowed, to my delight, as if we were old acquaintances and colleagues. When I told him about my project on shamanism and about my view of uheer as the wretched souls of the unmourned victims of political violence, he immediately agreed. He told me about the Center's projects and generously shared brochures and papers that the office produced. I visited the Rehabilitation Center several times, each visit lasting for more than two hours, which were spent in conversation with Dr. Rinchin, before I finally inquired about the film on the mass burials.

When I requested a copy of the film about the mass burials, to my surprise Dr. Rinchin told me that he did not have a copy and that I should not bother trying to find it:

> The film brought me so much suffering and trouble. The first time the film was shown, I was accused of "smoking up" the blue screen of the national television station with death and negative energy. I had acquaintances call me at home and request that I stop the showing of the film. Over the next few years, I was constantly accused of reopening old sores, digging into the garbage heap of history, creating anxiety, and ruining social life. People I did not even know threatened to beat me up. Even some of my friends severed their ties and acted as if they did not know me. Acquaintances stopped talking to me. It has been a difficult few years, and I advise you to stay away from that film. I was chased by a car a few times. Sometimes I was even afraid to walk the streets.

Although many individuals felt that rehabilitation was necessary, a surprising number of people expressed indifference, disregard, and even resistance to the discoveries. Some suggested that it was best to "move on and not hold a grudge about the past"; others opined that it was pointless to do this kind of digging, that it was simply a way for desperate historians to build a career on the bodies of the dead. Said Dr. Rinchin, "It is shocking to see how even people who were victims of false accusations and imprisonment now came to the state's defense. The state was able to produce its cadres. The film was never shown on TV again, and I never managed to get a copy."

I was intrigued by Dr. Rinchin's remark that even people who had been victims of violence disapproved of his work and wanted him to stop. How was that possible? Dr. Rinchin mentioned a few names in passing that I brought up later on with some of my older friends. They immediately recognized all the names and explained to me that these people had been persecuted by the state, but then had been rehabilitated publicly and awarded various state honors and medals. It appears that the state used not only the cycles of repression and rehabilitation but also its reward system in order to silence the critics of state violence.

Once, as we were discussing shamans and their suppression under socialism, Dr. Rinchin asked me if I believed in spirits. This caught me off guard. No one in Bayan-Uul had ever asked me if I believed in spirits; most people seemed to assume I did, that it was why I was there. I mumbled something along the lines of what was believable for the people of Bayan-

Uul. Then Dr. Rinchin told me of something that had happened when he was excavating the mass graves. Spirits do exist, he said.

> Several years ago, when we were trying to locate the mass graves in the north [Khövsgöl province], we were walking with shovels. We were very close to the burial site but still could not locate it. Then we suddenly saw a lizard. Now, note that we were in the north, in a place with permafrost, dark, damp soil, and thick forests. Lizards live in the south, in desert areas. That lizard was clearly displaced—it was not from there. And the lizard was not afraid of us, of people. It was climbing up our shovels and running around them. Then it would run and come back to us. It was as if it wanted to tell us something. So, out of curiosity, we followed it. The lizard actually brought us to the sites. When we started digging in the spot where it had brought us, it climbed up a small cliff and watched us dig. It held its head up and seemed very satisfied. When we began finding the bones, it became restless, came back to us, and started climbing up our shovels again, as if it was trying to say something. I do not know exactly what that lizard was. I am convinced, though, that it was the spirit of that place or of one of the dead people. Most likely it was a displaced spirit who wanted to show us the right way. Without that lizard we would probably have found the place eventually, but I am not entirely sure. So, yes, spirits do exist.

I do not know exactly why Dr. Rinchin told me this story. I interpreted his receiving help from a spirit as a form of intuitive knowledge in the face of forgetting and of the state's attempt to keep the past out of the reach of the public, including scholars. Dr. Rinchin was a historian and believed in hard facts. He even mentioned that the state archive must hold all the names of the people who had been shot in various places and then buried in the graves because the Soviets always recorded the names of the victims who had been transferred from a "delivery" officer to the executioner (from hand to hand, with signed documents). The Mongols must have followed the same strategy. But it was impossible to obtain those lists from the archives. Dr. Rinchin's story of a lizard spirit had some implications for me in terms of thinking about the people of Bayan-Uul, incessantly searching for the missing, the presumed dead, and people whose identities are impossible to discover. The persistent lizard spirit is an image of resistance to the state's inhibition of remembering.

Obviously, Dr. Rinchin's film about the mass burials would not have helped the people in Bayan-Uul (or most people, for that matter) to find many clues about their missing relatives. I see the film not as a source for identifying victims, but as a barometer for identifying the impact of the implementation of forgetting and the force of its momentum even after the end of formal state-socialist-style forgetting. Formal state-implemented forgetting had ceased. But it survived (practically before my very eyes) in the minds and actions of individuals. The agency of state socialism was embedded in people's behavior. And when the state stopped the implementation of forgetting, individuals continued it. The state was able to get to Dr. Rinchin through colleagues, friends, and ordinary people who eventually convinced him to quit his endeavors or attacked him for the knowledge that he made public. In some ways, state socialism had been embodied by people who continued to disseminate the interests of the state even after its collapse. The neoliberal state encompasses many of the elements of the socialist state, and the repercussions of forgetting have continued to create specific types of silences even during democratization.

Numerous other mass burials have been found in different parts of the country. On the outskirts of the city of Ulaanbaatar are several trash dumps where trucks bring trash to be burned. In 2002, near one of them, a place called Hambiin Ovoo, a construction company that was digging for sand found piles of human bones. The Association of Political Victims asked the Central Intelligence Department to determine the identities of the bones. The department replied in writing that despite the numerous bones being found, Hambiin Ovoo was not included on the list of places where executions and burials of political victims took place in the 1930s and 1940s. A single document regarding this particular place was found in departmental archives. As the construction company continued to acquire sand from near Hambiin Ovoo, it encountered several layers of burials.

For the past fifteen years the outskirts of the city, including Hambiin Ovoo, have come to be heavily settled with migrants from the countryside. The media documented that the human bones were everywhere—children were playing with them, dogs were chewing on them. But when the construction company encountered burials of Buddhist monks in yellow silk robes, along with wooden bowls, leather hats, boots, and other items with which the monks were identified, some leading figures of the Buddhist monastery stepped in. A team from the City Rescue Office led by a chief lama of the central monastery and composed of several doctors of forensic medicine collected the bones and established that the mass grave contained the skeletal remains of about a thousand individuals. Two truckloads of bones were cremated. The ashes were powdered and mixed with yellow clay, and the material was used to build a large Buddhist stupa on the top of a nearby hill to commemorate the victims. Although the majority of the

Figure 11. Hambiin Ovoo Buddhist stupa

victims were lamas, some were laypeople. The identities of the victims remain uncertain: the Central Intelligence Department insists that Hambiin
Ovoo was not listed as a killing field and that there is no archival evidence
of any kind that people were shot there. A few newspapers did speak of it
as a killing field, but the archives continued to reject this description.

Some journalists and historians have closely questioned the hastiness
of the cremation and the fact that there were no further attempts to establish the identities of the people who had been killed, through either
archival documents, forensic medicine, or DNA testing with the help of
the international community. The question of whose bones these were will
never be answered.

In 2006 two other anthropologists and I hiked to the hill to see the
Buddhist stupa that had been erected from the remains of the Hambiin
Ovoo victims. Upon our descent from the hill into the valley, we were surrounded by terrain densely packed with human bones. Only a part of the
mass grave had been excavated and cremated; additional layers of bones
continue to be discovered. No one knew the names of these victims or anything else about them, except that most were lamas. I expressed my sorrow
to our guide because the identification of the dead, their names, and the

places of their birth has been a prime concern of the Buryats, who carry the memories of their ancestors through their shamanic practices. It was their inability to identify the spirits of the dead who nevertheless trouble their descendants that led me unexpectedly to the mass graves.

I see the mass burials as material versions of uheer; they exist as groups, defy individual recognition, and are the outcome of state violence. But they also encompass some controversial meanings. Both the mass burials and the uheer are at the same time sacred and polluting. They are worshipped and respected, but they are dangerous and frightening, and thus the living try to get rid of them. Buddhist practitioners, who have disproportionately more political and economic power than shamans, ritualize at least some of the burial sites by cremating the bones of the dead, building stupas, and performing mourning rites for the collective deaths. They turn the polluting, frightening, and eerie into something sacred, valuable, and worthy of respect. Such meanings bring peace to the general public and some solace to the family members of the persecuted. Yet the stupas that the Buddhists erect out of the acres of burnt bones do not help to identify individuals; death continues to be anonymous, and identities remain unknown. Stupas do not replace the origin spirits—the verbal memorials for individuals. Rather, like the state narrative, they cast the political violence as a national tragedy that absorbs individual tragedies.

Like the uheer, the bones from the mass burials are mute, even though stories swarm around both. Yet in the midst of such an abundance of narratives about the past, many individuals continue to search for one particular story, to the exclusion of another. They seek knowledge that would help them speak to the uheer and hear their stories, not just stories about them, or turn them into origin spirits. Shamanism is about these specific stories. A proliferation of stories cannot make up for the ones that are missing.

THREE

Genealogies of Misfortune

A brisk walk from one end of the town Bayan-Uul to the other took me about two hours in good weather, over a terrain of sand mixed with yellow soil and patchy grass. It could be an exhausting trek during the spring sandstorms or the rainy days of fall, when the roads became flooded. As I approached Bayan-Uul's administrative, commercial, and cultural center, there were fewer roaming dogs—or, at least, they were less aggressive than the ones on the outskirts of town, where I had to carry a wooden stick with which to beat them off.

The market, a big white building, was the busiest place in town. I frequented it to catch up on news and buy local bread and imported apples. Each time I went my batch of goods was more expensive than the last. If the price remained the same, the weight of the package decreased. When buyers grumbled about being ripped off, merchants complained about their sources' increased prices. Goods and sellers constantly changed in this unpredictable trading.

Outside the market, a few scattered brick buildings housed the district's administration, a comprehensive secondary school, the police station, a bank, a hotel, and a post office. Streets lined with tall plank fences stretched from the center in different directions along the Ulz River for more than seven kilometers. These fences separated individual families' plots of land, with their log cabins and gers, from each other. Four thousand people lived in the town, another thousand in the surrounding countryside. While physically the sedentary town is different from the nomadic countryside, with its grasslands and livestock, socially the two constituted a single fluid unit. Many families had residences both in town and in the country and moved between them depending on their needs. Since schoolchildren lived in the town during the school year (and because the state stopped financing the dorms), often grandparents or other family members moved from the countryside to live with children, and in the summers, most moved back to the country.

The ruins of the power plant and a dismantled machine repair shop in the town's center were the largest remnants from the socialist era. Before the collapse of socialism in 1990, Bayan-Uul was a relatively wealthy district. Signs of Bayan-Uul residents' recent impoverishment contrasted with the remnants of prosperity under socialism. The glass had been broken out of the windows of some of the spacious brick houses built during social-ism and replaced with cardboard. Once-plush wool carpets were worn out. Hardwood floors needed varnish. Without electricity, Soviet-made refrig-erators and electric stoves became storage cabinets. Families stashed their televisions, vacuum cleaners, washing machines, and irons in closets.

People reminisced nostalgically about their modern hospital, the ac-claimed school, and the "cultural center," an abandoned large pink build-ing where the young organized their discotheques and older people gath-ered for Mongolian-style swing and ballroom dancing. Even the wooden carcass of a Buddhist temple—a local initiative that began after socialism in the early 1990s—remained unchanged for the next decade. The pov-erty that followed the end of socialism was a new phenomenon, for be-tween 1960 and 1990 the district of Bayan-Uul had been the richest of the Buryat districts (which included Bayan-Dun, Dashbalbar, Ereentsav, and Tsagaan-Ovoo) and had one of the most prosperous state farms (SFs) in the country.

Wealthy during socialism by every account I came across, Bayan-Uul be-came a wretched place after the collapse of the socialist state in 1990. As I wandered among the ruins of the state farm, listened to the desolate sound of squeaking fences, and turned away from seeing dogs feed on human feces, I wondered how Bayan-Uul, one of the most economically successful districts in entire country, had turned into a place of such destitution. The people I have known sought ways to overcome their suffering in both prac-tical and spiritual terms. They have not been dealing with their misfortunes simply in in religious terms, at least not as defined by Geertz (1973)—finding ways to make suffering "bearable, supportable[, and] . . . sufferable" (1973:70), but through action, investigation, and experiment. Why, despite their efforts to rebuild their lives, did the people of Bayan-Uul keep getting poorer? What were the global and local circumstances that influenced this drastic impoverishment, which in turn had intensified suffering and mis-fortune?[1] What kinds of obstacles prevented people from sustaining their businesses, keeping jobs, and otherwise finding ways to rebuild their lives and care for their families?

In this chapter I take a cue from Veena Das, who argues that "a theory of suffering must break away from the traditional mode of conceptualizing suffering—as an intellectual problem of theodicy alone" (1995:138). She suggests that "we need to explore how the conditions for suffering were created" (1995:22), as well as the social mechanisms that create and distribute pain and suffering and theodicies of suffering, both of which legitimate the social order. But because individuals also resist that order, it is important to explore "the dialectics of the individual and the collective that develops in the context of that social order" (Das 1995:138).

The conditions, events, and discourses that have contributed to suffering following socialism, based on my research, amass into what I call the "genealogies of misfortune." I use the term "genealogies" to indicate the Buryats' views about heritability and their belief that ancestral deeds influence the lives of future generations in tangible ways. For Buryats and other Mongols, a teleological explanation, such as a Buddhist notion of karma, is only one possible explanation for suffering and misfortune.[2] This is partly because the Buryats have not one, but at least two spiritual systems. Buryat shamanism explains misfortune by exploring human actions—violence, neglect, and forgetting—in multiple contexts and generations. I also use "genealogies" to indicate the connections among events and policies in the socioeconomic life of the country and their cumulative consequences on individual lives. I show that misfortunes, both those that affect individuals in the present and those that were suffered in the past by their ancestors, are not just incidents or mistakes made by individuals and families; they are closely tied to national and global politics and are the repercussions of and resistances to them.

In so doing I argue that many external causes of suffering (such as the privatization of state enterprise, inequality, and the end of state services) have stirred up the local circumstances that exacerbate competition, rivalry, and particularly the assumption of bad intentions regarding other people's behaviors and actions.[3] The proliferation of shamanic spirits and their ability to act on behalf of their masters makes the possibility of harm real and the suspicion of ill-will somewhat legitimate. Often the most impoverished and unfortunate individuals tend to suspect others of malice—partly because they, more than the relatively fortunate, need to try and make some sense of their ongoing suffering. While such suspicions often constitute a form of resistance to power, oppression, and discrimination (usually represented by a more powerful person), as I show, it also makes the sufferers' lives more complicated.

The new, uncertain condition that the people are battling is a complex one. Both the repercussions of socialism and the effects of neoliberal policies, as well as the emergence of new practices and structures based on combinations and hybridizations of these two in various forms, continue to influence the country. At least for me, the kind of postsocialism that has taken place in Mongolia almost automatically implies the presence and effects of neoliberal capitalism. The ordinary citizen of Bayan-Uul or Ulaanbaatar may not know the term "neoliberalism" (or "postsocialism"). But everyone I met has been affected by neoliberal policies, such as the privatization of state assets, the liberalization of prices, and the loss of state services, among others. Neoliberalism in Mongolia may not exist as theoretical knowledge, as an ideology that is articulated to the masses, or as an explicit state-led lifestyle-teaching campaign. Ordinary Mongolians may not be familiar with the term "neoliberalism," so they might be unlikely to attribute certain events and programs to its effects. Nevertheless, it exists, primarily as a set of impositions and demands by the Washington Consensus and by organizations and enterprises operating upon neoliberal principles. To qualify for loans and aid and to open up a market economy, Mongolia needed, for instance, to complete the privatization of state assets, end state services, dismantle the socialist infrastructure, free up prices, liberalize trade, and enact tax policies that favored foreign investment. As explained to the public, the goal of these reforms was to leap from one system to another as fast as possible in order to shorten the painful "transition" period, to destroy the old system in order to avoid reversion to it, and to prevent the old powers from reestablishing their rule. The consequences of overhastiness and corruption in carrying out these policies led to lasting and, in most places, irremediable impoverishment.

The linear transition from socialism to capitalism, propagated and implemented by developmental economists, never took place the way it was predicted. As anthropologists have demonstrated (Burawoy and Verdery 1999, Humphrey 2000, Buyandelgeriyn 2008), not only did the process bring about complex and unexpected outcomes, but also in many places it revived networks, values, and practices from the heyday of socialism. Instead of the result of an orderly transition from one system to another, postsocialism in Mongolia has been a combination of repercussions of neoliberal policies with processes of the "unmaking of socialism" (Humphrey 2000) from the early 1990s. The two systems (neoliberal and postsocialist) are not always contradictory, but they enable and complement each other, for behind the processes are some extremely powerful international and domestic agents, which are manipulating circumstances and politics.

But seen from the economic margins, from places such as Bayan-Uul, the uncertainty, the system's instability, and rapid shifts tend to undermine the efforts of ordinary citizens to make their lives and find their place in the world. Mongolia's postsocialism cannot be imagined without the highly specific repercussions of common strategies of neoliberalism as practiced by its international advisors and communities. Ignoring this would mean also to forget the nationwide life-transforming experiences of "shock therapy," the role of foreign aid on transforming communities and political leadership, and the redistribution of the country's economic and political resources.

The genealogies of misfortune that I build in this chapter are not limited to neoliberal policies. Many major economic processes that took place during socialism also contributed to these genealogies, though not because the country's leadership intended to oppress its population. Projects under socialism were intended to function and bring fruitful results within the system, although they did not always do so. Once the system collapsed, the repercussions of these socialist projects turned out to be unexpectedly harmful, especially in the new market economy. For instance, if, during socialism, individuals were expected to remain stable and dedicated to their jobs in order to advance in their career, capitalism favored experiences in multiple places and entrepreneurial and opportunistic drive. Thus, individuals had not only to acquire new professional skills, but also to adopt new rules—rules that often contradicted their moral and ethical values—in order to operate successfully in the market economy. There are many such examples. My main goal here is to show the intimate link between individual misfortunes and larger global events and processes. I discuss the ways in which individuals deal with the incongruity between themselves and new capitalism, as well as their resistance to and maneuvering in the new conditions. I start with collectivization in the 1950s, shift to the dismantling of collectives in 1990s, then move on to local and global obstacles that ordinary people experience in their attempts to rebuild their lives and the sense of fear and mistrust within the communities, which further deepens their suffering and misfortunes.

The Collectives and State Farms

Collectivization in Mongolia began in the 1930s and lasted for more than three decades (until the 1960s), owing to resistance movements—that at times engaged in armed battles—in various parts of the country. Through collectivization the state controlled the nation's biggest assets—livestock and the herdsmen's labor that sustained its growth. Stalin also wanted to make Mongolia the Soviet Union's meat supplier and closely watched the country's policies on the increase of livestock. Collectivization in Bayan-Uul was completed in 1956. The initial confiscation of livestock was effected with violence and left bitter memories among the older generation. As an old horseman told me, "The district officials would arrive on horseback with accounting sheets, stamps, and whips to collect, count, brand, and take away our herds. Our wives and old people would weep and beg the officials to leave some of the livestock we were especially attached to, but the officials did not care."

Although violent at the outset, once established the collective farms (CFs) greatly aided the herders. The poorest nomads benefited the most, because CFs provided guaranteed salaries and allowed each family to own a small private holding of livestock. Unlike farm animals, which are housed in shelters—such as chickens and pigs—pastured livestock are highly sensitive to their environment. The herdsmen's intuitive and technical knowledge about the ecosystem, geography, seasons, and animals is indispensable. Every few years, however, life-threatening droughts or *zud* (deadly snowstorms) cut off the animals' access to grass and culled the least fit animals—and people—from the rest. In those cases, the state supplied emergency brigades, as well as technology and machinery to combat the natural disasters. Some of the services were extremely efficient. For instance, emergency brigades helped nomads fight steppe fires and move to new pastureland during floods, and helicopters supplied hay and other necessities to herdsmen and their livestock stranded by zud. The state insured CFs against the losses and underproduction that often occurred during such emergencies. Through centralized amassing and distribution of gains, as well as subsidies, the state covered enterprises that worked at loss (at least for some period).[4]

The dry continental climate on a high north Asian plateau provides just enough moisture and heat to sustain suitable pastureland for the kinds of livestock raised in Mongolia. To increase livestock, the state invested in protecting the herds from natural disasters and supporting their growth. During ordinary times, organized student groups traveled and lived with nomads to help with seasonal relocation and herding and to build wells and livestock fences. Nationwide vaccination campaigns to prevent and eradicate most of the infectious diseases of livestock and enforced quarantines during regional outbreaks greatly improved the lives of herders and aided their labor. In traditional nomadic life, each herding family was solely responsible for all its livestock; under the CF system, however, the farms were organized into brigades that specialized in raising a specific type of livestock or pursuing a particular segment of animal husbandry (i.e., sheep brigades, cattle brigades, calf brigades, milk brigades, hay brigades, even specialist herders for newborn lambs and kids). Those arrangements and investments helped the nomads in their strenuous work, but they also put pressure on herders to meet herding quotas. Still, individual families, instead of struggling on their own during natural disasters or relying on informal help from kin and neighbors, as they had prior to collective farming, now had an official system of support from their CFs and state emergency services.[5]

State socialism also tried to make economic production, transactions, prices, and exchanges as predictable as possible. Because the state was the main and often the only client, the marketability and competitiveness of products were not a concern for CFs so long as they met established standards. Similarly, the CFs were not worried about appealing to buyers, competing with other CFs for customers, or, in general, predicting demand and adjusting their strategies. Although the system limited (and sometimes prevented) individuals and enterprises from making a profit, it also freed people from having to search for a market and from traveling long distances with highly perishable products for which the sales outcome was uncertain. For many, the CFs were a better system than individual domestic herding of private livestock. Of course, the CFs had many shortcomings, both systemically and as individual enterprises. But in the context of postsocialist impoverishment and uncertainty, many herders missed the security and safety that CFs provided.

My analysis indicates that collectivization was not the sole precursor to the impoverishment of herders after socialism's collapse. Bayan-Uul was disproportionately run-down and deprived compared to neighboring districts: there basics such as bread, meat, and dairy were plentiful; gers and log cabins, though modest and simple, were well kept, with no signs of abandonment; and most people seemed to be calm and busy with their daily tasks and chores. Overall, life seemed to be much more orderly outside Bayan-Uul. When I asked people of Bayan-Uul why the district was so much poorer than all the neighboring ones, they replied: "It's because they had CFs and we had a state farm [SF]." I invited former accountants, laborers, tax officers, and herders to my place and listened to their generously detailed and emotionally charged explanations about the differences between the economics of CFs and SFs.

CFs were cooperative-style livestock herding enterprises based the common ownership of herds and a division of labor. They had a local bottom-up elected administration and devised their own plans for production, both with the approval of the state. They also had some limited opportunities to barter or sell any excess products after submitting their quota to the state. Because CFs were mostly on their own (with limited state subsidies, loans, and involvement), they also operated on a smaller limited budget. And thus many CFs struggled to purchase newer technology and machinery; they spent substantial effort to ensure that sufficient raw material was delivered on time and to maintain sufficient cash flow for distributing salaries and rewards. CFs also assumed certain risks and responsibilities, as their relationship with the state was at least in principle distant, although in practice it varied. Most CFs were based solely on livestock herding.

But the Mongolian state also strove to increase livestock numbers and make the pastoral production as efficient as possible through modernization, financial investment, and more stringent bureaucratic control. It also sought to develop industry and agriculture in addition to livestock herding. In the 1960s some of the CFs in different parts of the country began expanding into SFs—a different system of rural socialist enterprise.

Only the Bayan-Uul CF was transformed into an SF in 1961, shortly after collectivization.[6] Other districts kept their CFs. The SF was an economic extension of the state, not a cooperative establishment like a CF. The SF had top-down management, worked to fulfill state-mandated requests, and sold its products directly to the state. SF members and even administrators had little say in planning the SF's production but were expected to work toward filling orders received from the state. By contrast, the CFs had at least some independence from the state in planning and managing their production. The state directly supplied SFs with resources and directions. CFs had to put in requests to buy equipment and supplies and to get support from the state. To a certain extent, SFs had a supply system, whereas CFs had a demand system and were thus more in touch with reality and exposed to challenges.

The SFs strove to become more comprehensive production centers, so in addition to livestock herding, they also had agriculture, such as wheat and vegetable harvesting, and industry, such as dairies, garment factories, logging, furniture factories, and other small centers for metal- and iron-work. The state invested heavily in SFs—relocating entire settlements of people from different parts of the country, providing start-up funds, and supplying machinery and raw materials. In economic terms, the SFs were superior to CFs. Bayan-Uul was supplied with technology and machinery, and it produced a diversity of products—industrial, agricultural, and livestock—whereas the neighboring districts produced only livestock. The residents of Bayan-Uul, almost all of whom were employed by the SF, were more cash-rich than their neighbors. Even the salaries of the Bayan-Uul SF herders—provided directly by the state—were significantly higher than those of herders in the neighboring CFs. In the 1980s an SF shepherd in Bayan-Uul earned ninety möngö (cents) per head each month, whereas herders in the neighboring districts' CFs earned only fifty möngö. In addition, a large proportion of the population employed in agriculture and industry also received state salaries.

At the same time, however, while the SF had more money, it had fewer head of livestock per capita. With 5,000 inhabitants, Bayan-Uul was far more populous than the other districts in Dornod province, which had a population of about 2,000 each. Almost two-thirds of Bayan-Uul's population lived in the town; each of these individuals owned only a few head of livestock privately or none at all. The remaining one-third of the population had some privately owned livestock. Bayan-Uul's prosperity during socialism thus lay in cash and in SF equipment and subsidies, not in livestock. In the late 1980s Bayan-Uul's approximately 5,000 residents had only 60,000 head of livestock, whereas the neighboring districts, each with a population of 2,000 to 2,500, had 100,000 to 150,000 head. This means that for each person in Bayan-Uul there were twelve head of livestock whereas in the surrounding districts there were sixty. In contrast, neighboring districts, which were based on CFs, were almost exclusively rural. Their small percentage of the population who were in nonherding jobs, such as teachers, nurses, truck and tractor (and other machinery) drivers, and administrators, were mostly the members of herding families. These districts were rich in livestock but cash-poor. (This was to be one of the reasons for Bayan-Uul's deeper postsocialist impoverishment compared to that of its neighbors.) The small number of livestock per capita worried the district leadership as early as the 1980s. In an attempt to increase their livestock, in the late 1980s the Bayan-Uul SF began leasing livestock to selected herdsmen, with insignificant results.

One problem was that the younger generation was more attracted to an urban lifestyle rather than a traditional nomadic one. Many younger women opted for "nice," "clean" jobs indoors—for example, positions as accountants—or at least in industry, such as making bottled lemonade. They preferred to avoid the backbreaking labor of livestock herding, which required enduring freezing temperatures in the winters and burning sun in the summers, along with this way of life's attendant inconveniences and hardships. Many younger men were also more interested in driving tractors and trucks or working at the power plant than in being herders, although men were less eager to leave the herding lifestyle than women were.

The sedentary center of Bayan-Uul offered a more modern and a less physically and mentally demanding lifestyle than the countryside. Administrators, physicians, and teachers all received higher salaries than the herders. But their main source of pride and distinction was not so much money as their access to electricity, media (televisions and newspapers), social events in the "house of culture," amenities, services, and consumer goods, all of which made life in the town of Bayan-Uul more comfortable and culturally satisfying. Younger people enjoyed dressing up and taking a stroll through town, simultaneously people-watching others and putting themselves on display. Parents were especially keen on being able to show their children educational and cultural programs on TV and to watch TV shows and movies themselves. Consumption and access to goods that were available only intermittently (such as clothing, school supplies, and certain kinds of foods, including imported candies, jams, or conserves) was also an attraction in Bayan-Uul, for there were no shops in the countryside. Most families in Bayan-Uul lived in a cash economy. Household-based, more or less self-sufficient livestock production was limited to a small number of herders in the countryside. On the other hand, exactly the opposite situation held in the neighboring districts. Their lifestyles and economies were centered on livestock herding, and economic transactions were predominantly done through barter and exchange; cash was used less often. The individual herding families were relatively self-sufficient in supplying themselves with meat and dairy products. There were no retail sales of meat, milk, or even bread (usually baked at home) in the few small grocery stores outside of Bayan-Uul. No one needed to buy meat for dinner when everyone had livestock to supply it. In the Bayan-Uul center, on the contrary, most people were dependent on store-supplied meat and milk, as they had no livestock in their town. Some had extended families in the countryside who provided them with meat and milk, but intermittently, and there were many families who were fully dependent on the salaries that they received from the state. So the general picture during the heyday of socialism was that Bayan-Uul was more modern, wealthier, and technologically and culturally superior compared to the neighboring districts. Its residents were proud of their town and their identities as townspeople.

But the collapse of the socialism and the dissolution of the SFs and CFs brought much more devastating impoverishment to Bayan-Uul than to the neighboring districts, which were based on CFs. There are at least two major aspects of SFs that contributed to the impoverishment of Bayan-Uul after socialism. One, Bayan-Uul had fewer livestock head per capita, but more cash and machinery; and two, SFs were fully dependent on the state, so once the state collapsed, the agricultural and industrial units that were directly supported by state money ceased to operate. The SF workers received very little private livestock to sustain them over the long term. Plus, once the state collapsed, SF machinery, buildings, and tools quickly lost their value. It was only the livestock that supported life in the countryside.

Mongolia's livestock is pastured year-round almost exclusively in a cold, dry continental climate. The need for large pastures forces the nomadic families to live far apart, often several miles from the nearest neighbor. Most herders have small holdings of livestock for everyday needs and for provisions. They need horses for transportation to fetch the daily drinking water, herd their other livestock, and travel to town; camels to move to the next pasture; and cows and sheep for milk and meat. A nomadic lifestyle requires a certain level of self-sufficiency unless there is a constant supply of goods through some kind of delivery service to the most remote valleys. Unlike workers in industry and agriculture, who are fully dependent on state salaries for their livelihood, herders have some independence as owners of small holdings of livestock and as nomads who live more or less on the margins of a cash-based economy. Many herders can subsist on their own without state services, modern equipment, and even cash—for months, if necessary. As long as they have sufficient livestock, they travel, produce food, and make fire with dried cow dung and firewood.

With the end of the state salaries, herders suffered less than did the sedentary workers, who were fully dependent on state salaries and who had insufficient livestock to allow them to survive for an extended period of time. So it was the former workers on the SF, who had more money and easier access to amenities, services, and "culture"—accountants, machinists, factory and agricultural workers, and clerks—who had the most difficult time after the dismantling of the state farms. In contrast, the privatization of the CFs in the neighboring districts transformed the cash-poor herders into independent herdsmen with sizable herds. Thus, at least to some extent, it was the shift from CFs, centered on livestock, to the more comprehensive SFs that caused a whole segment of the rural population to become proletariats, creating the main conditions for impoverishment after socialism. Although eventually many herders in Bayan-Uul became impoverished, for reasons that I explain in the next section, most state workers (e.g., clerks,

tractor drivers, and smiths) were given very little opportunity to raise sufficient livestock for survival, and their lives deteriorated almost immediately
after the dismantling of the SF.

Dismantling the State Farm

The privatization of state assets throughout the country was, for the most
part, corrupt and mismanaged. The individuals in power had more opportunities to get larger shares, whereas the people at the bottom were left out.
It was a complex and chaotic process that sorted out what had previously
been a relatively homogeneous population, economically, into haves and
have-nots.

The privatization of livestock in Bayan-Uul took place rather suddenly
and haphazardly on December 10, 1993. It led to the deaths of large portions of those livestock throughout the district because, as Purvee, one of
only a few successful herdsmen in his fifties (he was also a blacksmith and
forged shamanic paraphernalia), explained to me, the sedentary people
had no warning to prepare shelter and food for receiving their livestock in
the coldest time of winter. The livestock should have been distributed in
summer when there was grass on the ground, and when people still had
time to build fences, cut hay, adjust to their new lives, and learn new skills.
In December, the people in the town of Bayan-Uul had no time to prepare
shelters and no hay with which to feed the livestock. One man told me:

> My wife, who was a clerk at the SF, went to work that day in the morning as
> usual. In the evening she came back holding a long stick and herding a few
> sheep and a cow. I asked what happened and where she got all the livestock.
> She told me that she did not know, but that people were saying the SF had
> been dismantled. She looked awkward with the stick because she had not
> had much experience with livestock ever since she was a little child. We shel-
> tered the livestock in our yard that night but had no hay to maintain them
> for longer.

Upon receiving their livestock, the townspeople panicked and rushed
to locate a relative or friend among the herdsmen in the countryside who
would agree to take care of their livestock. The herdsmen themselves, however, had not known to prepare extra hay or fences and could provide little
help to their relatives from the sedentary center.

More disconcerting, many people simply did not understand that privatization signaled the end of the SF jobs and salaries, and that the livestock

was given to them to enable them to subsist independently of the state. They either slaughtered and ate their share of the livestock or sold their animals to traders. Some even assumed that the livestock distributed to them was a one-time gift from the state; others thought it was an annual bonus or a reward from the state. Overall, people were confused about the distribution of animals. Purvee lamented to me: "No one explained to us that from now on we would be on our own and that the state would not provide us with the services and direction it had for many decades. We did not know that we now had to take care of ourselves, without any support from the state! We did not understand what privatization really meant!"[7] Because the Bayan-Uul SF also had fewer livestock per capita, compared with the neighboring districts, individual families received fewer head. Almost overnight, the wealthy SF had become an impoverished settlement with insufficient livestock, whereas the families in the neighboring districts, previously poor, now became the owners of large herds. Without jobs and other activities with which to generate a living, people continued to eat and sell their livestock.[8]

Some town families contemplated moving to the countryside, becoming herders, and raising their share of the livestock. That was not feasible for the majority. The number of animals the families received was insufficient to sustain an independent nomadic household. Each person received about five sheep; every five people were allotted one cow and a horse; and camels were scarce, so only a few got them. But a nomadic household needs at least several dozen sheep, camels, at least two or three cows, and a number of horses to function as an economically self-sufficient unit. The industrial and agricultural workers often had smaller families, so they received fewer animals—too few to allow independent subsistence. Furthermore, most had no experience herding livestock.

The non-Buryat groups from the western provinces who were settled in Bayan-Uul during the establishment of the SFs in the 1960s moved back to the lands of their birth, buying up animals from the families who had the fewest (since otherwise they would have frozen or have had to eat them anyway) to sell in Ulaanbaatar on their way back home. All of these combined continued to drain Bayan-Uul. Within a year the overall number of livestock had decreased by more than half, from 60,000 head in 1993 to 28,000 in 1994 (Galsan 1994).

The agricultural and industrial units were also privatized and turned into eleven private enterprises: a wheat farm, a grain mill, a bakery, a restaurant, a hotel, a vegetable farm, a hay farm, a logging and furniture industry, and several livestock farms. All of these except the haymaking and livestock-herding "companies" went out of business shortly after starting. Among the many reasons for these business failures was the dispersal of machinery to different owners. It became almost impossible for individual businesses to gather all the necessary equipment in time to complete production. With time and poor maintenance, the machinery began breaking down. Getting the new parts became a problem because the factories that produced these machines in the former Soviet Union had been either privatized or demolished or had ceased to manufacture certain them. Thus, many individuals had to seek new suppliers or comb through used "technical markets" in Russia. These activities proved so time-consuming that they were not cost-effective, so many owners of these agricultural machines and vehicles hastened to sell them before they became completely worthless. With the money they made from selling their tractors, combines, trucks, harvesters, and other machinery, most bought Soviet-style jeeps for personal use and occasional trading. The machinery that did not sell ended up rusting on the outskirts of Bayan-Uul.

The issue of value has been one of key concerns of privatization. The values of objects, as Alexander argues (2004), are constituted through networks with other objects and institutions; thus, changes in one area might lead to changes in an object's value. This is precisely what happened with

Figure 12. The last of the Soviet machinery, 1996

SF property: without the SF system, the values of individual machines, buildings, and other assets decreased. More, as Verdery (2004:140) argues, privatization in postsocialist countries has entailed not only a distribution of the right to own objects, but also a distribution of risk, liability, or even debt. And the right to own objects did not include a right to control their prices and fix their values. Thus, through privatization some people ended up inheriting the troubles of a defunct economic system without its securities and subsidies. Verdery's insight is crucial for understanding privatization in Mongolia and the reasons behind the ongoing impoverishment of large segments of the population.

There were also less visible impediments to ordinary people's attempts to work themselves out of poverty. Because the socialist state kept some of the workings of the economy secret, many people after socialism ended up pursuing businesses that were not economically profitable and were therefore heavily subsidized by the state. Humphrey (1998:101), who conducted a comprehensive study of a Buryat CF in the Soviet Union in the late 1960s, concluded that socialism was built on illusions of success and prosperity. The CF farmers had no control over their production and profits and did not fully understand the economic system in which they lived. Humphrey explained that CFs appeared to function well, but in reality prices (both those charged to farmers for their materials and those at which they sold their products) did not reflect costs. Because of this inherent discord, there was no way to devise a profitable production plan for the CFs. Instead, the centralized state management simply canceled the losses of some farms using the profits from others.

As has become more widely known since the collapse of socialism, the Soviet Union subsidized up to 30 percent of Mongolia's economy. It also appears that agriculture in many SFs operated at a loss during socialism. The copper and other mineral mining in Erdenet that began operating at fuller capacity began bringing enough profit into the national economy to make up for losses in other areas of national production. After socialism, then, without state support or adequate infrastructure and technology, private farming could not compete with cheap imports from China, and thus all local initiatives failed. Therefore, owning a private business in Bayan-Uul also meant dealing with problems produced by the socialist economy, in addition to the new dilemmas from a market economy, such as uncertainty, price fluctuations, and competition, but without the infrastructure of established capitalism. Although Mongolia received a significant amount of international aid and loan money in the 1990s,[9] it was not necessarily intended to support private businesses.

"Slaves to Livestock"

"Give livestock to herders!" was one of the campaign messages of the Democratic Party (DP) in the 1990s in their struggle for recognition from the populace and their attempt to end the MPRP's decades-long rule. The DP leaders were convinced that herders were eager to own livestock, and as much of it as possible. In practice, many herders, especially in the livestock-rich districts of Bayan-Dun and Dashbalbar, were not interested in having extra-large herds. According to a former SF worker, after the initial distribution in those districts, plenty of livestock was left over and up for grabs. Someone even went around asking, "Who wants livestock?" He was told, "Why do we need livestock? We do not want to become slaves to livestock." The distribution of leftover animals took a few weeks: reluctant herders took some of them, and the rest were sold to traders. No one imagined that soon many people in Bayan-Uul would become desperate for livestock and would live to rue their decisions.

While in the context of Bayan-Uul's destitution it is almost unbelievable that people refused to accept the free livestock, I can also understand that raising livestock, especially as a self-sufficient family unit without any outside support, is a mind-boggling endeavor. In springtime, during the birthing season, the herdsmen "have no time to pick up their hats that had been blown by the wind," and during the summer many manage to get only two or three hours of sleep before rising again to milk the cows at the crack of dawn. Some even say that "to follow a farm animal is to become one." That is not a derogatory statement; rather, my observations and very limited experience with livestock tended to convince me that the phrase describes the state of complete mental and physical exhaustion that prevent one from attempting to pursue any outside activities and interests—thus, over time, making one feel like an animal rather than a human. The nonstop, repetitive, unavoidable, and time-sensitive tasks that require instant attention force herders to be on duty around the clock, largely ignoring their own needs and wants. Unlike in western-style farms, where technology, systematization, schedules, and business management help to create flow, predictability, and a controlled environment, nomadic pastoralism requires flexibility, maneuvering, and constant decision-making. For the most part, it is the people who structure their lives around the livestock and not vice versa.

In addition to hardships stemming from mismanagement during privatization and from their limited resources, herders now had to make up for the state services and protection that died with socialism. Without state support for firefighting, helicopters to distribute hay during the zud, and veterinarian services, human and livestock casualties soared. For instance, during the steppe fires in Bayan-Uul in the fall of 1995 and the spring of 1996, many locals lost their livestock and gers, some were severely burned, and others became partially disabled. Some of those families now hunt gazelles and marmots and, as the shaman Tömör put it to me, "live in a stage of savagery, outside of civilization." Some worked as herders for the few affluent families, in return for which they would receive a portion of the upcoming year's lambs, calves, and foals. Some were grateful, but many, unused to patron-client relationships, expressed their discontent with having constantly to negotiate for their needs.

The distinction between the haves and the have-nots was sharpened, but the distance between the two was as short as one zud, flood, or other natural disaster. Without state support, livestock was constantly under threat. For instance, without state extermination brigades, wolves and foxes regularly raided the herds. The price of a bullet almost equaled the price of a sheep, so many herdsmen could not afford to shoot the attackers regularly. Family members took turns guarding their livestock, and it was rare for a nomadic family to pass an uneventful night. Both men and women complained about the backbreaking labor and about not being able to get away from their household duties in order to see a doctor or visit a sick relative in the hospital.

Many people lost their livelihoods several times over in the 1990s and 2000s: first their salaried jobs, then a portion (or all) of their livestock owing to rapid privatization during the winter, and finally money invested to launch a business that subsequently failed. Some of the reasons behind the bankruptcies and losses of private entrepreneurs are clear. The privatization of SFs was a matter not only of property ownership, as Verdery revealed (2004), but also of the ownership of risk, liability, and debt against properties that were losing value. And specific to Mongolia, the new owners also most likely took on a share of the debt. Some of the economic programs instituted during socialism were never intended to generate profit; their purpose was political and ideological—settling the vast land, managing the population, and creating an illusion of prosperity and development.

In Bayan-Uul I came across only three herdsmen who were able to raise sizable herds. One was Purvee, who by 2000 had more than seven hundred sheep, twelve camels, thirty-five horses, and about forty cows. After much hesitation I asked Purvee how he had managed to raise such large herds. Without any sign of displeasure or surprise, Purvee told me the story behind his success.

I already knew from Dolgor that during socialism Purvee was an acclaimed SF shepherd. Purvee himself told me that upon privatization of the SF he received a slightly larger portion of livestock than did other herders: thirty sheep, ten cows, and a few horses and goats. Then an opportunity came: a herding company that was established following the privatization of the SFs in 1993 offered Purvee a job as a shepherd. He accepted and was given one thousand head of sheep to herd. His payment was half of the newborn lambs every year. By the next spring approximately seven hundred of the sheep had given birth. Half the lambs and all the original flock belonged to the company. Purvee received the rest of the newborn lambs as compensation for his labor. After three years of herding and receiving his portion of newborn lambs, Purvee had accumulated enough sheep to have his own flock.

I walked with Purvee through his enormous partitioned livestock fence, which consisted of separate enclosures for cattle, sheep, camels, and horses; smaller ones for sick sheep; and a separate one for hay. Contrary to my assumption that Purvee built the fence after the collapse of the SF, he told me that it was built during socialism, in the 1970s, when the general secretary, Yumjaagiin Tsedenbal, encouraged herders to build fences in order to help keep livestock from scattering during storms. Before the fences were built, the herders rode on horseback to restrain the herds until the storms were over. Purvee was convinced that the SF was a better arrangement than the new capitalism, in which every family struggled alone. He opened up his storage cabin to show me a mountain of sheep's wool, cattle pelts, sheepskin, and other animal hides; they were about to rot, and he was waiting for traders to come and pick them up. Overall, Purvee recognized that he was exceptionally lucky—hardly an average Mongolian herdsman in the current free-market system. He was certain that without some kind of communal or state support, family-based herding was not sustainable—not even his own herds, which had little chance of surviving the zud that came every few years.

The Intangible Obstacles

Many people tried to start businesses in wheat harvesting or herding, as well as operating a clothing stall, a café, or a bakery. But the only activity that generated any profits was importing cheap Chinese clothing and shelf-stable foods (e.g., flour, sugar, conserves). The rest tended to fail, and thus life in Bayan-Uul mostly continued to deteriorate. Although many people understood the ways in which the end of socialism and the privatization led to impoverishment, they were somewhat perplexed about why their businesses kept failing, impoverishing them still further. They believed, given the information they had, that they were doing the right thing, and their goods and services seemed to meet the demands and needs of their clients.[10]

It is difficult to know the extent to which Humphrey's discoveries apply to the Bayan-Uul SFs. However, a story about a family struggling to run a business clarifies some of the global, national, and regional obstacles that impeded their success. Their story gives some answers to the question of why ordinary people were unable to work themselves out of poverty. Ganba, a former SF engineer, and his wife, Tsetseg, were among the first people in Bayan-Uul to start cross-border trading with China in 1992. They obtained a number of assets from the privatization of the SF—trucks, a jeep, a grain mill, tractors, and plows—and planned to run a multifaceted business of herding, haymaking, wheat harvesting, shopkeeping, and cross-border trading.

The Russian border was sixty-five kilometers north of Bayan-Uul, but Russia offered fewer opportunities for profit than China because of economic collapse, local politics, and lack of security.[11] Trade with China was much more robust, even though it was three hundred kilometers away. China's Heilongjiang province, which borders eastern Mongolia, is home to some of the Buryat diaspora, known as Barga Mongols, who are scattered in both rural and urban areas.[12] The Bayan-Uul traders collaborated with the Bargas and exported animal hides, copper, scrap metal, and raw cashmere to China, bringing back dishes, clothing, and other consumer goods.

In 1993 Ganba and Tsetseg began working with a Barga couple in the exporting of wool carpets from Mongolia to China. At the beginning of their entrepreneurship, Ganba and Tsetseg had a two-room log house and a ger on their plot of land. Their two older children were studying in private colleges in Ulaanbaatar, and the three younger ones attended the local school. Their home was fully furnished, the floors and walls were covered with wool carpets, and in their glass cupboards were proudly displayed tea sets, crystal glasses, and vases. Ganba and Tsetseg described their Buryat trading partners in China to me:

> When we first met, we were shocked at their poverty: the couple lived in
> a bare, cement-floored mud hut with no furniture but a bed and table,

and meager kitchenware consisting of a few bowls, a pot, and some chop-sticks. They drank beer instead of water because the former was cheaper and stretched the meat from one sheep through a whole year, while we [Mongo-lian Buryats] slaughtered a sheep almost every week. . . .

But after a couple of years of carpet retailing, they [the Chinese Buryats] were able to renovate and fully furnish their house, updating their kitchen with new dishes and modern appliances. After a couple more years the fam-ily built a new house, signed up for cable TV, purchased a telephone with long-distance international service, and even hired a cook.

Unlike their Chinese partners, Ganba's family was by this point strug-gling just to keep the business running. Because of the long distances they had to travel to the Ulaanbaatar carpet factory (six hundred kilometers round trip) and from their home to China (more than three hundred kilo-meters), all on dirt roads, Ganba's Soviet-style trucks wore out, and it took over a year to get parts from Russia to repair them. With outdated vehicles and little cash, he had to stop not only his trading, but his wheat-farming business as well. The couple lost something at practically every step. Nearly every trip required more effort and money than the one before. Ganba and his wife worked harder, but the family was growing poorer every day.

Ganba and Tsetseg's losses were embedded in the challenges that Mongolia, as a whole, was fighting at the time. In the early 1990s infla-tion reached 400 percent. An underdeveloped banking system, incom-plete knowledge about markets, and unfamiliarity with customs and ways of life in other countries impeded the growth of individual businesses. If the Chinese traders' prosperity had been sustained by the country's recent economic growth, Mongolian traders were in the opposite position: they were hit by a tidal wave of economic crisis. Mongolian traders were disad-vantaged in other ways compared to their Chinese counterparts: the Mon-golians travelled over 1,600 kilometers during a single trip, spent about a week on the road, and had no control of either retail in China or the bulk purchasing of carpets from Mongolian factories. Given all this combined with an inadequate banking and loan system, a lack of business experi-ence, poor infrastructure, and Bayan-Uul's isolation, private businesses had little chance to survive.

Ganba's experience encapsulates the struggles of many individuals who are going through the juncture of the old, dissolving socialist economy and the new, barely present capitalism. The stories of his trips elucidate mainly external reasons for misfortune, such as inflation, a shortage of gas owing

Figure 13. Consulting a spirit

to problems in the Russian-Mongolian trade relationship, the demolition of the carpet factory due to the rapid privatization of state assets, and the uncertain supply from the Russian factories that were to supply machine parts. Not fully aware of the external, often global conditions plaguing their businesses, Ganba and Tsetseg have sought answers to questions about their business failures from shamans. As I was getting ready to leave Bayan-Uul, the couple was consulting the shaman Tömör and sponsoring rituals for Tsetseg's Hoimorin Högshin, who had been neglected after Tsetseg married and began participating in the rituals of the origin spirits of her husband's family.

So far in this chapter I have been discussing the conditions for misfortune that came mainly from outside, such as the neoliberal imposition of rapid privatization, the socialist state's withholding of information about economic losses, the lack of infrastructure and markets in rural areas, inflation, and political instability, as well as the economic transformations China and Russia were undergoing. These conditions influence not only businesses, but the local social world, the relationships and networks. Gossip and rumor feed existing feelings of competiveness, jealousy, and suspicion and also create new ones. The local community also breeds the conditions for misfortune in its own way.

Everyday Conditions for Suffering

The velvet or "blood" antlers of the deer that inhabit northern Mongolia and the Manchurian regions of China,[13] which are still fleshy and not dried (bone), are used in some places to make medicines.[14] There are only two ways to get velvet: by killing a deer or by searching for the freshly shed antlers in summer. After the collapse of socialism, the deer population dropped drastically due to hunting. The government then banned deer hunting and the export of antlers. The tedious work of collecting the shed antlers, at least in Bayan-Uul, had been done mostly by impoverished women; the smuggling of antlers, which was prohibited regardless of whether the deer was killed or the antlers had been shed naturally, was men's work.

The seasonal and uncertain job of collecting antlers, and especially the ways in which the collectors themselves were forced to learn the circuits and routes of the buyers, illustrates some of the unique aspects of incipient capitalism in postsocialist Mongolia. Capitalism in this part of the world is different from that based on the visible, organized labor of mass manufacturing in factories. There is no official employment of a large segment of the local population by capitalists, no resistance to factory discipline by the townspeople, and no noticeable emergence of new patterns of consumption and lifestyle transformation that I could attribute to the arrival of capitalism, as were found in Bolivian mines (Nash 1993), Malaysian factories (Ong 1987), or South African towns (Taussig 1980). Neoliberal capitalism in Mongolia thrives on extraction without investment and oppression without interaction. The extraction and export (often illegal) by local people of raw cashmere, antlers, gold, silver, timber, coal, and other resources produces the illusion that these people are agents rather than victims of global capitalism. Often "absently present," thriving on chaos, active but untraceable, capitalism in Mongolia's rural area has a ghostly presence. Neoliberal notions of self-care and self-sufficiency make individuals look as if they are of their own volition taking up foraging, artisanal mining, and the collecting of antlers. Thus, they lack the status as workers that would give them a moral claim to the rights and benefits accorded to workers who can document their employment through official channels and who have defined workplaces. Since they have no registration or visibility in capitalist production, the contribution of "unofficial" workers to the global economy is not recognized.

My traveling companion, Tegshe, is one such disowned laborer in this type of capitalism. A widow and mother in her early fifties, she had collected deer antlers in the summers in the mid-1990s to sustain her always-hungry family. Although she had trained herself to endure the hardships of living outdoors, such as walking barefoot several kilometers a day and subsisting on dried cheese, dried beef, tea, and broth cooked over an open fire, she never imagined that her life would become such a battle for survival.

Under socialism she had a respectful and decently paid job. She worked for the district's nature preservation department and was known as "Forest Tegshe." One of her responsibilities was organizing communal tree plantings to regenerate and sustain the local forest. Her husband and brother both worked for the SF. The family lived in a large two-bedroom log house insulated against the winter cold; they also owned a ger and had a separate summer cabin. Tegshe occasionally traveled to Ulaanbaatar to shop at the state department store, and her husband owned a motorcycle—all signs of a comfortable lifestyle.

Then everything began to crumble. With the dissolution of the SF, Tegshe's family members lost their jobs. Tegshe's husband began to drink heavily and died in a car accident soon afterward. Yet she had to feed her own four younger children (the oldest of whom was by then working in a factory in Ulaanbaatar) as well as two younger siblings whom she describes as "slow." Beyond her deceased husband's small pension of ten dollars a month and a few sheep, she had nothing.

Her everyday existence was a heroic endeavor. To soothe the pangs of hunger she trapped marmots, fished in the river with a spear, collected and sold berries, and grew potatoes and other vegetables. Collecting antlers was the riskiest endeavor in which she was engaged, although it paid relatively well.

"Aren't you afraid?" I asked. "It must be dangerous."

"Predators are not the most terrifying things," Tegshe said with a grin. "It is the two-legged predators that are most frightening. They might rob you of your findings." A modest person, Tegshe did not mention the risk of being raped, but she told me that she and her sister were once attacked by an unknown man with a gun who threatened to kill them unless they took off their clothes. Tegshe always built a big fire at night and kept a stick and a knife by her side for protection, and she and her sister fought with the man until dawn. "Ever since that night, my sister has hated men," she said.

For Tegshe, her gender and other attributes of identity, such as being a widow, a female breadwinner, a de facto head of household, a solitary traveler, and impoverished, were indeed conditions for suffering. Like most women who collected deer antlers, Tegshe did not know the long-distance traders, who paid higher prices, because their visits were irregular and unpredictable. Since she was always desperate for cash, she usually sold her antlers for less to local middlemen.

Tegshe's misfortunes seemed to pile up. Her unmarried sister became pregnant, so there was soon another mouth to feed. Destitute, Tegshe pawned her deceased husband's pension book before the bank distributed the money so that she could get wheat flour to make bread for her sister while she was nursing her baby. The family that took her pension book held it for almost a year, so Tegshe could not use it to claim her husband's monthly pension payments. Instead, the family "paid" her with the flour they sold in their shop, forcing Tegshe to be their customer and support their business. Tegshe tried to talk to them, but they simply refused to give her the book. Her poverty, status as a widow, and gender seemed to make her vulnerable. I suggested to Tegshe that she make her case by telling the shopkeeper she needed cash to buy medicine that their shop did not have. When she went and talked to his family, they were surprised by the firmness of her decision. They promised to return her book the next month, but they did so only several months later, when they had profited enough (in their view) from the payments to which her book had entitled them. It was distressing to hear other stories in which Tegshe, in her effort to hang on to life, became a victim of exploitation by the locals.

Tegshe consulted with the shamans, seeking some relief for her plight. Unfortunately, like most people's, Tegshe's trips to the shamans did not soothe her anxieties but exacerbated them. According to one shaman, Tegshe's misfortunes persisted because her deceased husband's soul had turned into an uheer who had returned to his family. This forced the distressed Tegshe to go to other shamans and to a Buddhist lama to inquire about the truthfulness of the first shaman's diagnosis. She was somewhat relieved when they told her that no such soul had returned. But other shamans told her that she suffered because multiple spirits of her birth, adoptive, and husband's families were requesting rituals from her.

During her life Tegshe had been a part of several families. Tegshe's first family was that of her maternal grandparents. Because her father left and her mother remarried, Tegshe lived with her maternal grandparents until she turned sixteen, when she rejoined her mother to help her raise several more small children from the mother's second marriage. That was when Tegshe's grandfather brought her to her new family on a horse cart. He also brought a cart full of sacks of dried cheese, bread, meat, and clothes for his beloved granddaughter. As she recalls, at the time she did not realize that her life as a beloved granddaughter was ending and that she was becoming responsible for bringing up her half siblings.

Soon afterward her grandparents died, and then her mother and step-father passed away, leaving Tegshe to care for her younger siblings. After the collapse of socialism, when the previously suppressed origin spirits returned to their descendants, Tegshe became solely responsible for staging rituals for three sets of vicious spirits: those of the grandparents who raised her, those of her dead stepfather's family (which included her half siblings, with whom she now lived), and those of the parents of her dead husband—an only child.

Each family had a different set of spirits who requested offerings, mostly in the form of livestock. The most specific requests came from her adoptive family; the origin spirits needed a sheep to be sacrificed, its deity of the smithy—Dorlik—needed a goat, and the Hoimorin Högshin needed "forest" offerings consisting of birch trees decorated with the figures of animals, plus food and drinks. These rituals were supposed to help release her half siblings from their depressed states and free Tegshe from supporting them full-time. Her in-laws' household spirits as well as those of her own birth family were also demanding attention and rituals. Yet Tegshe did not have the resources even to ascertain the names of the spirits and the types of gifts and rituals they wanted from her. The shaman who offered to perform all the rituals claimed to need seven head of livestock altogether. Tegshe was appalled by the shaman's greed. Even if she wanted to sponsor the rituals, she had no resources.

As Tegshe's life worsened, she came to believe that the origin spirits had been punishing her for not staging the rituals. While helping out with other people's rituals, Tegshe was able to speak to the shaman Tsend, who offered to worship most of the spirits with just one sheep. Over the next few months Tegshe prepared for the ritual.

The day before it was to take place, Tegshe and I erected my little tent as we lined up with Tsend's other clients for the ritual. It was a chaotic event. Tegshe's brother, as the man of the household, had to put himself forward in the community, taking responsibility for the sheep, the ritual, and the trees to create a ritual forest—a very difficult task for him because he was shy and had a hard time admitting his ignorance. Instead of asking for advice, he avoided doing some of things that were necessary and tried to send Tegshe to bring sheep, talk to the shaman, and organize the ritual. Some of the elders intervened and yelled at him, and the women scolded him. But it was commonly understood that people sought rituals to ease their misfortunes and not to celebrate their happiness, so the etiquette was to show humility, not hostility. Various people who were conducting their own rituals recognized the situation and helped Tegshe with whatever they could. When Tegshe walked to the next valley to bring her sheep from the flock of the surrogate family that cared for her few head of livestock, one of the men took Tegshe and her sheep home on the back of his motorcycle. When Tegshe got up at dawn to get her dairy products from another family, someone offered her his horse so she would not have to walk. Another woman who was conducting a ritual and had brought a stove offered it to Tegshe, along with firewood, so that she could bake bread to offer to the spirits and to feed the shaman. One person's ritual, as someone put it, was only possible with communal support.

With much effort on everyone's part, it was finally Tegshe's turn for the ritual. It was full of awkward moments and difficulties. The shaman Tsend, a man in his seventies, crippled and suffering from arthritis and other ailments, was exhausted and grumpy from nonstop shamanizing. Tegshe, usually so eloquent during other people's rituals, seemed to panic when it came to her own. She could not utter the right words and forgot the rules, for which Tsend yelled at her and even poked her with a ritual instrument. I recoiled with awkwardness and pain on Tegshe's behalf and worried that she might give up the ritual altogether. At one point Tegshe cried and, unable to carry out the ritual, asked for help. At that moment our close friend Dolgor stepped in and helped her by substituting for Tegshe whenever she needed to speak with the spirits. I was relieved when the ritual was successfully completed. I could not tell that the ritual made much difference in Tegshe's life, but it changed her brother a little bit, who, I was told, became more sociable and responsible and improved his connections with the people of the community. Tegshe seemed pleased that the ritual had apparently awakened him and enhanced his sense of self, to the point that he was finally asked to help build a log house in a nearby district.

Tegshe's story illuminates a number of external and internal conditions of suffering, such as the end of SF jobs, the loss of her husband, becoming the sole provider for her family, engaging in unsafe efforts to make money, and, finally, dealing with a shaman who was vying for customers and whose claims she found to be false (until she found Tsend). In her efforts to survive, she has had to deal with violence, discrimination, and exploitation. The forest is a source of subsistence, but in order to utilize it, she must simultaneously become a potential victim of robbery and rape. In the next section I discuss how Tegshe's resistance to this multilayered condition of suffering through rumors and complaining brought about additional conditions of suffering from within the community in Bayan-Uul. Doubly poignant is the fact that her resistance worsened her situation.

The Community of Mistrust

Mistrust and suspicion of ill intent seemed to prevail in Bayan-Uul. Even people who thought well of others often assumed that those same people had negative attitudes toward them. The words, gestures, and actions of others were perceived as being loaded with "a presumption of malice" (Ashforth 2001:313). Even if these assumptions were unfounded, they still affected social relations, networks, and structures of everyday life in the district.[15]

While I was aware from many oral accounts of the problem of accusations of malice, several times I had an opportunity to observe these accusations closely and even to be a part of them. Once I visited Tömör's family accompanied, although not very enthusiastically, by Tegshe. When we arrived, Tömör and his wife, though always gracious to me, were indifferent to if not downright dismissive of Tegshe. The situation was most awkward. At first I hoped that Tegshe and Tömör's family would be kind enough to suspend their hostility toward each other, and I tried repeatedly to involve both sides in the conversation. Yet they pointedly ignored each other. When Tegshe, perhaps no longer able to bear the tension, went outside, Tömör's wife told me why she disliked Tegshe: she had once seen her quarreling loudly with someone at the market. Quarrels at the market were frequent, so I did not ascribe too much significance to her comment.

After a few moments Tegshe came back inside the ger. While discussing various questions with Tömör and his wife, I mentioned in passing that in the next day or two Dolgor's daughter Zaya (a young shaman) was performing her *naiman* (a worship of her origin spirits that all shamans perform once every three weeks). Since Tegshe still was not participating in the conversation, I decided to end my visit much earlier than planned, as the silent unpleasantness between her and Tömör's family was becoming intolerable.

The next evening I attended Zaya's naiman. It lasted for many hours because some of Zaya's origin spirits would not respond to her evocations. She called on them repeatedly, but although she was able to summon and become possessed by two of the spirits, the rest did not arrive. I had attended many of Zaya's previous naimans, and they were all different. Sometimes her origin spirits were slow to arrive, while at others they responded to her on the first call and conversed eloquently with the audience. At first Dolgor thought Zaya was doing something wrong. She scolded her daughter and instructed her to sing louder, drum more rhythmically, and toss more libations. After a while she decided that it was not all Zaya's fault—something must have happened in the spirit world, or perhaps someone was blocking the naiman. We ended the ritual, and after midnight Dolgor and I walked back to my place. Worried, Dolgor speculated about the incident while smoking her cigarette and sipping tea, then left, refusing as usual to take my flashlight and instructing me to close my chimney cap and bolt my door.

Early the next morning I decided to visit the female shaman Chimeg, which I did frequently. I found her sitting on a rug in her full paraphernalia, possessed by a spirit and talking to Dolgor with a libation in her hand. She was focused on her possession and was deciphering something for Dolgor. From the conversation I figured out that Chimeg was possessed by Demid Baavai (one of Zaya's origin spirits, who liked snuff). Dolgor told the spirit that Zaya had held her naiman rituals last night and was expecting her origin spirits, but that not many came, including Demid himself. Demid, the spirit, replied:

> Ha!! When we arrived at your home, your front gate was blocked with a black rock the size of a bull. It took us a long time to move that rock out of the way, so we did not make it to your naiman. A man from the south decided to tease Zaya and test her powers and blocked your gate with that rock. It was a provocation. But our *ulaach* [mediator, in this case Zaya] is much younger and has fewer shanars than that person. This will not harm our ulaach, but it was an annoyance nevertheless.

When Dolgor heard this from Demid Baavai, she became upset and felt unsafe. Zaya had had only two shanars and was already being provoked to compete with others. Who was that person? Dolgor was determined to find out.

The next time I saw Dolgor, she told me that she had found out who had challenged Zaya during her ritual of naiman.

"Undeniably, that person was Tömör," she said.

"Why?" I asked, thinking, Why would Tömör, who is so powerful and wealthy, ever consider provoking someone as poor and insignificant as Zaya?

"The last time you visited Tömör, you mentioned that Zaya was going to perform her naiman. Tömör's daughters winked at each other and made faces. Did you see that?"

"No," I said, becoming more perplexed.

"Well, that's what Tegshe told me. She said that Tömör's daughters were giggling and that she felt very uncomfortable. Please do not circulate information about shamans."

Tegshe was annoyed by Tömör's family's indifference, but it did not occur to me that she would pass on to Dolgor such unfounded accusations, as they seemed to me. I was also aware that, at least to a certain extent, Tömör was aloof toward poor people such as Tegshe because he was constantly being asked for help, especially the "loan" of a sheep or a horse. As far as I knew, Tömör was generous. Many times I saw him, after a long conversation, load a sheep onto someone's horse or motorcycle. The sheep, however, were rarely returned to his family. Tömör could easily have assumed that Tegshe had come to request help.

In return, Tegshe took Tömör's aloofness and his daughters' giggling as a prelude to Tömör's "blocking" of Zaya's ritual with "a rock the size of a bull." Tömör's daughters, who were fifteen and sixteen years old, liked to mock people. I had seen them shrugging their shoulders, giggling, and winking at each other during some conversation or other. I had not thought that someone would ascribe significance to behavior characteristic of most girls of that age. They seemed to laugh at me all the time. To Tegshe and Dolgor, however, such acts were nothing less than dangerous signs of jealousy and potential harm. Dolgor was operating on the presumption of malice and was convinced that in Tömör she had an enemy who would create obstacles in Zaya's quest for shamanic power.

Living with an Assumption of Malice

Dolgor's presumption of malice on the part of Tömör and some other shamans greatly complicated her life. The next time I went to see the shamans Tömör, Luvsan, Purvee, and Tsend in the nomadic countryside, Dolgor wanted to join me to visit Tsend and Purvee (who is Dolgor's older brother) and to get a ride to the country to visit her son, who was raising their few head of livestock. She wanted to avoid Tömör because he was now her family's enemy. She also avoided Luvsan, because he might thrust some of his spirits on her and so gain control over her.

The journey was a tricky endeavor, mainly because of my attempt to visit in a single trip two hostile camps of shamans—Luvsan in one and the other three shamans in the other. In order not to fuel intershamanic rivalries, I usually visited only one family at a time (two at the most) and stayed for several days. But this time—shortly after the Mongolian Lunar New Year—I was getting behind in paying customary holiday visits to people with whom I was well connected and who had been of great assistance in my research. Transportation was scarce, so I needed to visit them in one trip, but I had to make it look as if I were making a special trip for each of them. In particular, I had to conceal the visit to Luvsan from the others and also hide my other trips from him. That was difficult to do: visitors quickly spread the news and whereabouts of travelers from one ger to the next. We needed to figure out the right place and time to drop Dolgor off and then pick her up.

The day before the trip the jeep driver, Dolgor, her brother, and I all sat down around my dining table with a large sheet of paper. We sketched out a map of the Bayan-Uul countryside, planning every point of our trip so that it looked as if I were coming from the center of Bayan-Uul directly to each shaman (or at least looked ambiguous) and to hide the fact that I was traveling from one shaman to another. We made alternative plans and imagined anticipated encounters, questions, and events. All four shamans lived within fifteen to twenty-five kilometers of each other, their gers divided by hills, ditches, and occasional bushes. In order to pretend that I was coming from the Bayan-Uul center to each family, we had to zigzag back and forth along the same road and take some rough, little-traveled paths with which my driver was familiar. We also decided to bring along some traveling companions who completely understood our challenge and kindly agreed to act as shamanic clients; that way, if someone asked me why I was at Luvsan's first before coming to Tömör, I could say that the other two travelers had sought Luvsan's help. The driver was also prepared to take on some of my travels as his own "business" to head off closer questioning.

On the day of the trip, we dropped Dolgor off at her son's ger before I visited Luvsan. Afterward we went to Tömör's ger and stayed with his family for a couple of nights (the driver and the other two travelers stayed with an acquaintance nearby), then traveled all the way back to pick up Dolgor. Next we all went to visit Purvee and finally Tsend. The trip was very successful, and I was able to ask almost all the questions I had been saving up.

With all our planning, however, we did not foresee how extensive the customary gift giving would be. Luvsan's son gave me an enormous sack of frozen milk disks, Tömör gave me a leg of mutton, and Purvee's wife gave me a bag of frozen buuz and a loaf of bread. It was winter, so the frozen food was easily transportable, and everyone hastened to take advantage of the natural refrigeration. When I got back to my place in the center, I offered some milk disks and meat to Dolgor. As poor as she was, she refused to take them, saying that they might carry "dangerous things" (spirits or pollution) from their givers. "The gift is not from them, but from me," I insisted, stuffing her sacks with provisions. Finally Dolgor took them, saying: "OK. I will purify them with *arts* [dried juniper]; you do the same. Food is the easiest medium for transporting pollution, attaching spirits, or simply having influence on a person." The assumption of malice almost kept Dolgor from getting a few meals' worth of supplies. I also wondered if she would have been offered even more provisions (and who knows what else in terms of opportunities and help) if she simply accompanied me everywhere.

Dolgor's suspicions affected her daily life and the atmosphere in her household. She tried to protect and control her grown daughters, who lived with her, but they in turn tried to limit her involvement in their personal lives. They would leave home for hours at a time without telling her where they were going, hide their relationships with men, and resist doing household chores. And every time her daughters, especially Zaya, the one initiated as a shaman, roamed around, Dolgor assumed that a spirit or person was manipulating her daughter through invisible means.

Shamans hustling for recognition and competing with each other, as well as thoughts of uncontrolled spirits saturating the space, further sustained Dolgor's presumption of malice. Her poverty, hunger, and feelings of insecurity against the background of the market economy made her feel vulnerable to bullying, marginalization, and shamanic and spirit attacks. Dolgor attempted to protect herself against this kind of oppression, especially spirit attacks, which is why she severed her connection with Tömör. I believe that in doing so, however, she made herself and her daughters even more vulnerable and isolated from the community. Without realizing it, she had placed her neophyte shaman daughter in opposition to Tömör, inadvertently perpetuating the shamanic rivalry and competition that she detests. Although in the popular imagination shamanic rituals are associated with healing, sometimes they become a condition of suffering, along with external impositions in the search for markets and resources and internal powers that maneuver to take advantage of both external wealth and a shaman's own people.

FOUR

Thriving and Silenced Stories

Imagine a beam of moonlight piercing the cloudy sky and illuminating the faces of a dozen men and women traveling through the grassland in three horse carts. The pointed tops and long earflaps of their lambskin-trimmed hats indicate that the travelers are Buryats. Their carts are loaded with pots and pans, containers of water and milk, and a sheep. It is well past midnight, and the travelers can hear wolves howling in the dark. They need to be on their guard to avoid meeting anyone, but exhaustion defeats some of them, and they doze off. The familiar road seems unending at night, but the barking of dogs and the bittersweet smell of smoke from burning *argali* (dried cow dung used for fuel) indicate that they are getting close to their destination.

It is the heyday of socialism in the 1960s, in the northeastern Mongolian countryside. The travelers are all members of an extended family and are going to see a female shaman who survived the religious persecutions of the political purges in the 1930s. The shaman practices her rituals in secret, and on this night she was expecting her visitors. In the dark, the travelers pick up the shaman, load the carts with a trunk containing her paraphernalia, and fasten the door of the shaman's ger with a leather rope. Then the carts continue their journey far into the mountains. Finally they arrive at a secret spot, well hidden from roads and settlements. For the rest of the night the female shaman beats her drum and shakes her bell to invoke the origin spirits of the family she is helping. After the shaman has sent off the soul of the sheep to the origin spirits, the men of the family slaughter the animal, the women cook it, and the family presents the meat on a wooden plate to the origin spirits of their family. As the darkness that shielded their rituals thins, the family pours the rest of the water over the short blue flames still rising from the piles of cinders. The smoke from the fire hangs over the trees and dissipates slowly. By dawn, they arrive home to get ready for work at the state farm, where they agree that religion is the opiate of the masses and a way to fool the innocent populace.

The scene recounted above is my reconstruction, based on Buryats' memories of the propitiation of their origin spirits with the help of female shamans who practiced in secret during socialism. I have never come across a description of a secret ritual. Instead, memories of underground practices that remained largely unarticulated were scattered throughout conversations about any number of subjects. For instance, inconspicuous specks of memories emerged throughout my stay when someone's child was sick and needed a shaman. "There were officers who would stay in the shaman's ger so that the latter could not attend to a sick child, even when the child was burning with fever," some older women remarked to me while reminiscing about the socialist era. During a conversation about the local state officers, some told me: "At the local level, in Bayan-Uul district, for instance, it was not so bad. It was only on the *aimag* [provincial] level that shamans were persecuted. Locally, the officers themselves secretly sought the help of shamans when their own children got sick. After all, they were Buryats too."

I heard many stories about two female shamans in particular, Genen and Khorlo, who practiced in secret during socialism. In this chapter I explore the politics behind the memories of these two shamans. I focus on the ways in which hierarchies of power, gender, and social position of their current disciples, family members, and clients have shaped the public memories of these two women in different ways. The disparity in the degree to which contemporary audiences were exposed to memories of these female shamans, in turn, allowed disciples and family members to acquire completely different levels of economic and political powers for themselves. Genen had survived the persecutions of the 1930s. She initiated Luvsan and then Jigjid as shamans. After she died in 1971, she came back to the community as an origin spirit. Khorlo, who also practiced in secret during socialism, died in 1982. She secretly initiated Molom (Tömör's father) and other people as shamans. Having been harassed by the state during her lifetime, Khorlo promised her family that after her death she would not return as an origin spirit to her descendants, in order to save them from state persecution. But in the early 1990s, during democratization, she returned as an origin spirit to her sixteen-year-old granddaughter, Baigal, who was also initiated as a shaman.

In the process of learning about Genen and Khorlo, I encountered a problem related to the construction and distribution of memory. People contended that Genen and Khorlo were equally powerful shamans and that both helped the sick and troubled, but there were more stories circulated about Genen than about Khorlo. The stories of Genen were widespread, vivid, and colorful, while the memories of Khorlo were scattered, seldom articulated, and held in reserve—scarcely even made into stories. Genen's stories were detailed, personal, and intimate. But little was known about Khorlo even by her family members, although her powers were revered. Clearly, the memories of Genen were privileged over those of Khorlo. Why were the details about one person's life being recounted and shared collectively, but not another's? Why there was a discrepancy between the powers that were attributed to the shamans and the extent to which they were remembered?

The community did not simply choose to cherish the stories of one shaman and disregard the other. What appears to have affected the stories about them is the difference in power between the contemporary descendants, disciples, and families of these two shamans. Genen's son Tsend and her two disciples Luvsan and Jigjid have become some of the most powerful shamans in the area and beyond. But Khorlo's son became an atheist and a communist while she was alive, and their relationship was essentially severed. Since Khorlo now had no male descendant, her spirits returned to her teenaged granddaughter. Yet it is not only the power of descendants to attract spirits that matters in the articulation and circulation of memories, as will become clearer in this chapter; intergenerational bonds and love and caring for one's elders are factors as well.

Stories and silences, and their contexts, are equally important in finding the ways memories are constructed. How do differences in the gender, age, wealth, and social standing of these descendants affect the powers of the spirits and the memories of these two female shamans? How do people of different social and economic standing talk about their memories, and to what kinds of audiences? In the first half of the chapter, I discuss the production of the stories about Genen and their meanings, uses, and interpretations by her relatives and the community. In the second half, I discuss the production of the silences that dominate the memories of Khorlo.

Remembering is a gendered process. Gender, in turn, is fashioned by the politics and structures of power. The descendants who have the power to construct, distribute, and maintain the memories of one's powerful origin spirits tend to be successful shamans. In contrast, the shamans who are unable to do so tend to struggle in their quest for power, despite their once-powerful shaman ancestors. The power of a shaman and that of an origin spirit construct each other dialectically: successful shamans make obvious the powers of their origin spirits, whereas the origin spirits who are known to be powerful (especially if these are the spirits of shamans whom their communities respected and regarded as powerful) automatically elevate the credibility of a shaman. Given audiences' skepticism and suspicion toward shamans' motives for practicing, the memories of powerful origin spirits are crucial. They make a shaman credible and help to recruit clients, who in turn bring material rewards. Ever since the end of the socialist disruption, credibility has been a rare commodity. In addition to enhancing the memories of origin spirits, which in turn aid shamans' political power, the stories that circulate within the community beyond the descendants also serve the intentions of individual narrators. Therefore, the meaning of the stories depends not only on their content, but also on the narrative context and the motives of the narrators.

As I traveled through a nomadic terrain as an outsider, I encountered the most widespread stories first, a consequence of my meeting with more powerful persons in the beginning of my fieldwork. I heard the less frequently articulated ones after that, often from women or men who were not shamans or who were not at the center of social life. I mostly heard the stories about Genen first, and mostly from male shamans, for I met them before I met the female ones. Khorlo's stories came later on, and mostly from female narrators who were not shamans. In telling stories about Genen and Khorlo, I have maintained the order in which I encountered them in order to keep explicit the relationship between power and memory.[1]

If the frequency and scope of the storytelling and the distribution of the stories were based on the narrator's political powers in the community, the shifting content of the stories was based on their own political subjectivities. By political subjectivities I refer to what (Hall 1977:128) calls "structures of feelings" that people gain in the process of living through historical changes, and the kinds of political engagements they develop as "an effect of experience" (de Lauretis 1984:159). There is a complex relationship among subject, experience, and narrative: "the self-as-subject is continually produced and dispersed in experience; experience is generated and distributed in social practice; and the subject of experience is engendered in narrative" (Steedly 1993:21). Such an analysis calls for a double contextualizing of narratives. First there is the formation of a subject through an experience of sociopolitical changes, and then there is the act of storytelling, which is influenced by those changes. But there is also a possible third element in the politics of storytelling: while the stories are shaped by the narrators, the narrators are also being influenced by the stories. The narrators tend to tell the stories that affected them the most. Like those of the audiences, whose relationships change each time they listen to the stories, the narrators' subjectivities also change.

In that sense, the stories can be seen as an extension of the storytellers' own political subjectivities.[2] Though subtle, a dialectical relationship exists between the content of the stories and the narrator's subjectivities. And so individuals' memories of the female shamans are presented below in the context of the narrators' own experiences, as a story within a story. Each memory constitutes a form of personal political project through which individuals represent their own subjective identities, make meanings out of their own experiences, and place themselves within the historical continuity of their survival on the edge of the violent state. My goal is to reveal these multiple narratives, which show the dynamic, intersubjective character of memory. A unifying issue that emerges from these narratives, however, is the narrators' contentious relationship with the state. They provide the reader with a brief look at the state from the margins that contest its powers through shamanism.

The term "personal political projects" is a modification of the term "moral projects," used by Cole (2003) to address the ways in which different generations remember a violent anticolonial rebellion in Madagascar in 1947. Cole argues that in understanding the heterogeneous ways in which people remember certain events, it is important to consider not only the relationship between the narrative and its context, but also the agent. Inspired by Taylor (1989), she develops the notion of a "moral project," which has to do with the ways the locals' understanding of "good" and "the good life" may shape a given individual's selection of the narratives and the particular uses to which they are put. In the case of the Buryats' memories, I prefer the term "political projects," because the ways in which people draw on their narratives are not limited to their understanding of a good life. I argue that the Buryats' memories are situated in the specifics of the micropolitics of the local as well as in the overall structures of feelings of anxiety, fear, and despair produced by instability and an ongoing economic crisis. The term "personal political project" is more suitable to showing the narrators' attempts to express their political stances, including their resistance to the state, while its oppressive attributes were still fresh in people's memories.

Although both male and female shamans secretly practiced "underground" during socialism, two female shamans stand out in the memories of the people of Bayan-Uul. During socialism, shamanism became feminized: women practitioners became more prominent than men. During the state violence of 1937–1940, the Buryats lost most of their adult men. Many elders recall that some Buryat settlements had no adult men left at all. So I speculate that there was a period when more female shamans remained than male. Yet this distorted ratio was not the only reason women became more prominent in shamanic practices during socialism.

Certain political and social circumstances value and marginalize specific attributes associated with one gender over those associated with the other. Marginality, as Tsing argues (1993), is a conceptual space where certain groups enable their creative possibilities in resistance to as well as in conversation with the dominant—within as well as without—discourses. The Buryat feminization of shamanism during socialism is a particularly fine example of Tsing's conceptualization of marginality. An offshoot of general notions of gender, which consider women to be inherently and generally weaker than men, the socialist state considered men to have more political agency than women. To some extent, the state privileged but also scrutinized men more than women. I use the word "feminization" because not only were female shamans able to subvert the state ideology that suppressed shamanism, but also they did so specifically by using their distinctly marginal position to their advantage. They were doubly empowered: they subverted the official power of the state by engaging in shamanism, and they did so by using not their advantages, but their disadvantages (i.e., marginalization). Women were perceived as meek, weak, and compliant. "With long hair and short intelligence," as a Mongolian saying describes them, women belonged to the domestic sphere and were suited only to the menial tasks of herding, cooking, and sewing. The state saw female herders as incapable of political leadership or ideological transgression, and thus it scrutinized women less than it did men. It was precisely the hierarchical assumptions of gender and the stereotypical view of herder-women as uneducated and unenlightened that freed them from close scrutiny and allowed them to carry out secret shamanic practices underground during the state suppression of religion. Men were more visible than women in almost all spheres of life and thus had fewer opportunities to take part in activities prohibited by the state. As the stories make clear, in order not to attract unwelcome attention from the state, women employed a variety of strategies that did not look like resistance. Indeed, by performing some of the belittling stereotypes of women, such as ignorance, submissiveness, modesty, and quietness, women averted the state's gaze.

Within their immediate circles the female shamans were mostly respected and relatively safe. But they were wronged by the socialist state. In this context feminization, in which women dominate a practice, does not imply empowerment in any official sense. Engaging in shamanism was prohibited and carried the threat of imprisonment. Female shamans' empowerment was limited economically and socially. Even if female shamans could accumulate some wealth, they could not use it, because that would draw suspicion from the state. They either declined gifts from their clients, distributed them among their friends and relatives, or hid them. Denying wealth was a way of diverting the state's watchful gaze and escaping scrutiny. Their relationship to the idea of power and money was different from that in capitalist societies: for them, wealth was taboo because it brought problems, and fame led to future suffering.

Contending with the State

I heard about Genen for the first time from the shaman Jigjid, a disciple of Genen's. I met him in 1996 before I traveled to Bayan-Uul. He lived in a spacious three-bedroom apartment in a four-story complex in Nalaikh, a former coal-mining town about fifty kilometers east of Ulaanbaatar. After obtaining his degree in biology from the State University of Mongolia in the 1960s, Jigjid became a well-respected high school teacher and enjoyed all the privileges the socialist state could offer its midlevel *seheeten* (intellectuals). From his living room window, we could see the town's main square, the town's most massive monumental-style building—the "palace of culture"—and, in the center of the square, a statue of a miner in his work clothes, chin up and chest thrust out, a proud proletarian vanguard of modernity.

Jigjid owned Soviet-made furniture, including a stocky sofa, a dining table with six matching chairs, and a large cabinet with sliding glass doors for displaying fine crystal, china, and silverware. The neighborhood in which Jigjid lived, the family furniture, and other accoutrements indicated status, taste, and a relatively high income. During socialism, modern apartments with indoor plumbing and central heat were coveted by almost everyone in cities and their outskirts, but since demand was higher than the supply, they were given first to individuals who excelled in their service to the state or to people of high rank—political elites, professionals, and intellectuals.

Jigjid was a scientist, a Marxist, and a humanist, as he told me during our long conversations. He taught his students that religion was the opiate of the masses and that science was the only legitimate reality. At the same time, he was a shaman-healer in disguise. By working as a part-time physical therapist in a local hospital, he discreetly evoked his origin spirits and sought to heal patients who needed help beyond what biomedicine could provide. In the hospital, when a person's life was hanging by a thread, the state pretended not to notice Jigjid's special powers. To me, he said that the magic powers of the spirits superseded science, biomedicine, and the modern state. Perhaps that is why, when I asked him to tell me about his teacher, he described the magic powers with which Genen would resist state persecution.

It was said that she [Genen] alone survived the terror [the persecution of 1937–1940]. During that time [the Internal Ministry] compiled a list of the names of its intended victims.[3] And she could erase her name from that list. . . . Yes, from a distance. If someone tried to take her picture, the [film] would come out blank. She was powerful. Every time her name appeared on the list, her origin spirits would censor it and erase her name. That is how she survived the persecution. Every time a group of people were taken, she stayed. The locals were surprised. Later she confided to me that this was how she saved her life. And she asked me not to tell anyone, because she was worried that she could be discovered, and then anything could happen.

I nodded, and Jigjid continued:

You know, my teacher could disguise drunkenness from the police. Everyone could smell the alcohol. She would be completely drunk. But every time the police officer tried to register this as a formal fact with their special chemical device, it would not work. The device would indicate that she was not drunk. The police in the city of Dornod [the provincial capital] had to leave her alone. My cousin there was a chauffeur, and he liked to drink a lot. Every time he drove my teacher around, he would drink. He would get caught by the police, but they could not accuse him of breaking the law, because the device, which worked on other people, did not work on him. The police would ask, "Did you drink alcohol?" And he would reply, "Yes, I drank a little bit." Many people who drank less than he did would get caught and lose their driver's licenses. And my teacher would say, "As long as I am with you, I will not give you away to the police." I asked her to share her magic with me, but she told me that when the time came, I would learn about it on my own. I have not found that magic so far. Maybe it is not yet my time.

The state was able to control its people by ordering time and space.[4] But Jigjid contends that shamanic powers are also capable of structuring time and space as well as human relationships. The spirits traveled "at the speed of light" and, like an invisible telephone, delivered information from one person to another over long distances. They shifted among different historical epochs, free from linear Marxist history. "Aren't the spirits and souls pure intellect?" asked Jigjid. He said that he uses Hegelian idealism against Marxist materialism to prove the existence of spirits: "Since the spirits are eternal, then they correspond to the Hegelian notion of eternal soul, of eternal intelligence, right? It's all a matter of naming and categorizing. We need to rethink what has been named in a certain way and how we were misled about things that have been taken as truth." Jigjid used scientific rhetoric purposefully, to portray shamanism as having equal authority to science. In the future, he said, the advances of "sciences" such as physics, "brain and cognitive science," and chemistry will explain the existence of spirits and possession. At the moment the sciences were not advanced enough to explain something as complex as the existence of spirits. Jigjid was convinced of the powers of spirits over science because he had once been cured not by biomedicine, but by his teacher, Genen.

> I came to my teacher for the first time in the late 1960s. I was almost bedridden. My teacher was direct and uncompromising. She gave me an ultimatum: "You have two choices. You either go back to let your body rest forever, or you become a healer." I really did not want to become a healer—such a backward and shameful thing to do—but decided that it was better than death and followed her instructions. I was cured of "schizophrenia" and of the troubles in my liver, kidneys, stomach, and lungs and was able to complete my studies at the National University of Mongolia.

After Jigjid became a healer his teacher told him that he was not a body healer, but a soul healer. Unlike a biomedical practitioner, he treated changes not only in the body, which are merely a manifestation of illness, but in the soul—the real site of illness. In his treatments, Jigjid scarcely touched the client's body; instead, with the help of his spirits, he sent "biowaves" from a distance.

During my next few visits, he took me on a tour to visit his former clients, each of whom told me of their experiences with Jigjid. In the 1980s he had saved a six-year-old boy who had been diagnosed with meningitis but had not responded to treatment in a local hospital. Jigjid discovered that the soul of the child was disturbed by a curse placed on the family after a fight with a neighbor who had tried to steal their new radio. For several nights he evoked his spirits, offered them food and gifts, and asked them to lift up the curse and protect the child from the affliction. "My son is now ten years old," the boy's mother told me. "He has a good brain; he is doing well at school."

Another time Jigjid saved a ten-year-old child who went to sleep and would not wake up. The doctors tried every possible treatment, and the chief doctor of the children's hospital went through "piles of thick books," but in the end he concluded that the illness was unknown to science. Jigjid found out that the family's homeland spirits in western Mongolia were calling them to come back; if the family didn't return, the spirits were going to take the child. Apparently this situation was common among people who had been relocated at the state's mandate to work in industry or state farming. Jigjid appeased the spirits with offerings and explained to them that the family had moved in order to work in mining. The mother of the child was proud that for the last few years the boy had been doing well in school and had not had any problems related to his brain.

Jigjid's seemingly apolitical healing rituals were his way of contending with the modern state. He turned insignificant elements such as a radio and relocation into deep symbols that mediated such state operations as industrialization, forced resettlement, and material deprivation. The state essentially claimed ownership of its citizens' bodies and health as a resource for developing its economic base and the body of the nation.[5] Jigjid competed with the state by managing the bodies of individuals through spiritual intercourse with their souls. He emphasized his magic healing rituals in the context of Genen's magic in transcending both the state's power and modern technology (e.g., police devices and "death lists"). By situating his own magical healing in the context of Genen's, he showed that he was a political extension of his teacher.

"An Armored Tank"

"This is my teacher, the shaman Genen," said Luvsan, and he showed me a five-by-seven-inch black-and-white photo of a woman wearing a Buryat fur hat. Luvsan handed me the picture and asked me to make several copies out of it when I traveled back to Ulaanbaatar. The photograph puzzled me. No one knew who the photographer was or when the picture had been taken. Genen's granddaughter told me she had heard that an unknown foreigner who had crossed Mongolian lands took the photo. Long after Genen passed away in 1971, the image was sent anonymously to a local Buryat man named Sergei who now lives in Ulaanbaatar. After the collapse of socialism in 1990, Sergei made several copies of the photograph and

Figure 14. Genen

gave them to some people in Bayan-Uul, including Luvsan, who kept it on his altar.

Pouring himself a drink from a bottle of Polish vodka (my gift) into an exquisitely handcrafted silver bowl that he had crafted himself, Luvsan continued:

> [Genen] initiated me as a shaman when I was fourteen. The first time I was possessed by a spirit, I was scared; I ran over the treetops. Genen led six of my thirteen shanars.[6] Genen was difficult and demanding. She would scold us for being *asman* [self-appointed] shamans. As she aged, she became capricious and difficult. She also became interested in drinking. She was often drunk, and her son and daughter had to tie her to her bed so she wouldn't

fall out. One day, when she was quite old, she had gotten very drunk. She wanted more alcohol but, alone in her ger, was struggling to open a bottle. At that time bottles did not have a screw cap, only the snap-off ones you open by knocking hard on the bottom. When the door opened, Genen asked angrily, "Who the hell are you?" The person replied: "I am Dondogma [her daughter]." Genen pleaded softly: "Please open the bottle."

Luvsan laughed quietly while sipping vodka from his bowl. He continued:

When Dondogma opened the bottle, Genen shared it with her daughter. What can you say? When Genen grew old and weak, she also had to cooperate with others and even find ways to please them. Genen's daughter-in-law was also a very strong-willed woman, and she used to scold old Genen all the time. At the end of her life, Genen was almost impoverished. She went through life alone, since her husband was taken as a "terrorist" in the 1930s. Her entire life was a struggle.

Luvsan's gloomy memory of Genen contrasted with the relative glamour of his own life. A shaman and also a Buddhist monk, Luvsan was one of the few who had embraced the advantages of the market economy and successfully transformed his cultural capital into material goods. Luvsan had large herds of livestock, cash, and luxury items, including a windmill for electricity and a video camera. He had traveled extensively through Italy, France, Germany, Korea, and Russian Buryatia. He and his family were among the few who managed to raise a significant number of livestock. As a Buddhist monk, he was also able to raise money to build a personal Buddhist temple, complete with brand-new furnishings and religious accoutrements. He also built an office for his shamanic rituals and was talking about building a small hotel for visitors like me. He was well-known outside of Bayan-Uul, unlike the other shamans in the area. Indeed, attracting long-distance audiences, including international visitors, was his personal strategy for empowerment (see chapter 6). His consumption was more luxurious than that of most people in Bayan-Uul: he drank instant coffee, ate potato chips, and wore flip-flops—still a rarity in the remote countryside of the 1990s.

Yet, despite his present comfortable situation, his memories of the past under state socialism have kept him fearful and suspicious. It seemed that his experiences of state violence in the past, of the collapse of the state, and of the uncertainties of the present tormented him. Further contextualization of his life and his relationships with the state are needed to understand his memories.

Luvsan feared the possible return of state surveillance. Under socialism Luvsan was taken to jail in 1973 and again in 1985 for "shamanic activities." His belongings were confiscated both times, and he was accused of accepting *barits'* (gifts) for his shamanic services. The state even accused him of taking children for his shamanic services, a reference to his son and daughter, whom Luvsan and his wife had adopted (they had no biological children).

> In the prisons I worked at the brick factory. Gloves never lasted, and our fingers would get chapped and bleed. The guards used to beat some prisoners with resin pipes until midnight. . . . Then they arrested my wife as well because she would not tell them where she hid my shamanic paraphernalia. They deliberately put her in the cell next to mine. We used to have conversations disguised as Buryat songs. The guards did not know what we were doing. They thought we were just bored.

"What did you sing about?" I asked Luvsan's wife. She laughed and said, "Ah, I do not remember, but I did sing to him that I did not give his *sahius* [paraphernalia] to them."

Luvsan, like almost all herders, was also tormented by the volatility of the market economy and the uncertainty of political instability. His material success came with no guarantee that it would last; he was aware that both money and fame were temporary and that he would be dependent on caregivers in his old age. Without state support, his livestock could vanish in a single storm; without pensions, he could starve; and without filial children, he could suffer abandonment and loneliness. Luvsan did not trust his adopted son because "he listened to his wife." Luvsan also dreaded that his daughter-in-law would eventually gain power over him and he would become dependent on her. He worried her large impoverished family of former SF workers would take over his belongings. He wanted her out of his household, but, having forced his son to divorce twice, he could not let this one go, as he needed a daughter-in-law to do the housework. His most vivid memory of his teacher was from her old age, when the once powerful and proud Genen became bedridden, drunken, and fully dependent on her children—a memory that in part reflected his own fear and uncertainty.

Luvsan was one of the first persons to tell me about the state violence of the 1930s. He blamed Stalin and Choibalsan as the main players and expressed his sorrow for all Buryats. Later, he and his wife told me that

Luvsan's father had been persecuted as a counterrevolutionary. His mother, unable to provide for all her children, gave Luvsan up for adoption at the age of three to one of his uncles. He did not want to leave his mother, so his future stepfather gave him treats of sweet bread to lure him to his new home. His identity as a child of a counterrevolutionary prevented him from getting into high school, so he could not continue his education after middle school.

Despite (or perhaps because of) his rather traumatic childhood and political marginalization, he became a relatively successful herder, skilled in woodcarving and carpentry; and, most important, he became one of the few shamans to practice during socialism. He gained additional powers quickly after socialism. The locals called Luvsan "an armored tank," referring to the numerous shamanic spirits and Buddhist deities with whom he surrounded himself for protection. He was impenetrable to curses and to various spells against him. Luvsan constantly "domesticated" new spirits in order to gain more power. When his shamanic powers had reached their limit or were not the right fit for solving the problem, he used the powers of his Buddhist deities. Most people respected his powers, but Luvsan was worried about his competitors' intentions. From a shamanic point of view, his ability to gain protective spirits was a sign of power. But in the larger context, his spiritual armor was an indication of his acute terror and suspicion of powers beyond his reach. His paraphernalia, which weighed over 135 kilos and was loaded with protections from every possible deity and spirit, was a symbol both of his shamanic power and of his insecurity. Like most people I met in Bayan-Uul, Luvsan too lived under the presumption of malice. He assumed that he was surrounded by people trying to control or harm him and that the state could interfere with him in some way.

"I Will Never Leave You"

"My mother used to tell me that she would never leave me," said Tsend, Genen's son. "I did not really understand her words at the time and thought she was going to live a long life. Only when she came back to me as an origin spirit did I realize what she meant." The locals recall that when Genen died, Tsend was so unwilling to be separated from his mother that he could not put her paraphernalia out in the wilderness, as the rules of shamanic practice decreed. The locals attributed Tsend's reluctance to stage a farewell ritual for parting with his mother's paraphernalia to emotional attachment, but Tsend blamed it on his poverty. "I never had all the resources for the farewell ritual at once. When I tried to do the ritual the first time, my borrowed car broke down; the second time, the sheep did not arrive; and the third time, the wheels of the horse cart broke." Yet at some point he decided that these obstacles were messages telling him to keep the paraphernalia.

Genen's spirit returned unexpectedly to her son in the late 1980s, fifteen years after her death. She arrived during Luvsan's performance, and while possessing him she demanded to speak to her son. Tsend was so moved that his voice trembled, and he asked his countrymen to speak to his mother's spirit for him. The spirit of Genen had come to initiate her son as a shaman. She requested her drum from Luvsan, who had held it since she passed away, and said that his time to own her drum was over; it was now Tsend's turn.

Of all the people I spoke with about Genen, Tsend was the most hesitant to share his memories of his mother. At first he did not trust me, even hinting that I might be spying for the state, or that I might be willing to sell out the Buryats' culture to foreigners. By the time Tsend felt comfortable telling me about his mother, I had heard about Genen from other local people. As I listened to Tsend, I realized he too was familiar with the locals' stories of his mother, and that he purposefully framed his own memories in response to those stories. Tsend was aware that the locals mostly glorified Genen. He spoke not of her glamour, but of her modesty and powerlessness, and he emphasized her struggles to survive as a single mother.

> My mother spent her childhood on the edge of the livestock flocks. She was one of ten children and was poor. All her siblings died from illnesses before reaching the age of five. She was also constantly sick, as her soul kept leaving her body. Her parents repeatedly brought her to a shaman to recall her displaced soul, and it soon became apparent that she needed to be initiated as a shaman to stay alive.

I knew from other people that, like many other Buryats, Genen had come to Mongolia to escape the turmoil of civil war (1905–1907) and the Bolshevik Revolution (1917) in Russia. In Mongolia Genen married and raised a daughter, who died in childbirth at the age of eighteen. Genen and her husband adopted Tsend. But during the state violence of 1937–1940, Genen's husband was arrested and never came back.

When I asked Tsend how his mother survived the persecutions, he said rather somberly: "She was a poor widow and unworthy of attention!" In the next instant, however, he brought up a different point: "The officials were afraid of her origin spirits." He recalled how, during one search for evidence of shamanic activities, an officer lifted up the lid of a wooden trunk where his mother kept her shamanic paraphernalia. The officer looked somewhat stunned at the *ih amitai* (an antelope-skin gown adorned with elaborate metalwork) and *uulen amitai* (a metal headdress with antlers and adorned with prayer scarves). He shut the lid of the trunk and walked out of the ger without saying a word. "He was intimidated by the sahius," said Tsend.

> Before collectivization our life was particularly hard. My mother had to leave me alone in a ger. She fastened one end of a long sash to me and the other end to the wall, so that I could not wander out of the ger and get lost or freeze while she collected firewood and argali, caught water from a stream, or hunted marmots. Winters were the hardest. She extinguished the fire and hid the matches and dried cow dung, because she was afraid that I might make a fire during her absence and burn myself and the ger up. By the time my mother got back home, I would be cold and hungry, and I would often have fallen asleep on the dirt floor of the ger. Sometimes a neighbor's child would come to check on me, but most of the time I was left alone crying. I have rheumatoid [arthritis] in my legs because I was always cold while growing up. She had very little livestock and was barely making ends meet. People helped us out of pity. Someone would bring a piece of meat, another one some milk, or a little cash.

"Did her life improve at all after she began to resume her practice, even if it was in secret?" I asked.

"No," said Tsend. "But joining a collective farm was helpful. That is when we began having bread every day. But we were still very poor."

Tsend's emphasis on poverty and powerlessness (his mother's and his own) was an example of "the arts of political disguise" (Scott 1990:136): protection from state persecutions during socialism and from jealousy-fueled "white talk"—a kind of rumormongering that describes one's condition in an exaggerated way—during the competition and hostility that sprang up in the wake of the market economy. White talk can be dangerous: it can trigger competitiveness and jealousy, which can in turn trigger the infliction of harm by others. With livestock, loyal clients, and frequent trips to Ulaanbaatar for medical checkups and shopping, Tsend and his wife were well-off by local standards. Yet, like Luvsan, Tsend found that his material comforts relieved neither his fear of the state nor his anxiety about the ongoing economic crises and political instability that followed the collapse of socialism. Luvsan repelled these dangers by displaying his power through his rituals, his paraphernalia, and the temple; Tsend behaved with humility and disguised his power and wealth in order not to incite jealousy and white talk, which might spur curses and pollution.

Tsend strategically refrained from advertising his powers in order to confirm that he practiced not for the sake of money, but because his mother had returned to him, so that he could "alleviate people's misfortunes." That is why, in his practice, he presented Genen not as his mother, but as one of his origin spirits. From his clients' point of view, Tsend could afford to be modest. He did not have to worry about attracting an audience or persuading clients of his power or the credibility of his spirits. Of all the origin spirits in Bayan-Uul, Genen was the most "real," because people had known her personally. And of all the shamans of recent years, Tsend was the most credible, because so many people had known his mother.

Settling Accounts with the State?

Sergei was Genen's client. He had made multiple copies of Genen's pictures when he received them from an anonymous traveler back in the 1980s and then distributed them to his friends and relatives. Sergei portrays Genen not as a shaman with supernatural abilities, but as a brave and powerful individual who possessed and created power through her daily interactions with others. She confronted the state not with the powers of her spirits, but directly through her wit and courage. Not poverty but wealth, not diffidence but audacity, and not hiding but her very public visibility saved her from persecution by the socialist state.

> When Genen became aware of the persecutions of religious practitioners in the late 1930s, she traveled to meet the commander-in-chief of the local camp of the People's Revolutionary Army. Surprised at the appearance of an unknown herder-woman traveling alone with several cloth-wrapped bundles, the guard at the gate asked Genen to wait outside and went to the chief to inform him that an unknown *avgai* [a neutral way to describe a woman] requested a meeting with him. After a prolonged wait at the gate, Genen entered the office of the military commander carrying her cloth bundles. She introduced herself as an *udgan* [female shaman] and said that she regretted that the new government had decided to prohibit religious practices. Nevertheless, she said, she would comply with the decisions of the state, and since the Mongolian people no longer needed her services as a shaman, she was resigning from her practice and becoming an ordinary woman. Also, she was donating all the money she had received from the people for her ser-

vice to the local army camp. Having said so, Genen opened her bundles. Old and new bills scattered across the desk and onto the floor. The money totaled 30,000 *tögrögs*—roughly the equivalent of three million tögrögs, or US$3,000 in 2000. Thrilled, the commander-in-chief said that Genen would be treated with all the respect and privileges of a hero, and he arranged to give her a ride all the way back to her home village in his jeep. He also told the Internal Ministry in Ulaanbaatar to remove Genen's name from the list of people to be killed. If she was targeted, the commander said, the local army group would protect her. Genen's name, which was at the top of the list, was deleted.

We can read these stories in at least two different ways, in two different contexts. First, we can read the content of the story on its own terms, literally, outside of the postsocialist context, without taking account of Sergei's intentions, and simply placing it within the official discourse of state socialism. Second, we can place the story in a postsocialist context and read it from Sergei's point of view, by considering his political subjectivity.

In the first, literal reading, the story is a triumph of socialism and atheism over superstition. In it, Genen accepts the virtues of secularism, voluntarily gives up her identity as a shaman, and becomes a "new socialist citizen." The state is not a set of distant, obscure, and controlling institutions; rather, it is represented by a warm, compassionate person who is willing to negotiate with her. The story promotes the state project of liberating, enlightening, and modernizing the citizens. Genen leaves her dark, barbaric past and transforms into a model citizen of the socialist state. The story is perfect propaganda, suitable for a textbook or newspaper glorifying the state's success in creating the new socialist individuals.

For my second reading, I return to Sergei's intention of showing Genen as a brave woman. If Genen remained a shaman her entire life, then, the story is Sergei's fantasy, or possibly someone else's retold by Sergei. In it, Genen deceives the state by convincing the commander-in-chief of her conversion from shamanism to secularism. It is a well-performed farce. How is it that the commander-in-chief is so easily tricked by Genen? After all, is he not an agent of the state, carefully chosen for his post on the basis of his abilities to suspect, detect, and reveal deception and lie? It is possible that the commander knew Genen's intentions and still decided to perform his part in this farce.

If so, what were the commander's motives? First, the officer could tell his supervisors that he had completed the ideological refashioning of a new socialist citizen. The commander would receive credit for his success-ful conversion of Genen from religion to secularism. It was not difficult for both Genen and the commander to perform their respective parts. The script for the performance, although unwritten, was well-known and ex-pected—it was the plot of socialist propaganda. Comfortably performing their roles, both reached their respective goals: Genen got freedom, and the commander got credit, and perhaps a reward, for his work. So there was no reason for the commander to disturb the show, especially when the rules were followed and the state was not disturbed.

How was such a farce possible? Some anthropologists offer insights that may help explain this situation. First, the power of the state was porous, and as Watson (1994:2) argues, "state socialism was never as omnipotent as the cold war warriors of the 1950s claimed it to be, nor was it the paper tiger that some present-day celebrants of its demise proclaim." Second, Mongo-lian socialism was coupled with Soviet oppression, and thus state power was to some extent seen as having been imposed from outside. Therefore, as Humphrey notes (1994:23), the relationship between superior and sub-ordinate was never fully antagonistic: to some extent, everybody felt op-pressed. The fact that the socialist state was partly seen as an imposition from outside was also apparent in individuals' actions. For many, the state was a resource for economic and political advancement. To gain access to that resource, one needed to skillfully perform a role in its propaganda play, the "triumph of the state." In this interpretation of the story, then, the commander performed his role as the state's agent and Genen performed hers as the subject of transformation; in this interpretation, the state exists as the product of a performance, but not as an entity on its own. The state has substance only when individuals utilize it as a resource for achieving their personal goals.[7] At the same time, all the signs of violence are present, although indirectly: the "death list," the Internal Ministry that compiled the list, and the military, which is ready to defend or invade whenever nec-essary. In the story of Genen, Sergei tends to deconstruct the state. But in the story of his own experiences with the state, he depicts it as a tangible, omnipresent, and fear-inducing entity. I think of the following story, of Ser-gei's encounter with the state, to be a precursor of and a background for better understanding his story about Genen, as well as his personal politi-cal project as a narrator. Indeed, he told me this story after that of Genen, as if to explain why deception or lying was in general a part of everyday life.

Sergei's encounter with the state during the 1970s left him agonizing about the state's ubiquitous but disguised penetration into his life.

In the early 1970s, after I moved from Bayan-Uul to Ulaanbaatar, I was working in a steel factory. I was a bachelor, and I would stay at work until late and come home only to sleep. My ger was on the outskirts of the city in a ger district. One day two men and a woman, none of whom I ever met before, appeared at my door accompanied by our district chief. They were dressed well in leather coats and carried attaché cases. "We are scientists at the meteorological station," they said, and presented their IDs. Our district head explained to me that my ger was in the best location for conducting meteorological observations. They had decided to use it as an office while I was away at work during the day. They needed my approval, which they got immediately, and I gave them extra keys to my ger. Over the next couple of months, I hoped to find these people at work in my ger, but they were always gone before I got home from work. There were very few signs that anyone had been in my ger; I would find everything the way I had left it in the morning except the occasional cigarette butt or candy wrapper—nothing else. I was very puzzled. After two months, I was told that the meteorological observations were complete, and I got my keys back from the district head.

"So what was this whole thing about?" I asked carefully, afraid to show my impatience to hear the secret behind the story. "What do you mean?" exclaimed Sergei, troubled by my cluelessness. "These people were not scientists of any sort! These were secret agents from the Internal Ministry in civilian uniforms, trying to find evidence of my involvement with the shaman Luvsan! They were looking for material evidence of shamanic practice, or for people who might visit me from Bayan-Uul. But I am not so stupid as to bring home anything related to shamans. I am sure they went through my stuff."

I asked him what made him think so. He talked about Luvsan's imprisonment, the suppression of religion, and the surveillances by the Internal Ministry. He said that when he realized that the two months of "meteorological observations" were actually two months of state scrutiny, he became terrified of the state. "The state is extremely powerful, and it can do anything to you," concluded Sergei.

Sergei does not believe these were bona fide scientists, and he associates their suspicious appearance with the state's surveillance. The crucial aspect in memory is not "truth"—"not what really happened, but why individuals remember events in one particular way and not another" (Steedly 2000:838). In the context of Sergei's chilling experience with the state penetrating into his life in the guise of scientists, I see his memory of Genen's triumph over the state as his way of settling with it for the injuries it had inflicted in his youth. Sergei's experience of the state's deceitful invasion of his life provides a context for understanding his memory of Genen. By seeing in her a champion who triumphs against the state, he is able to settle his own emotional accounts with it, balancing his own sense of defeat with the evidence that Genen was able to prevail. That is why, in Sergei's story, Genen maneuvers the state into acquiescing to her requirements. She makes the state useful, transparent, and a negotiating partner. She essentially "buys" the state, rules it, and parodies it, all at once. Sergei shows that the state's existence depends on the performance of people who resist it, and on whether or not the state can serve as an economic and political resource, as it did for the commander-in-chief. It is not only the dialectics of power and resistance, but also the many deviations within it—for instance, not only do the powerful state officials temporarily get on the side of the transgressors, but also the transgressors themselves assume positions of power—which cause the state to function not as a monolithic entity, but as a porous and shifting set of structures, networks, and institutions.

For Jigjid, Genen was a magical contender with the state. Luvsan commented on Genen's decline of power. Tsend emphasized his mother's hardships. And Sergei saw her as triumphantly overcoming the state. Far from being congruent depictions, each of these stories was the teller's political project, and thus they differed in content and purpose.

I now turn to the memories of the shaman Khorlo, who is surrounded by silence. These stories of Khorlo told by her descendants are woven together with my stories about producing silence.

Khorlo: Silent Memories

My friend Tegshe brought me to meet Jargalma and Baigal, the daughter and granddaughter, respectively, of the shaman Khorlo. Tegshe felt proud to bring me to Khorlo's descendants, exclaiming: "For sure, the children of Khorlo would have the best stories to tell, and a lot of them!" With high expectations and some trepidation, I followed Tegshe into Jargalma's ger. I was a bit shocked to see that the ger lacked the usual white canvas cover over the felt; it had only a brown felt cover and was exposed to mid-February's icy storms. Inside, its neatness was due not only to its owners' meticulous housekeeping, but also to the paucity of household items they owned. No clothes, towels, or bags were hanging from the walls; no dishes were stacked up on the cupboard. After a moment, sitting on a small wooden stool, I noticed that a small brick stove in the middle of the ger was cold—a sign that the family had not built a fire in at least the last three hours. Jargalma was stitching up a degel for someone on a sewing machine. Her husband was bedridden with cancer of the liver, and Baigal went to their log cabin to bring some food. I asked them not to bother cooking for us, but the family cooked the last few frozen dumplings that they had prepared for guests celebrating Tsagan Sar (Lunar New Year).

Our conversation flowed easily over topics such as surviving the winter, making a living after the collapse of the SF, and some folk methods of curing liver cancer. After a while I felt comfortable enough to change the subject, so I mentioned that I was interested in learning about the shaman Khorlo and asked if they could share some stories about her. Silence. They then said that they did not know anything. More silence. At last Baigal said that she did not know much about her grandmother because she was only two years old when she died. Jargalma sighed: "I know nothing about shamans. And I never saw my mother performing a ritual. She always hid it from us, her children. I am sure she did so to keep us all from getting into trouble with the government. I am sorry that we are of no use to you. You should go to Luvsan and others to conduct your studies." I emphasized that I would like to hear about her mother's life as a person, not so much about her rituals. Jargalma repeated that she really had nothing to tell me: "She just lived like anyone else—nothing interesting or special."

Having heard so many stories about Genen, I was surprised by Jargalma's emphatic claim not to know about her mother. I did not believe her. Yes, I was a stranger to the community, and if I wanted to hear informants' personal memories, I needed to develop closer relationships with them. But I had the impression that Jargalma's silence was not due to the fact that I was a stranger. I guessed that she might just never have had an opportunity to share her memories with others. Even Baigal had not heard much about her grandmother from her mother. Baigal had been initiated as a shaman a few years earlier. It was unusual for a family with a shaman not to know about their spirits, especially the spirit of an ancestor as recent as Khorlo, who had died in 1982. I was convinced that just because Jargalma had no stories to tell me at the moment, that did not mean she had forgotten about her mother. I had an intuition that if I waited for Jargalma to feel at ease talking to me and then asked her about her mother, she might recall something.

Jargalma's silence was, for the most part, the result of the state's implementation of the technologies of forgetting: disrupting the transmission of shamanism, silencing memories, preventing opportunities to make memories into narratives, and making the remembering of the past irrelevant and dangerous to her family. Most regrettably, Jargalma devalued whatever memories she retained of her mother; to her they did not seem worth recounting, even to someone who was interested. But there was more to Jargalma's silence. After all, I had already heard a bit about her mother from other people—mostly Dolgor, Tegshe, my neighbors, Luvsan, and Tömör. It seemed strange that although Khorlo's clients and acquaintances were willing to tell me about her, the shaman's own family was silent.

If Jargalma's silence was the outcome of state-imposed forgetting, then other people would not be talking about Khorlo either. Why did the silence surrounding Khorlo persist among certain people but not others? The current politics of power also influence the construction and distribution of the memories of origin spirits. Who has the power to narrate? How do Baigal's gender, age, and social and economic standing limit her ability to take charge of the memories of her once well-known grandmother? In the following, I show how the success of Baigal, a shaman and granddaughter of Khorlo, is being hindered because the necessary resources for constructing, distributing, and thus empowering the memories of one's origin spirit lie in a gendered realm dominated by men.

Producing Silence

Like stories, silences are produced through social relationships, politics, and events. It was peculiar that memories of Khorlo had skipped over her children and spread among other people, forming a kind of vacuum of silence around the memories. This silence was a protective cushion during socialism, because family members of a shaman were under even tighter scrutiny than the rest of the community. I could see that forgetting—Khorlo's deliberate hiding of her practices from her children—had created an odd picture of distribution of and gaps in memory within the same generation. This was an understandable repercussion of the technologies of forgetting created under socialism.

But now it was the year 2000, and it had been more than ten years since shamanism began to thrive again in the area. Jargalma's daughter Baigal had been initiated as a shaman a five years ago, and one of her main origin spirits was Khorlo herself. Everyone who mentioned Baigal spoke positively and promisingly about her and urged me to include her in my studies. It seemed to me that the descendants of Khorlo would have had every reason to be proud of their heritage and reputation. Instead, the family knew less and talked less about Khorlo than did her non-kin. Why did the silence among Khorlo's descendants persist while shamanism thrived? And what circumstances allowed memories to resurface in the form of a narrative?

Often silences are a sign of powerlessness, not of the lack of a story to tell. As Tsing (1990:122) argues, power consists, at least in part, of the ability to convene an audience. According to Steedly (1993:198), this ability requires telling a compelling story that is strategically designed to meet the interests of the listeners. Shamanic rituals, as far as I saw in Bayan-Uul, were the most suitable spaces for sharing stories, because it was for these rituals that various individuals gathered who might not otherwise be sharing the same space. But I also knew that female shamans in the sedentary area drew smaller audiences than the male shamans in the nomadic countryside. This was partly because of space: the rituals in the sedentary areas were performed indoors in order not to disturb (and sometimes in order not to alert) the neighbors. Yet that same proximity enabled more frequent encounters for sharing stories. Given all this, Jargalma and her family had plenty of opportunity to be part of the collective memories about Khorlo. But they were not.

I thought about the gendered aspect of storytelling as well. Some anthropologists have proposed a "muted group" framework in which, in a male-dominated social structure, men determine the communication system while subordinate groups such as women and children are made "inarticulate" (E. Ardener 1972, 1975; S. Ardener 1975, 1978:21–22). Furthermore, "the language of a particular culture does not serve all its speakers equally, for not all speakers contribute in an equal fashion to its formulation" (Kramarae 1981:1). But others argue that women are not made inarticulate—it is just that their voices have gone unheard in public speech. And even if they are heard in public, "if they are to gain an audience" they have "to present their stories in the borrowed phrasings of men's interests and men's experience" (Steedly 1993:185). Therefore, if we are to find women's speech (beyond official phrasings), we should move toward exploring the "misfit" by listening to women tell stories in ways other than the official, "culturally appropriate" ones (Steedly 1993:177–178).

Buryat men are often more articulate and speak more authoritatively in public than the women. Yet the stories that I heard about Khorlo were mainly told to me by women while I was talking to them individually or in their family circles—a setting similar to that in which I met with Jargalma and her family. According to most standards of gender hierarchy and power, Buryat women were not a muted group. And even if their voices were subdued by male storytelling during large gatherings, my individual meetings with them yielded rich narratives. In short, I found Jargalma's insistence that she knew nothing about her mother unbelievable.

In order to unpack some of the structures that perpetuated Jargalma's silence and to see whether her unarticulated memories would resurface, over the course of three months I frequented Jargalma's house, shared meals with her, and attended Baigal's rituals. It became apparent that Jargalma was embarrassed by her acute poverty, and she refrained from speaking authoritatively, including sharing her memories, in the way successful people did. Because the generation that was born after World War II had had jobs and salaries all their adult lives, this crushing poverty, which arrived almost overnight, was new to them. Jargalma and her husband, Damba, had been accountants for the state farm, but since its dissolution they had had no means of earning a living. Too young to qualify for a pension, Jargalma earned some occasional income sewing degels, but it provided no more than a couple of pounds of rice or flour, which the family stretched as far as it could possibly go. Baigal's brother quit school and herded someone else's livestock in the countryside in exchange for two small sheep a year. Since graduating from high school, Baigal had had no job prospects. The family owned no livestock. With a sick husband, Jargalma was in despair. This family was in a far worse situation than most others I knew.

A certain degree of economic prosperity is crucial in order for a shaman to produce memories of a client's ancestors. More resources allow a shaman to sponsor big rituals, which are followed by banquets. After the rituals, a shaman converses eloquently with the audience as they enjoy the feast. The possession rituals proved the existence of spirits to the audience, but storytelling accentuated their powers. With few resources, Baigal's family staged rituals intermittently, and they were almost never able to afford follow-up parties. Thus, there were few opportunities for the family to convey stories about Khorlo and their other ancestors.

The poverty and powerlessness of Khorlo's descendants silenced them, as did culturally appropriate gendered notions of visibility, speech, and body movements. But shamanic performances are a kind of antidote to silence: they provide opportunities to be heard and to hear stories from others. In order to succeed as a shaman, a woman needs to behave in a way that is almost the opposite the prescribed norms for a proper woman. Not only must she speak and make herself visible, but she must do so in order to display her powers in direct and indirect ways both during and outside of rituals. When I asked Baigal why she did not perform more ceremonies, she expressed her fear of competing with other shamans for clients: "I stay out of shamanic politics and try not to compete for clients and services with other shamans. If someone harms me and my family by sending their spirits, I have no one to help or to protect us. When my parents ask for favors from others, people joke that Jargalma and Damba have nothing to give back unless they give their two children, and that's my brother and me. To make matters worse, Baigal's teacher, Undarmaa, a well-respected female shaman, had moved to Ulaanbaatar two years ago. Baigal had since lost touch with her, and she had no money to travel to see her teacher. Before she left, Undarmaa told Baigal to watch out for gossips and stay away from shamanic politics. She said that because Baigal was poor and alone, there would be plenty of people who might harm or take advantage of her. Baigal was convinced that attracting clients (which was necessary to a shaman's continued ability to practice) was extremely dangerous, because if other shamans in an area learned that their clients had begun employing her, they might launch rituals against her. Too careful to convene an audience, Baigal was losing out on all opportunities to gain money and influence. That kept her in poverty, which in turn robbed her of the confidence to socialize and to speak.

Baigal's fear of pursuing clients resonated with her mother's discomfort at putting herself forward in the community to advocate informally for her daughter. Dolgor once told me that the family's poverty was due to Jargalma's timidity—that she needed to learn more about spirits in order to tap into their powers, to forge networks with more powerful shamans, and to promote her daughter as a powerful shaman. Although conceptually I agreed with Dolgor, I also saw how, in reality, age, gender, social standing, material situation, and the degree of power held by a woman's male relatives all prevented Baigal and Jargalma from engaging in the local competition for shamanic power.

Although attracting an audience directly was not easy for Baigal, networking with better-established shamans and attending their rituals was an indirect way of securing one's allies and opportunity to gain at least some audience. I once witnessed Jargalma's shy attempt to build a network with other shamans on behalf of her daughter. It was when Tömör was staging his shanar. Jargalma's neighbor, Radna, the hospital jeep driver, and his wife were going to go to the ritual, and Jargalma was keeping an eye on their house while they were away. She asked Radna to give several meters of silk and a bottle of liquor to Tömör and ask him to take Baigal under his tutelage. Radna agreed. When we arrived at Tömör's place, Radna presented the fabric and the liquor to Tömör but did not mention anything about Jargalma's greetings and her desire to have Tömör's protection for her daughter. I almost blurted out Jargalma's request to Tömör at that moment, but refrained from doing so because I was not sure about the relationship between Tömör and Baigal (among other politics among them). Later I learned that right before Khorlo died, she had initiated Tömör's father, Molom, as a shaman. I thought that Tömör probably would not refuse to take Baigal under his wing if Jargalma asked him. But Jargalma could not come herself, as she needed to take care of her sick husband. Her neighbor's failure to convey her wish was another sign of her exclusion from the reciprocity network. I thought that Baigal herself should have come to Tömör's ritual, delivered the gifts, and talked to him in order to strengthen her ties to the more-established shaman. She also would have probably learned a lot about her grandmother and other spirits in that ritual. But poverty, the burden of her father's illness, and her fear of rumors, and the risk of inviting harmful rituals from competitors kept Baigal from attending other people's rituals, causing her to miss out on the precious stories of her grandmother—her distinctive source of shamanic power and credibility.

People shared stories in the ritual arena and beyond, among kin and different generations. Although Buryat women were not silenced, storytelling, to the degree that would lead to the distribution of stories, suited men's daily activities better than those of women. Depending on the scope of distribution and level of influence, storytelling was a gendered practice. Genen's memories were popular partly because their narrators were all men. Men traveled more frequently, had more time for storytelling, and attracted bigger audiences, so their stories were better publicized. Women were not expected to tell stories in public. That was not because they were not taken seriously or could not articulate them well. Rather, cultural notions of gender and gendered divisions of labor impeded women's storytelling. Women were expected not to jump ahead of men or talk more than men when men were around. Preoccupied with child care, livestock, serving in-laws, and feeding family members and guests, women had fewer opportunities to speak to visitors uninterruptedly. As Steedly (1993:175–186) keenly observed during her research among Karo mediums in Indonesia, the stories that women told were interrupted, shortened, and diverted, and they sometimes ended inconclusively. As a result, they sounded unauthoritative, uncertain, and not as easily shared by others. In a similar way, Buryat women's narratives did not make a well-formed story that could be easily circulated and shared.

Ideally, spirit possession rituals are arenas for storytelling. Women's storytelling during possession by spirits was better accepted than their speaking outside of such ritual events. This was not because women were better performers than men. During possession, it is not actually the shamans themselves who speak to the audience, or at least they are not supposed to; rather, they are taken over to serve as intermediaries for more powerful, more authoritative origin spirits. Women gain audiences as "someone else speaking" by a temporary subversion of identity (Steedly 1993:175). But once the spirits leave, as Steedly (1993:196) has shown, there is little trace of them left; their desires and advice disappear with them, and the actual women's lives remain largely the same. Because the audience believes that someone else is speaking, the shaman's voice is not acknowledged behind that of the spirits. At least, this is how it is supposed to be in proper possession rituals; otherwise, possession is not needed, and the audience can consult the shamans without having them become possessed by spirits. Shamans become possessed by spirits, as Baigal told me, so that clients can hear the stories of the spirits, not the shamans. For that, the voice of the spirit during possession "merges with the intention of her audience, marks the official limit of women's narrative experience. Stories about mediums do not restore her speech" (Steedly 1993:186). On the contrary, men, especially elder ones, are charismatic storytellers and possess the culturally prescribed authority to draw audiences. Some of the male shamans hold just as much authority speaking in their own voices as they have delivering the voices of the spirits through possession.

From this point of view, there was little hope that the stories of a twenty-year-old fledgling female shaman such as Baigal, or an unemployed middle-aged woman such as Jargalma, would receive wide acceptance outside the ritual arena. Baigal's possession ceremonies drew at least a few devoted clients. And although she could have inserted her own stories or opinions in between her possessions by individual spirits, she spoke little during her rituals. Although I attributed this to her modesty, sometimes I wondered if she preferred to stay quiet because she thought that most people came to listen to the voices of her powerful origin spirits during the possession and had little interest in her own non-possessed voice. The Buryats are keen to separate spirits from shamans. Hearing the spirit's authentic words is the client's ultimate goal, even if the shaman or the audience repeats the spirits' words afterward. Of course, most people are also aware that spirits are not agents that are completely separate from shamans. The spirits are influenced by shamans, even though it is impossible to pin down the degree of separation or overlap between spirit and shaman. The reason many people considered Baigal a reliable shaman was that she was Khorlo's descendant, and, given her modest demeanor, her clients regarded her incapable of faking and lying.

In addition to descendants, disciples also played a significant role in producing and silencing the memories of their teachers. Khorlo's disciple Molom silenced her memories unintentionally. I met Molom in 1996 and

1997; he died in 1998, in his seventies, from what I believe to be stomach cancer. As his son, Tömör, recounted, Molom was initiated as a shaman late in life, in the 1980s. Molom did not contribute to making memories of Khorlo after the collapse of socialism because he chose to limit his shamanic practice, attending only to his white (healer) origin spirits and not his black (aggressive and assertive) ones. Instead of loud rituals of spirit possession, during which various spirits from the past would possess him and tell stories about their past, he practiced by whispering to his spirits and sedimenting their powers onto herbs. He rarely told stories, including ones about Khorlo. Ultimately, the memories of Khorlo were not as popular as those of Genen. Molom's death, Jargalma's family impoverishment, and more traditional structures of age, gender, storytelling, and leadership all contributed in specific ways to the silence surrounding Khorlo. But silence did not mean that the memories had vanished.

Memory Triggers

In order to further develop my relationship with Khorlo's descendants, I asked Jargalma to make me, for compensation, some items of shamanic paraphernalia. Jargalma enthusiastically agreed, and together we sewed the numerous tassels, beads, bells, and rings on the silk cape and headdress. I wanted to be in the right place and time for stories about Khorlo to emerge from Jargalma's silence. Eventually fragments of memories began to emerge, but they differed from the neatly packaged and well-performed stories about Genen that were narrated by men. Often a chance event would trigger a moment of memory. Jargalma began reminiscing about her mother's paraphernalia. "I do not remember if shamans during socialism had anything like this," she said, stuffing the snake figure with cotton.

"What was the paraphernalia like?" I asked.

"My mother's paraphernalia was worn out and plain, consisting only of a cloth headdress and a gown. It was nothing like what shamans have nowadays, no bright silk and velvet, no flashy beads and tassels."

"How did she hide her paraphernalia from the state officials?" I asked.

"My mother had a tiny drum with a drumstick that she hid in a school bag hanging from a wall in our house."

We would have conversed more, but Jargalma's housework, her preoccupation with her sick husband, and her efforts to find ways to make ends meet kept interrupting our conversations.

The lasting trigger for Jargalma's purposeful remembering was my meeting with Khorlo's spirit. The meeting happened during Baigal's *yoholgoon* (the thrice-monthly worship of all of a shaman's origin spirits). There were three clients seeking her help at the ceremony: a young man with a sick mother, a woman named Baasan who was concerned about her nephew's soul (and whose biography I tell in chapter 7), and Baigal's brother (Khorlo's grandson), who came from the countryside because he was suffering from nightmares. Baigal became possessed by the spirit of Khorlo, who sang to the young man that his mother was sick because a Buddhist deity in her house was abandoned and needed propitiation. As for Baasan's nephew, she suggested summoning his soul, because it had left his body. Khorlo told her grandson (Baigal's brother) that he had fallen ill because of pollution from a silver bridle he had picked up in the wilderness a few days ago. The bridle needed to be returned to the place where it had been found.

After the spirit took care of the clients, Baigal suddenly turned her face (hidden behind the black tassels of her headdress) to me. Khorlo sang in an energetic and assertive voice, "*Shchuuu*! Darling girl-child of mine, whose child are you? And where do you come from?!"

Momentarily startled, I introduced myself to her and said that I was doing research on shamans in the area. Everyone else supported my assertion and explained to the spirit that I was writing a book on shamans. I also repeated the rhymes after Baigal's father whispered to me in a low voice: "I had the honor to meet your quick and remarkable mediator [shaman]. I came to your mediator's [shaman's] *yoholgoon*, and I am very happy to take part in this ceremony."

THE SPIRIT: *Shchu*, shhhh. You have arrived to do your work, have you not?
THE AUDIENCE AND ME: Yes, yes, I did/she did.

The spirit of Khorlo began singing while beating her drum:

The time was difficult, the time of fog and clouds,
The time [I] used to hide in fog was rough,
Write the truth, write it all up, darling girl-child of mine,
Write down the difficult time that we struggled through.
The time was difficult, but [I] never surrendered,
Write that well, it is the time to reveal the truth.
In the face of harsh times [I] never gave up;
The people condemned and blamed me: what a devilish she-wolf I was!
Shchu, shchu, nowadays things are easier, *shchu, shchu*.
Many kinds of shamans are everywhere. . . .

The spirit sobbed, and the audience pacified her. Then, all of a sudden, Baigal's father asked the spirit a question about my mother's health: "Burhshuul, this scholar-girl's mother is not feeling well. . . . Advise her what to do." The spirit of Khorlo beat the drum for some time and then sang:

Your trip will be fruitful. Your journey is safe. Your goal will be met.
No afflictions by spirits. A square white building is your destination.

Before I comprehended the meaning of her last words, the audience replied to the spirit: "OK, thank you, Burhshuul, understood."

The spirit left after a sip of milk. The ceremony was ending. Then the people in the ger turned toward me and explained: "Take your mother to a hospital. A 'square white building' is a hospital."

Chased by the Spirits, Watched by the State

One afternoon, Jargalma came to my place, wearing her only "going-out" embroidered polyester blouse, which she shared with her daughter. After a few preliminaries, Jargalma sat down at the table and began talking about her mother. It took me a few minutes to realize that Jargalma had made a special trip (and hence the fancier blouse) to tell me about her mother. With the curtains closed, leaving us free from outside distractions, my room was a suitable place for long conversations. We used up half a dozen candles, drank a big thermos of milk tea, and munched on cookies all night long. It was only toward the end of our long conversation that I understood that my meeting with the spirit of Khorlo during Baigal's ritual was taken as a sign of the spirit's approval for Jargalma to share some personal stories about her mother.

Jargalma carefully distinguished memories of her own experiences from the stories she had heard from others. Since she had not talked about her memories before, most of them were not neatly packaged into complete stories. Thus sometimes she began her story somewhere in the middle, adding the context or the beginning later. Sometimes new stories emerged before she had finished the one she had started telling me. I tried to maintain the "fragmentary and inconclusive" (Steedly 1993:180) character of her memories as I wrote this chapter. But over time, that became difficult. Nor could I ignore the stories other people told about Khorlo. As had happened when I was getting stories about Genen, by the time Jargalma told me about her mother, I had already collected some stories from others. I have put them together here in a vaguely biographical fashion, still trying to maintain their randomness and interrupting them to provide the contexts from which they had emerged. "I heard that that my mother suffered from delusions as a young girl," said Jargalma. "She used to push her head into the cinders in the stove. The people attributed this behavior to the fact that she might have inherited Dorlik, who yearned for the touch of fire and metal. My mother was initiated as a shaman early in her life. But since female shamans propitiated the origin spirits of their natal paternal clan, their husbands and in-laws tend to be hostile to their endeavors."

In rural patrilocal and patriarchal marriages, women's spiritual connections disturbed the husbands' families' lines of power over their daughters-in-law. Dolgor told me that Khorlo's mother-in-law was especially brutal in controlling Khorlo. Dolgor was preoccupied with the ways parents-in-law treated their daughters-in-law, because she was the mother of eight girls and always worried about the older ones, who lived with their husbands' extended families. This is the story she told me:

> At the end of a long day shepherding, Khorlo would be given some *hiaram* [a mix of water with a little milk and salt] and then some *bantan* [broth thickened with flour, sometimes with pieces of meat] in her little wooden bowl. During the day in the pasture, Khorlo used a sharp rock to scrape out the bottom of the bowl so that she could deepen it and get more food. Her tricks did not escape the eyes of her mother-in-law. The deeper Khorlo made her bowl, the further the food was from the brim of her bowl. When her first-born child died, Khorlo decided to quit being a shaman. If her spirits allowed her to suffer so much, what was the use of propitiating them? She left her paraphernalia at the top of a mountain and ran away, all the way to the city of Ulaanbaatar, wanting to get as far from her origin spirits and her in-laws as she possibly could.

Just to make sure I understood the moral of the story, Dolgor added: "Women must avoid brutal in-laws and abusive husbands. That is what I tell my daughters, but I don't think they listen to me." At the age of thirty-four Dolgor became a widow with ten children, the youngest just three months old. She ended up living with her mother-in-law for the next ten years. Although the mother-in-law was not physically abusive, she was nevertheless controlling and extremely cruel, which used to sap Dolgor's energy. But with her older girls, she realized, matters were worse. Some of them were harshly exploited and bossed around the house and eventually came back to Dolgor. The other, younger girls could not find good husbands and lived with Dolgor.

Jargalma's story continued, following her mother from Bayan-Uul to Ulaanbaatar.

> When my mother arrived in Ulaanbaatar [probably in the 1940s], she found a job as a seamstress in an army-clothing factory. She married an army officer who was ethnically a non-Buryat—he was a Khalkha. Khorlo was convinced that her origin spirits would never find her again. Yet, a few years later, in the midst of her happily married life, she began seeing uncanny signs. Crows would sit on her shoulders, and street dogs followed her. Soon she fell ill with stomach ulcers. She became a living skeleton; her kidneys almost stopped functioning. She had hidden the fact that she had once been a shaman from her husband. Yet he guessed her secret because she was a Buryat: "Are you sure you do not have any special spirits following you? You are a Buryat, and Buryat people are known to have some 'special forces' to take care of." And my mother lied: "No."

When she became bedridden, her husband took a monthly leave and brought her to Bayan-Uul. "My father basically left the army and settled here," said Jargalma. "He told his commanders that his wife needed his attention. He was a very easygoing man, my father. He worked as a carpenter for the local state farm and stayed here because my mother's origin spirits demanded that she stay in her homeland."

"And how did your mother become initiated as a shaman?" I asked.

"I do not know the details," Jargalma said. "My father traveled around and found some elders among her people. . . . Alone, my mother would stay awake late at night. She would tell us to go to sleep; when we woke up in the morning, her rituals would be over. We never saw her rituals."

Khorlo did not gather an audience, and she condensed her rituals to the barest minimum. Her visitors left quickly after consulting with her, leaving sweets that Khorlo would imbue with the powers of her spirits and then toss out at night on behalf of her clients. To her spirits Khorlo explained the impossibility of carrying out proper rituals because of the "difficult times."

Modesty was Khorlo's political strategy for keeping herself safe at a time when fear of the state and mistrust ordered people's lives. Gifts and goods attracted suspicion from the state, so she avoided collecting them.[8] She used the cloth she received for making degels, headscarves, and shirts, but instead of keeping them for herself, she distributed them to relatives and guests as holiday gifts. Khorlo also kept the gifts of sheep she received in the flocks of their donors, rarely claiming them for consumption. She was so careful not to spread the word about herself that in 1977, when a group of her relatives who lived in Russian Buryatia heard about her and came to Bayan-Uul in a jeep to look for her, she pretended she was someone else: instead of saying that she was the shaman who took care of their family's origin spirits, she said she had never heard of such a shaman in the area. When her relatives left, Khorlo quietly tossed some libations to her origin spirits for these new-found relatives. When Jargalma asked her mother why she did not reveal her true identity, Khorlo said it was unnecessary. She needed neither veneration nor gifts for herself; she would simply take care of her relatives by propitiating their origin spirits, even if her relatives were unaware of what she had done. Jargalma represented one of the most extreme examples of the generation of non-knowledge, the victims of the disruption of knowledge within families. Although Khorlo performed rituals for others, exposing them both to the risks of being arrested and to the knowledge of shamanism, she refrained from exposing Jargalma and other children to her practice and the dangers it entailed. Jargalma told me that even the generation after hers knew more about shamanism than most people of her age, because the later generations were able to learn, even though what they found out had to be kept secret. But her generation was the most alienated from the past even though they were closer in age.

Injured by the State

The state never managed to arrest Khorlo, but it inflicted emotional injuries on her family. Khorlo's only son, Ivan, became an ardent atheist and turned against her. The locals told me that Khorlo spoiled Ivan, serving him the biggest portions of food and the choicest pieces of meat, and freeing him from all household chores. In return, Ivan threw the food at her, called her a charlatan, and ignored her in her old age. He demoralized Khorlo every day until her death.[9]

I learned about the state's destruction of this mother-son relationship accidentally, on a hot afternoon when Baigal and I were sitting in her ger, avoiding the midday sun. A middle-aged, poorly dressed man came into the house, opened the drawer of a cabinet, took out a hammer, and left without uttering a word or even noticing us. I was taken aback by the way he ignored Baigal, who was the authority in the house (at least in the absence of her parents), and inquired about him. He was Ivan—Baigal's maternal uncle. He had seven adult children, and his family was on the verge of starvation. Baigal attributed his misfortunes to her grandmother's curse.

Baigal was not the only person who was convinced that Ivan's poverty

Figure 15. Ritual with a young female shaman

was a punishment for his brutality toward his mother. The people of Bayan-Uul told me that when the spirit of Khorlo arrived at Baigal's initiation ceremony for the first time, she immediately began scolding her son. Khorlo's spirit had stated that Ivan's sufferings had only begun and that he should expect to "hit bottom" with respect to his poverty. Apparently Ivan's family was even poorer than Baigal's and often had only one meal a day—and sometimes not even that, subsisting on tea. There were no jobs in Bayan-Uul, and Ivan's family did not own any livestock. Some of his children rummaged through garbage for scrap metal to sell to traders; others herded livestock for the more affluent. Khorlo's revenge against her son, who had become "permeated" with the state's ideology, was also her revenge against the state.

Before Khorlo died in 1982, she told her daughter that because of *hestuu tsag* (hard times, referring to persecution), she was taking all of her origin spirits with her and would not return to any of her children. Khorlo meant that none of her descendants would become shamans, because she did not want them to suffer the repression she had known during her lifetime. But her origin spirits did not remain dormant. Fourteen years later, in 1996, Khorlo's spirit returned to Baigal. I asked Jargalma why. In reply, she simply described to me the seizures, nightmares, and hallucinations Baigal had had in the ninth grade. She sometimes had to skip school for days in a row and got to the point where would ran away and lie in a ditch with the pigs. "We were very reluctant to initiate Baigal as a shaman. But as Tömör noted, all the signs were there, and we thought it was better for Baigal to become a shaman than to lose her mind," said Jargalma. "We did actually ask the spirit of my mother why she decided to return and demand a shaman, and why she broke her promise not to return. Her answer was that it was not she, but more powerful origin spirits in our lineage, that demanded propitiation."

Once I asked Jargalma if she had a picture of her mother. No, her mother was all against picture taking. But she pulled out a collection of family photographs and showed me a tiny little photo, half an inch by a quarter of an inch—a passport photo. It was a black-and-white portrait of a woman wearing a headscarf tied in back. Jargalma expressed her desire to enlarge the photo for herself and her children. I offered to do so during my next trip to Ulaanbaatar. Jargalma got excited about this, but then changed her mind. What if the picture got lost on my trip? Then she would have no visible memory of her mother at all.

Memory, Gender, and Power

The variety of stories about Genen and Khorlo present individuals' personal political projects in relation to the state, both during socialism and after its collapse, to community politics, and as a part of their subjectivity. For many, the stories of female shamans were ways of contending with the state. Just because there were sites of resistance does not mean that state socialism was weak. Some scholars who concentrate on power pay less attention to resistance, worried that if they mention resistance then the forces of the oppression, of the uneven dynamics of power, and of exploitation will be diminished or dissipated. And resistance does not necessarily imply empowerment on the side of the oppressed. Just as Luvsan's "armoring" implies the existence of vague powers that he cannot pin down, resistance gestures toward powers the extent of which we cannot always know.

Laced with magic, the stories disclose the obscurity of the past and index the present disenchantment with the democratic order. The more magic employed in a narrative, the greater the opacity of the past and the stronger the disenchantment of the present. The narrators purposefully play out their beliefs in magic and spirits to destabilize, parody, and even attack state propaganda, modern technologies, and institutions of neoliberalism. Through the memories of shamans and their magic, they mourn their painful past by reminding themselves about state violence, which is scarcely acknowledged in the official histories. By remembering the socialist past, they show that their conflicting feelings about the state persist in the new historical setting.

In the context of their present-day communities, the narrators negotiated their positions by building their memories discursively against each other to stake a claim for "truer" and therefore more authoritative memories about the shamans, especially Genen. The fact that these female shamans practiced under the fear of persecution, with few material incentives, made them "real." In the context of suppression of the past and disbelief in shamans, the affiliation of contemporary shamans with Genen and Khorlo became an especially useful tool for gaining credibility.

The memories of Genen and Khorlo inform us about the structures of gender and the position of women in socialist and postsocialist rural Mongolia. The female shamans during socialism were powerful in the spiritual realm, but they were marginalized according to the state ideologies of gender and antireligious ideology. Since the end of socialism, men have gained power for themselves and for these spirits as well by telling stories about these female ancestors. These memories are crucial in contemporary shamans' competition for audiences, when the market economy and the outcomes of past state violence have created a particularly rational, skeptical, and choosy audience.

Female shamans, marginalized during socialism, had to die first in order to become spirits and gain power. Only through their death and return, as embodied in narrative, is their power legitimized among their living descendants. For them to gain power, someone else must speak for and about them—the male disciples, clients, and family members who have been successful in advancing their own as well their female ancestors' powers. However, it is significant that it is these female shamans, out of all others, who were chosen to be remembered; they were powerful on their own account. Memories of female shamans have been framed by the contemporary anxieties of Mongolian life amidst ongoing crisis and have shaped modern-day shamans' political subjectivities.

Finally, an interesting pattern emerges from studying the memories about Genen and Khorlo. The more closely related the storytellers are to the shamans, the more modest and less imaginative the memories are. Disciples and clients seem to use the memories for their own agendas in more pronounced and distinct ways (this is especially noticeable in the case of Genen). The farther the memories radiate, the more popularity they gain, and the more subversive and magical they become. But there is always a limit to the usefulness of the memories. This can be seen most clearly in

Khorlo's case, since her presence does not assist her descendants in terms of their success in daily life. Khorlo was persecuted during socialism. But the fact that she returned as an origin spirit during neoliberal capitalism does not make her suited to or supportive of the new order. The spirits remain separate and resistant to both orders while requesting worship, thus maintaining the parallel world even during the most challenging times.

FIVE

Ironies of Gender Neutrality

While traveling through an unfamiliar terrain during my initial summer visits in 1996–1999, I lived for days in a row with families of male shamans, and, occasionally their kin and clients. Nomadic herders, they lived in the grasslands, outside the sedentary town. There I met with origin spirits that these shamans summoned to their rituals, and among them also the origin spirits of female shamans from the past, including Genen and Khorlo, whose stories I retold in chapter 4. As time passed, I encountered many memorable and dramatic stories about female origin spirits. But I began to wonder about the whereabouts of living female shamans. The abundance of female origin spirits against the absence of living female shamans reminded me of the words of Edwin Ardener (1975), who noted the contrast between the glorious presence of women in poetry and stories and their scarcity in real life at the sites of officially acknowledged prestige and power.

Indeed, during those three summers (1996–1999) I barely managed to meet two female shamans. One insisted on postponing our conversations because her paraphernalia were incomplete. She wanted "to be studied after the completion of her shanars." Another female shaman was Chimeg—a woman in her late forties. She was Tömör's disciple and had completed three shanars, only one fewer than her teacher. During the ritual she called on her origin spirits to protect Tömör from spirit attack. At a break, I saw Chimeg and Tömör arguing with each other outside the ger. Then Chimeg suddenly walked away crying. Since I was more closely acquainted with Tömör at that time, I asked him first what had happened. Tömör refrained from giving any details, saying that the matter was trivial. Then I went to Chimeg and inquired about the situation. She linked her arm in mine and said: "These male shamans always dismiss women. They think that just because we are women we cannot be as good shamans as they. . . ." We were interrupted by the resumption of the ritual, and then, like the other female shaman, Chimeg suddenly left. Over the next two years she traveled through Russian Buryatia, and the local people lost touch with her.[1] When she returned, we became neighbors and friends. Much of this chapter grew out of our frequent conversations and my observation of Chimeg's trouble-some relationship with the Bayan-Uul community.

However, before Chimeg and I met again, and while I was still living with my initial hosts—the male shamans—I asked them about Chimeg and the existence of other female shamans in the area. My questions stirred some unexpected reactions from the male shamans. Tömör told me that, together with his mentor, Tsend, he would provide the most truthful infor-mation for my research. He was clearly upset that I was searching for other shamans despite all his help. Luvsan suggested that I stay away from all other shamans in the area, as most of them were either fake or, if real, had questionable motives. In short, as other people warned me, talking with one shaman about another could heat up existing rivalries. It was better not to bring the issue up.

As I continued to travel, I had hoped to meet female shamans with little effort, and preferably at the center of the rituals, just as I had male sha-mans. I suspected that this idea perhaps was naive but remained open to it nonetheless. After all, now that it was no longer suppressed, as it was under socialism, shamanism was now proliferating as individual families rushed to discover and propitiate their forgotten origin spirits. And since, at least in principle, shamanism was also gender-neutral, if not egalitarian, why could female shamans not reach the same success as male shamans? According to shamanic principles, male and female shamans perform the same rituals, are possessed by male and female spirits, have disciples and clients of both sexes, and use the same ritual paraphernalia. The principles not only wel-comed but even facilitated women's empowerment. To acquire the highest title of zaarin, male shamans had to complete thirteen shanars. In order to acquire the equally powerful title of duurisah, women needed to complete only seven shanars, because women were considered more gifted than men in connecting with spirits.[2] Unlike in the larger Buryat Mongolian society, where patriarchy is the norm and men are seen as superior to women, sha-manism did not discriminate on the basis of gender.

I expected that female shamans would have a status and recognition similar to that of as male shamans because before I came to Bayan-Uul, much of the literature that I read on spiritual practices and women empha-sized women's empowerment (Atkinson 1989; Balzer 1981; Kendall 1985,

1988; Tsing 1993). Although it is crucial to examine women's empowerment, it is equally important to attend to the gender-based complexities that women face in gaining powers and to investigate the structures, circumstances, and discourses that impede their advancement. And for shamanism specifically, it is also necessary to make explicit the political and cultural significance of shamanism with respect to other powers and practices. That is because shamanism often had a contentious relationship with other powers that led to the marginalization of its practitioners—for example, during imperial Russia's expansion to Siberia, and under the Buddhist missionaries in Mongolia in the seventeenth, eighteenth, and nineteenth centuries.[3] In twentieth-century socialist Mongolia, shamans, regardless of their gender, had no official power. Whatever power the shamans gained at that time was secret and risky. Shamanism became dominated by women, who also had to refuse material rewards from their clients in order to avoid being noticed by the state, which would expose them to the risk of persecution. Thus, I thought that with the end of the totalitarian regime, when shamanism finally brought economic opportunities and freedom, female shamans would benefit from their practice the same way as male shamans. Yet throughout my research in Bayan-Uul I met no duurisah and no female shamans whose economic situation and social prestige were comparable to that of male shamans. So while there was no shortage of female shamans and many had gained several shanar, overall they lagged behind male ones.

Thus, a part of my argument is that simply participating in the practice of shamanism does not automatically make women powerful. We need to look much further to gauge their empowerment, because in Mongolia shamanism is open to both men and women and its principles are gender-neutral. Female practitioners also start from the premise that as shamans, they are equal to men and are thus entitled to the same respect and benefits as their male counterparts. Because both female shamans and the larger society expect them to take the same path in pursuit of power as male shamans (and because that is what they ultimately do), it is important to look deeper into their experiences.

The gendered hierarchy of shamanism became obvious to me after I moved to the sedentary center of Bayan-Uul for my yearlong stay in 1999–2000. I discovered that the center was full of female shamans. Unlike the male shamans in the grasslands, these female shamans were poor and struggled to maintain their practice. Many had completed a number of shanars and offered the same services as the male shamans, and the women were seen as being as powerful as men. Their skills in the rituals and spiritual powers, however, did not translate into material or political power on the same level as that of their male counterparts. Others lagged behind in their shanars because they could not afford to stage the rituals. Shanar rituals are elaborate, labor-intensive, and very expensive. But a shaman must stage them every two to three years until reaching the title of zaarin or duurisah. Shamans who fail invite trouble: their own origin spirits, instead of serving and protecting them, begin to harm them or leave them exposed to the attacks of other shamans and spirits. Thus, economic impoverishment led to spiritual stagnation, which in turn diminished the shamans' competitiveness, clients, income, and prospects for staging shanars, creating a downward spiral.

I met numerous shamans, both male and female, who were at different stages of accomplishment. The ones who had achieved the highest rank were almost exclusively male, whereas a disproportionate number of female shamans were stuck somewhere in the middle, having performed only three or four shanars out of the seven needed for them to reach the title of duurisah. Of the numerous bases for individual shamans' success and failure—some gender based and others that have nothing to do with gender—how does gender figure in the process of the shamans' quest for power? In what ways did the postsocialist transformation benefit male shamans more than female ones?

Figure 16. A female shaman

I explore these questions by analyzing the experiences of a female sha-man, Chimeg, in her quest for power. I start with Chimeg's experience as a child, a young woman, a wife, a mother, a shaman, and a divorcee. In addition to engaging with Chimeg, I learned about her from numerous in-dividuals, including Chimeg's cousin Dolgor and my confidante and trav-eling companion Tegshe, who invited Chimeg to live in her house for free. Chimeg is representative of most of the female shamans I encountered in the area: she had a troubled personal life and financial difficulties that de-layed her rituals. She is unique, however, in that she has become one of the most powerful shamans in the area and dares to contend openly with male shamans. Because she pushed and transgressed the boundaries of public expectations of what it means to be a woman and a female shaman, she revealed to me the glass ceiling in shamanic practice, the workings of the fragmented and dynamic systems of gender, and disguised forms of power and subjugation.

A Beloved Daughter

Before Chimeg was two years old, she was adopted by a childless couple. At first Chimeg's adoptive parents pampered her, showering her with rare and expensive clothing and treats. Her grandfather was especially loving and af-fectionate. Dolgor, Chimeg's cousin, told me:

> We [Chimeg and Dolgor] were about five years old when I saw Chimeg for the first time. She almost blinded me with her beauty. Chimeg was wearing a white satin dress decorated with ruffles, with puffed short sleeves and a bell skirt. I had never seen anything this crisp and airy, so white, shiny, and beau-tiful! Her two braids were fastened with red nylon ribbons made into big flowers. Her sandals were also white. At that time, we [Dolgor and her sib-lings] did not wear anything like that during the summer—we went barefoot and we all wore degel, but we could not even dream of Western-style dresses.

A few years later, Chimeg's adoptive parents began having children of their own. Chimeg, feeling neglected, often rebelled. Sharp-tongued by nature, she often argued with her parents and tested their patience. She remembers that her mother would get so angry at her that she would whip her with a horse's bridle made of leather straps. When her grandfather was in the house Chimeg used to hide behind his back and provoke her mother: "Dulma, Dulma [Chimeg's mother's name], do you want to beat me? Can you beat me now? Can you beat me now?" Her mother used to mumble: "Just wait; once grandpa leaves, I will skin you!" After her grand-father died Chimeg felt especially lonely.

While the abuse and neglect of stepchildren is strongly condemned by the society at large, it is indeed a common concern throughout Mongo-lia. In addition, the concept of child discipline in Mongolia often includes physical punishment, although not for everyone. It is impossible to discern the motives behind the beatings Chimeg's parents gave her. It is also worth noting that a child's status changes drastically with the arrival of younger siblings. Older sisters and brothers, even at an early age, are expected to look after the younger siblings, protect them from mishaps, entertain them, and carry them around. In addition, the older ones may receive less affec-tion, entertainment, and treats as a way of marking their status as older children or simply due to the limits of the resources. However, Chimeg's transition from a singleton to a big sister had been rather difficult because she lost her grandfather at about the same time.

As Chimeg grew older, she became known for her beauty, and many young men sought her attention. When she was sixteen a married local doctor began courting her. Chimeg's parents hoped that he would divorce his wife and marry Chimeg, and they seemed to ignore his advances to her. Chimeg, however, disliked him and avoided him as much as she could. In the meantime, one evening two unknown men from neighboring districts arrived on a motorcycle and stayed in their house for two days. After long conversations with Chimeg's father, one of the men asked Chimeg if she would marry him. He was eleven years older than Chimeg and worked as a tractor driver at the collective farm. She had no interest in him. But she ac-cepted his proposal in order to end the unwanted advances from the mar-ried doctor. She imagined that once the doctor left her alone, she would divorce her husband and start her life anew.

Arranged marriages—once dominant in prerevolutionary Mongolia—were banned from the early days of socialism, back in the 1920s. But even informal arrangements such as Chimeg's were far from commonplace by the late 1960s, when Chimeg got married. Most people of Chimeg's gen-eration met their mates on their own at school, extracurricular activities, dance clubs, and after-school volunteering (state-mandated), as well as at the livestock pastures and through friends. Even if parents were interested in a particular mate for their children, the young people were given time and opportunity to become acquainted and get to know each other be-fore marriage was proposed. Furthermore, marriage proposals among the Buryats have been highly ritualized and staged and (purposely) took a long time, with each party paying long visits to the other, engaging in gift exchange, heavy drinking, ritualized friendly humiliation, feigned hiding and stealing of the bride, and finally Bakhtinian carnivalesque festivities that continued all throughout the engagement and wedding preparations. Obviously, the purpose of these parties was to break down the distance between strangers and allow them to become an extended family. And even if families did not stage the traditional Buryat wedding, at least some of its elements, especially the visits and parties, were kept almost intact. Overall, even if parents arranged the introduction between their children, it was made to look like a serendipitous rendezvous, and the two parties' parents pretended to know nothing about it (even if the young couple did).

Chimeg's marriage was nothing like that. She told me that she felt lonely during her wedding because the event was dominated by the groom's side. She was embarrassed to be marrying so early—before finishing high school—and was worried that her classmates would show up. We have little information that would explain her parents' motives behind hastening to marry Chimeg off. Some people told me that Chimeg had to agree on the marriage because she got pregnant out of wedlock. Chimeg never told me this. But even if Chimeg was pregnant, the arrangement is still surprising. Many Mongol women have their first child out of wedlock, and their parents usually tolerate it; some even welcome it. It is possible, however, that Chimeg's parents wanted to hide her out-of-wedlock pregnancy from the public by marrying her off as soon as possible.

Intimate Subjugation

After settling down with her husband, Chimeg realized that getting a divorce would be more complicated than she had expected. Her husband threatened to kill her if she divorced him. Every time he sharpened a kitchen knife or chopped firewood with an ax, he reminded her that she could not leave the house. "I was so naive!" exclaimed Chimeg. "I really believed that if I left, he was going to come after me and kill me! After many years of marriage, when I asked whether he was really going to kill me, he said, 'Of course not! Are you stupid? I was just trying to keep you!' And I was so devastated!"

Chimeg's husband also used to beat her violently. He was jealous.

> I always had many men vying for my attention. Even after I got married, I used to receive love letters. Sometimes my husband would discover them before I did, and he would beat me. I would say that I had nothing to do with the letters and ask why he was beating me and not the men who wrote

the letters. Then he would say that they [the men] were sending me letters because I must have made the first move and thus given them reasons for sending the letters. He would beat me more. Ironically, I did not even know some of those people who sent me letters.

A few months into her marriage Chimeg got up the courage to leave her husband, but then she found out that she was pregnant. After her first child was born she tried to return to the home of her adoptive parents, her baby in her arms. Her parents refused to take her back, saying she would be a burden, absorbing the resources needed to bring up her younger siblings. Chimeg was devastated: "My father even contacted my husband and asked him to take me back on the condition that he would treat me better. It was a deal between the two men." Chimeg also sought help from her biological father, but he dismissed her. Chimeg's mother had died before her arranged marriage, after many years of being ill and bedridden. Dolgor remembered Chimeg's attempts to return to her parents. "It is actually true that her husband used to beat her very often from the beginning of their marriage. At the same time, she [Chimeg] was a character too. I do not know the details, since my family lived further away from Chimeg's, but she definitely has a 'mean mouth.' And I heard her husband would beat her because she would say mean things and make him angry."

Rejected by her adoptive family and disowned by her biological father, Chimeg had no choice but to return to her husband. Chimeg told me that he considered her one of his possessions and demanded that she obey him unquestioningly. "My husband told me that since I was his wife, I was at his disposal and had to satisfy his sexual needs, even if I did not want him and even if I had my monthly matters. He was so stupid, he would force me to have sex with him even when I was attending to our sick child staying up all night. He just said that I should shut the child's mouth."

Once Chimeg realized that there was no one to help her, she resisted her husband by ignoring her housework or doing it halfheartedly. She jumped at the chance to go to a two-month-long course at a nursing school in Ulaanbaatar and then worked part-time as a district nurse, in which capacity she was on call for the local hospital. Among repeated beatings, there was one particularly violent episode that caused Chimeg to resume her search for ways to leave. Coming home from seeing a patient one rainy day, she was delayed by the muddy roads. Soaking wet, she arrived to a cold house and hungry children. She took off her rubber boots, made a fire in the stove, put on water for tea, and held her two-year-old to her chest to warm him up. Her husband entered, took their child from Chimeg's arms, and threw Chimeg on the floor, where he beat her, kicking and stepping on her with his hard-soled work boots. When their five-year-old son ran to his mother, Chimeg's husband threw the child against the wall and continued to beat Chimeg. She told me: "I could not do anything. I just screamed, 'Kill me! Kill me! You're always threatening to kill me. Now is the time!'"

When he had finished beating her, Chimeg could not get up by herself, so her husband had to pick her up from the floor and then nurse her in bed for several weeks. Two of her ribs and her left arm were broken; her kidneys were injured, and she urinated blood for two weeks. "'I will leave, just wait, the kids will grow up and I will leave,'" she said. "I promised my-self. I understood that I could not and should not live like this."

While Chimeg was thinking about ways to leave, her husband accepted a job as a herder on the collective farm and moved his wife and children from the sedentary town at the district to the nomadic countryside. At least in town Chimeg could maintain her job and built a network. But in the countryside, Chimeg had no place to go and no social life. Herding sheep and cattle was lonely work, and she felt isolated and even more oppressed by her husband than when she lived in the sedentary center. Chimeg de-scribed for me how her day began: "Every morning before sunrise, winter or summer, my husband shouted to wake me up. I would get up while he was still in bed, light a fire in the stove, and make tea. I would bring tea, sliced bread, cream, and sugar on a little table next to his bed. My husband would only get up after he had had his morning tea in bed and after the house had gotten warm."

It was during the years that Chimeg lived in the countryside that she and her husband had most of their children. That was due in part to the fact that most of Chimeg's married life coincided with Mongolia's pro-natal policy (1965–1989). The state prohibited birth control and abortions.[4] With limited control over her body, Chimeg became pregnant almost every other year throughout her twenties and most of her thirties. She described her life as that of a childbearing machine, saddled with children that her body carried: one inside, another "dangling from her neck," another riding on her back, the rest clutching her skirt, and all of them "hanging" from her heart, for she loved them all despite everything. A few times she would feel ready to leave her marriage, then realize that she was pregnant again; so she waited to leave until the child could be weaned and learn to care for its basic needs. Chimeg gave birth to more than ten children. Yet once, when she left her husband, her youngest child died during her absence. Just a year and a half old, the child died of dehydration caused by a gas-trointestinal infection. By the time her husband took the child to the hospital, it was too late. After that, Chimeg promised never to leave her children until they could fend for themselves.

The Politics of Gendering in Socialist Mongolia

It is now time to pause and explore the politics of gender that would explain, at least partially, Chimeg's struggle to leave her violent marriage as she was being weighed down by motherhood and a lack of social and other support. So far I have retold Chimeg's life prior to her initiation as a shaman. Her life is influenced by the construction of gender in the rural household, ethnic identity, and the socialist state. In general, I take gender as "the socially and culturally produced ideas about male-female difference, power, and inequality" (Gal and Kligman 2000:4). During socialism, the Mongolian state attempted to use the fluidity of gender to its own advantage by creating highly nuanced and well-promoted policies. In turn, those policies further shaped the differences between men and women. Women were promoted at work, in some professions to the same levels as men. In some professions women adopted some masculine features as marks of equality, such as short hairstyles, minimal jewelry, and menswear-inspired work clothing, suits, and accessories.[5] At home, however, women were expected to accept male dominance and perform their traditional housekeeping role. Men's traditional superiority over women had been denaturalized in most public and professional spaces, since men shared power, resources, and prestige with women. At home, however, they returned to their dominant positions, occupied the most prestigious spaces, and expected to be attended by their wives. As many scholars noted, during socialism women held two jobs: the official state job and housework.[6] Indeed, the domestic sphere was exactly the place where "considerable gender inequalities in Soviet life increased, but became 'unsayable'" (Gal and Kligman 2000:47). Even if a woman had a high social position, neither that nor gender equality at work changed the gender hierarchy at home.

The basic notions of the gendered division of labor in a traditional nomadic household are similar, at least in rhetoric, throughout much of Mongolia. In a nutshell, women are expected to do most of the housework, including cooking, cleaning, dairy processing, and child rearing; they are also responsible for managing and taking care of sheep and goats, and cattle. Men take care of the "outside" matters, such as fetching firewood, tending to the horses, locating good pastureland, and searching for lost livestock. The Buryats enforced gender hierarchy in their households much more diligently than the Khalkhas, and the gendered hierarchy is rigid. I regard this as one of the ways in which the Buryats maintain their ethnic identity in response to the Khalkha-dominated state propagation of gender equality.

Although the state penetrated the most intimate spaces, such as uteruses and sex lives, when it came to the birth of children, it refused to involve itself in cases of domestic violence. Rape in nuptial families was not criminalized until 2008. Under the guise of protecting domestic privacy, the battering of women is still considered *ger bulin asuudal*, a family matter that needs no outside intervention, including that of the police. There are cultural pockets that accept (or even celebrate) wife beating. For instance, I heard the following unsolicited remarks: "A wife and a dog need to be beaten once a month"; "A beaten wife is a tough wife"; "A wife needs a slap on her face once a day"; and "Monthly wife beating reinvigorates men's spirits."

The only people to whom women could appeal for protection when they were mistreated by their husbands were their kin, mostly fathers and brothers, and sometimes an older brother-in-law. The arrangements for help are not official or customary, but rather incidental, and depend on individual relationships. Some male kin refuse to help and protect women, for one reason or another, so they do not guarantee a woman protection. While in practice such patronage saved many women from abuse and misery, in the abstract it also reconfirms male domination.

By ignoring intimate violence, the state indirectly supported male domination in the domestic sphere, in contrast to the public and work spheres, where men and women were for the most part considered to have equal rights. There men could not automatically and explicitly dominate women and claim superiority. The relative gender equality in public and in the workforce (up to a point) helped the state reach its economic and social goals. Equally, gender hierarchy within domestic sphere and male superiority was also in line with the state's pro-natal policy and the promotion of a uniform, family-based lifestyle.

As I have already mentioned, most of Chimeg's married life coincided with the state's pro-natal policy (1965–1990). It openly encouraged and tacitly forced women to give birth to as many children as possible. The state justified the policy in several ways. It made use of Mongolians' nationalist sentiments, fueled by anxiety about the country's underpopulation and by Sinophobia—in this context, a fear of becoming absorbed by the Chinese. In meeting its grandiose economic goals for industrialization, urbanization, and modernization, Mongolia, like other socialist countries, was "dependent on the availability of labor, of human capital, and reproduction and the labor force" (Kligman 1998:4). The increase in population was also one of the major indicators of socialist development and modernization. It was a sign of the successful implementation of medical and technological advances that reduced mortality and increased longevity. For instance, the 1950s cultural campaigns also aimed at improving the reproductive health of the population through the treatment of syphilis and other sexually transmitted diseases.[7] As Gal and Kligman argue, "The health of a state has long been linked to the rapid reproduction of its inhabitants; the vigor of individual body has served as a sign of the health or infirmity of the body politic" (2000:18). The Soviet Union supported Mongolia's pro-natal policy not only because it demonstrated the superiority of the socialist welfare system over capitalism, but because the country was a military buffer zone for the USSR. In the media, arts, and cinema the Soviets were represented as the saviors of a population that was *ustaj baisan* (on the verge of extinction).

The state conveyed the pro-natal propaganda through political rhetoric and cultural productions. Slogans such as "Children Are Our Future," "Devote Everything to Children," "For Mothers and Children," and the like were posted on the tops of the buildings of Ulaanbaatar's main streets. In addition, the state also provided some economic incentives. Families with four or more children received monetary rewards on a monthly basis. Mothers of four were awarded the state medal for "Mother Heroine of the Second Degree," and a mother of five or more children would be lauded a "Mother Heroine of the First Degree." The most laudable aspect of the pro-natal policy was the state's investment in a robust day-care system; comprehensive schools; hospitals; and spaces and resources for extracurricular activities, entertainment, sports, literature and the arts.

The pro-natal policy, however, conflicted with those of its citizens, especially in urban settings. In the popular view, women who had a lot of children were stigmatized as uneducated, uncultured, and passive. Yet most women, especially in rural areas, had little control if any over their reproductive lives, which conflicted with their plans for succeeding in their careers and pursuing their education. Even if men and women had equal education, that hardly translated into equal job advancement and equal rights in general.[8]

Mongolia's pro-natal policy was tremendously successful. Its population tripled, going from 647,504 in 1918 to over 2 million in 1989.[9] The increase in population came at a high personal price for women, who bore the physical and emotional burdens of the policy. Not only did women suffer from multiple births, complications from illegal abortions, and even maternal mortality, but motherhood became a convenient, unacknowledged way for men to exert control over the women in their families.

Men openly observed that women who were "piled up" with children, like Chimeg, could not easily move and so had to put up with their husbands. To a large extent, women's childbearing became a tool allowing men to control their wives.[10] Although most people are extremely affectionate and love their children, sometimes women often spoke of children as *mahan tsoij* (flesh padlocks) or *ginj* (shackles), and they complained to me about being unable to engage in any activities beyond those of their household. There is also a fine line between a woman's desire to have many children and the effects of external pressures on her to do so.[11]

Rural women had far more children than did urban women, who had (highly limited and often of questionable safety) birth control and (illegal) abortions. The average household in the rural area of Bayan-Uul prior to the 1990s included eight children, and patrilocal residency made women almost fully dependent on their husbands and in-laws for support in child care.[12] Such a large number of children made the issue of divorce and separation practically impossible for most women, even though divorce was legal. Among the Buryats, the father's family claims the children, so women who divorce and leave their marriage have to endure the emotional burdens of being separated from their children. A woman's departure could lead to fatal outcomes for younger children. In addition to Chimeg, I met two other women whose young children died during their absence, mostly from infection and dehydration. Many women confessed to me that the main reason they stayed in an abusive marriage was their children.[13]

In addition, divorcees faced financial hardships, were stigmatized in a world where everyone was expected to be married, and were in danger of being bullied, harassed, and treated as second-class citizens. The perpetuation of gender roles of men as breadwinners and women as childbearers meant that for women, divorce brought consequences that discouraged them from initiating it. Many men I spoke to were confident that their wives did not have courage to leave them, and that they accepted the flaws in their husbands' behavior: "If women divorce their husbands, they become orphans. It is not in their interest to initiate divorce." The cultural value of men as heads of the household made their mere presence an invaluable asset to the household and to a woman's social status.

As mothers, women were expected to tolerate certain imperfections in their marriage such as their husband's infidelities, lack of support, and even emotional and physical abuse for the sake of their children. By officially recognizing men as heads of the households,[14] ignoring domestic violence, and reinforcing the pro-natal policy, the socialist state prevented gender equality, especially behind closed doors.[15] Gender during socialism was heavily influenced by the state by means of pro-natalism, the construction of child-centered families, gender equality in the work force, but gender hierarchy in the domestic sphere, and ignoring domestic violence.

The Shaman Chimeg: Gender and Shamanism after Socialism

By now it should be clear that Chimeg's experience was heavily influenced by the state construction of gender coupled with Buryat traditions and the rural nomadic lifestyle. In telling of Chimeg's experience as a female shaman after the collapse of socialism, I redefine the notion of gender in the context of the public proliferation of shamanic practices in postsocialist rural Mongolia. Simultaneously, because the collapse of socialism transformed the social construction of gender—it is no longer solely influenced by the state's politics—it is necessary to weave those changing notions of gender into the experiences of Chimeg as a female shaman.

As in a quintessential story about shamanic illness, prior to becoming initiated as a shaman Chimeg suffered from acute illnesses. By then she was in her late thirties and her doctors could no longer give her a diagnosis. Chimeg was fairly certain that her illnesses had something to do with her abandoned origin spirits. She knew that her biological parents had shamanic ancestry, but because they lived during socialism, they never became shamans. Chimeg reasoned that her siblings and cousins died young because none of them had become shamans and propitiated the family's origin spirits. In addition, her mother was bedridden for years. Toward the end of her life, she could not move and speak; she could only hear and see. Chimeg told me, "The spirits did not let her die peacefully. Instead, they made sure that she had been tortured and dried up slowly." Chimeg thought that she survived because she used her adoptive family's name, so the spirits could not find her. At the same time, she also gave agency to the spirits: they allowed her to go to a different family so that she would have a chance to be initiated as a shaman. In any case, she was convinced that she had to become a shaman.

Chimeg learned the shamanic skills quickly, and at her first shanar it became clear that her origin spirits were extremely powerful and aggressive. She completed her first two shanars without too much effort and immediately began to get constant requests to worship various families' abandoned origin spirits. She traveled extensively. It seemed to me that she traveled in order to get away from her abusive husband. Chimeg explained her travels, as did many other shamans, as the will of her spirits, which guided her actions.

Despite her husband's violent restrictions, Chimeg expanded her travels beyond the district of Bayan-Uul and went to Russian Buriatya, where she acquired numerous disciples and clients. In the early to mid 1990s there were only a few shamans among the Buryats in either Mongolia or Russia, but demand was high. Although she had completed only three shanars of the seven required, Chimeg had become one of the most renowned and financially successful shamans of that period.

More, Chimeg's travels to Russia coincided with a period of nationwide trading. Upon the collapse of socialism, both the former Soviet Union and the Mongolian state withdrew their respective monopolies over the importing and exporting of goods and services. The two nations' populations had to fend for themselves, but that also meant that opportunities opened up for individuals and private businesses to fill functions previously performed by the state. Chimeg used these social changes to her own advantage and found a profitable outlet. At the time Mongolia was suffering from a shortage of wheat flour. She took the payments and gifts she had accumulated from her shamanic practices and started importing flour from Russia into Mongolia while still practicing shamanism. She brought a truckload of flour from Russia (usually five tons) to her district of Bayan-Dun and exchanged every bag of flour, each weighing between eighty and a hundred pounds, for a sheep. Within two years Chimeg had accumulated a large number of livestock, including a camel caravan. She built a new log house and filled it with expensive carpets, furniture, and dishes.

Despite these material comforts, and despite the fact that Chimeg had managed to acquire them during a time of economic collapse, Chimeg's travels infuriated her husband. He was jealous and assumed that whenever she traveled and stayed in other people's houses, she was cheating on him. Not only that, but her frequents absences from the home meant he no longer had anyone to serve him his meals, take care of children, and clean the house. He also felt emasculated because he had failed to provide for the family after his job ended with the collapse of the SF. His wife, on the contrary, who had always been dependent on him, was now a successful breadwinner and enjoyed her freedom. Because his pride was hurt, he preferred to stay poor and maintain control over Chimeg. The new and unexpected gender roles and reversal of power in the household were not acceptable to him. He was still the man and she, Chimeg, was his wife. But it was not until Chimeg's husband tried to harm her shamanic paraphernalia that Chimeg left him. She told me:

> One evening my clients, disciples, and I returned home from a trip to Russia to get the rest of my shamanic paraphernalia from the house. We were about to go to the countryside for a bigger ritual. My husband was not home, and I went to the local store to buy bread for my family and guests. When I returned, my guests were sitting quietly, each embracing an item of my paraphernalia, which were stored in separate cases. I asked what happened, and they told me that my husband had tried to throw them into the stove and burn them. My guests had to wrestle with my husband to save my paraphernalia. I thought that I should leave before my husband burned my paraphernalia one day.

When Chimeg finally left, her husband refused to let her have her share of the household items, including bedding, and he forbade their children to give anything to their mother. Since her husband controlled the possessions, the children did not dare to confront him openly. The oldest son secretly continued to give her provisions from the family's storage cabin.[16] "He told my children: 'Your mother will not be gone for too long. Once she gets cold and hungry and has no clothes to wear and no friends and relatives to help her, and no place to stay, she will come back home; she will not disappear.' I will not go back even to my district!" repeated Chimeg to herself over and over. Chimeg's husband refused to officially divorce her, and she could not claim her share of household property. She had no livestock, house, or access to her garden. Chimeg's state employment as a district nurse, which she took up during the short intervals between her ten pregnancies, did not qualify her for a state pension. Chimeg received limited help from her grown children; they remembered her struggles against their violent father and sympathized with her. But since they lived in the family compound with their father and all their food was stored in common, they had to be secretive about helping their mother.

Chimeg moved to the district of Bayan-Uul (adjacent to Bayan-Dun) to be close to her cousin Dolgor and her friend Tegshe. She had expected that by leaving her husband and pursuing her shamanic practice, she would gain even more power and expand her practice. Having done well in the past, she was confident she could survive on her own, have a home, and bring her younger children to live with her. But her attempts to make a living as a shaman were highly problematic. Partly, as I argue in chapter 6, at least in a place such as Bayan-Uul, the well-to-do shamans were also wealthy herders and entrepreneurs, and they had a highly efficient and supportive system of family and kin. Their shamanic practice ensured them social prestige, protection from burglars, and various networks through which they consolidated and increased their wealth. It is hard to say whether these male shamans would be able to gain so much wealth through their shamanic practice along and with no start-up capital. Regardless of gender, shamanic practice as a full-time job, without other support, both financial and social, was hardly the most gainful occupation for either male or female shamans. Consider that Chimeg gained her wealth in early 1990s by supplementing her shamanic practice with a lucrative business—importing the main local staple, wheat flour. In other words, shamanic practice alone, at least in impoverished rural Mongolia, does not bring wealth. Here, gender mattered less in making money, but it mattered a great deal in having the rights to retain and own property. Chimeg was able to earn money and livestock, but she lost it to her husband due largely to the male domination of Buryat-Mongol households, and to state policies that perpetuated the male hierarchy and failed to defend women.

If earning a large income was now out of the question for Chimeg, then how about a modest one as a shaman? Why did Chimeg have to struggle to sustain herself and maintain her practice? My partial answer to these questions is that the loss of many attributes that constitute a woman, attributes that are associated with marriage and family, had undermined her shamanic practice in a way that it would not have done if she had been a male shaman.

Before I delve into issues about the acquisition of shamanic powers, let me situate and define gender as it transformed from the state-shaped notions and practices under socialism into a more fractured and contested notion after socialism. As I situate gender in relation to what it means to be a shaman, I define it in a more contingent way by borrowing Heather Paxson's notion of gender "as a system of virtues" and follow her chosen definition of virtue as "moral standards" and "manners and customs and ways of living" (2004:11). Paxson argues that "gender in Greece entails a personal responsibility to behave in a morally proper manner" (2004:250). She is inspired by Michael Herzfeld's (1985) argument that masculinity is not a set of ideal characteristics and values, but rather entails a person's ability to enact those characteristics and values. Thus, masculinity, as Herzfeld argues, is less about "being a good man" than about "being *good at* being a man" (1985:16). Paxson calls the capacity to enact the values and characteristics of a particular gender "gender proficiency." Motherhood completes a woman not because it realizes her biological capacity, but because by being a good mother a woman can demonstrate that she is good at being a woman—that is, she can demonstrate gender proficiency.[17]

Paxson's notion of gender as a system of virtues is well suited to thinking about the construction of gender, and particularly the female gender, in Mongolia. Ideal women are perceived as virtuous—selfless, nurturing, and giving. They are expected to be able to appease, manage, and find the way to settle conflict in the household, and steer their loved ones out of trouble. Such capabilities develop from the activities related to rearing and raising children as well as from learning to accommodate and attend to one's husband. Both motherhood and marriage are equally important for completing a woman as a moral being. They create necessary structures, borders, attachments, and demands that make the actualization of women's virtues possible, and make them publicly visible and recognizable.

Although the Buryats do not compare the abstract category of shaman with an abstract notion of woman, the ideologies behind being a shaman coincide almost exactly with the female gender as a set of virtues. Both shamans and women are expected to serve others, renounce egotism, attend to the suffering of others, and provide emotional support. Although conceptually the meanings of the work of a shaman and that of a woman can be considered the same (serving, helping, and resolving issues), in practice the work of shamans as ritual performers differs from the work of women in that the latter's work is rarely seen *as* work. And here is the culprit. For a woman to be a shaman, she must have a spotless reputation as a woman. That means that she has to be a mother and a wife. Marriage brings prestige and status for women and protects them from public intrusion in the form of gossip and rumors. At the most basic, marriage fulfills women's supposed biological need for sex. Furthermore, women's emotional attachments to their husbands and children make them responsible, tying up their desire to seek sex, since they must then protect their honor. In addition to being virtuous, giving, and nurturing, women in Mongolia are also judged on their intelligence and their ability to influence their husbands, keep them away from trouble, and manage conflict in their relationships. If a man engages in extramarital affairs, there is a tendency to seek the flaw in the wife, whether it is a lack of astuteness or a loss of appeal and attraction. It is seen that women are *narin uhaantai* (perceptive), whereas men are naturally *gunduugui* (lenient). It is women's work to guide their men in the subtleties of life.

But Chimeg, violating all the norms and expectations associated with being female, left her children, husband, and home, thus failing triply at being good at being a good woman. Worry-free single women are seen as having unbridled sexuality—a potential source of danger and conflict. Married women were suspicious that Chimeg might seduce their husbands. The local men responded to Chimeg's fleeing her husband with roaring disapproval. Chimeg was transgressing the established norms of womanhood and the structures of male domination. Most of the local men I talked to expressed the feeling that Chimeg was wrong and that her husband was right. Their reaction was so uniform that it was as if they had agreed on it beforehand. They said that he raised the children while Chimeg was traveling and performing shamanic ceremonies. It was rumored that while she was traveling she had an affair with a married man. According the locals, Chimeg was betraying her husband, who despite her infidelity stayed at home and took care of the house and children. And even after all she had done, he was willing to accept her back into the family. So he must be a good man. Some people said that maybe even Chimeg deserved her husband's violence. Many men claimed that Chimeg's husband was a quiet and decent person, that he would never even bloody a mouse's nose. Surely, they said, Chimeg's husband knew her best and treated her the way a husband treats a wife who runs off, engages in love affairs with other men, and does not take care of the house and children. Not one man I talked to sympathized with Chimeg. While it was clear that her children were mostly grown and could fend for themselves, by leaving her children with her husband Chimeg also inadvertently transferred all the credit for raising them solely to him. Her husband gained social support, prestige, and sympathy, all at her expense. Unexpectedly, Chimeg's freedom was detrimental to her practice. She was deemed amoral and unkind for leaving her children. And rumors began circulating about her "failed rituals," "loose sexuality," and "greed," which only contributed to her marginalization and undermined her shamanic practices.

Chimeg was convinced that by freeing herself from the domestic sphere she showed her dedication to her practice. But the local people—her current and, potentially, future clients—did not separate the idea of the domestic sphere from Chimeg. The conflict between Chimeg's expectation that by leaving her husband she would become an independent shaman devoted to her clients and the locals' negative perception about divorced women set the stage for Chimeg's losing her hard-earned prestige.

Women's identities are defined by their attachment to their households and children, and by belonging to men. Chimeg was able to acquire wealth and succeed as a shaman in her earlier years partly because she had the status and prestige of a married woman, even though her husband was not traveling with her. Her travels as a married woman were not a threat to other women, since she was attached to (and controlled by) a man. And since she had a man to control her, she was also not a threat to other shamans (especially male ones). Marriage also protected women from public intrusion into their personal lives, shielding their privacy. By leaving her household and her husband, however, Chimeg lost the protection of her private life while she shamelessly and improperly imposed her presence upon the public sphere. She lost her status as a proper woman.

Chimeg's situation became even more complicated when she also lost her house. When she left her domestic sphere (which was a hindrance to her shamanic pursuits) in order to enter the public one, she expected to be perceived as a public persona—a shaman. But she did not realize that her identity as a woman, and thus her association with the domestic sphere, would be attached to her in a conceptual way, despite her physical departure from her home. Just as men carried their social spaces wherever they traveled, women were associated with the domestic sphere even if they were away from their households. Women were associated with the domestic sphere beyond its actual physical presence. For the locals, especially men, even if a woman was a powerful shaman, she was still a *woman*, which meant that she belonged to a domestic sphere. The notion of domesticity followed her as a principle that defined women and limited their entrance into a public sphere.

The Materiality of Shamanic Powers

If being a female conflicts with shamanic power and the methods by which it is acquired, despite the rhetoric of gender neutrality, what constitutes power for shamans? How do shamans acquire those powers? And how do audiences and clients recognize them? For the sake of clarity, I divide shamanic powers into two categories, official powers and unofficial ones. The official shamanic powers consist of completing thirteen shanars for male shamans to become zaarin and seven for females to become equally powerful duurisah. The shamans stage their shanars at intervals of two to three years; thus, the entire process of becoming a zaarin or duurisah usually takes between fifteen and twenty years. Timely, well-organized public performances of shanars are the most well-accepted and visible manifestation of a shaman's power. For each new shanar, a shaman acquires corresponding items of paraphernalia (e.g., a bracelet and a mirror for their first shanar and an antelope-skin gown for their final, culminating shanar) and enlivens them with newly connected origin spirits of the shaman's family or clan.[18] Each new origin spirit is given an item of paraphernalia as a place to descend when it arrives at the rituals.

The shanar ceremony is also a training session for a shaman. A teacher shaman brings the disciple and the new origin spirits together into a potentially productive union. The disciple becomes acquainted with the new origin spirit first, when the teacher becomes possessed by it, and then learns the spirit's huudal buudal and masters the ability to summon the spirit him- or herself. The shanar succeeds when the disciple becomes possessed by the newly introduced origin spirit, which then communicates with the audience. The new origin spirit expands the shaman's power, knowledge, and skills. A shaman's growing collection of paraphernalia indicates the number of shanars performed, thus making the power visible.

In order to stage the shanars, a shaman needs other kinds of unofficial power—material resources and social networks. The road to acquiring resources necessary for shanar starts at one's home and family. Because women marry outside of their birth homes and join an unfamiliar patrilocal residency, female shamans start with extremely limited resources, support, and shamanic networks. Female shamans must build their networks and find resources in an unfamiliar setting, and they must travel longer distances to solicit help from their birth families. In this most male shamans have advantage over women to begin with. They remain in their communities and sometimes in their extended family's household. As heads of the household, male shamans tend to have far more resources at their immediate disposal, including those needed for staging their shanars.

Moreover, the shift from state farms to domestic production after the privatization of livestock and the institution of family-based livestock breeding brought drastic changes to the lives of families and to the perceptions of gendered hierarchy within families. During socialism, women were state employees whose status was more or less equal to that of men. Following the end of the salaried state jobs after socialism, the domestic economy became the primary form of production, in which women are the main producers even though they do not necessarily control domestic production. During socialism women were reproducers of their husband's families ("lineages" were supposedly destroyed) as well as of the state, while they were also producers of material value as workers for the state. After socialism, lineages "revived," private property thrived as a result of domestic production, and women became the reproducers for lineages and producers for domestic production—both ultimately owned by men and intended primarily to enhance male privilege. Women's tasks and responsibilities increased because they now carried the burden of feeding their families through domestic subsistence food production. Without state jobs, women became workers for their families and often for their in-laws and their husbands' extended family as well.[19] Women's labor and reproduction are valuable, but at the same time women have no claim to the products of their labor; women are suspect and dangerous "outsiders both in their natal and marital households" (Steedly 1993:184).

And yet, in order to achieve the status of a full-fledged shaman and then to maintain that status successfully and continuously, a person must be free from daily household and family duties while still receiving services and benefits from their family members and utilizing the domestic space and the household money. To some extent, a shaman, whether male or female, needs a "wife"—a virtuous and nurturing individual who is versed in shamanic knowledge and who voluntarily structures her life around the often unpredictable life of a shaman. A "wife" is needed to run a rural no-madic household and to produce food (baking bread, processing animal skins, and making dairy products) that herders used to get from state farms or buy with cash. Shamanic ritual is a highly labor-intensive and time-consuming endeavor. It requires a shaman's full engagement often for days in a row, as well as immediate assistance from family members. Such ritu-als conflict with the daily demands on women, demands associated with nomadic herding, housekeeping, and caring for family members in the ab-sence of job opportunities and services once provided by the state, includ-ing medical care, day care, and help with livestock, with moving livestock to new pastures, with building fences for livestock, and with purchasing raw materials. The state used to support all these activities, but now the households were on their own. During rituals led by male shamans, it is his wife and children who serve him. But husbands rarely agree to serve a female shaman as an attendant, since that is a subordinate role. I have seen husbands serving their wives during rituals only if they were much younger than their wives, or if the couple were both shamans and exchanged the "conversationalist" services with each other.

In more traditional households, by performing at the center of her household a woman contends with the traditional male-centered values, competes with her husband for space in the household, and challenges his power and prestige, even if she never intended to do so. In the coun-tryside, where there are no hotels and restaurants, traveling guests create social space within a household. Guests can stay overnight, dine with the family, and even share the hosts' housework. The domestic sphere (that is, the ger) at the same time serves as a social space. And a shaman's house-hold is usually the center of the ritual. The traditional gendered division of labor—women serving and men entertaining the guests—is challenged when women become initiated as shamans. Unless a husband agrees to serve his wife during rituals and gives up his central role when entertaining the guests, female shamans must find people to assist them during rituals. They also have to deal with their husbands' resentment, which might stem from their losing their space and prestige to their wives' shamanic performances. At the same time, a female shaman, just like a male one, needs a physical and stable station where she can perform her rituals and support from her immediate family. Without a permanent station, shamans tend to lose their clients, and it hinders their further advancement.

By leaving her home Chimeg lost that station. Without a home of her own, it was difficult for her to invite teachers to lead her shanars and follow up her rituals with parties and meals. She had no place to accommodate clients who came from far away for long-lasting rituals. Her unstable situation made her difficult to find by distant clients, scholars, tourists, and media, who searched for "authentic" and powerful shamans. At the most basic level, Chimeg lost her material base for her shamanic performances and thus undermined the potential expansion of her social networks.

In turn, without sufficient support and resources, Chimeg could not obtain her paraphernalia, especially the antelope-skin gown, metal cask, and other items that were necessary for her to stage her next shanar and advance in her powers.[20] In addition to the lack of money and sheep that she needed to offer to blacksmiths so they would forge the metal parts of her paraphernalia, she did not have the same network of acquaintances as male shamans, who easily forge working relationships with blacksmiths. She needed to make a special trip and put forth extra effort to find a blacksmith, even though her connections and means for travel were limited.

Among various sources of power, certain forms of time and space are crucial to a shaman's success. The nomadic countryside is the preferred space for a shamanic performance; it allows the staging of large-scale rituals because it accommodates large audiences. The most profitable time to practice was from May 15 through September 15, when the most expensive shanar rituals were staged and the "doors" to the celestial world were open for accepting clients' gifts of sheep and birch trees adorned and represented as "a golden army." Powerful male shamans resided in the countryside and spent most of their summers performing rituals. Yet female shamans, whose clients were often even poorer than themselves, staged their rituals within dimly lit gers or in log cabins enclosed by wooden fences. Such indoor spaces could accommodate audiences of no more than fifteen and made it difficult to conduct the complex space-requiring rituals that involved the sacrifice of a sheep. Partly owing to these kinds of space constraints, despite their advanced skills most of the rituals conducted by female shamans were limited to smaller-scale activities, such as appeasing a spirit or calling a lost soul, rituals that also had no time constraints. Without sufficient livestock and without families to take care of them, most female shamans lived in the sedentary part of Bayan-Uul and not in the nomadic countryside. They were accessible for drop-in rituals and consultations during the winter for clients who did not want to travel to the countryside to visit male shamans. Unlike male shamans, female shamans in the town of Bayan-Uul possessed neither appropriate space nor the most lucrative time for rituals.

Mobility and Power

Travel is an arena where men may have several advantages over women. Many cultures have places where women are not allowed to visit.[21] In Mongolia, however, both men and women, including Buryats, travel widely. In fact, one reason I met fewer female Buryat shamans was also that so many of them traveled incessantly. Male and female Buryat shamans travel to get their paraphernalia from blacksmiths and seamstresses, to consult with their teachers, and to perform rituals in their clients' homes as well as elsewhere. While there are no official restrictions on women's travel, owing to their vulnerable sexuality and, often, economic challenges, women had to limit the travels that would have enhanced their empowerment. But even overcoming this presented a double bind: sometimes shamans lost their local clients as a result of too much travel.

Following the collapse of socialism, however, women's opportunities for travel diminished owing to postsocialism's gendered labor division. With the dissolution of the state farm, a relatively gender-equal employment system also ended, and production shifted from the state to the domestic sphere, where men and women resumed their traditional gendered divisions of labor. Men took back their conventional role as obtainers from the "outside." Women remained "inside" their homes as producers of food and caretakers of livestock. Owing to the family's dependence on home food production, extensive travel by a woman caused irrecoverable lags in her household productivity and risked the loss of her untended livestock to predators, disease, or malnutrition. Women's travel, then, was not only unsafe and risked generating unwelcome gossip; it was also structurally impractical for the survival of a nomadic household in the economy of nomadic livestock herding.

Although men and women could travel the same distances and to the places, sometimes those same travels produced different meanings and discourses because of gender. Travel for men is an opportunity to gain prowess and knowledge and to expand their networks. Traveling men engage with their surroundings: they converse with strangers, party with acquaintances, and stay overnight in their friends' gers. These activities correspond to shamans' travels, through which they acquire clients, knowledge, and support. Such activities, however, contradict the behaviors expected of women. Most married men expect their wives to travel to return to their homes, but not to pursue empowerment in public. Women's minds must stay bound to their households, even if their bodies are crossing the same geographical terrain as men's. While traveling, they are supposed to maintain a self-protective, "closed" demeanor and avoid the public's gaze, possible male advances, and even influences from "bad" women who might corrupt them, encouraging them to party and visit others. They must remain disengaged and detached, and the knowledge, networks, and renown that women gain from travel must be limited to its immediate purpose. Unlike men's, women's social network and intelligence are not expected to expand due to travel.

Men speak freely in public and engage in extended conversations when visiting families, and they therefore have more opportunities to narrate their own travels in the most favorable light. Women, for the most part,

Figure 17. A female shaman performing a ritual at home

are more constrained in public and seldom speak in public about their experiences. They do not make new acquaintances as easily as men, and they engage in long conversations only with their close friends and kin. In other words, women create little public knowledge about themselves. Yet others may comment on a woman's travels even before she has a chance to narrate her own experiences or become aware of what others are saying about her. Men produce stories about and during their travels, while women's travel generates talk among others, not all of it favorable. Most travels of divorced women were commented upon with a focus on their sexuality. And although even married women were not immune to rumormongering, they were better protected. That is one reason Chimeg was able to acquire wealth and succeed as a shaman while she was a married woman. But as a divorced woman she lost her womanly virtues. Instead, she acquired negative female stereotypes—promiscuity, immodesty, and impudence. Because her failed personal life seemed to imply an inability to attend to other people's problems, Chimeg's credibility diminished. And because of the increasing number of shamans in the area, it became harder and harder for Chimeg to compete for clients.

An unattached, traveling, single woman not only has a dangerous and untamed sexuality in the eyes of a conventional patriarchal community. In addition, because her identity does not fit the female gender norms of virtuousness, she is treated as an outsider. A male shaman who has all the attributes of a respectable person—family, home, wealth—is preferred over a woman with a confusing lifestyle and suspect behavior. She is a woman with no man to control her, so every man feels justified in dominating her. A single woman's sexuality becomes the center of public discussion and a chance to undermine other women's reputations through her example.

Chimeg's reputation suffered particularly when she became involved with other men. The male shamans pointed at Chimeg's relationships and claimed that she was using shamanic practices for personal gain: to find a new husband. Indeed, Chimeg dreamed of romantic love, a caring husband, and a household based on an equal division of labor between husband and a wife. She contrasted her oppressive husband with her gentle new lovers. Her dreams challenged the patriarchal system, where women complained that as workers and servers, they had become *barlag* (slaves) and *togoonii bariul* (potholders). She became involved with men much younger than herself—a transgression detested by many. Her interest in perfumes, lingerie, fashion, and cosmetics also challenged the boundaries set for middle-aged married women. She refused to give up on herself as a woman. That was decidedly not what was expected of a woman in her fifties: older women were supposed to be modest, display little or no sexuality, and care more about other family members than about themselves. Chimeg's fashionable clothing and makeup were considered inappropriate for her age.

Chimeg's spiritual powers no longer translated into material gain. Even for a shaman who had completed only four shanars, Chimeg was poor and marginalized. Having stagnated in her quest for power, Chimeg was pitied, not respected. She was visited by clients but underpaid, receiving compensation only in proportion to her impoverished situation, not her skills. Even if she carried out a complex ritual, her clients paid her the lowest acceptable sum. Her poverty precluded pride; she accepted the smallest compensations and served the poorest clients, who did not dare seek the services of wealthy shamans. She was visited for services when no other shamans were around, but otherwise people avoided her. She was called for emergencies, for drop-in consultations, and to perform small rituals. Requests for big rituals were awarded to more prestigious (male) shamans in the countryside. Chimeg's story continues in chapter 7, since her life and practice are intermeshed with others'. There I present how gossip, the interpretation of divination, and storytelling by clients can affect a shaman's power and faith in a profound way.

While Chimeg is unique in her achievement of success and fame, even though she could not retain them, the experiences of other female shamans reveal some additional transformations in gendered structures and economic changes that affected their quest for power. Both practicing in their homes and traveling to clients' homes introduced serious conflicts into female shamans' marriages and disrupted the household economy. In a nomadic household, women serve and men entertain guests. Female shamans tended to transgress that order. Married female shamans often came into conflict with their husbands over the respected positions they sought as entertainers, hosting their own clients as guests. Female shamans who practiced rituals in their homes claimed power by creating a public space within the household—a space that traditionally belonged to their husbands.

Transgression

By now it is clear that being a female shaman inevitably involves a certain degree of transgression of official female gender norms, such as performing in public and seeking visibility and fame. While female shamans are for the most part able to adjust the extent of their transgression in order to

appear modest and compliant when necessary, female shamans still constitute an uncompromising challenge to patrilineal and patriarchal structures. Both male and female shamans propitiate and derive power from the
origin spirits of their birth families. While non-shaman women leave their
natal origin spirits at home when they marry, female shamans bring their
natal origin spirits with them to their marital home. They are not expected
to serve the origin spirits of their husbands and thus do not contribute to
the enhancement of their husbands' status or their families' memories. In
fact, many men disapprove of their wives being initiated as shamans, since
they contend for public space, attention, and resources and establish their
own sphere of influence and network.

Unmarried female shamans receive support from their birth family.
Their kin gather their resources to obtain the shamanic paraphernalia and
stage shanars. After marriage, however, these same women's shamanic
practices tended to decline, unless their birth family's support persisted.
Married women's shamanic activities contradicted (and were of no use to)
patriarchal kinship structures: children ultimately belonged to their male
kin; families lived in a patrilocal setting; and children were raised by their
paternal grandparents and inherited their father's clan name and the clan's
ancestral spirits.

I met many women who claimed that unless their husbands' families
propitiated their origin spirits, their children were in danger. One woman
named Oyun was especially keen to propitiate the origin spirits of her birth
family, as she had two sons from a previous marriage. She was worried
about her sons being treated the same as the rest of the children of the
extended family and wanted to ascribe value to them. The women's natal
origin spirits were "outsiders" to the family and were ritually "sent off" to
her male kin. Families had no reason to support the "outsider's" practice.

And yet, even if the origin spirits of a woman's birth family were sent off,
their memories remained, because they would be summoned to the ritual
and fed and entertained before being asked to leave the family. Some of
these spirits left for a few years and then returned, thus keeping their memories alive among the family. When Tömör's youngest daughter got sick, he
attributed her illness to the origin spirit of an old woman in his wife's family. That spirit was particularly harsh toward children, Tömör told me, and
occasionally requested the sacrifice of a duck or other bird. She had escaped
her abusive husband and fled to Mongolia on her own, walking through
forests and mountains and eating wild animals and birds. She never
reached the settlements in Mongolia and died in a forest. Although Tömör

placed the old woman in his wife's lineage, I encountered this story in a chronicle about the Buryats' ancestors, documented by Nimaev (1983).[22]

In some households, women have specific roles and duties that are owed their husband's parents. A daughter-in-law, especially one married to a youngest son, is expected to take over the personal care of her in-laws and respect and respond to their every wish. Physical and verbal abuse; dramatic intimidation using gestures, eye movements, and unpleasant tones of voice; and public humiliation through loud scolding, beating, or simply talking badly about her incompetence in her work or her low moral standards were often employed by extended families. Daughters-in-law had to appear to be working at all times, and they were expected to look tired.[23]

Figure 18. A female shaman after a ritual

People accepted female shamans as long they were not their own wives or daughters-in-law. By becoming shamans, women were empowered by their spirits, by their clients' and disciples' support, and by the income and respect others accorded them. Unlike ordinary women, they could explain their bad moods as afflictions from spirits. Their shamanic practices and spirits enabled women to skip chores, travel, and spend time with company outside their immediate circle of family, friends, and neighbors. Shamanic activities also helped women evade the societal expectations for their domestic and kinship roles—that they would always be obedient and hardworking, expecting few or no privileges.

At the same time, as I illustrated earlier, the women who dared to pursue shamanic activities put their marriages at risk. I met many female shamans who chose to leave their husbands in order to pursue their careers in shamanic practice. Chimeg's experience shows all too well what it means to be a divorced female shaman in postsocialist rural Mongolia. Unable to claim their own property, shifting between temporary homes, attached neither to a man nor to the homes of their birth, divorced female shamans occupy an uncertain transitional space. With their constant travel, they easily acquire bad reputations, which prevent them from attracting new clients and generate suspicion in their existing clients about the quality of their rituals.

For female shamans, travel is both necessary and dangerous. Marriage helps a woman build her reputation and gain clients, but it also limits her advancement. Divorce or separation allows women to devote their time to shamanic practice, but the stigma attached to their status as divorcees can cost them not only their reputation but also the resources needed for obtaining paraphernalia and staging shanars. Such structural limitations—the shamanic glass ceiling—prevent women from becoming full-fledged shamans and keeps them at a mediocre level. Either way, women are put in a double bind. Married or unmarried, traveling or at home—each gain generates a loss or erodes their achievements.

For Chimeg, as for most women I met, the activities that are necessary to achieve the status of a full-fledged shaman, such as public performance, traveling, networking, and being at the center of attention, often conflict with being a mother and wife. Because women's activities as shamans tend to disrupt her service to her loved ones, and also because the quest for charisma and being at the center of their households conflict with the traditional male space and challenge the overall gender hierarchy, many female shamans must tailor their performances to accommodate their husbands. That means they must tone down their practice and become content with partial success. If a female shaman decides to leave her marriage in an attempt to free herself to pursue her shamanic practice, she often damages her reputation as a virtuous and morally proper person. Such a woman is treated as a second-class citizen and receives little if any of the support and empathy accorded her married counterparts. Her shamanic practice stagnates. The culmination of my argument in this chapter is as follows: female shamans, unlike male ones, are squeezed in the culturally and socially mediated constraints of a double bind. Married or unmarried—either way, because of gender norms that inhibit women's progress as shamans in both the domestic and the public spheres, they are able to gain only partial shamanic powers and to advance only partway through the levels required for her to become a full-fledged shaman.

Many female shamans I met were either divorced, unmarried, or married to younger men. If they were not in a traditional marriage, they were stigmatized and marginalized. The freedom these women had to pursue their practice came at a high price: their private lives were subjected to public scrutiny, rumor, and judgment, and their bodies were vulnerable to men probing their sexuality, and even to rape. Even though these women refused to be subjects of regulatory power who produced and exploited "the demand for continuity, visibility and place" (Butler 1997:29), they were still oppressed by intrusive rumors that controlled and limited their shamanic achievements.

A female shaman named Sarnai divorced her husband after enduring an abusive marriage for almost twenty years. At the age of fifty she married her twenty-eight-year-old disciple. Sarnai's unconventional move caused much gossip and disdain. Sarnai did not let the talk affect her. She traveled with her husband, who helped her during rituals by serving as a conversationalist with the spirits and as an altar attendant. Sarnai succeeded as a shaman when she was married (even if her marriage was abusive). When she got divorced, her clients began leaving her. Yet because her new marriage allowed her to travel, she was a particularly strong performer, and because her husband helped her during her rituals, together they were able to build a new clientele.

Female shamans were often underpaid, receiving gifts in proportion to their perceived lower economic status, not according to their shamanic skills or a given ritual's complexity. The basic established gift among the shamans in Bayan-Uul for a ritual to appease an origin spirit was four meters of cloth and a sum of money, the amount left to the client's discretion. No matter how many spirits the shaman evoked, for one ceremony only one piece of cloth was offered to all the spirits.

A female shaman named Uyanga in a district neighboring Bayan-Uul made a big splash by breaking the one-cloth-gift rule. She requested not only individual gifts for each sets of spirits, but also gifts for every person in the audience from her pupil shaman and his parent. She demanded that the guests and the people who served in the ritual be fed the best food and served alcohol every two hours.

But then Uyanga developed a problem. True, women who did not request gifts received insufficient compensation compared to that given to male shamans who had homes, family, and livestock. But women who requested gifts ran a serious risk of losing dignity in the eyes of the public, since gifts that were demanded harmed a shaman's status. Money made by shamanic practice already had less moral value than that earned through labor or even trading. Such money was "barren";[24] it did not bring virtue and was supposed to be either given away or spent on things unrelated to the most intimate aspects of one's life. There were "moral doubts" about the money shamans made,[25] based as it was on someone else's suffering. If that money was not freely offered, but demanded, then the shaman might lose any prestige she had gained by successfully ministering to the client. After being shamed, Uyanga was pushed to reduce her requests regarding the one-cloth rule. She also could not require additional gifts for the participants in the ritual, backstage workers, and other helpers. Uyanga, who was flourishing, had to scale down her requests and accept what others gave her.

Despite the difficulties facing them in their efforts to succeed as shamans, female Buryat shamans are compelled to portray themselves as equal in power to males. These women conceive of a public performance in which they are surrounded by an audience as their socially legitimate arena. The conflict between the public expectations that female shamans can become as powerful as male shamans and society's unwillingness to recognize the concrete obstacles that limit women's quest for power results in a double disadvantage for female shamans. Female shamans both lag behind men in their advancement to power and are also blamed for being unable to reach established norms of power.

In different ways, both state socialism and the market economy limited the means for women's empowerment while facilitating men's greater access to economic and cultural value, and thus greater shamanic success. Because the state destroyed family genealogies, the shamans operate under an added onus of disbelief in their credibility: they can only imply, not prove, the authenticity of their knowledge about origin spirits. Discrepancies in information revealed by clients who solicit additional opinions from either male or female shamans create a feeling of anxiety and uncertainty among audiences searching for proof about the authenticity of their origin spirits, since often the "truth" comes from collecting answers that match. Sometimes, however, only the shamans' reputations and persuasive performances offer any hope of mending lost family ties after the state's decades-long campaign of memory suppression.

SIX

Persuasion and Power

In the previous chapter I revealed the gendered constraints that female shamans experience in their quest for power. Although shamanism was feminized while it was suppressed under socialism, with the advent of democratization and a market economy the trend has been mostly reversed: male shamans have taken center stage, while female shamans have been marginalized. In this chapter I explore some of the strategies that shamans use in order to obtain their power and persuade their audiences of their shamanic skills. "Power" and "persuasion" in the context of shamanism are closely related: "persuasion" constitutes a form of as well as a means for obtaining power, because someone who is able to persuade others is in the process of increasing his or her already existing power. Although shanars are the official markers for shamanic power, all the necessary preparations for staging a shanar are embedded in shamans' everyday economic and social life.

Shamanic practices have proliferated as the Buryats have solicited help from their shamans in their attempts to deal with the challenges brought by an ongoing economic crisis and a volatile market economy. The shamans explain the misfortunes as the revenge of the origin spirits after decades of socialist suppression, and they offer rituals to ameliorate them. Both the ongoing economic crisis and the urgent need for families to propitiate their abandoned origin spirits had been conducive to local shamans' success.

At the same time, Buryats are concerned about the authenticity of the shamans and their credibility regarding the knowledge that they brought into the ritual arena. Skepticism towards spiritual practitioners is not unique to postsocialist Mongolia; it is found all over the world. As Pigg (1996:185) has convincingly argued, skepticism is a necessary part of a belief system that helps to make shamanism believable and enduring. In Nepal, communities determine believable shamans by finding the fake ones as a point of comparison, and they generate the criteria for a shaman's authenticity and truthfulness on the basis of what is available.

Pigg's (1996) argument sheds light on the agency of shamanic clients as they partake in the remaking of shamanism in the context of ongoing social and cultural transformation. The shamanic clients and audiences are not passive spectators or consumers of shamanism; rather, they constantly scrutinize practitioners' authenticity and skills and solicit the opinions of others in order to gauge the credibility of the shamanic knowledge. They also constantly revise and recreate their own methods of determining a shaman's competence. While skepticism is an integral part of shamanism, the Buryats' skepticism toward their own shamans is also historically conditioned. In other words, the Buryats' skepticism is not based only on their desire to find the most competent shaman and the best solution to their problems, but also on both actual and a perceived lack of knowledge about their past and about shamanism owing to past state suppression and disruption of shamanic tradition. Entire generations had been kept from being exposed to shamanic ritual and cosmology, sometimes by their own families. While most Buryats believe in the probability of spirits and shamans, they remain skeptical about individual shamans' power and integrity. Many clients simply lack the knowledge they need to informally evaluate a shaman. They also seek ways to determine the authenticity of particular spirits, especially of those claiming to be their ancestors and thus demanding lavish rituals. But because many families' genealogical records have been destroyed and some of the remaining ones damaged, audiences cannot check the basic facts about whether a particular origin spirit belongs to their lineage. Lacking a point of reference, they have to base their decisions on a combination of inductive and deductive reasoning, intuition, alternative opinions, and piecing together incomplete information. Intriguingly, the people who are seeking the services of shamans in order to find solutions for their misfortunes end up taking part in the reconstitution of the suppressed shamanic practice through their search for the most powerful shamans and spirits. Skepticism is crucial in this process. The reconstitution of shamanism occurs as a result of clients' skeptical questioning and their search for alternative meanings and solutions to their problems.

Often, after the completion of a ritual, audience members share their observations about possible moments of slippage in a shaman's possession, discuss whether or not the spirit's words revealed anything new and useful, or retell some of the most amusing or difficult moments of the ritual. Most shamans rarely carry out a completely flawless performance that is accepted in its entirety. On the other hand, a ritual hardly ever fails completely. The Buryats do not use the categories of fake versus real for shamans themselves, but they do use these categories in gauging details and parts of individual shamans' rituals, spirits, and consultations in a dynamic and contingent way. Also, in Buryat shamanism the ranking of shamans, based on the number of completed shanars, the expectations that correspond to those ranks, and the taboos on prematurely performing harsh and complex rituals, all help to prevent the shamans from completely failing in their rituals. Nevertheless, shamans need to build up sufficient trust and power that in cases of real or seeming mishaps, their reputation remains intact. This requires more than completing shanars and serving others.

So how did successful male shamans such as Tömör and Luvsan obtain the powers that brought them fame, global and local networks, and material wealth? What do they have that female shamans who possess the same skills and accomplishments lack? What do they do differently from female shamans?

To give partial answers to these questions, I explore some of the tactics of shamans' persuasion and ways of gaining followers that I witnessed both during rituals and enmeshed in the micropolitics of everyday life. Then I narrate the ways in which the shamans Tömör and Luvsan have gained their respective powers. Tömör made use of conventional forms of power, family and kin support, local networks, and his entrepreneurial prowess. Lacking these resources, Luvsan created a global and national network and traveled extensively to places as far away as Parma, Italy. Both Tömör and Luvsan were able to curb and make use of their audiences' skepticism.

In addition to their material and political gains, these shamans' practices also contributed to the re-creation of the world of Buryat spirits that is presided over by the celestial court. The celestial world is a structure that represents the Buryat past as a spiritual nation to which each individual Buryat's past belongs. The celestial court—its governing body—is recreated at all large-scale rituals, such as shanars. Its structure and constituent members (spirits and gods) are the same for all Khori Buryats in Mongolia. But because Tömör and Luvsan staged well-attended, large-scale rituals more often than did other shamans in their community, their representation of the spirit world of the Buryats has become the most well-known. The celestial court is a body of structured communal knowledge around which the Buryats build their family genealogies, nurture their sense of belonging to a group with a distinct identity as Khori Buryats of Mongolia, and create their connection with their ancestral homelands, history, and memories of their family members.

Shamanic Microtactics

Shamans use many microtactics to attract and maintain followers, including clients and disciples. Some shamans gain clients and recruit disciples during their rituals from the audience members who came to attend the ceremonies along with the clients. While being possessed by a spirit during a ritual, a shaman can simply and suddenly point at or grab a person in the audience and announce that he or she must become a shaman. I saw this happen a few times. Each time, the shaman's directness and spontaneity drew awe and disbelief from those chosen. The shamans' method for convincing the chosen individuals (and their families) to have faith in becoming shamans was consistency and persistence. Despite those individuals' resistance, refusal, and disregard, shamans tended to continue announcing those "chosen by spirits" while being possessed by different spirits both at the ritual and outside the ritual arena. The individuals who had thus been "nominated" by a shaman tended often to attribute their misfortunes to their refusal to be initiated as shamans. The shamans were perfectly aware of the limitations of this method; after all, not everyone agreed to be initiated as a shaman. And even if these people believed the prognosis and propositions of that shaman, they also consulted diviners, lamas, and even other shamans before making their final decision. Even though it was only partially successful, this was the most fundamental and common way for a shaman to expand his or her pool of disciples.

Aware of people's skepticism, the shamans also use tactics that do not look like tactics for the implicit, everyday recruitment of clients and disciples. Woven into friendly conversations or enmeshed within rituals, these might include anecdotes about other shamans' rituals and their failure to persuade clients of their shamanic powers, which are surely greater than those shamans whose rituals have failed. Indeed, gossip about other shamans is a widely used tool for undermining the power of one's competitors. In addition to stories of other shamans' failed rituals, mentioning their harmful rituals, such as placing a curse on someone, and the consequences of those rituals, as well as their utilization of filthy, unusual, and frightening substances in their rituals, such as dog's blood or an unusually large number of needles, or adopting an especially vicious spirit were effective in frightening people away. I was consistently warned by my friends to avoid certain individuals who presumably were both powerful and malicious, and whose harm was irreparable.

In addition to sending out frightening messages about their competitors, shamans engage in discreet recruiting by giving a shamanic diagnosis to persons in a casual rather than a ritual setting. For instance, a shaman might point out as an aside, in a conversation over tea, that a person is polluted and may need a cleansing ceremony. Or a shaman might note that one of the visitors, who has stepped outside for a moment, is being followed by spirits. Most likely, the other visitors and the person's friends and family would relay the shaman's remarks. To some extent being given such a message by family members has more impact than being told directly by a shaman. In such cases the implicitness, seeming casualness, and ambiguity of the remarks serves as bait. A few times during my stay in Bayan-Uul, I was approached by shamans and lamas who told me that I was either being followed by a spirit (one was a five-year-old girl with long pigtails) or that I had lost my soul, upon which these shamans immediately staged rituals for me and gave me various protective essences, amulets, and purifying water.

Although clients attempt to separate business shamans from real ones, the boundaries between the two are often blurred. It is often impossible to pin down which words were part of the politics of maintaining power and which deeds focused on helping the client, or what the shaman had in mind while doing or saying something. What matters is how the client received the shamans' words and deeds and how they affected that client's condition. A shaman who performed a ritual primarily to serve his own needs might yet end by positively affecting a client who, because he or she believed the shaman, felt better after the ritual. How a client reads a shaman's intentions may matter more than the shaman's initial motive.

Because many people in Bayan-Uul who sought shamanic services were struggling economically, in addition to their other problems, some shamans felt the need to attract a rich audience beyond Bayan-Uul,[1] and to that end they would travel to urban and international communities. Even then, shamans had to summon their audiences well in advance, especially for shanars. If they are able to summon a larger audience for a shanar, they can also obtain resources and paraphernalia faster for their next one. With each shanar, the expectations of shamans are raised; the paraphernalia become more intricate and expensive, the audiences larger, and the ritual preparations more expensive and labor-intensive. Therefore, shamans must travel farther to acquire more resources, attract larger audiences, and involve a wider kin network.

Overall, obtaining shamanic power is expensive, labor-intensive, and time-consuming. In order to become a full-fledged shaman, the shaman must not only complete the requisite number of shanars but must also obtain shamanic paraphernalia, twenty-one objects ranging from coral bracelets to an antelope-skin gown. The shamans stage a shanar every two to three years and accumulate their powers and paraphernalia gradually. The average shaman needs at least a decade to become fully accomplished. Only by staging their shanars in public do the shamans prove the advancement of their powers. During a shanar a shaman publicly performs possession by all of his or her origin spirits (both known and newly found) and displays the designated paraphernalia to the new origin spirits. Each origin spirit corresponds with a specific item of paraphernalia. If there is no shanar, the origin spirits assume that they have been abandoned by their shamans. In such a case, they torment the shamans, expose them to attacks by other spirits, or, worse, turn against the shamans and gradually kill them.

Economic success and spiritual powers are interdependent; a delay in one causes the decline of the other. Without spiritual power, a shaman is in danger of losing clients; without clients, he or she receives less income; and with insufficient income, he or she cannot stage subsequent shanars and obtain more paraphernalia. Because of this correlation between economic and spiritual status, impoverished shamans are seen as spiritually weak. One of the most successful shamans in Bayan-Uul was Tömör. He had completed only four shanars at the time I met him, but his fame and reputation has already traveled beyond Bayan-Uul. In the next section I analyze some of the resources that helped his practice and the ways he obtained and maintained his powers.

Tömör's Father

Tömör's empowerment was no mystery: he was a charming and entertaining host, a dramatic performer, and an eloquent storyteller. Unlike female shamans, who undermined their immediate support by leaving their birth families to join their husbands' families, male shamans stayed with their kin and family and further expanded that support. Tömör was also the only son of a well-respected shaman-healer, Molom. His shamanic spirits had been strengthened while resisting Buddhism during the seventeenth, eighteenth and nineteenth centuries. At the same time, Molom was also an officially trained Buddhist lama-healer, a master of dharani and herbal medicine. Molom combined white (healing) shamanic spirits and the skills of a Buddhist healer. According to Baasan, a family friend, Tömör possesses only a fraction of his powers but is still efficacious.

According to Tömör, his father was sent to a monastery to become a Buddhist lama at the age of three. Back in the 1920s, this was the usual path for many boys before the state purges in the 1930s; the monasteries were Mongolia's dominant political, spiritual, and economic institutions. While in the monastery, at the age of eight, Molom began seeing shadows and hearing voices. His monastic teacher determined that Molom's shamanic spirits were rebelling against his Buddhist teaching. Molom often could not sleep at night because he saw unexplained shadows and felt short of breath. He would call on his teacher, *"Bagshaa!* [Teacher!]." His teacher would come, touch his head lightly, sometimes purify him with juniper smoke, and whisper dharani, after which Molom went back to sleep. After many years of consistent Buddhist suppression, the shamanic spirits finally stopped returning to Molom. By the age of eighteen he had become a fully ordained Buddhist monk and a healer and was an expert in reciting sutras, healing with herbs and dharani, and bone setting.

Molom's monkhood was interrupted by the state violence against religion that began in the 1930s. The monastery where he grew up was burned, and his teachers and the higher-ranking monks were killed. Molom was not yet twenty years old. Along with many younger and lower-ranking lamas, he was recruited into the army and sent to Mongolia's eastern border to fight the Japanese. There, in 1939, he fought in the Battle of Khalkhin Gol, which takes its name from the Khalka River. Japan's attack on the Mongolian border endangered the Soviet Union's lands in the Far East. Soviet troops were stationed along Mongolia's central and eastern borders, and Mongolian soldiers fought alongside the Soviets against their common enemy.[2]

Molom, like most Mongolians who experienced the Soviet influence in the second part of the twentieth century, respected and adored the Russians. When I mentioned Stalin's brutalities to Tömör, he interrupted me:

> Stalin was one person who made tremendous errors. We cannot go back and fix them. But my father told me that the Russian soldiers truly believed in protecting the Mongols. They really did have *tsagaan setgel* [a white—i.e., good—heart]. It was my father who told me that the Russian soldiers saved the lives of many Mongol soldiers on the battlefield. They prevented the Mongols from going on suicide missions from the trenches. They would say, "There are so few of you. You must live, but we are a bigger nation." And they would pack up grenades into their pockets, leave the trenches, crawl in front of the tanks, and blow themselves and the tanks up. My father would not make up such stories.

Tömör's narrative highlights the immense discrepancy between the Soviet leaders' policies of Mongolian domination at the top and friendship among ordinary Russians and Mongols from the decades after World War II.

After World War II was over, Molom returned to Bayan-Uul and worked for the state farm. He got married and had two children, Tömör and his sister; the family adopted another girl, one of their relatives. Religion remained repressed by the state throughout socialism, so Molom did not return to his Buddhist practice but lived as an ordinary herdsmen. But in the late 1970s, when Tömör returned from his three-year mandatory military service, he could not recognize his father. Delirious, Molom was roaming the mountains on horseback. Without food or sleep, he had finally collapsed; Tömör's mother, who nursed him, was overcome by grief. Tömör sent his father a few times to the state mental asylum, where powerful injections made him lethargic. He turned into a shell of a man, his mind no longer in touch with reality.

Tömör consulted with the local people and decided to ask for help from the female shaman Khorlo. Within a short time, powerful origin spirits were revealed, and Molom was initiated secretly as a shaman in 1980, just two years before his teacher, Khorlo, died. Right after Khorlo's death, the state had another round of cleansing of what it deemed the remnants of superstition and religion. The shaman Luvsan went to jail for his ritual activities in 1973 and again in 1985. And in 1984 Khorlo's daughter Jargalma was ordered to go the police station in the provincial center, in Choibalsan, to present her mother's death certificate; the police, unaware that she had died in 1982, suspected her of practicing shamanism.

Because of the threat of arrest, Molom pursued only minimum-level shamanic powers, just enough to keep his origin spirits more or less appeased. He never completed all thirteen shanars and did not become acquainted with all his origin spirits. In fact, he completely blocked his black spirits and worshipped only his white spirits, because the rituals and paraphernalia necessary for propitiating the white spirits were small, less labor-intensive to make, and easier to hide. The white spirits also required much lighter paraphernalia, ritual instruments, and offerings. Instead of a drum they required a bell with which they were summoned. A white shaman needed a gown, vest, cape, and headdress; these were all made of cloth and thus could be easily hidden and transported. White spirits feasted on *tsagan ide* ("white food"—dairy products and tea). In contrast, attending to the black spirits required heavy paraphernalia made of steel and animal fur, loud rituals with drum beating, and the sacrifice of sheep. Molom remained as a *tsagani böö* (white shaman) without taking up on the *harin ongod* (black spirits). He combined these white shamanic skills with his

Buddhist lama-healer skills in dharani, herbal medicine, and bone setting, and thus was known as a *tulmaashi*—a syncretistic practitioner who focused primarily on healing.

Molom figured out ways to hide his practice from visits by inspectors or others. He wrapped a towel around his bell to quiet its ringing and uttered his evocations in a whisper. Like other families who secretly practiced shamanism, he placed his butter candlestick and the offerings in a closet with doors. "If someone came in while Molom was performing a ritual, he would pinch the lit top of the butter candle, close the door of the closet, toss the drink, and pretend that nothing was going on," Jamtsa, an old man who had been Molom's client, told me. The community revered Molom, for he took risks himself and saved many people's lives. No local person denounced him to the state. Even some of the party officials pretended not to know much about his religious activities: after all, he saved the lives of several of their children.

Having lived through the persecution and terror of the 1930s, fought in the Mongol-Soviet war with Japan,[3] and experienced the collectivization of the 1950s, and the state's constant propaganda campaigns, Molom did not want his grandchildren to grow in terror or to lose their loved ones. Yet at the same time he knew well that his black origin spirits, whom he had blocked, would eventually return. There will come a time, he often warned Tömör, when he would run out of ways to hold them back. Molom also knew that his white spirits and Buddhist deities shielded him from harm, but he lacked the protection of his black spirits. By giving up his black spirits, Molom was balancing his shamanic practice against the state's prohibition, since he could not satisfy both. He knew that eventually something tragic would happen: either his black spirits would take revenge on him for having abandoned them or some other harm would reach him because his black spirits were not there to protect him.

Tömör's Inherited Powers

Molom's black spirits finally reproached him. Instead of troubling Molom, however, they attacked his son, Tömör. The first manifestation was that Tömör went mad. Molom had attempted to shield his family by blocking the black spirits to prevent them from attacking his family, but they had apparently found a way to reach past him and torment his son. Tömör was sick and wanted to die. During Tömör's tormented years, Purvee, a family friend, would come by on horseback every day to take Tömör hunting or go for a long ride. Purvee played Buryat-style poker with Tömör and more or less took care of him until he recovered, after he had been initiated as a shaman. Sunjidma remembers only that Tömör was in bed much of the time. Molom had exhausted his healing skills on his son, and he knew that if he held the black spirits back much longer, they would try to take either Tömör or him away. In the 1980s the state still suppressed shamanism and persecuted its practitioners, so Tömör's initiation rituals were performed in secret and with little fanfare.

Origin Spirits: The Powers of the Ancestors

Tömör told me that he recalled little from the time when he was being initiated as a shaman. He remembers only that he was puzzled about being constantly accompanied by two women, an older and a younger one. Later, when he became a shaman, he learned that the older one was his origin spirit, Saran Ejii (Beloved Mother Silverhair), a powerful female spirit from six generations back. Far removed from her current descendants, she had become a full member of the celestial court and held a prestigious position as the keeper of the keys for the Fifty-Five Good Western Tengris. The younger female spirit turned out to be Saran Ejii's granddaughter. Her name was Baljima, and she was a *buumal*—a special person, designated by the tengris for initiation as a shaman and designated to attend all the members of the celestial court, not just her family's origin spirits, as was the case with most shamans. People like Baljima were considered to be of celestial origin and had to avoid crowds, public places, abandoned houses, and funerals. She was also prohibited from going to festivals, markets, and parties. She was to bring the powers of the tengris to her community to assist in their survival during the difficult periods of colonial oppression and intraethnic wars. But at sixteen she fell in love with a boy her age. She pleaded with him to bring her a horse secretly so they could sneak out to the festival together. But when the young couple went to the festival, blood began seeping from Baljima's nose and ears. Polluted by the crowd at the festival, she died soon afterward. When she possessed Tömör, Baljima often cried about her premature death. Tömör was convinced that these two female spirits, especially Baljima, had had a profound effect on his life, and he strove to keep them happy.

Since 1980 Tömör had had dreams about mountains and other places in Russia. He made several trips to Russia over a three-year period and visited his ancestral homelands. "My dreams were the messages of my origin spirits summoning me to visit their lands," Tömör explained to me. Although he could travel to places thickly inhabited by spirits, he could not be in crowds. He would sweat profusely, his legs and hands would shake, and sometimes he would faint. He would always get sick after such experiences. He had to avoid busy public spaces and large crowds and was convinced that Baljima, who was expected to avoid crowded places but did not, was influencing his bodily reactions to the outside world and commanding his actions.

Tömör did many things to appease Baljima. He made her the possessor of his *zurhevch* (heart pendant)—one of the most important objects of paraphernalia, and one that encompasses the essence of a shaman's life. He had a white stallion sacralized for her, made a nice saddle for it, and offered her numerous sacrifices of sheep. But Baljima was happiest when Tömör exchanged his zurhevch, which was made from a reshaped bullet, for a jade-colored rock in the shape of a heart—something that happened unexpectedly. Once, when Tömör was visiting a friend's family, he saw the friend's child playing with a heart-shaped piece of rock and thought that it could make a nice zurhevch. When Tömör asked if he could have it, the family gave it to him. The next time Tömör evoked Baljima, he wore the new zurhevch. She was overjoyed. I was present when, in 2000, during one of the rituals, Baljima possessed Tömör. But during that particular ritual he had forgotten to wear his zurhevch; he had left it hanging on a leather rope with other objects of paraphernalia. When Baljima possessed Tömör, she requested her zurhevch: "Where is the Rainbow Princess's childhood toy, my precious stone zurhevch?" After the ritual, the audiences and Tömör had a long conversation about the rock. Tömör and the people in his ger listened over and over to my cassette recording to hear the voice of Baljima's spirit requesting the zurhevch. Tömör was surprised that Baljima was fascinated by it. He himself thought that the rock was an industrial remnant, perhaps something left over from mining, a limestone or granite quarry, or a construction site.

When I lived in Bayan-Uul, the place was infested with unknown spirits who had returned from suppression and were trying to find their descendants. If they could not, they would attempt to find any human host who would adopt them either willingly or by mistake. Many shamans I had known were overwhelmed by the multiple spirits vying for their attention, claiming to be their family's abandoned origin spirits. These shamans struggled to figure out which ones were their own origin spirits and send away the ones from outside. For recently initiated shamans, who were still mastering their skills and who had limited knowledge about their own past, this was an especially difficult task. Some shamans were approached by origin spirits of several different clans who represented different sides of their families, such as their in-laws and adoptive families. Although the spirits of one's in-laws or adoptive family were not strangers in life per se, a single shaman could represent and serve spirits of his or her natal clan only. Instead of sending away these challenger spirits from other clans, some shamans befriended them and even invited them to join their own family's origin spirits. These shamans had to worship and appease spirits of different clans. But in that case, the spirits of different clans competed against each other for exclusive patronage of the shaman. Such spirit battles, I was told, distressed and weakened the shamans. The origin spirits also needed to be agreeable with each other for a shaman to succeed.

Tömör's power rested on his close relationship with his origin spirits and his knowledge about them. Unlike most shamans, who struggled to figure out the identities of spirits that approached them, Tömör had shunned them all. He was confident that his origin spirits were complete for his current four shanars and five *shandruus* (initiation for a white shaman). If new spirits claimed to belong to his lineage, Tömör was ready to block them with the help of his existing origin spirits, who in their turn were happy to keep their shaman exclusively for themselves. (If a shaman serves additional origin spirits, the amount of attention each spirit receives diminishes.) Thus Tömör shielded himself and his rituals well, ignoring any other spirits that tried to get his attention. Unlike other shamans who felt uncertain of their decisions to accept the new spirits or send them away, Tömör felt safe because he believed if an important origin spirit came up, then his existing origin spirits would let him know. He also thought that the new spirits would wait for his next shanar to appear and introduce themselves because real origin spirits would obey the rules of shamanism.

Unlike some shamans who worshipped a large number of spirits, Tömör was certain that the number of his origin spirits was complete. He had only eight origin spirits, but they all were powerful and distinct. The most important characteristic of Tömör's genealogy of origin spirits was their kinship continuity: there were no interruptions between the generations, and it was made clear how the members were related to each other (see chart 1). Unlike other shamans' genealogies, which have interruptions, disconnections, and zigzag structures, Tömör's is clear and certain. With the help of one of Tömör's uncles, I recreated a part of his genealogy that represents Tömör's origin spirits—Delger; Saran Ejii; Ülzii, the son of Delger; Namjil, the daughter of Bazar; Baljima, the daughter of Ülzii; Erdene, the son of Erdene; Dugar, the son of Bayar; and his father, Molom, the son of Davaa. This continuity between the spirits ensures that there is no space for any outside spirits with whom he is unconnected to torment Tömör, and he ritually protects himself and his family with his origin spirits. Thus, by strategically maintaining the completeness of his genealogy, Tömör did not allow space for new spirits.

While Tömör's stories about his origin spirits made them memorable and thus contributed to his fame, the most credible source of his empowerment was his father. The fact that the locals had been acquainted with Molom and that many had been cured by him led them almost automatically to seek Tömör's services after Molom's death.

Molom died in the fall of 1997. His health deteriorated rapidly while I was visiting with Tömör's family in 1996 and 1997. He was suffering from stomach cancer and could no longer eat solid food. Less than two years after his death, Molom became one of Tömör's origin spirits and joined the rest to contribute to his son's shamanic powers. But even before he returned as a full-fledged origin spirit, while still on his eighteen-month journey to the celestial court to accept his highly esteemed position of *khaan tenngriin altan shargal takhilchin* (golden altar keeper of the tengri [celestial god] king), Molom was looking after his son. Tömör described his first encounter with his father's spirit:

A few months after my father's death, I had an accident. It was a windy day, and I was outside the ger talking to someone. I wanted to light a cigarette, so I struck a match against the side of a matchbox. The head of the lit matchstick broke and flew into my eye, where it made a sizzling noise. My eye was burned, the black part turned white, and I was certain that I had been blinded in one eye. Desperate and in pain, I began putting compresses on my eye made with the urine of my five-year-old son to reduce the inflammation and pain. Then, a couple of nights later, I had a dream. My father came to me and said: "Son, what have you done! I have not even reached my final destination, and already you have hurt yourself." Then he blew into my eye, and I felt something like a warm, wet tongue licking my damaged eye. When I woke up that morning I washed my face and sat down to drink tea. Sunjidma [Tömör's wife] reminded me, "Don't forget your urine compress." And then both of us were startled. My eye was normal, as if it had never been burned. I even forgot about the pain and the urine compress. Then I remembered my dream. My father was looking after me.

Unlike other families, who often initiate into shamanism at least two members (one white and one black), Tömör insisted that none of his family members be initiated as a shaman, and he attended to both black and white spirits all by himself. In the district it was rumored that his adopted

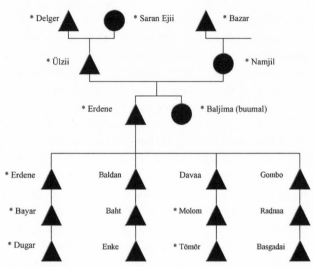

Chart 1. Tömör's kinship chart

sister had been appointed to be initiated as a white shaman and attend to the white spirits. Tömör opposed her initiation, arguing that there was no point in everyone in the family becoming a shaman. Tömör did not trust others to care for the origin spirits properly. Amidst chaos, uncertainty, and despair, he consolidated his spiritual safety as well as his social standing by setting up boundaries against the spirits and people who wished to enter into his relatively well-balanced life. Although many shamans I knew searched for powers by contacting and sometimes adopting new spirits, preferably relatives belonging to the shaman's lineage, Tömör blocked and limited his interactions with various spirits, even if they might have been from his lineage. Partly because Tömör was confident in the powers of his origin spirits and set out "fences" to guard his ritual space from outside intrusions, his rituals were smooth and structured, with little deviation from the original plan. The rituals of many other shamans were full of surprises, deviations, and uncertainties and were sometimes invaded by unknown spirits. The shamans often became sidetracked by outside spirits, got stuck figuring out new questions, or simply encountered something unknown that further complicated their rituals. Those adventurous and flexible rituals were far more interesting and sometimes more entertaining, but they made the shamans more vulnerable to the scrutiny of the community, as the shamans had little control over the outcome of their rituals.

Having his spiritual and material resources largely under control did not necessarily mean Tömör and his family had no problems. Tömör was in poor health during the period in which I did my fieldwork. His theory was that when he became a shaman, he indulged in possession rituals without taking any precautions, and did so too often for his early stage. "Ah, I loved being possessed by spirits when I first discovered I could do that," he told me. "Many new shamans struggled with it. But I would let a spirit in and then out, and then the next one. I was thrilled to be able to do that." Since the spirits carry all the illnesses of their human lives, they deposit them into the shaman. Tömör was careless and did not protect himself.

Dolgor had a different theory about Tömör's illnesses. She thought that Tömör had an assertive character and liked to evoke his black spirits, who brought immediate results but were also harmful to the shaman. Dolgor believed that Tömör should employ his white spirits, who were slower but much less harmful. That would ensure some balance. But, according to Dolgor, Tömör also needed more cleansing ceremonies for himself.

Although Tömör's health was not improving as quickly and as steadily as he had hoped and he worried about his daughters when they left Bayan-Uul to go to college in Ulaanbaatar, he remained optimistic that everything would go well. With his extensive network in the city, he could pour money into his problems and pay other people to take care of things he could not handle himself. Tömör considered his origin spirits complete because he had a nuanced explanation for his illnesses, and he was very much in control of his life, compared to others who seemed simply to go from one crisis to the next.

Throughout the world shamans are considered to be healers as well as patients. Taussig (1987) presents, how in contrast to university-trained Western doctors, shamans and folk healers embark on their professions as a way of healing themselves as well as their patients. It is a way of allowing "the sickness causing trauma and the healer's ministrations to reweave the creative forces of his personality and life experience into a force that bestows life upon himself and upon others through that bestowal" (Taussig 1987:448). Taussig's idea is applicable to the Buryats' case as a general principle. But the issue of shamanic healing is also very complicated, with many contingencies. For one, by healing others a shaman exposes his or her body to the forces of both helpful as well as harmful spirits. Therefore, shamans must limit their exposure to harm and be able to cleanse and re-store themselves. But that is not always possible, and some shamans need rituals themselves, performed by their teachers or other shamans. While most shamans I met no longer had any of the psychological and mental

problems that they claimed to have had before becoming shamans, few
if any solved their other health problems. Tömör, for instance, was over-
weight and suffered from pain in the pancreas, heart, and lungs. He had
trouble walking and moving and needed help to perform some of the
more strenuous work associated with herding. Thanks to Tömör's extensive
support network, his livestock was intact and taken care of. And he also
received constant attention from his clients, who helped him with medi-
cations and supplements and arranged hospital visits and stays when he
managed to get to Ulaanbaatar. In other words, the widespread notion that
shamans heal themselves while healing others is not an abstract or elusive
phenomenon. Based on my observations of shamans' different relationships with their clients and followers, shamans heal their own illnesses not
so much by their supernatural powers, but by having a network to share
the burdens of their illnesses.

Tömör's "Mobile" Intelligence and Stable Support

Tömör was initiated as a shaman back in the 1980s, when religious practices were still prohibited by the state. He practiced in secret. The risky endeavor seemed to present him with some exciting challenges. "During the
day I was a communist, and at night I was a shaman," Tömör told me mis-
chievously. In order to be a successful shaman, Tömör had to be a proper
socialist as well. He combined performance of the spirits and performance
for the state. He was the herder extraordinaire of the state farm, also known
as a "thousander"—his flock of sheep had reached one thousand head.
This showed his commitment to the state and the party and also made
him a valuable member of his state farm. In fact, he was too valuable to be
dismissed easily, so he felt a bit safer than other shamans. He was also such
an eloquent propagandist of the MPRP's ideology against superstition and
religion that party officials could not detain him even if they did suspect
him of being involved in religious practices. "Some of the officers would
try to accuse me of being involved in shamanic practices. I would tell the
person: 'What are you talking about? Are you saying that I am involved in
such stupid superstitions? If you want to arrest me, then do it now!'" Usually the party official or officer would simply drop the argument and leave
Tömör alone.

One day, however, someone denounced Tömör to the provincial center.
He was summoned by the police and questioned about his activities. He
explained to the officers that he was performing a *zan uil* (folkloric tradi-

tion) of worshipping the mountain spirits. Such activities serve as an incentive to the locals to protect the environment. The chief accepted Tömör's explanation. He said that there was nothing wrong with doing zan uil–related things and that the other officers should have better things to worry about. Tömör was a quick problem solver and enjoyed outsmarting others. Often his speech was rhythmic, playful, and sharp. His ease in coming up with ornate and exciting phrases and jokes and his ability to make up stories and come up with unusual interpretations of the mundane and banal greatly enriched his shamanic abilities. In many ways he attracted people with his social skills and personal charisma, which clearly expanded his shamanic practice. He had, as many people remarked, a "mobile" mind.

Shamans strive to appear materially independent and morally indifferent to gifts. In reality, they are heavily dependent on social support, clients, and gifts. Yet they must demonstrate an air of indifference in order to show that they are shamans not for the sake of money, but for the sake of helping others. To persuade his clients that he had no need of gifts, for instance, Tömör practiced a form of potlatch after big rituals.

I attended many potlatches. At one that he gave at the end of the annual worship of his origin spirits—a large-scale ritual during which Tömör became possessed by all his origin spirits—Tömör gathered the audience members together. At least fifty people were gathered in his ger, all tightly packed together, sitting on beds or chairs or standing. He brought out the cases of liquor people had brought him as gifts. He then arranged for everyone to distribute the bottles that they brought to the spirits of the local landscape or to any other spirits they wished to honor, and ask those spirits to look after them and their families. When all the bottles had been emptied and stashed under the tables again, Tömör threw an overnight party. Guests were pressed to eat and to drink. Tömör's four teenage daughters graciously served his guests liquor, his wife cooked soups and stews throughout the night, and the happy audience began to sing loudly. Tömör asked everyone to stay at his home until sunrise so that he would not be responsible for lost or injured horses, or for people getting hurt while making their drunken way home.

This ritual was not a service for clients in the audience; it was Tömör's worship of his own origin spirits. To show that he gained no material advantage from the alcohol people brought as gifts, Tömör made sure that it was used as a libation for the spirits only. Every single bottle was tossed to the spirits at the completion of the ritual. At the banquet Tömör served alcohol bought out of his own pocket, proving that he was not doing "business" with his clients. Yet by giving the party afterward, Tömör also expanded his existing network, since almost every guest brought a friend or family member—each one a potential client.

Besides constantly expanding his network of followers, Tömör was well supported by his teacher Tsend, the female shaman Genen's only son, and by a blacksmith, Purvee. Unlike many shamans, especially female ones, who struggled to complete their paraphernalia, Tömör was friends with a blacksmith. A shaman's paraphernalia consists of twenty-one items. For the first three shanars, the shaman's gown, headdress, and cape are all made of cloth. Usually female family members make these items, though skilled seamstresses may also be involved. The subsequent shanars, however, require an uulen amitai, several ritual instruments, and an ih amitai adorned with metal parts that represent the skeleton and internal organs, as well as wildlife and other shamanic symbols that must be made with steel and cast only by a specially designated blacksmith. Forging shamanic paraphernalia is time-consuming and labor-intensive, and the metal is not easy to come by. Purvee told me that it took several weeks and thirteen men working full-time in his smithy to complete Tömör's paraphernalia. Most shamans' shanars are postponed specifically because they lack sufficient resources and a large enough network to complete the metal part of their paraphernalia.

Unlike most shamans I knew, Tömör was supported in every possible way. He used his wealth to expand his social network and strengthen existing ties. His father's reputation was perhaps his most valuable asset, coupled with his teacher Tsend's fame, which came from his mother, Genen. And last but not least, his immediate family, consisting of his devoted and hardworking wife, Sunjidma, and their eight children, all worked incessantly under his "leadership," as he put it. Sunjidma worked around the clock, like a robot. She barely stopped to take a break to eat, and then usually only after everyone else was finished eating. Otherwise she continued to cook, clean, manage her children's labor and chores, take care of the livestock, and serve her demanding and almost immobile husband. And even though Sunjidma at times challenged Tömör's leadership and felt tired and overworked, she steadfastly continued her motherly and wifely duties. Without his family, and especially Sunjidma, Tömör would not have succeeded as a shaman.

Luvsan's Global Networks

With the end of Soviet domination in the late 1980s and 1990s and the beginning of democratic changes, a wave of nationalist sentiment swept through Mongolia, and the elites began to revive traditions that had been ignored or suppressed. As a part of this effort, some Mongolian scholars came to study Buryat shamans in Bayan-Uul; they focused on male shamans, such as Luvsan, Tsend, and Tömör, in part because female shamans in Bayan-Uul had such low visibility.[4] Luvsan was a disciple of the female shaman Genen and thus benefited from her fame and skills. He was the only shaman who held the title of zaarin. In the early 1990s, when it was time for Luvsan to stage his next shanars, there were no higher-ranking shamans to lead the ritual. Luvsan led his last few shanars all by himself, and he bestowed a title of zaarin on himself.

In addition to his dramatic performances and powerful origin spirits—the conventional, well-known powers—his travel and international fame afforded him experiences that many others could only dream about. In June 1996 a combined scholarly and lay group that regarded shamanism as an authentic Mongolian religion (as opposed to Buddhism, imported from Tibet) organized the International Symposium on Central Asian Shamanism on the shores of Lake Baikal. Scholars, shamans, and spectators from Central and Northern Asia and other parts of the world spent a week holding ritual festivities, filming, and networking. Several male shamans were asked to participate, amongst them Luvsan and Jigjid. Luvsan was one of the most charismatic; he led the worship of the island of Oikhon in Lake Baikal, where the Thirteen Lords of the Island of Oikhon, members of the shamanic celestial court, resided. He also bestowed the title of zaarin on other shamans from all over Siberia, Russia, and other Central Asian countries. With his double identity as "the highest-ranking shaman in Mongolia and a Buddhist lama"—and with paraphernalia weighing over 140 pounds—he impressed the international audience, comprised of New Age spiritualists, tourists, media figures, filmmakers interested in the "exotic," and scholars who sought the "authentic shamanism."[5]

One of the symposium's attendees, Bernardo, was a spiritual seeker and a traveler from Italy. He travelled extensively and made films on "spiritual masters" around the world, including the Dalai Lama. He was fascinated by Luvsan, and in the summer of 1997, a year after the Lake Baikal symposium, Bernardo traveled to Bayan-Uul, where he stayed for a week in Luvsan's felt tent, filming his rituals. While there, Bernardo got the idea of inviting Luvsan to Italy. After he returned home, he organized an international conference in Italy in December 1998 in association with the University of Verona. Luvsan and other shamans were invited to provide live performances while scholars discussed the trance rituals.[6]

Luvsan's trip to Italy was a triumph. He reached one of the most prestigious destinations in the world, one that most Mongols can only dream of. To appreciate his success, we must also consider the challenges and significance of international travel for Mongolians. Those who live in the first world mostly travel "down," to places where their powerful currencies and passports help them to overcome obstacles and cross borders much more easily than the population in the rest of the world. Mongolians who can afford to travel "up" to more affluent counties. Mongolians' meager average earnings mean that they not only struggle with money, but also with obtaining visas to first-world countries.

Geopolitical and economic circumstances in Mongolia made international travel a prominent marker of distinction particularly during socialism and only slightly less so since its collapse. During socialism, one way the Mongolian state controlled its people was by restraining their mobility. Foreign travel destinations were limited to socialist-bloc countries, mainly the Soviet Union, and travel was restricted to students studying abroad, diplomats, and state officials. Ordinary citizens did not have international passports allowing them to cross the border.

Since the collapse of socialism, all Mongolians have been able to have an international passport and travel anywhere in the world. But travel has been geared toward survival: for trading or for finding migrant work in other countries. Luvsan's travel to Italy was not about survival, but prestige. What could have been more prestigious than to have Italian money, a visa acquired easily, and his ticket paid for? For ordinary Mongols, getting a visa to a Western European country such as Italy is extremely difficult.

Luvsan Travels to Italy

The nature and meaning of travel changes over the course of a shaman's career: it is both a marker of social status and a means of acquiring material wealth. Through different types of travel, individual practitioners lose or gain powers. The purpose, final destination, and route of an individual shaman's travel may all help determine his or her status and power. Among the Buryats, neophyte shamans at first travel in order to learn and serve. They go and see teachers to increase their knowledge and skills, seek out blacksmiths and seamstresses to order paraphernalia, and visit clients upon request. After performing three to five shanars, a shaman is usually seen as having gained enough power to progress in status from neophyte to mid-level shaman. Shamans' increased empowerment also leads to a corresponding transition from what I call "service travel" to "prestige travel." As a shaman gains power, he travels locally less and less; his nearby clients more often travel to see him than he them. However, when a relatively high ranking shaman travels, he or she is mostly summoned to more prestigious destinations, such as Ulaanbaatar or abroad.

A correlation between travel and shamanic power has also preoccupied anthropologists working in other parts of the world, including Indonesia. Travel is not just about moving physically from one place to the next; it is also about gaining an audience and occupying a terrain. And travel produces knowledge, stories, and traditions—intangible assets that are essential to or that further enhance the shaman's engagement with a community.[7] The knowledge, stories, and resources he gained from his travels gained Luvsan further prestige and respect among the locals in Bayan-Uul. He was a person "who had seen the world and who had open eyes," meaning that he had gained intelligence, compassion, and an open heart—what men's travel was supposed to yield.

When I visited him in the summer of 1999, Luvsan's biggest news was his trip to France, Germany, and Italy. Five thick photo albums were neatly filled with photographs from his visit. And he had a story to tell about each and every picture. Luvsan pointed his finger to a photograph of a cherub that he took in a church in Italy and said informatively: "This is Angela, a messenger to gods."

I told him that it was fascinating that he remembered so many details about his trip.

"It took us only a few hours to get the visa! It was all arranged by the Italian side!" Luvsan's son remarked proudly.

On the international flight Luvsan wore a burgundy velvet degel with a golden silk sash and a zaarin hat he had designed himself. With its golden ornaments, it resembled a throne of the Bogd Khan, the last emperor during the period of theocracy (1911–1921). Luvsan checked his baggage—a trunk he himself had hand-carved elaborately and filled with his shamanic paraphernalia—at the airport and enjoyed seeing how people turned to look at him.

At the conference people wanted to see Luvsan's spirit possession ritual. "I was careful and did not really lose consciousness. I made sure that I was OK—I was not going to take any chances that something might go wrong," he told me in a low voice. He was received royally. His host family had a farm on the outskirts of Parma. The family baked bread with their own wheat, which they harvested with their own small tractor. Luvsan and his son liked the tractor immensely. The lady of the house constantly offered Luvsan food, vodka, and other drinks, as well as smiles and good-morning and goodnight kisses. "They kiss all the time, on the cheeks, regardless of the degree of relationship," he noted. In restaurants, he ate special a Mongolian-style noodle soup consisting of pieces of lamb and spaghetti noodles made specifically to suit his Mongolian palate. After the conference Luvsan toured Italy, Germany, and France with his hosts and shopped for gifts for his family.

Luvsan talked about the "strange" customs of Italians, such as meals that took three or more hours, with "too much loud discussion." He drank only vodka, which was "pure, clean, and harmless." He refused to try wine because he was told that it was made from grapes pressed with the feet, "which was unclean and barbaric." He was surprised that the Italians liked to keep "old" things and were indifferent to modern-style furniture and houses, and that they were such religious people. Once he spent all night turning watches, jewelry, and pens that people set out on a table before him into amulets by enlivening them with the powers of his origin spirits.

The churches and medieval castles that he saw made the strongest impressions on him. During one of these visits Luvsan was even able to show off his shamanic skills. At the entrance of one castle he said he "saw" a warrior riding a black stallion and wearing a black cape with a red lining billowing in the wind behind him. The Italians guessed that this figure must be the ghost of the owner, who died defending his castle back centuries ago, probably from Christian missionaries. Luvsan told them that without a libation to the ghost he would not go inside the castle, and he sprinkled alcohol to appease it. The local pagans were impressed with Luvsan's' ability to communicate with spirits and asked him to teach them how to do the same. Luvsan was especially pleased to hear that these Italians were interested in his shamanic practice as well as reviving their traditional pre-monotheistic pagan religious practices. He felt especially connected with them despite their many differences.

Before Luvsan left his hosts in Italy in the winter of 1998, he invited them to his home in Bayan-Uul. Then, early in June 1999, a bus full of Italians arrived at the ger in his summer pasture. Happy and loud, the guests spent a week camping next to Luvsan's ger. Luvsan has received so many international visitors since then that he has become selective: he has restricted some who looked as though they were cash-poor from attending his rituals, much to the dismay of the local people, who feel sorry for the occasional backpackers and students who were being prevented from participating in rituals unless they had paid or given gifts. Luvsan also became selective about invitations abroad: only the most prestigious ones were worthy of his effort.

This exclusive behavior is consistent with Luvsan's rise in status overall.

As we have seen, the farther a shaman travels and the more powerful an audience he reaches, the less he travels locally. Ceasing to travel in local areas means that a shaman has become well established and has no need to search for new clients or expend effort making house calls on existing ones. Subsistence-related travel is thus no longer necessary for an affluent shaman. Travel abroad supports intangible needs that go far beyond mere survival.

Since I met Luvsan in 1996, he has gradually transformed his valley's single log cabin and ger into a bustling ritual center. He built a Buddhist temple, complete with furniture and ritual objects; a wooden temple for his shamanic activities (his "office"); and a new log house for his grandson. He also bought a windmill to generate electricity and was planning to buy a video camera and build a sauna and a small guest house for tourists and anthropologists.[8] But most important, in summertime, the valley was full of visitors' cars, trucks, and tents, waiting for their turn at a ritual.

"I am turning the money I received into something virtuous for the people in this district. I used the money to build the temple," Luvsan told me as he opened a large padlock on his freshly painted temple and let me inside. A few years ago he used to send clients who needed Buddhist rituals to temples in the city of Ulaanbaatar or other provincial centers. During the last year of my fieldwork, however, he completed the construction and interior decoration of his own temple, built to serve clients that needed Buddhist rituals. (By contrast, the communal temple in the center of Bayan-Uul remains unfinished due to a lack of funds.) Two sets of clients offered the gifts that supported Luvsan's building and acquisition activities. One, a group of local Bayan-Uul clients seeking Buddhist rituals, used to go to Ulaanbaatar before Luvsan's temple was built. The others, long-distance shamanic clients, were mostly from outside Bayan-Uul.

Young Mongolians dressed in Levi's, T-shirts from the Gap, baseball caps, and fleece hoodies came mostly from Ulaanbaatar. Others, the diaspora Mongolians, observing the same universal youth dress code, came from Munich, Seoul, San Francisco, New York, and other global cities. In his shamanic office, a round ger-like wooden building, Luvsan proudly displayed amulets, photographs, musical instruments, eagle feathers, seashells, and other exotica from Italy and from other shamans in Mexico, Korea, Brazil, and Siberia. He decorated his brown drum with images of wolves. The display of memorabilia and stories of his trips attracted and impressed clients. Local people pointed out that since his faraway clients did not know much about Luvsan's history of failed rituals and saw only his successes, they may have had more faith in him than did some of the

Figure 19. A shaman with his new global clients

Figure 20. A shaman with his disciples

Figure 21. Inside Luvsan's shamanic office

locals. And because the potency of the ritual depended on belief, Luvsan was perfect for such clients.

At the same time, however, the influx of faraway clients elevated Luvsan's status among the locals. That was not because the people of Bayan-Uul believed that an audience from far away was better able to judge Luvsan's shamanic power. Rather, the local people referred to his qualities as a person, indicating that Luvsan's exposure to a diverse clientele increased his dignity, tolerance, and compassion. I heard people say: "Shaman Luvsan has been to many places and seen the world. He has such an open mind, he will understand everything."

Tricking the Spirits

Aware that he was being watched by the locals, Luvsan was keen to keep up with gossip about him. He sought to show that he practiced because he was chosen by his spirits to help people out, not simply for the sake of money. Although he kept an eye out for rich clients prior to becoming known to people in Ulaanbaatar and especially to international audiences, he served everyone who sought his help to prove that his motives were not based on profit. By serving the poorest clients often almost for free, he displayed his dignity, power, and credibility. In shamanic epistemology, a shaman is a trickster of spirits, convincing them to serve humans. In evocations of the spirits, a shaman transforms the meager offerings to his or her origin spirit into gifts of mythological proportions and exquisite beauty and quality. Seven small spoons of clarified butter are depicted as seventy-seven *boshik* (barrels); a dozen butter-candle offerings are transformed into a hundred candles; a simple wooden table laden with offerings is depicted as made from exotic sandalwood. That ability to trick the spirits is crucial in meeting clients' requests: most clients cannot supply the amount of butter and luxury items the shaman offers to the spirits in evocations.

Regarding Luvsan's ability to trick the spirits, Dolgor told me a story (even though she avoided him in person specifically because she was wary of his motives). "Luvsan is a person with great vision," began Dolgor.

Sometimes he can see things in such extraordinary ways. Once Luvsan told his family: "My lord, a very poor and exhausted person is coming to us! Make food and tea." In a few hours, an old lady from a faraway district came with her grandson on their last surviving horse. Over the past few years she had lost her sons and daughters, and her livestock had gotten lost and been eaten by wolves. She was barely alive herself. Her origin spirits had not been worshipped for too long and, infuriated, they were destroying her *golomt* [hearth]. Everything in her life was out of balance. In order to get her rituals completed, she needed to present something to a shaman to deliver to the spirits. She gathered all her money, which was less than a hundred tögrögs [US$0.10]—nowhere close to buying anything for the ritual. When she presented the money to Luvsan, he managed to launch a full-scale ritual for her. He gave fifty or so tögrögs to his son and said that the old lady would "buy" a sheep from "this family" [he meant his own family]. He gave ten tögrögs to his daughter-in-law to "buy" sweets, milk, cream, and other dairy items needed for the spirits. He gave another ten tögrögs to his wife to "buy" cloth and prayer scarves to put on the altar to give to the spirits. He then put the remaining money on the altar as a gift to his origin spirits. After Luvsan completed the spirit possession rituals for the lady, he told her to stay overnight and get some rest instead of traveling late at night. The next morning he loaded the meat of the sacrificial sheep onto the old lady's horse and saw her off.

The impoverished woman's visit enhanced Luvsan's power and popularity. The story about his treatment of her also elevated his status in comparison to the other shamans in the area, who had refused to help the poor old woman. The more independent of the clients' gifts a shaman was, the more credible he became. The shaman who could show he practiced on the basis of goodwill alone was highly respected and showered with gifts.

Shamanism is a tricky business. It is not supposed to look like business. Shamans depend on their audiences' gifts for their livelihood, but they must appear independent of them. Based on the examples of Luvsan's and Tömör's successful shamanic practices, we can see that the empowerment and visibility of male shamans take place at least on two levels. At the local level, the gendered division of labor and unequal access to primary resources, networking, and kinship structures often impede females' and enhance males' access to shamanic power.[9] At the national and international levels, scholarly symposia, tourism, and research projects further facilitate men's visibility and empowerment locally—a direct extension of local male empowerment. Men are invited to these larger events because they are already visible in their local setting. Also, since most researchers, organizers of scholarly symposia, and national-level rituals are male, they tend to invite male shamans; female shamans remain largely unseen. And whenever one meets female shamans, it is easy to make an assumption that those female shamans must be powerful against the invisibility of others.

The Community of Spirits

One outcome of shamanic practice is the representation of the Buryats' spirit world, the result of searching, identifying, interacting, and worshipping spirits and gods. I briefly sketch out that representation by providing some details about the names, images, characters, and identifications of the spirits. This is the heart of the rituals that shamans offer to their clients. The clients then operate within this realm in their quest for "completing the list of their origin spirits"—the topic of the next chapter.

Three distinct but interrelated cultural spaces emerge from individuals' interactions with the spirit world. These three spaces also encompass meanings in their own right. One space is the ruling hierarchy of spirits and gods in the celestial realm—the celestial court. The second cultural space emerges with the compilation of genealogies, which include origin spirits. These genealogies are not just lists of the names of dead ancestors; rather, they are a form of interactive history. They are constituted from historical personae impersonated by possessed shamans, who present specific instances of the past in the present, or of the present in a form from the past. Rather than thinking of shamanic performances as forms of historical memory no longer accessible in discursive form, I see the performances as enacted memories realized through multiple media, such as gesture, language, food, music, and material objects. And third, communication from the evoked origin spirits also allows the mapping of the historical landscape of the Buryats (discussed briefly in chapter 1).

The spirit world is an alternative political space. It represents the idealized nation where the Buryats tap into their gods' and spirits' powers and also enact periods of oppression that have been present throughout their own history. The Buryats' subordinate positions are carried in the stories of spirits in various ways, especially the stories of female spirits. Both male and female shamans can become possessed by spirits of either gender, indicating that both are subject to the embodied memories of violence.[10]

The Celestial Court

The Buryat origin spirits are ruled by a hierarchy of communal spirits and tengris that I call the celestial court. Structurally, the celestial court can be divided into parallel white and black spiritual groups.[11] Burhan Garval,[12] the most powerful spirit in the celestial court, stands alone above any of the black spirits' leaders, heading the white spirits in general and overseeing those white origin spirits that are endowed with healing powers. The black spirit pantheon's divisions parallel those of the white spirit pantheon (except for Burhan Garval), with three levels: (1) the tengris, divided into fifty-five western (benevolent) tengris and forty-four eastern (evil) ones;[13] (2) the Oihoni Arvan Gurvan Noyod (Thirteen Lords of the Island of Oikhon in Lake Baikal);[14] and (3) the common spirits of particular realms important to the Buryats, such as Dorlik, Manjalai (leader of shanars), Hoimorin Högshin, Danchhai Noyon (lord of the underworld), and others. Like the white pantheon's Burhan Garval, the black pantheon rules origin spirits who share similar properties with them.[15]

Shamans evoke the celestial court in almost every ritual. Despite their mandatory presence, however, its top members (Burhan Garval, the Thirteen Lords, and other tengris) rarely possess shamans; rarely do they involve themselves in human affairs. The highest members of the celestial court make major decisions that the shamanic origin spirits transmit to the human world, but they remain distant and elusive, like earthly governments. "They are like senators," Tömör told me. Most of the Buryats I met were familiar with these members, and some even knew their evocation poems. When I asked Tömör what the tengris actually do, he laughed. "Where have you seen any lord doing much at all? They discuss things and sit around, like our big-bellied members of parliament."

The common spirits—Dorlik, Manjalai, and Hoimorin Högshin, among others—are also well-known to the Buryats. Unlike the highest members of the celestial court, these common spirits possess shamans and communicate with humans in the same way as the origin spirits do. They serve all shamans, and every shaman can attain his or her own "copy" of the common spirits and personify them for his or her household without placing them alongside his or her origin spirits in genealogies, as is the case with Hoimorin Högshin. Because all Buryats are familiar with the celestial court, it provides a way of creating imagined communities and maintaining a sense of ethnic unity and coherence.

The origin spirits constitute a populace under the rule of the celestial court. They have different ranks, occupy designated spaces, and perform duties. The more powerful origin spirits secure permanent *huudal* (seats) with the celestial gods, while the less powerful ones oscillate between the Earth and the celestial realm. On Earth those spirits become *ezed* (lords) of landscape features such as mountains, rivers, and lakes, and they also play and bathe on Earth. But they "work" in the celestial court as *tahilchin* (altar keepers), *emeelchin* (saddle men), *haalgachin* (doormen), and *tulhuurchin* (keepers of keys). Thus, when the shamans evoke their origin spirits, they call them not only by their names, but also by the spaces they occupy, their burial sites, and the jobs that they hold in the celestial court. Several things take place simultaneously through evocation: place-making on earth, mapping the spiritual realm, identifying an origin spirit, and repeating the celestial court hierarchy.

The white and black members of the celestial court and the corresponding origin spirits that they rule have different powers, and this divides their tasks as well. The black side is in charge of the *khatuu* (hard) rituals. The word *khatuu* refers to the dangerous nature of the task, the intensity of the physical labor involved, and the aggressive dispositions of the spirits and tengris in this category. These rituals include the saving of the soul from the underworld, the *ami nasnii andaldaa* (fight for life), reproduction, and the delivering of the souls of the dead to the underworld court. The black spirits are indispensable in times of emergency and disaster, but the effects they are able to achieve are often short-term ones. The white spirits are less aggressive than the black. They perform almost all the functions of the black ones, but their effect is not as immediate and condensed. Instead, they ensure that the rituals yield a consistent and lasting effect that is distributed evenly through time. For individual shamans, the black pantheon is good for helping others, but the white is necessary for maintaining one's safety and well-being.

Some of the origin spirits who have been unable to get powerful and re-

spected positions with the celestial court become landscape spirits only—
the lords of mountains, rivers, cliffs, small hills, or even just the slope of
a mountain. The origin spirits who are affiliated with the celestial court
tended to be more benevolent than those who have been unable to ascend to the celestial court because the landscape spirits protected their
lands from outsiders. They are also unhappy about having been abandoned by their descendants as the Buryats moved off their land to escape
colonialism.

Although it looks empty to human eyes, the landscape is densely popu-
lated with spirits. At a lake or river one must be wary of *lus* (lords of the
water)—urinating next to a stream might cause kidney and bladder problems. While in the forest, one needs to watch out for *savdag* (lords of the
forest, plains, and ditches)—breaking off branches or taking wood from
the forest could result in broken limbs or accidents. People especially
avoid ditches, abandoned homes, and ruined settlements, where the spirits
called *albin* (evil spirits of the landscape) and *tiiren* (demons) lived. Associated with substances such as filth, dirt, and mold, the social environs
they inhabit are riddled with quarreling and violence. As discussed earlier,
uheer are the lowest tier of the Buryats' spirit world.

In a world filled with spirits—on the land, above it, and below it—it is
impossible not be engaged with them, as either a shaman or a client. To
be able to protect individuals, shamans need to achieve mastery over their
own origin spirits, while clients must complete the worship rituals their
family's spirits demand. The last chapter shows how one particular individual engaged with the spirit world and illuminated the challenges that
she faced in her life: the repercussions of state suppression, economic survival, political marginalization, and, most important, gender hierarchy. As
a result of finding, worshipping, and learning about the spirits, genealogies
expand and grow, the lost historical landscape becomes illuminated, and
stories feed into and thicken the dispersed and fragmented history of the
Buryats' survival on the borders of violent states.

SEVEN

Incomplete Lives

I met Baasan in 1996 when I first came to Bayan-Uul. At that time a physics teacher at the local high school, she wore flowing skirts and cardigans and carried a handsome purse over her shoulder. Gracious and alert, she radiated energy and confidence. By 2000 she had retired, but she still lived in her home in the district center. She seemed to have aged more than most other people I knew, and she seemed less energetic than before. After encountering Baasan a few times at various shamans' rituals, I began to suspect that something had happened in her life for which she might have been seeking resolution. I learned about her tragedies when Baasan stopped at a ritual performed by the female shaman Baigal (see chapter 4) to ask about her nephews' health. That night, after the ritual, Baasan and I walked back to the district center together arm in arm, each of us holding a stick to beat away the dogs that roam Bayan-Uul at night. Baasan began telling me of her grief. We each took turns walking the other home, but upon our arrival, unwilling to say goodbye, we continued to talk, walking each other back and forth several times through the narrow moonlit alleys. I invited her to sleep in my spare bed. She agreed and dozed off just before dawn. After that night, we spent almost every evening for the next two months talking about her search for the reasons behind her misfortunes.

Everything began with her brother's sudden death two years before. Since then, she had been trying to find out why he died, which led her to search for her unknown origin spirits. Her attempt to put an end to her misfortunes became, as it was for most other people, a search for a missing, unknown, and often unknowable past. This chapter details Baasan's travel stories, tracing how she learned of her ancestral past, partially rebuilt her lost genealogy, and found meaning behind her misfortunes in the light of her fragmented knowledge about her past.

Baasan gradually wove together her family's genealogy out of narratives of suffering, loss, and love. In retelling them, I cast those narratives within the larger history of the Buryats' struggle against colonialism, migration, and political violence. Her work of reconstituting the past involved gathering *tuukhe* (history) from shamans, books, and official documents, and accessing her own *sanahan yum* (memories) of the events that took place in her childhood, and the narratives of (and about) her parents and grandparents that she heard at various times in her life. Like most Buryats, she learned anew about the origin spirits who returned to torment their descendants for forgetting. And she also encountered some extraordinary knowledge that lay somewhat outside of shamanism. That was the female ancestor who never became an origin spirit but who yearned for remembrance. And by pushing the limits of the known and knowable past, she also reached the irrecoverable gaps in her family's past. For Baasan, and for most Buryats, these gaps often tell stories of violence and forgetting and demand further search and commemoration.

In this chapter I also retell Baasan's interpretations of the events in her family's life that led to her brother's death, her travels to shamans and lamas, and the contribution of the community members to her knowledge through their interpretations of dreams, divination, and explanation. The reader will learn about the circumstances and events that influence clients' belief and disbelief in a particular shaman. In chapters 5 and 6 I discussed the shamans' maneuvering through a gendered social terrain in their roads to empowerment. Here I elucidate the clients' influences on that process as well.

In her experiences, Baasan is representative of other Buryats who have long lived with incompleteness and disruption—their past suppressed, the future unknown, and the present out of control. Much of the opaqueness stems from the destruction of Baasan's genealogical records. One of her uncles had burned them in an attempt to save his extended family from arrest during the political violence and repressions of the 1930s. The family's remembering now only stretched as far as the living members, who had heard some stories from their elders, could recall.

Shamanic clients receive little attention in anthropological studies on inspirational practices, as they usually center on the practitioners. Shamans are the community's leaders, storytellers, and innovators (Tsing 1993). Spirit mediums carry their communities' histories (Lambek 2002), and keep them in touch with their own past (Steedly 1993). Shamans among the Buryats of Mongolia also fulfill these functions, but they are not the only agents of cultural production. Clients organize, distribute, and interpret that knowledge. And they filter, recreate, and expand it. Stories recounted by a spirit-possessed shaman in the ritual arena are scattered fragments within the larger narrative of the family's and the Buryats' past. An origin spirit is a shaman's impersonation of a historical personage who conveys the stereotypes of a particular time and place. Clients must piece together a larger narrative by connecting various strands and constellations of stories and people to compose at least a partially coherent past.

Furthermore, a shaman is not supposed to retain his or her knowledge beyond the period of the possession itself;[1] it is the client who must absorb the stories by individual spirits and shamans and assemble them into a narrative as they continue to gather more nuanced elements. Because clients often consult with multiple shamans and spirits, they have to sift through an array of details and narratives to pick the ones that make the most sense. They learn to draw the big picture of their genealogical history on the basis of their collected knowledge, which is something that shamans may not be able to do for all of their clients. Much of the work of making the past is dialectical; it is based on the communication between clients and shamans.

In gathering and collating information, a client may see more of the overall situation than the shaman and be better able to situate fragments of knowledge within his or her own genealogical map. Clients can also thereby better judge their shamans' knowledge. In order to verify shamans' truthfulness and the authenticity of their knowledge, clients keenly solicit second or third opinions from other shamans.[2] The truth thus comes to be a kind of consensus among shamans. But it is certainly not the shamans who compare and contrast their findings with each other. It is the clients who solicit multiple opinions in disguise from individual shamans, compare, and then selectively amass them.

An Unexpected Death and the Mystery of the Golden Box

One October morning in 1998, Baasan's brother Bat was found dead in the grasslands between his own ger and that of a friend he had visited the day before. Neither the police nor the doctors could establish a reason for the forty-five-year-old's death. No heart failure, wounds, or internal bleeding were found. He had had a drink of *shimin arhi* (a traditional spirit distilled from dairy products) in his friend's ger the night before, but the friend testified that Bat did not get drunk. The doctors suggested that he might have frozen to death, but the people of the district argued that the night was too warm for anyone to freeze. Lacking any other explanation, Baasan suspected that Bat's death might have been related to his initiation as a shaman two months ago. His teacher was Chimeg, and Baasan wondered whether she had done anything wrong.

As time passed, Bat's death came to be less of a topic of the locals' conversation. Baasan, however, remained restless and tormented, because she had learned that her brother had died prematurely, yet she still did not know the reasons behind his death. Like all Mongols, she had sought, as a part of the funeral rites, the divination services of Buddhist lamas and inquired about Bat's life. Called "the opening of the Golden Box," this practice involves retrieving information from a sutra titled "The Golden Box" and charting the trajectory of the person's life and afterlife as given by Burhan Bagsh (the Teacher Buddha). Based on this information, the diviner advises survivors of the course of their late kinsperson's reincarnation and next life. The written notes based on the Golden Box are expected to be buried with the dead, but Baasan kept Bat's notes with her so that she could read them more carefully after the funeral, when she had a "clearer mind."

The notes indicated that Bat should have lived until the age of sixty. They gave three reasons for his premature death.

1. *His soul had already left his body the year before his initiation as a shaman*. This meant that Bat's teacher, Chimeg, had neglected to summon his soul before his initiation ritual.[3]
2. *Although Bat became a shaman and propitiated his family's origin spirits, the origin spirits remained neglected*. In other words, the rituals had not reached the origin spirits. The purpose of Bat's shamanic initiation was to make sure that the angry origin spirits did not harm him or his other living relations.
3. *Bat died because "he uttered an inappropriate name."* This one was the most unclear, and Baasan had no explanation for it.

"My brother was not supposed to die!" said Baasan. "He was initiated as a shaman; that must have been what killed him!" For more than two years Baasan visited numerous shamans hoping to find the reasons for her brother's death and her other misfortunes. Sometimes, caught in the claustrophobic politics of shamanism, her travels seemed repetitive and meaningless, like putting the same stitches over and over into a ragged piece of cloth. At other times she encountered lacunae in the records destroyed by the state and struggled to find her next step. Often, however, she found unexpected knowledge, when the shamanic (and sometimes Buddhist) rituals and divinations led her to explore the forgotten corners of Buryat past and to ancestral lands her family had lost to Russian settlers.

Crippled Health, Incomplete Lives

In their family, Baasan and Bat were the only two surviving children of eleven siblings. When Baasan was seven her mother died in childbirth, and Baasan began having the seizures that have lasted throughout her lifetime. She contracted bronchitis at ten and tuberculosis at eleven, developed ovarian cancer at twenty, had kidney problems, and then wrestled with infertility in her thirties. As the illnesses spread around her body, she moved around the country, switching hospitals and doctors and seeking suitable treatments. Nevertheless, Baasan did well in school with little effort. In her Mongolian State University graduation class photograph, she is the only woman among fifty-one men. She earned her degree in physics in 1956.[4] After graduation she returned to Bayan-Uul, where she lived with her father and brother and taught in the local school. Her health continued to trouble her, and she spent all of her summer breaks in hospitals.

Her brother Bat, on the other hand, was excluded early on from schooling and social networks. His father refused to send him to school because he could not let his only surviving son go and live in a crowded dormitory. (As a girl, Baasan was less precious to her parents than her brother.) Although healthy and smart, Bat never gained a vocation or established a career. Having never gone through formal schooling and the state system of job placement, Bat struggled to find a job in a system where all jobs were state jobs. Unable to find permanent employment, Bat switched from one temporary position to another. He went from working as a guard in a bank to being a manual laborer, an administrative officer, a policeman, and other such temporary occupations. With no qualifications or networks, he could not find a space within the state that controlled the job placement in its entirety. He was left out of the system.

Following the end of socialism, when, in 1993, the state farm livestock was privatized, Bat's family received enough to enable them to move from the sedentary center of Bayan-Uul to the countryside. But just when they thought they might be able to have a better life, their livestock began dying. Bat saw this as a spirit attack. He even transferred his livestock from his own name to his son's to try to deceive the spirits who were harming him. Broke, depressed, and lonely, he refused to leave his ger, and his wife became the breadwinner of the household. Baasan may have struggled with physical ailments, but Bat was dying emotionally and socially; his soul was lost. Each sibling's life was incomplete, but in different ways: Bat had been socially unfit, and Baasan was physically ill. He was excluded from the state, while she was embedded in the state through school, work, and hospital treatment.

A Past That Refuses to Be Revealed

Restless and anxious, Bat had a vision of an unknown man that persisted for months, so he turned to the shamans for help. They interpreted his vision as an affliction by spirits: "The Hal'bin clan has long been known for their famous shamans. Their spirits have now returned to torment their descendants for having abandoned them; they request propitiation." Bat's family became a center of rituals for chasing away albin, appeasing lus, worshipping Hoimorin Högshin, and propitiating the family's origin spirits, both with and without the sacrifice of sheep. But none of the rituals seemed to work; Bat's situation did not improve. All of the diviners said the same thing: their worship was not reaching the family's origin spirits. The spirits received nothing.

The reason was that, like most Buryats, Baasan and Bat had no knowledge of the individual identities of most of their origin spirits. They evoked and conversed with a couple of origin spirits whom the shamans discovered. But they had no knowledge about the rest of the origin spirits who belonged to them. They did not know the names of some of the origin spirits and their *duudalga* (evocation), which included huudal buudal. Therefore, unable to evoke each origin spirit by its name and huudal buudal, they had to send the offerings and requests to the origin spirits of their clan as a group. Amending this lack of knowledge (i.e., identifying the individual spirits and their huudal buudal) was crucial to Bat's healing. To find the names and places they needed, Baasan and Bat, over the space of a year (1997–1998), made eighteen long trips and countless shorter ones to every diviner, shaman, and lama they could find. They traveled by horseback, camel, horse cart, Soviet jeep, and foot. They attended other people's shamanic rituals to ask those individuals' origin spirits about their own— some origin spirits can retrieve the names and evocations needed to call other spirits. But Bat and Baasan's origin spirits remained as lost as their destroyed genealogical records.

After numerous rituals, the shaman Tömör finally revealed a great origin spirit from three generations back. Tömör suggested that they find a shaman from their clan (Hal'bin) to contact it. Bat and Baasan borrowed money and traveled to see a young female shaman named Undarmaa, who attended the origin spirits of the Hal'bin clan. Undarmaa had migrated from Bayan-Uul to Ulaanbaatar. When I visited her in 2000, she was living in the crowded ger district with her elderly mother and two small children. There Undarmaa and a shamanic colleague revealed to Baasan an abandoned landscape spirit whom Baasan's ancestors had apparently propitiated long ago but had neglected over the past few generations. The curse of this spirit—once the lord of a local mountain in their ancestral homeland in Russian Buryatia—must have been strengthened after several generations of neglect. "That mountain spirit must have been abandoned by my grandparents, when they emigrated from Russia to Mongolia at the turn of the twentieth century," said Baasan. Like most Buryats of their day, they had come to escape the turmoil of the Bolshevik Revolution and the Russian Civil War. The spirit requested the sacrifice of a blue goat to call off his curse.[5] A few days later, with the help of other Buryats who had migrated to Ulaanbaatar, the sacrifice was made to this mountain spirit with all proper respect.

A few days after the ritual, Bat began having a recurring vision of two human skulls resting on his hearth. Hoping to inquire about the meaning of such an inauspicious vision, Bat and Baasan made another trip to see Undarma. She was not home, so they went to Undarmaa's colleague to ask about the two skulls, pleading many times with the origin spirit who possessed him, once entranced, for an answer. The origin spirit finally said that a spirit named Navaan of the Hal'bin clan, from their ancestral homeland of Ul'han, requested worship of them. At least one major spirit of the Hal'bin clan was a direct ancestor of Bat and Baasan.

Baasan knew the spirit named Navaan and his son, the spirit of the famous zaarin Dugar, from attending Chimeg's rituals. As a shaman of the Hal'bin clan, Chimeg regularly evoked and was possessed by both Navaan and Dugar, among her many other origin spirits. Bat and Baasan did not receive explicit instructions that one of them be initiated as a shaman, but they felt so troubled and desperate they decided to have Bat initiated, hoping that with proper ritual attention to the origin spirits, he would be able to stop all these misfortunes from being inflicted on them.

Desperation: Bat's Initiation as a Shaman

Baasan thought that Chimeg was the right person to be Bat's teacher because she was a powerful shaman of the Hal'bin clan who attended directly to Navaan. But she was also reluctant to seek Chimeg's services because of the shaman's controversial reputation. Chimeg was just then divorcing her husband. Rumors about her "greedy," "moody," and "sexually loose" behavior circulated widely. As I discussed in chapter 5, most male shamans were temporarily united in their opposition to her divorce. Chimeg's bad reputation was hurting her credibility, and she was losing clients. Her incessant mobility was also inconvenient for clients like Baasan and Bat, who sought her services consistently and repeatedly in an effort to resolve their troubles. Tormented about going to Chimeg, Baasan checked with diviners, who confirmed that despite Baasan's reservations, Chimeg was a compatible mentor for Bat. So Baasan and Bat pooled their resources and staged Bat's shanar.

In the first shanar, called *altan tsereg örgöh* (to enliven the golden army), a neophyte shaman acquires protection from malevolent spirits and becomes a *bariashi* (healer). Chimeg led Bat's first shanar, introducing him to five origin spirits, including Dugar and Navaan. Each origin spirit received an item of the paraphernalia to enliven them with sacred healing and protective powers. These objects were also their descending places when Bat summoned them to his rituals. The mirror and headdress were expected to protect Bat, while his coral bracelet and prayer beads gave him healing powers. Bat also got a bell for evoking his origin spirits. When Bat acquired the power of five origin spirits, Baasan hoped to shake off her illness and save her brother, who was decaying inwardly in his desolation. But instead of acquiring safety and security, two months after Bat was initiated as a shaman, he died mysteriously.

Baasan was essentially accusing Chimeg of Bat's death. She worried that Bat should never have become a shaman. Had Chimeg just thrust some incompatible, random wandering spirits on Bat, instead of his own origin spirits? Were the rituals sloppy, so that the origin spirits simply refused to accept the new shaman? Or were there additional origin spirits who had been left out but were expected to be revealed? There were so many questions. Baasan feared that if she did find out Chimeg's mistakes and did not fix them, then someone else in her family would die, including possibly herself. The question of who would die next kept her awake at night.

Finding Shamanic Errors

Baasan needed to clarify the shamanic ritual's errors and discover which obscure, angry origin spirits still seemed bent on avenging their fury on their descendants. In so doing, she built a particular kind of Buryat history around her family, piecing together the stories and explanations of

the spirits, shamans, diviners, and lamas she encountered. Into these narratives she included her own memories and elements from locally and
state-constructed histories, spinning all these threads into a long narrative.
Alternating between belief and skepticism, Baasan pushed to their limits
the possibilities of knowing, remembering, and revealing what she could
accept as truth. She learned that truth is not always knowledge; it is also
empty spaces left for missing knowledge, represented in her case by the
legacy of losses from the socialist state's suppression of religion and its efforts to erase communal and individual memory. Finding errors also led to
identifying the truth, which ultimately differentiates between the shamans,
dividing them into bad and good, weak and powerful, fake and authentic—the process that accompanies the reproduction of the past.

Baasan, however, did not know how to find the errors that might have
taken place during rituals. So she filed the task in the back of her mind
and went on with sending off the origin spirits who were still attached to
her dead brother. This was the first thing she needed to do anyway. She
needed to let the origin spirits of Bat know that their shaman had died and
then send them away; otherwise they would remain around her family and
cause trouble, maybe even request that the family provide another shaman.
However, she hoped that some clues about the shaman's errors might be
revealed from the sending-off ritual.

Baasan invited the shaman Tsend, son of the legendary female shaman
Genen, to perform the ritual of *ongon hariulah* (sending off the spirit). The
ritual seemed to be successful. But a few days after it took place, Baasan
suddenly recalled that the main origin spirit of her family, Dugar, had not
been sent away. Bat had been initiated as a shaman particularly to attend
Dugar. But Baasan remembered that at the sending-off ritual Tsend did not
call Dugar's name and ask him to retreat. Did this mean that Dugar was
absent from the pantheon of origin spirits? Or did Tsend forget Dugar?

At dawn the next morning, Baasan mounted a horse and galloped off
to Tsend's house. She told the shaman that Bat's main origin spirit had
not been sent back at the ritual the other day. Tsend's wife became worried
about Baasan and scolded her husband: "Why did you not ask the names
of the origin spirits? How could you make such a mistake?"

But Baasan was convinced that the mistake was not Tsend's fault. Tsend
did not send off the spirit of the zaarin Dugar during his ritual for some
reason that was related to her brother's death. She hypothesized that Dugar
had not been invited to the first shanar, led by Chimeg, when her brother
was first being initiated as a shaman, and Dugar had never been connected
to Bat to begin with. Baasan told Tsend about the strange message that she

found in the Golden Box, which said that Bat died because he had "uttered an inappropriate name." With his prayer beads, Tsend began divining about each of Bat's origin spirits. He discovered that two of his five origin spirits were responsible for Bat's death: Domhor, the possessor of Bat's headdress, and Dugar. Domhor was a low-ranking female spirit, a savdag, and it was she who possessed Bat's headdress—one of the main attributes of a shaman's paraphernalia.

"Chimeg said that Domhor was eighteen years old," said Baasan.

"That is where things went wrong," responded Tsend. "Chimeg should have given the headdress to Dugar, who was a high-ranking spirit [he was a zaarin in his lifetime], instead of giving it to a lower-ranking spirit. If Dugar had had the headdress or the mirror, then he would not have let Bat die so easily."

Dugar was not among Bat's five spirits, but he was supposed to have been. This is where it all went wrong: Chimeg had not connected Dugar with Bat.

Baasan's Interpretation of Her Brother's Death

At first Chimeg had said that Bat was to be initiated as a shaman in order to attend Dugar, and she had promised Dugar the headdress. But during the actual ritual, when she was designating each item of the paraphernalia to individual origin spirits, she forgot or became confused and gave the headdress not to Dugar, as she had planned, but to an insignificant spirit named Domhor. Dugar got nothing, and thus he did not become Bat's origin spirit. However, because Chimeg had said that Dugar would be Bat's major spirit, Bat assumed that he had been connected to the spirit. So if Baasan's belief about Chimeg's forgetting to give Dugar the headdress is correct, then it appears that both Bat and Baasan also overlooked the fact that Chimeg missed Dugar's gift. Either lacking sufficient understanding about the shamanic rituals or by failing to pay enough attention to Chimeg's performance, neither Bat nor Baasan noticed Chimeg's mistake at the ritual.

After his first shanar Bat began staging his rituals, and he evoked Dugar in all of them. Now, the message from the Golden Box saying that Bat died because he had "uttered an inappropriate name" meant that during the rituals Bat called the name of the spirit Dugar. Because the spirit was not given the appropriate paraphernalia and did not become a part of the origin spirit pantheon, he "shot" Bat for calling on him essentially to nothing. Baasan concluded that Chimeg's sloppy ritual killed her brother. She became convinced that Chimeg was a business shaman who would do any-thing to make people stage rituals solely for her benefit.[6]

Tsend's Explanation of Baasan's Misfortune

The following was retold to me by Baasan because Tsend provided me with only a bare-bones account of the event in order to maintain the privacy of his clients.

According to Tsend, Bat was not supposed to be initiated as a shaman to begin with. (Again, Bat and Baasan received the same message at the beginning of their journey to different shamans.) The family would have been in better shape if it had just consistently worshipped the origin spirits with the help of an outside shaman. Chimeg should not have supported Bat and Baasan in their desperate quest to initiate one of them as a sha-man. Chimeg undoubtedly is a powerful shaman: she had "glued" the ori-gin spirits to a person who was not meant to be a shaman. That is a dan-gerous maneuver, and Bat was not the only victim. Tsend had to clean up Chimeg's mess for several people and separate them from their glued-on spirits. Most important, Chimeg made a terrible mistake when she told Bat that Dugar was his major spirit and promised Dugar a major piece of para-phernalia, only to forget it during the actual ritual. Had Dugar received a headdress or a mirror, he probably would not have harmed Bat.

Chimeg's Counterargument

Chimeg was well aware that Baasan blamed her for her brother's death. She disagreed with Baasan's accusations, but could not confront Baasan because she felt sorry about Baasan's brother's death. ("You cannot really start a fight with someone who is grieving over her only brother's death," she told me.) Chimeg explained to me that Bat died because he had pre-maturely called on the blacksmithing deity, Darhan Dorlik. Chimeg was against Bat's evoking him, because in order to call on Dorlik, a shaman needed to have performed at least three shanars, and Bat had completed only one. He did not listen to Chimeg's warnings and evoked Dorlik on his own. Bat died because he lacked the power and experience to handle a deity as powerful as Dorlik.

Chimeg explained this to me as we were passing by Baasan's house on the way to my place. "It is really terrible that Bat died," she said. "And I am so afraid of Baasan, because she accuses me of the death. But I did nothing wrong. Had he listened to me, he would have been fine." Chimeg linked her arm in mine. She spoke quietly, lowering her head. She never mentioned this story to me again, and I never heard her tell it to anyone else. Other shamans in the area knew Baasan's version—that Chimeg had made a mistake in giving a headdress not to Dugar, but to another spirit—because she consulted them in her search for the reasons behind her brother's death. Hardly anyone, however, knew Chimeg's explanation. Even if some of the shamans knew about it, no one mentioned it to me. Sunk in grief over the death of her disciple and taken aback by the powerful accusation against her, Chimeg was silenced. Bat's death and the stories around it further damaged Chimeg's reputation, and she continued to lose clients.

Within the tightly woven network of shamans, who are mostly (although not exclusively) male, female shamans tend to be pushed to the margins. In chapter 6 I discussed how male shamans advance in their quest for power faster than female shamans because they possess distinct gendered advantages owing to the patriarchal setting. Men's privileged situation in the patriarchal structures of kinship and in the domestic economy, not to mention their access to travel, allows them to build networks, stage shanars, and obtain paraphernalia much faster and easier than women, who lack these supporting structures. As a result, male shamans have a better chance of gaining the attributes necessary for them to be persuasive in their powers. Such powers are crucial in a place where truth does not simply consist of fact, but includes consensus, persuasion, and the display of power. In this male-dominated social setting, it is difficult to gauge the extent of the clients' objectivity, which they claim to employ in their search for truth. While I do not think that Baasan discriminated against Chimeg on the basis of gender, her decisions were heavily influenced by male shamans who were more influential and powerful than Chimeg. Even if Baasan is aware of the gendered disadvantages that curb female shamans' power, how would she balance that against the male shamans, who are able to provide more convincing answers because they happen to live in a society that enhances male power to begin with?

Within the realm of shamanic cosmology, it seemed to me that Chimeg's story was just as truthful as Baasan's. Darhan Dorlik is one of the most powerful deities in the pantheon of common spirits of the celestial court. He is not an origin spirit, but a communal deity, and as such is ranked above the origin spirits. An individual family will have its own personalized version of Dorlik, which is either inherited as a family divinity or created for a shaman as he or she gains power. In either case, Dorlik worship requires a high-ranking shaman. Every shaman's goal is to connect with Dorlik, since that provides the best shield from affliction. But not many shamans dared evoke him. And it was possible that Dorlik had killed Bat.

Laying shamanic cosmology aside, I thought that Bat could have died from any number of things associated with the harshness of daily life in Mongolia, including poor diet, bad alcohol, undiagnosed illnesses, and acute infections. Mongolian rural doctors are usually highly skilled and have great sensitivity, developed from working in harsh conditions without access to latest equipments and lab tests. Still, neither the experiences of the local physicians nor an autopsy that was performed on Bat by doctors at the provincial center could explain his death.

Hypothesis and Revelation: An Old Woman Who Settled on a Hearth

Baasan had figured out the main reason behind her brother's death: the shaman's mistake. She knew that the mistake needed to be fixed to avoid further consequences. In addition, she also had to prevent the misfortunes inflicted by her unrevealed and unworshipped origin spirits. She was also troubled by the two skulls that her brother saw before his death and by the fact that, despite all the rituals, they remained unidentified. Who were they, and why did they come to Baasan's family? In order to find answers to these questions, with her brother gone she had to continue her efforts on her own.

The night after Bat's death, Baasan's friend Sara, a fledgling female shaman, told Baasan that she saw in a dream that the spirit of a sad old woman had taken over Baasan's hearth. Baasan felt that this spirit was the human image of one of the two skulls her brother had seen in visions before his death. She went on to solicit advice. The diviners and shamans suggested that the old female spirit needed to be driven out from the hearth with a ritual. Two male shamans, Sergei and Jargal, volunteered to help Baasan with this ritual to express their condolences for her misfortune. (Later Baasan encountered the old female spirit again and discovered her identity, but at first she simply tried to drive her out.)

Having cleansed her hearth of the old female spirit (or so she thought), Baasan then propitiated her family's major protective deity, Higan Tengri— the deity of warfare and a member of the celestial court. The shaman Tsend had warned her many times, from early on, that Higan Tengri was her family's most important deity. Baasan chose the shaman Tömör to conduct the ritual; she believed in Tömör's efficacy because his father, Molom, had been most helpful to her family in the past. For two days and two nights Tömör beat his drum and sang to Higan Tengri, with only a two-hour break to prepare for the sacrifice of a sheep. The worship also required the staging of a small warfare scenario. Baasan's extended family rode around on horseback shooting arrows at an imagined enemy and imitated fighting with swords.

I was surprised that Baasan's family would worship Higan Tengri. What could they have to do with a deity of war? It was only later that I realized that the answer lies in the Buryats' history of oppression and resistance: Higan Tengri was the creator of Hoimorin Högshin, whom he had made in order to help the Buryats survive Russian colonial advances (see chapter 1). Meanwhile, the immediate benefit of the ritual was that it peeled off another layer of the unknown past. At the end of the ritual Tömör noted, "I 'see' there is someone in your family who exerts pollution." He could not, however, identify that entity.

In order to identify the entity that emanated pollution, Baasan then traveled to a diviner she trusted, a woman named Khorol. Divinations among Buryats usually follow a process of elimination. The client suggests several possible causes for their troubles, each represented by identical objects such as matchsticks (or identical rocks or sticks), without telling the diviner which one corresponds to which pollutant. The diviner tests the probability of each, rejecting the unlikely ones, until the most likely cause has been identified. Baasan suggested different pollutants, putting down one matchstick for each of the names of the origin spirits she suspected, some objects in the home that might have been polluted, the name of an ovoo, several potentially malevolent persons, and so on. Khorol eliminated everything in the first and second rounds; none of Baasan's nominees appeared to be the real pollutant. Thinking for a while, Baasan remembered Bat's Golden Box reading, which said that he died because the origin spirits had not been propitiated. But instead of putting down matchsticks representing the origin spirits whose names she already knew (and whom Bat *had* propitiated, if insufficiently), she put down a matchstick under the general term *övög deedes* (ancestors) in order to include the spirits of ancestors of whom she was not yet aware and who might be floating around unrecognized, not yet identified as origin spirits. In other words, she included the unrevealed or forgotten memory as a possible pollutant and a cause of illness.

Of the three suggestions put forward in the third round, each represented by a matchstick—the mountain spirit, objects, and the all-inclusive "ancestors"—Khorol picked up the last one and told Baasan, "This is the one who is making you sick." Properly called *övög deedsin uheerin buzar* (ancestral death pollution), it was a difficult one to eliminate. It indicated that unidentified ancestors were troubling Baasan. Now she had to identify them—find their names, where they had been born and died, and their place in Baasan's family's genealogy.

Once again Baasan frantically consulted various shamans and her friends about what she should do. She chose to follow the suggestion of Sara, a female shaman who also dreamed of an old woman on Baasan's hearth. She recommended, rather than a shamanic ritual, a Buddhist ritual that consisted of reciting the Luujin sutra, believed to be better than shamanic ceremonies for cleansing death pollutions and chasing away bad spirits from the hearth. It was considered to be a powerful ritual. Unlike a shamanic ritual, however, it did not reveal the identities of spirits, and it drove out the spirits collectively, without personalizing them. Baasan went around again to diviners to choose the right temple, settling on one in Ulaanbaatar. Pulling her resources together, she traveled about four hundred miles to a new temple called Ichin Choinhor. Baasan, accompanied by a city friend, was fascinated by it:

> We entered the temple through the main gates. There were three separate halls for sutra recitations and rituals: the main building, a little round building on the right, and a little round building on the left. In the administrative office on the right, there were an accountant and a secretary, then a big room for the *hamba* [chief lama or abbot] and his assistant. Everyone had a name tag. It was all very nice.

Baasan was too late to see the hamba at the temple that day, but she wanted her rituals to be held the next morning, since the date was auspicious. She asked the fire attendant, a young boy, how to find the hamba's house, and he gave her the address. Baasan met the hamba, an agile man despite his ninety or so years, in his ger. She told him about her brother's sudden death and that the Golden Box had revealed that her family had ancestral death pollution. The hamba divined with coins, suggesting that she have the sutra recited for the deity Choijoo (a messenger god to the Erlik Nomin Khan, or king of the dead), as well as having the Luujin sutra recited at her hearth. Baasan was pleasantly surprised at hamba's kindness and openness. It was quite unusual for a hamba lama to receive people at his home and immediately fulfill their requests.

Baasan was further impressed by the framed list of sutra titles with prices and accompanying offerings hanging on the wall of the temple. As Baasan saw, the Choijoo sutra was recited for seriously ill clients and was meant to cleanse curses from the dead. For the Choijoo rituals she needed 500 grams of barley flour, 200 grams of clarified butter, 500 grams of alcohol, and 2,000 tögrögs (US$1.80). Baasan described to me every single detail of her experience: the people's voices; the cashiers' faces; the furniture; the colors, shapes, and consistency of the offering cakes the temple made for the deities; the utensils and instruments used in the ceremonies; and the entire ritual procedure. "The recital of Luujin was so orderly, rhythmic, and convincing," she told me. "It was empowering to hear all the strong voices of the lamas merge into a single powerful chorus to deliver the recital. It was so enchanting, and they even shouted something that sounded like 'khui, khai, and khui, khai,' as if they were trying to startle or scare away the spirits."

Baasan had always visited Buddhist temples on her trips to Ulaanbaatar, and she was by no means new to temples. But her fascination with this particular temple suggested that it had something distinctive and special, creating a positive, persuasive, believable experience. What could that have been? Most people I met who had gone to other Buddhist temples remained elusive about their experiences, and no one enjoyed the rituals the way Baasan did. Like most Mongols, Baasan knew little about the ritual cosmologies, the meanings of the symbols, and the sutras' contents, since they are all in Tibetan. Unlike many other ambivalent clients, however, she was convinced that the rituals had their full effect on her. The pollutions were removed, her ailments were alleviated, and her body "felt lighter." I wanted to see what made this temple so persuasive and powerful.

So in August 2000, before returning to the United States, I went to the Ichin Choinhor temple in Ulaanbaatar to see if I could understand Baasan's fascination with it. The new temple specialized particularly in the *hatuu yum* ("hard" rituals) that exorcise demons and evil spirits in an unreformed Red Hat tradition of Buddhism, known as Nyingmapa. In addition, the temple provided all the services and rituals of the reformed Yellow Hat sect, Gelugpa—the dominant form of Buddhism in contemporary Mongolia. Built steps away from the last bus station at the edge of the northwestern ger district, it was easily accessible to both the rich, who arrived in their cars, and the poor, who came by bus. The temple was built into the natural landscape and supported by a high mountain to the north. When entering the temple, one sees not only the structured space in the yard, but also the mountain in the back.

I met with the hamba in his spacious, sunlit office. I asked him to divine my *noyon nuruu* (general well-being)—the most frequently made request. The hamba was humorous and easygoing. He joked that I had better get married soon, but also said that I should shun drunks and wife beaters, as there are so many of those out there. He was also concerned about the increase of births through cesarean deliveries as a result of increases in the age of childbearing. I came out of the temple thinking that the hamba's accessibility and unpretentiousness put visitors at their ease. Unlike in other Buddhist temples, this hamba's office was open every morning for a few hours so that visitors could consult him. It was rare for a hamba to serve the common people.

The temple had many other attractive elements as well: it specialized in "hard" rituals for ending ancestral curses, exorcising demons and evil spirits, and saving lives from the lords of the underworld. These ceremonies were in high demand. Every day at noon a chorus of more than twenty vigorous lamas, wearing black tasseled masks on their faces and tall pointed hats on their heads, recited the Luujin sutra to suppress bad spirits and demons. Their deep, robust, melodious voices filled every inch of space in the temple. The lamas' posture, their focus, the choreographed, dynamic twists of their heads, the synchronized swinging of their masks' black tassels, and sudden drum beating and cymbal clashing were captivating. It conveyed the sense of "formality, conventionality, stereotypy, and rigidity" that, according to Tambiah (1985:131), were the necessary elements for conveying the efficacy of a ritual performance. Overall, the rituals in this temple were more orderly and more meticulously choreographed than those in other temples I visited in Ulaanbaatar.

Besides the rituals, the mundane elements embedded in the structures of the temple's everyday life—the architecture, landscape, furniture, and attitudes of the staff—also contributed to a comforting sense of certainty, serenity, and completeness. They accentuated the power of the rituals and served as their prelude, continuation, and outcome. In that sense, the ritual began not at the actual sutra recital, but at the front gates, when a person entered the temple and left behind the bustle of everyday life. For people like Baasan, who lived in the nomadic countryside, the very existence of such a structure and act of entering the walled space of the temple would have made a distinct impression. Unlike in shamanic practice, where participants construct the ritual space within the living space and where the bustle in the kitchen, livestock husbandry, and other domestic tasks only aggravate the already hectic, messy, and labor-intensive shamanic rituals of possession, the temple was a quiet, meditative space removed from the stresses of daily life. The healing power of the temple of Ichin Choinhor lay at least in part in its empowering visual effect, therapeutic and stress-free environment, and competent management. For Baasan, who lived with bad spirits lurking around, settling on her hearth, and killing her family, the Ichin Choinhor temple was a place of refuge. It seemed that there could be no room here for bad spirits.

So far Baasan had gathered quite a bit of knowledge about her past. She had found a satisfactory answer to her brother's death in Chimeg's forgetting to give the headdress to the origin spirit Dugar, who then "shot" her brother. She had sponsored a ritual to send off the origin spirits whom her brother attended as a shaman. She had worshipped her family deity, Higan Tengri, which revealed that the source of her misfortunes was ancestral death pollution (presumably from the female ancestor who settled on her hearth and whom her shaman friend Sara had seen in her dreams). Baasan then had eliminated this pollution from her hearth by traveling to the Ichin Choinhor temple in Ulaanbaatar and having the proper Buddhist sutras recited.

Nevertheless, there was still a lot to uncover and take care of. Baasan wanted to find the identities of two skulls that her deceased brother saw

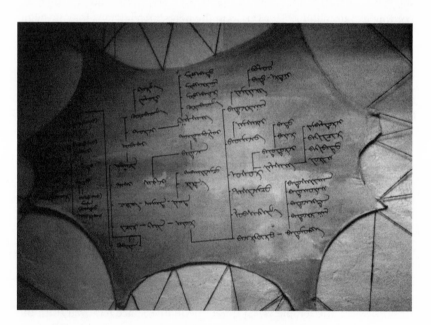

Figure 22. A sample genealogy in the local museum

Figure 23. A shaman in front of offerings for his origin spirits

Figure 24. Love and care across the generations

before his death. She drove out the ancestral pollution without identifying exactly which spirits were responsible for it. This is what most people in Mongolia do. The question is, though, to what extent is the driving out of the spirits without individualized rituals and without identifying them helpful? Such murkiness haunted her, and she strove to find her origin spirits and their individual identities. Baasan's search for her origin spirits will take her deep into her memories of her parents and her family history of loss, adoption, and love. She ultimately encountered the irremediable damage wrought by the state's violence against religion and memory and the impossibility of retrieving certain missing memories from the rubble of destruction.

Baasan's Memory of Her Father and Great-Grandmother

The images of the two human skulls that her brother saw on the family's hearth before his death and the old woman who was seen on her hearth continued to disturb and frighten Baasan. Who were they? What had brought them to her hearth? Even though she thought that the ritual of Luujin at the Ichin Choinhor temple had driven them out, at least temporarily, Baasan was still curious about their identities. In addition, although many of her origin spirits from the distant past were being revealed by the shamans, none of those spirits were identified as the two skulls at her hearth. As Baasan searched for answers to these questions, she suddenly recalled her father's three-generation biography and had an urge to read it.

The socialist state destroyed family genealogies as part of a campaign of forced forgetting. In the 1970s the state began requesting that everyone write an autobiography, a biography of their parents, and one of their grandparents—a three-generation biography-history of their family. Although the actual purpose behind this is not completely clear, one reason might have been to identify and weed out (or take note of) those individuals whose grandparents had been victims of political violence because they came from feudal, upper-class, clerical, or politically suspect backgrounds.[7] These three-generation biographies were one of many ways the state generated and controlled memories by fitting them into the parameters of socialist ideology.

Baasan's father lived and worked before the three-generation biographies became mandatory in the 1970s. He died without such a document. But the state acknowledged his administrative work, wrote his biography, and presented it to his children, Baasan and Bat. For the family, it was an honor. The biography was written to fit socialist ideology, but some facts also led Baasan to reconstruct an important part of her family history that up until then had been missing.

First, Baasan checked the dates during which her father, Sanjaa, had served in the army. They fell during the political repressions of 1937–1940, at the peak of Stalin's state purges. This was also the time when Japan was encroaching on the Mongolian border. Stalin accused the Buryats of being Japanese allies, and arrested Buryats on a daily basis. Baasan knew that while her father, Sanjaa, was serving in the army, both his father and his grandmother had died within a year of each other. She remembered what her father used to tell her about that time of terror and persecution:

> While in the army, my father received a note from home saying that his father [Amar] had died. My father [Sanjaa] felt rather peaceful and relieved to learn that his father had died a natural death at home, without experiencing the horrors of persecution, jail, and torture. But when he received a note that his grandmother [Otgon] died, he grieved for months and cried his heart out in bed. He was extremely close to his grandmother.

When Baasan recalled the dates and circumstances of the deaths of her great-grandmother, Otgon, and grandfather, Amar, she became convinced that the two skulls her brother Bat saw before he died represented these two ancestors. Otgon and Amar had died at a time of repression and could not receive proper burials, mourning, and rituals of sending their souls to the next destination. "There was hardly anyone courageous enough to seek a lama to recite sutras. Whispering a mantra was the best most people could do at the time," said Baasan. Without the proper rituals of mourning and grieving, souls do not leave the living in peace, but come back to torment them.

Otgon and Amar were ordinary people. They were not shamans or lamas, so after death their souls were not destined to become origin spirits. But even the souls of ordinary people need proper burials and rituals. With appropriate burials and mourning rituals, they would be able to find their next reincarnations and leave their living descendants in peace. But because they had been improperly buried and inadequately mourned, their souls were trapped on earth with the living, becoming uheer—malignant, tormented spirits—and settling on Baasan's hearth to trouble her and others.

It seemed logical to Baasan that the shamans with whom she consulted could not identify the two skulls on her hearth; after all, they were not origin spirits, but uheer, who, unlike origin spirits, have no identity. Shamans are possessed by origin spirits, but they avoid uheer. Baasan, however, needed either to drive them out or to appease them and make them benev-olent. But how? What were these uheer? And how could they be placated?

When a Loved One Becomes an Uheer

Trapped in the human world and trying to return to life, the souls of the unnamed, unmourned dead roam the human world. Although Otgon and Amar died peaceful, natural deaths, for example, they still became uheer because under the state's religious suppression they did not receive proper burials or mourning rituals. And if those who died natural deaths in the time of persecution became uheer, then what happened to the people whose lives ended prematurely—those who were killed, tortured, and dis-appeared? Did they also become uheer? Or did they turn into other in-visible creatures yet to be discovered? After all the worship of their origin spirits and their family's inherited Buddhist deities, why do the Buryats keep having requests for more rituals? Why is it that there is no end to bad luck, no end to the ancestral requests for gifts and rituals of respect, and no end to the rituals of *ugaal* (washing off)? These are not only the result of shamans' manipulation of the audience for gifts and power. One reason the Buryats' misfortunes do not end is that they are dealing with uheer, sometimes without even realizing it. Uheer, unfortunately, are eternal, and they torment the living without revealing themselves. Mute and elusive, they represent gaps in the historical memory and reveal the silenced world of the totalitarian regime in which the Buryats were caught for most of the twentieth century. By silently afflicting their descendants, uheer force the living to become aware of the suppressed tragedies of their past. Just as Baasan was forced to recover her memories, uheer force the living con-sciously to retrieve memories suppressed by the state.

As already mentioned, the most important problem is that appeasing ancestors (including uheer) in one setting—collectively, as many people, including Baasan, have done—does not work very well, because frequently the offerings do not reach each one of the many uheer roaming around. Every single ancestor has to be identified, recognized, and worshipped in-dividually, without discrimination, whether he or she became an unfor-tunate uheer or a revered origin spirit. Bat and Baasan's numerous rituals were ineffective because some of the ancestors became not origin spirits, but uheer. The problem is that the shamans are not uheer specialists—they are mediators for the origin spirits. Hypothetically, uheer specialists should be in great demand.

We might wonder why Baasan chose these two particular ancestors, Otgon and Amar, to identify as the two skulls on her hearth. What if these two skulls represent other ancestors? Obviously, no one can know the "truth" behind the two skulls. Instead, it is important to ask why Baasan identified the skulls with these two and not others. As Steedly reminds us, "The issue here is not truth, but memory, not what really happened," but why certain events are being remembered and retold in one particular way and not another (2000:838).

Baasan's associating of the two skulls with victims of state violence was a way of attending to the silences imposed by the dominant nationalist narrative. Most Buryats subscribe to the dominant Mongolian narrative that the violence of 1937–1940 was imposed on them by Stalin and that Mongolia (a "small nation") could do little about it. Yet just because the Buryats chose not to blame the Mongolian state does not mean that they had forgotten the pain of the violence or decided quietly to accept the abuse. The Buryats express their discontent not through explicit narratives about the violence, but through uheer—the product of violence. Baasan's identification of the two skulls with two ancestors who had died during the time of terror and had not received the appropriate rituals of mourning was an indirect reproach to the state. Thus, Baasan's identification shows the two worlds to which the Buryats belong: the national and the ethnic. As a part of the Mongolian nation-state, the Buryats bear the consequences of Mongolia's geopolitical domination by its more powerful neighbors. At the same time, within Mongolia the ethnic Buryats at various times in history had been oppressed by the dominant Khalkhas. What is poignant about the uheer is that while they symbolize the repercussions of both geopolitical and state violence, it is the most unfortunate and impoverished individuals, such as Baasan, who have to confront them and pacify them. Otherwise, the uheer were going to destroy Baasan's golomt (hearth). She was on the brink of yet more knowledge. When Baasan propitiated Amar and Otgon, new knowledge about the past was revealed.

Memory and Oblivion

The golomt is the core of the Mongolian family in both the physical and the conceptual sense. Physically the golomt is the center of the ger. Conceptually, the nuclear family is raised in the space around the fireplace. In the genealogical records, each name implies the existence of an individual hearth. Older children create their own golomts, but the youngest son is responsible for maintaining and continuing his parents' golomt. Hoimorin Högshin is the Buryat deity in charge of the well-being of the golomt and of protecting children from death and sickness. She is a communal spirit, but every family worships its own version. If Hoimorin Högshin gets upset, then children suffer from illness, the hearth cracks, and eventually a family might gradually die out. She is said to be especially hard on male children, because they are the carriers of their family hearth and genealogical records.

Baasan had identified the images of two skulls that her brother saw before his death as her grandfather, Amar, and great-grandmother, Otgon. Neither Amar nor Otgon was mourned properly during the time of terror, so they became uheer. Thus Baasan needed to make up for the inadequate mourning and rituals and give merit to their afterlife. To do so, she needed to find their identities: their full names, the places where they had lived, and the names of their parents, grandparents, and so on through the lineage. Baasan's task was to make enough merit and stage enough individual rituals for these two individuals so that their souls, which had been turned into uheer, could find their proper places in the afterlife and take different forms.

Baasan knew her grandfather's immediate ancestors from the stories that she had heard from her own parents. Baasan was the daughter of Sanjaa, who was the son of Amar, who was the son of Tseveg, Tseveg who was the son of Davaa. This was all that Baasan knew about her father's ancestral genealogy, because her family genealogy was burned during the political violence in the 1930s.

Baasan knew little about Amar's mother, Otgon, and her ancestral genealogy. Among the patrilineal and patrilocal Buryats, women rarely maintain the genealogies of their birth families. Their names are for the most part absent from the genealogies of both their marital and their birth homes. Once women marry, they also leave behind the origin spirits of their birth families. Leaving out the origin spirits of female ancestors from propitiation was customary. Otgon and her origin spirits were supposed to have little importance for her descendants.

Because the Buryats are patrilineal, most people logically assume that their ancestors are male. While this idea corresponds to the patrilineal ideology, the situation is different in real life. I think that Otgon appeared on Baasan's hearth as an old woman (the second time, after Bat died) specifically to make clear that she was not a male but a female ancestor.

It was not enough to appease only Otgon. Otgon's origin spirits and the deities whom she used to propitiate during her lifetime also needed propitiation. Only they could save Otgon's tormented soul from remaining trapped in the realm of the spirits. Once Otgon's soul found her designated place, she would leave Baasan and her family in peace. But Baasan knew almost nothing about Otgon, not even her full name. In addition to the fact that Buryat women's names are absent from their families' genealogies, Otgon's background was even more obscure because she was not Amar's biological mother, so her surname and her immediate ancestors were not remembered by her grandchildren. In her family, she was the *högshin eej* (old mother), the Buryats' kin term for a paternal grandmother that all grandchildren use.

Otgon had adopted Amar, and although he lived with her as a part of her extended family and continued her golomt, he never transferred his name to her genealogy. Amar kept the name of his biological father within his lineage and propitiated his biological father's origin spirits. Amar continued his biological father's lineage, but he procreated on his adoptive mother's hearth.

Baasan now realized that the fact that Amar was Otgon's adopted child did not mean that she was of no significance for Baasan and the other descendants. Baasan and the rest of the family could no longer trace themselves as belonging only to their grandfather Amar's birth family. They were leaving out the place where they came into being—great-grandmother Otgon's hearth. The place of origin was just as important as the lineage.

It was important to know the story of Otgon's adoption of Amar. Through it, Baasan reconstructed her lost genealogy. But this genealogy is not a list of names of ancestors that takes the reader into infinity. Instead of the expected lengthening, which implies perfect marriages, plentiful children, and neat relationships, this one widens, telling stories of love, death, misfortunes, and failed families. This is the genealogy that is built from women's perspective and with the inclusion of women. Constructed on emotionally moving stories about love, neglect, shattered hearths, and the pain of losing and building relationships, this genealogy is about the contradictions in a patrilineal society in which women play prominent roles but receive little official recognition. The genealogy, which shows Baasan's misfortunes, is a constitutive part of the Buryats' history, memory, and place-making.

A Genealogy of Love and Care

Otgon's ancestral past is surrounded by oblivion. And the most distant knowledge that Baasan learned about Otgon begins with a tragedy. Otgon initially had two children, a daughter and a son. A few years after they had started their own families, they both died. Otgon's daughter died while sailing across the Ingedei River in Russian Buryatia with her husband and their two small children; their boat flipped over during a particularly windy day, and they drowned in the river. Then Otgon's son died suddenly while chopping firewood in front of his ger. He left behind his wife, an adopted daughter, and their infant girl. Otgon was left with her daughter-in-law and her two small granddaughters. Her daughter-in-law was in a difficult situation. She could not decide whether to take her little daughters and go to her birth home or stay with her mother-in-law.

Otgon saddled her horse and traveled to see a local family, Tseveg and his wife, who had many grown-up children. Otgon pleaded with them to give her one of their sons to adopt. Tseveg and his wife told her that since all their children were grown, they would have to make their own decisions. Otgon was to talk to each of them in person. Three of the sons were at home, but none of them wanted to become Otgon's son. She was heartbroken. Seeing this, Tseveg and his wife told her she should also talk to their youngest son, Amar, just then at work in a Russian gold mine. When he came back late that night, Otgon begged him to become her son. Amar agreed; he was thirty years old and single. Otgon was so happy that she would not stop bowing in front of the family's altar to their gods and deities. The Tseveg family felt awkward; they wanted her to stop bowing. But instead of asking her to stop bowing, they graciously invited her to have tea and something to eat.

Otgon and Amar saddled their horses and went to Otgon's place that same night. Otgon's ger was next to that of her deceased son, where her daughter-in-law lived with the two grandchildren. Otgon was well aware that she was forcing an arranged marriage onto Amar and her widowed daughter-in-law. Feeling guilty about imposing her will and worried about whether the two would ever accept each other, she would secretly stand outside the new couple's ger and listen to hear whether they spoke to each other. The silence lasted for weeks. As Baasan remembered, "Otgon's birth son, who died from an accident during wood chopping, was a tall, handsome, and a charming man. But my grandfather [Amar] was short, quiet, and shy. It probably took a while for my grandmother to accept her new husband."

When Otgon finally heard the couple speaking to each other, she was relieved. They eventually had more than a dozen children, but only Baasan's father, Sanjaa, and three girls survived. They grew up at Otgon's hearth, and their childhood memories were filled with stories about their grandmother. Otgon spoiled her grandchildren, especially Sanjaa, her only grandson. Sanjaa slept in his grandmother's *övört* (chest) bed until the age

of seven. No wonder, then, that when his grandmother Otgon died while
was serving in the army in the late 1930s, "he cried his heart out," but
when his father died, he was not nearly so distraught.

Said Baasan:

> We have been propitiating the origin spirits of my grandfather Amar and
> his birth family [Tseveg] all this time, but we had abandoned Otgon, the
> woman who adopted my grandfather, Amar. She created a new family on
> her hearth by adopting Amar, and she was the most important person in her
> grandchildren's lives. We are the children of her hearth, and she is just as
> important to us as Amar's birth family. We were unable to properly bury her,
> so of course, she has been returning to us for propitiation.

Baasan speculates that as descendants of Amar's lineage who were born at
Otgon's hearth, they needed to propitiate both Amar's and Otgon's origin
spirits and their deities. But so far they had been propitiating only Amar's
origin spirits, forgetting about Otgon's side.

Otgon's return to her descendants as an uheer is remarkable on several
levels. It destabilizes the notion of a lineage and genealogy based on biological procreation or on a list of the names of male ancestors. Her claim to
be an ancestor has been nurtured through her strong emotional ties with
her grandchildren (particularly with Baasan's father) and on her tangible
effort to create and raise a family at her hearth. Here the emotional ties
and effort created by the hearth compete with the official patriarchal and
patrilineal norms through which males automatically become ancestors.
As Baasan put it, "Otgon is the most significant of all ancestors. We must
cherish her efforts, her merit, and we must create merit for her."

The God of Warfare, Hoimorin Högshin, and Forgotten Ancestors

In order to help Otgon, who had turned into an uheer, Baasan went to the
shaman Tömör and told him what she thought was going on. When Tömör
heard that Otgon's daughter had drowned with her husband while crossing the Ingedei River, Tömör almost jumped out of his seat. He quickly
made a connection between Otgon's misfortunes and the Hoimorin Högshin: "The Ingedei River is a place of habitation of Hoimorin Högshin. The
reason Otgon's daughter drowned in the Ingedei, and that her son died
too, must be that her Hoimorin Högshin had been abandoned. I'll bet that
the deity had destroyed the hearths of Otgon's ancestors as well as Otgon's

own hearth, and now she is continuing to destroy the hearths that Otgon had created by adopting Amar!"

Tömör told Baasan to have a ceremony of Luujin (driving off the demons and uheer) right at her hearth, and that he and another shaman, Dagva, would take care of the propitiation of Otgon's Hoimorin Högshin. Now Baasan realized that although for she had been propitiating the Hoimorin Högshin of Amar's birth family (Tseveg and his wife) all these years, it had never occurred to her to think about Otgon's Hoimorin Hogshin. Baasan was told to propitiate the deity of warfare, Higan Tengri, because it was he who sent Hoimorin Högshin to the Buryats. Baasan and her extended family were the biological children of Tseveg, Amar, and Sanjaa. But in the parallel shamanic cosmos, they were also the children of Otgon's hearth, whose ancestors should have been just as important to them as their biological ancestors.

The biggest problem was that Otgon built her new family by bringing Amar to her shattered hearth without reconstituting her family's Hoimorin Högshin. The future generations of her new family were in danger of dying out, just as her own two children had died. Amar's children survived at least in part because they were under the protection of the Hoimorin Högshin from Amar's birth lineage. Amar's son Sanjaa and three girls survived, but the other ten children died. Sanjaa also had more than ten children, but only Bat and Baasan survived their childhood, and Bat died when he was forty-five. Baasan is convinced that she and Bat, being the third generation of Amar's lineage, are too far removed from the protection of the origin spirits of their great-great-grandfather's biological family. Bat's suffering during his lifetime and his premature death, and Baasan's life-threatening illnesses and lack of children, were partially related to the fact that the protections from Amar's birth family were too distant and the ties had been weakened. At the same time, Baasan was convinced, they needed at least some protection from Otgon and her origin spirits and deities.

Although the shamans were able to create Otgon's vanished Hoimorin Högshin, no one could find anything out about her other origin spirits. Baasan had no leads to Otgon's origin spirits, either in her birth family or in the family that she married into. She did not even know Otgon's full name, whether she had any siblings, whether she was ever married, or where her two children who had died came from. Her genealogical records were absent, so there was no way to find out about her origin spirits and where they had lived.

Baasan finished her story by saying that she began hearing someone's voice at night from somewhere near the closet. It was a woman's voice,

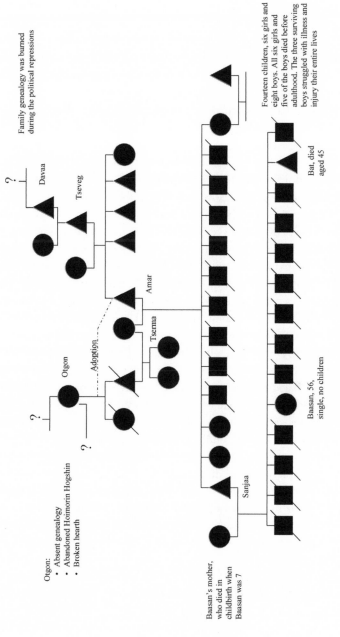

Otgon:
• Absent genealogy
• Abandoned Hoimorin Hogshin
• Broken hearth

Family genealogy was burned
during the political repressions

? Davaa

Tseveg

Otgon

? Adoption

? Amar

Tserma

Baasan's mother,
who died in
childbirth when
Baasan was 7

Sanjaa

Baasan, 56,
single, no children

Bat, died
aged 45

Fourteen children, six girls and
eight boys. All six girls and
five of the boys died before
adulthood. The three surviving
boys struggled with illness and
injury their entire lives

Chart 2. Baasan's genealogy chart

melodious and soft, and Baasan did not feel frightened. Then she felt that someone was following her as she walked home from gathering firewood with her nephews and nieces. She felt that figure, big and manly, coming close and wanting to put his hands on her shoulders. She went to several diviners, and they told her that these were her origin spirits, who would help her.

I have traced Baasan's journeys to find the reasons behind her misfortunes. People who had suffered the storms of the market economy also tended to have destroyed genealogies, opaque origins and pasts, and angrier origin spirits. The poorest people had the largest number of uheer and owed not only money to the shopkeepers in Bayan-Uul, but also gifts of sheep and cattle to the spirit world. Their lives were incomplete because their genealogies were missing, their origin spirits had gone unpropitiated, and the memories of their loved ones had been forgotten or suppressed.

Baasan made an explicit connection between Otgon's Hoimorin Högshin and the deaths in her extended family. Baasan's mother died in childbirth after having given birth to more than ten children, though only two survived. Baasan's paternal cousin (Sanjaa's sister, another of Amar's grandchildren) had fourteen children, six girls and eight boys. All six girls and five of the boys died in their youth or as children (see chart 2). The remaining three boys struggled with illnesses and accidents throughout their lives. One was brain damaged in a car accident. Another fell off a bridge and broke his back. (I knew this cousin; the accident happened when he was around forty years old. He went to see doctor after doctor, but without much luck. After years of living with tremendous pain, he died in 2001.) The third son is sick with an undiagnosed illness.

I charted Baasan's genealogy according to the stories she told me. It was more about people who had died than ones who had survived, and it developed more in width than in length. Baasan believes that the genealogy her uncle burned in 1937 would have helped her to find her origins. But without it, the memories she had lost remained empty spaces.

Fragments of the Past

Through Baasan's journey we have visited at least three realms: that of Buryat deities and communal spirits, that of shamans, and that of an individual family's origin spirits and genealogy. Each evokes certain kinds of knowledge from the past and carries a specific message. Together they contribute to the Buryats' attempt to complete their history, genealogical records, and worship of their abandoned origin spirits. They help to mend the Buryats' history, which was ruptured; their identity, which was suppressed; and their memory, which was manipulated.

Deeper meanings lie behind the many findings Baasan made in each realm. In order to find the communal Buryat deities Hoimorin Högshin and Higan Tengri, Baasan revisited the distant history of oppression and resistance, her ancestral homeland, and migration. The abandoned mountain spirit in Russian Buryatia whose curses she suffered was an ancestor whose awareness and importance were left behind when the Buryats migrated from their Russian-settled lands to Mongolia. Higan Tengri's cult, involving horseback racing, archery, and fighting, at first seemed out of place to me, but he appears to be a ritualized commemoration of the Buryats' struggle against their warring neighbors and the constant threat of colonialism. Higan Tengri was significant for the Buryats both in times of war and during periods of less violent resistance to Russian settlement, when Higan Tengri was said to have sent the Buryat people the Hoimorin Högshin, a deity protective of children and the hearth. Each Buryat family had its own version of the deity to help them survive the harshness of life under geopolitical oppression. In addition to these communal spirits, Baasan also became acquainted with the origin spirits of her lineage, Hal'bin such as the zaarin Dugar; his father, Navaan; and a lowland spirit named Domhor. Unfortunately, Baasan's belief in Chimeg's mistake as a reason for her brother's death made her connection with them unpleasant. Moreover, Baasan discovered that in addition to worshipping the spirits of her biological clan, the Hal'bin, she also belonged emotionally to Otgon's clan, whose identity was unknown. In this case, the stories of the spirits of the Hal'bin clan (i.e., Dugar and others) were actually less important than the stories about Otgon and her missing past.

Having lost her two children, Otgon in desperation adopted Amar as her son so that he would marry her widowed daughter-in-law, who was still living with her. That was how Otgon built a new family and became the head of it. But because she was a woman in a patrilineal and patrilocal society, after she died her descendants forgot her. After her death Otgon's soul clung to the hearth of her descendants—the descendants of the new family that she had built. Over time her soul became an uheer and began harming her descendants. Baasan nevertheless felt enormous regard for her great-grandmother, and so she continued her journey to save Otgon's soul. Like a child whose beloved mother has gone mad for reasons beyond her control, Baasan was trying to understand and accept the anger and pain, and the demands, of the uheer Otgon.

Baasan's journey has led us to explore the domain of the contemporary

shamans of Bayan-Uul, their politics, competition, and techniques of persuasion. Baasan is remarkably well situated within the web of shamans.
She was a client of the shaman Molom before he died in 1997. Afterward
she sought the services of his son Tömör. She also went so far as to solicit
help from Undarmaa, a female shaman who migrated to Ulaanbaatar. She
also consulted with Tsend, the son of the legendary female shaman Genen;
the shaman Jargal, who later committed suicide; Baigal, the granddaughter
of Khorlo, who also practiced in secret during socialism; Chimeg, whom
Baasan disbelieved from the first; Sara, a fledgling shaman; Khorol, a female diviner; and many other practitioners of various ranks, backgrounds,
and skills whom I did not introduce for reasons of time and space. Furthermore, Baasan also went to one of the best Buddhist ritual temples in
Ulaanbaatar, to the very home of the hamba. More Buddhist consultations
were involved—for example, the lama who opened the Golden Box and
Baasan's old acquaintance Sahia, whom I never managed to visit or become acquainted with. And this list includes only the names of major shamans. Baasan consulted many more whom I omitted from my narrative.
Shamanism operates in a larger network of religious pluralism, accepting,
competing with, but also negating Buddhism and other religious systems.

Baasan's greatest revelation was finding clues to her origins and learning to accept her loss, the empty frame for unspoken, absent, and erased
memories. These were things that shamans could not reveal and the origin
spirits could not talk about. For instance, Otgon and Amar were not direct victims of repression; they were not taken to jail, tortured, or killed.
They died natural deaths. Yet indirectly they were still victims of repression.
Their souls did not find their designated places and instead became uheer,
similar to the souls of people who had been the tortured, mutilated, and
murdered—the victims of repression.

The State through the Veins of Its Citizens

Baasan talks about the intimate nature of the state without necessarily
seeing its pervasive and ubiquitous presence. She told me about her experiences with a school and a hospital, the two most widespread state
institutions:

> When I was seven years old, I began having seizures. Then, when I was nine,
> my mother died in childbirth. That year the school administration failed
> to put insulation around the walls of the school building. The heat from
> the stove escaped with the wind that blew through the space between the

walls and the earth. In order to warm up, during breaks the teachers crowded around a stove in the directors' room while we students wrestled with each other in the classroom. At the end of a six-hour school day, I could not feel my feet; they froze even in felt boots. It was a difficult life; I was sick with chronic bronchitis and depressed over my mother's death, and I continued to have seizures. On top of all that, I contracted tuberculosis. It was in the late 1950s, when the state organized a campaign for eradicating infectious diseases. During the tuberculosis test, I was diagnosed as being free of the disease, but a month later I fell ill. I think it happened because my body's resistance at that time was so low that it got infected from the tiny amount of specimen in the test.

The school and the hospital represented the state's magnanimous ideals of socialism and its impoverishment in everyday life. Ideally, the school was a center for knowledge, but in reality, it was a place for wrestling to fight the cold, freezing one's feet, getting bronchitis, and having seizures. The hospital was more a display of the power of the modern state than a place where sick people came to be healed. During the state campaign for the eradication of infectious diseases, doctors and nurses in starched white uniforms enthusiastically performed their tests in regional hospitals, tents, and cabins, amazing the locals with the newest Soviet technology and an abundance of resources. Yet when Baasan got sick, she could not find the services and care promised by the state. The local doctors could not diagnose her, so she traveled to another clinic a two-day trip. Baasan was sick with a severe case of tuberculosis for an entire year.

Baasan's experience with the school and hospital shows that in reaching out to the bodies and minds of people to register and the population and take a census, the state stretched itself too thin. Instead of eradicating tuberculosis, as promised, the state ended up inflicting it. But the state had to maintain its power, and so it manifested its magnanimity in an eclectic and limited fashion. After Baasan graduated from high school, she was accepted at the Mongolian State University, then returned to Bayan-Uul to teach at the local high school.

I emphasized some of Baasan's experiences with the state in order to show how its presence in her life was consistent and taken for granted. The absence of the state from people's lives was more noticeable and more unusual than its presence. Bat, unlike Baasan, was excluded from the state. He did not get a formal education and thus never had a career. Bat was therefore considered an anomaly under socialism. His biological death was preceded by his social and emotional death.

Altogether Baasan made thirty-seven trips to shamans, lamas, diviners, and others to try to find the reasons behind her misfortunes. These were not brisk walks from one end of Bayan-Uul to the other; they involved long-distance transportation, the purchase of gifts for the shaman, and extensive planning. The trips allowed Baasan to create a departure from the state's presence in her life and to explore her desire for a closer connection with her origin spirits and communal deities, and to build a network of shamans that could support her through her ongoing misfortunes. Baasan's attempts to find meaning and her accumulation of multiple meanings in order to comprehend her experiences have served as a kind of healing. Her efforts relate to Kleinman's argument that the very act of making suffering meaningful helps a patient cope with it (Kleinman 1988). Shamans convey what is known and what can be known by bringing us the stories of origin spirits from the distant past. The clients travel to piece together those stories, and in so doing they attend to the missing and the silenced. If shamans bring us the stories of the spirits, clients such as Baasan bring us the continuity of such stories as well as the silence of the uheer, the outcasts of the spirit world and the outcomes of state violence.

NOTES

1. Each *sum* (administrative district) in Mongolia has a *sumin töv* (sedentary center), a settlement that is more or less equivalent to a small rural town.

2. The Buryat term *ug garval* literally translates as "origin beings." Since these are spirits of dead shamans returning to their descendants, "origin spirits" seems to capture the actual meaning of the term.

3. All translations are mine unless otherwise indicated.

4. See Rossabi (2005) for the details on the implementation of neoliberal reforms. The term "shock therapy" was coined by the economist Jeffrey Sachs, although he claims that the term has been misunderstood. For a more detailed discussion about "shock therapy," see the PBS interview of Sachs (2000) and his paper on the topic delivered at University of Utah in 1994.

5. For recent works on witchcraft in African countries see Geschier (1997), Comaroff and Comaroff (1999), Moore and Sanders (2004), and Ashforth (2005); for a treatment of the same material in the context of Indonesia, see Siegel (2006).

6. In Buyandelgeriyn (2007) I discuss in detail how shamans are constantly suspected of malpractice, manipulation, attaching spirits to clients who are not supposed to be initiated as shamans, and controlling their clients through their own spirits.

7. In a somewhat similar mode, Yang (2000:494) notes that "'capitalism' in rural Wenzhou is actually a series of hybridizations of different economic forms—indigenous (ritual, tributary state, and household/market economies), state socialist, and overseas capitalist elements—which combine and recombine in novel and contradictory ways."

8. While living among the Buryats, I too tacitly hoped that shamanic proliferation would bring at least some improvement in the local economy through payment to shamans, the emergence of temporary jobs such as making paraphernalia, and attracting long-distance clients and perhaps international tourists.

9. Some comprehensive accounts of Mongolia's postsocialist transformation and privatization are given in Heaton (1992), Broon and Odgaard (1996), and Rossabi (2005), among others.

10. For the purpose of clarity, I have delineated socialism from capitalism by using the letters H1A and H1B.

11. This is similar to the idea of building an "unofficial" history based on the stories

narrated by shamanic spirits. It comes from an inspiring book by Steedly (1993), in which she weaves together a history from the stories of Karo spirit mediums in a ritual arena in Karoland, Indonesia.

12. See Flaherty (1992) for details about Catherine the Great's Russification of Siberia and her persecution of shamans.

13. As some scholars of postsocialism (Verdery 1996, Burawoy and Verdery 1999, Humphrey 2002) have shown, instead of the promised transition to capitalism, a great range of socioeconomic and cultural configurations has emerged in Russia and Eastern Europe; some operate like feudal fiefdoms, others are based on merchant capitalism, and still others even reestablish the dismantled and privatized collectives.

14. Herzfeld (1985) argues that among Greek men there is a focus on "being good at being a man" rather than "being a good man" (1985:17–18). This notion emphasizes the value of performative skills in everyday actions, such as doing one's work with flair, performing a conventional dance with a slight twist, or even being good at stealing. The goal of this performativity is to imbue commonplace occurrences with specific meanings. Women, as Herzfeld (1991) discusses, play up their submissive role through exaggeration, cunning, deceit, and irony as ways of resistance. These silent acts of "protest may have little effect on the language-centered, legalistic, combative world of men," but they are nevertheless important for launching group action and ideological subversion. Still, Herzfeld is convinced that words would make these actions "binding . . . [and] official" (Herzfeld 1991:95–96).

15. There is no noun in either Buryat or Mongolian that corresponds to the English word "memory." The closest term is *sanamj*, meaning "memento"—a static object that triggers the act of remembering.

16. Like other Mongols, they use *tuukhe* in conjunction with *soyol* (*tuukhe soyol*) to mean culture as a product to refer very generally to their customs, habits, and distinctive identities; *tuukhe* is the term that comes closest to the meaning of "culture" in an anthropological sense.

17. In the anthropological literature, they are also identified as a segment of the Eastern Buryats (Humphrey 1983).

18. Mikhailov (1980, 1987) and others have written about the debates on the origins of the Buryats and the common identity that they have developed due to Russian colonial administration.

19. By "official history of Mongolia," I mean the textbooks produced during socialism. One was published in three volumes in 1956, 1968, and 1969 under the title *History of the Mongolian People's Republic* [*Bugd Nairamdah Mongol Ard Ulsyn tuukh*]; see Shirendyv and Natsagdorj (1956–1969). Another is by Bira and Natsagdorj (1984).

20. According to the 2010 census, there are 45,085 Buryats in Mongolia, making them the country's fifth-largest ethnic group.

21. Many different Buryat subgroups live outside of Mongolia, scattered over a vast area east of Lake Baikal in Russia and northeastern China. Although the Buryats are linguistically related, they consist of peoples of different tribes and ethnic origins. Because in the past they became parts of different political formations in Mongolia, Russia, and China, their historical faiths often diverge from each other.

22. See Meyers and Pels (2003) for a discussion on the relationship between magic, shamanism, and modernity.

23. See Flaherty (1992) on Catherine the Great's influence on shamanism in Siberia. On changes in the ways shamans have been represented in the Western imagination, print, and media, see Bernstein (2006).

24. Humphrey (1996) follows a similar line in discussing the terms "shaman" and "sha-manism." In order to deconstruct the established narrow view of the phenomenon, Thomas and Humphrey (1996) include various inspirational practices from around the world that conventionally lie outside shamanism.

25. Tambiah (2007 [1975]) discusses the "domestication" of spirits—the transforma-tion of the spirits from vindictive into benevolent forces through the simultaneous transformation of the afflicted from a sick person to a master of the spirit. In some instances healing among the Buryat Mongols is similar to this process. This is an example of the prevalence of the phenomenon and helps to blur distinctions made simply on a technical basis between shamanism and other inspirational practices.

26. I was told that some researchers who came to Bayan-Uul and neighboring districts could not study a number of shamans because of the antagonism among them. One of the researchers who followed one particular shaman closely was denied ac-cess to the others.

CHAPTER ONE

1. The Buryats do not use the term "celestial court." They prefer to name particular dei-ties, or they use euphemisms, such as *deedsuud* (the higher beings), *tenger ner* (the celestial gods), and *ongod* (spirits). Because these words do not distinguish between the origin spirits and the ruling hierarchy of spirits, I use the term "celestial court" to mark the differences and to encompass the group of generic spirits against origin spirits.

2. In Buryat, *högshin* specifically indicates an elder female relative; an elder man can refer to his wife as *högshin*, and children call their grandmothers *högshin ejii*. That is different from the ways in which Khalkha Mongolians use the same word, which means "old" and does not address nuances related to gender and kinship, as it does in Buryat.

3. *Chandagat* is also the general term for a species of rabbit.

4. Humphrey (1983) and Forsyth (1992:87–89).

5. Rumyantsev (1962), Humphrey (1979), and Batuev (1996:32–33).

6. The first Russian mention of the Buryats dates back to 1609. In a letter to Czar Vasili IV, the chiefs of the Tomsk district mentioned that they could not pay *yas-sak* (tribute) to the czar because the Bratskiye people had taken it before the czar's tribute collectors arrived. Other chiefs of neighboring districts also wrote to the czar that they could no longer pay tribute because they were constantly being raided by the Bratski people. The people referred to variously in these documents as Bratski or Bratskiye were the Buryats (Batuev 1996:29).

7. A Russian officer, Maksim Perfel'ev, who traveled along the River Angara toward Lake Baikal in 1626 and nearly reached Buryat lands depicts the Buryats as a "wealthy . . . sedentary . . . people" who had "plentiful horses, cows and camels," lived by farming and hunting, and dominated their eastern neighbors politically. The Buryats were the largest Siberian group, with at least thirty thousand people (Forsyth 1992:86).

8. Okladnikov (1976, 1979) and Mikhailov (1980, 1987).

9. By "official" histories, I mean most written histories, including Russian, Western, and Mongolian (socialist and postsocialist accounts), and those by Buryats trained in various scholarly trends and institutions: Tibetan Buddhist, prerevolutionary Russian universities, and Soviet and post-Soviet universities. There are also "offi-cial native" histories. Unlike Western-style accounts, which emphasize the common

traits and shared experiences of the Buryats, native scholars concentrate on the origin stories and genealogical accounts of their own tribes. They also use myths, oral narrative, archival materials, and Western-style scholarship as well as stories about the past that the shamans narrate during their rituals of possession. The best-known one is the *Chronicle of Buryat History [Buriadai tuuhe besheguud]*; see Chimitdorji'ev (1992).

10. The Soviet ethnologists G. R. Galdanova and V. V. Mantatov, in seeking to establish the Buryats' ethnogenesis, propose that landmarks such as ovoos indicate the formation of specific clans and other ethnic subgroups in Buryat lands. They also state that it might be possible to trace the Buryats' migration through the names of ovoos. Galdanova and Mantatov's claim adds to my idea about the ways in which the Buryats remember their lost ancestral homeland—by settling their lands with their origin spirits—particularly because ovoos are the spirits' residences. See Galdanova and Mantatov (1983).

11. The shaman also checks for the presence of each person's soul in his or her body. If a soul has been displaced, a shaman performs an individual soul-evoking ritual, since during shamanic rituals everyone must have his or her soul intact.

12. This story was published by the Mongolian scholar Dulam Sendenjav. He heard the story from the shaman Luvsan a few years before I began my fieldwork in the area where I met the shaman (Dulam 2000:168).

13. Forsyth (1992:87–89, 92) and Okladnikov (1979). The Russians have documented many instances of colonial brutality and massacres of the Buryats. For instance, a mass migration of Buryats to Mongolia occurred in 1658 when Ivan Pohabov, the founder of the Irkutsk settlement (near the western shore of Lake Baikal), tortured, mutilated, and killed Buryats and forced them to accept Christianity.

14. On shamanism and Christianity in Siberia see Znamenski (1999); on missionary activities among the Buryats, see Bawden (1985), Diment and Slezkine (1993), Grant (1995), and Konagaya (2002); on Siberia in Western mythology and the Western imagination see Diment and Slezkine (1993) and Hutton (2001).

15. See Bernstein (2011, 2012, and in press) for the contemporary development of Buddhism among Russian Buryats.

16. Krausse (1899).

17. Humphrey (1979) compares the genealogies of (western) Ekhirit-Bulagat Buryats and (eastern) Khori Buryats and their respective relationship to their lands. The Khori Buryats, nomadic pastoralists with vast common lands, united politically in order to claim their pastureland. Families had no reason to own individual pieces of land. Genealogically, they stem from a single mythological originator. In contrast, the Ekhirit-Bulagat Buryats had a sedentary lifestyle, and individual clans attached themselves to the land, so that they developed individual, internally inconsistent genealogies. They were not politically unified and lacked a single mythological originator.

18. While the sources to which Humphrey (1979) refers (most of them Russian and published in the nineteenth century and the second half of the twentieth) indicate a more peaceful relationship between Russians and the Buryats, Buryat scholarship published after the collapse of socialism and the Soviet Union emphasizes the brutality of the colonial administration. See Nimaev (1988), Natsov (1995), Batuev (1996), and Tsibiktarov (2001).

19. For English-language scholarship on the Russian administration in Siberia and the

Russians' relationship with the natives see Curtin (1909), Wood (1991), Kotkin and Wolff (1995), Konagaya (2002), and Reed (2002), among others.

20. In the international scholarly world as well as generally, the Qing Dynasty is known as Chinese. The "Manchu" usually gets dropped from the title. (The Manchus, who conquered the Chinese and established their rulership over them, had become assimilated into Han Chinese, and thus their voices are absent from this discourse.) However, the Mongols use the term "Manchu Qing" to separate the Manchu administration from that of the Chinese. The policies that the Manchu administration implemented in Mongolia during most of the Qing Dynasty differed drastically from those implemented by the Chinese government after the fall of the Qing. Specifically, the Manchus never settled Mongolia, and they prohibited Chinese settlements in Mongolia. The Chinese, however, after the fall of Manchu rule in the early twentieth century, initiated a politics of assimilating Mongolia into Han China politically and culturally. Thus both in official Mongolian history and in the communal memory, the Manchus and Chinese are more strongly distinguished than in international scholarship.

21. See Bira (1969), Shirendyv (1968), Perdue (2005), and Atwood (2006) for the Qing conquest of the Mongols. Many Mongol khans in the central area sided with the Manchus in their efforts to subjugate the western khans, thereby becoming more dependent on the Manchus and accepting their rule.

22. For instance, the shamanic communal spirit Hoimorin Högshin was replaced by a female Buddhist deity, Lham Burhan; Higan Tengri by Jamsran Burhan; and the Thirteen Lords of the Island of Oikhon in Lake Baikal were transformed into the Tavan Khan (five kings). See Heissig (1980:38) for similar transformations among other Mongol groups.

23. At the time of the Buddhist conversion in the sixteenth, seventeenth, and eighteenth centuries, the lamas substituted Indian and Tibetan folk-magic practices for the shamans' ritual functions (Heissig 1980:39). They taught the common people dharani, which kept demons and misfortunes at bay, destroyed evil, protected cattle and ensured their fertility, and cured various ailments. The lamas also offered personal identification with a particular protective Buddhist deity, a practice that corresponds with the shamanic idea of protection by origin spirits. Special categories of lama-magicians (dayanči and gurtum) replaced shamanic spirit possession through the performance of ecstatic rituals, driving out of demons, and foretelling of the future.

24. For Buddhism in Buryatia and its relationship with shamanism see Galdanova and Mantatov (1983), Mikhailov (1987), and Zhukovskaya (1991). Since the collapse of socialism, the Khori Buryats in Russia have been reviving and promoting Buddhism as a mark of their political sovereignty (see Bernstein 2012). The Buryats in Mongolia privilege their shamanism in order to distinguish themselves from the rest of Mongolia, which is largely Buddhist, but they do not engage in discourses of sovereignty.

25. The color white is a symbol of purity, kindness, and innocence.

26. Natsagdorj (1963), Ewing (1978), and Rupen (1979).

27. Mongolian People's Revolutionary Party (1985):67.

28. Socialist-period sources suggest that the Buryats received a warm welcome in Mongolia (Dondog 1988). But articles published since the collapse of socialism tell us that the local Mongols resented the migrants, called the Buryats "Russian convicts," and bullied them for using the forest for firewood and pasturelands for their live-

stock and for haymaking. The local Mongolian nobles imposed taxes and tortured those who failed, out of ignorance, to follow local customs (Galsan and Chuluun-baatar 2004).

29. The Russian-Mongolian relationship was more complex than the usual patron-client or dominator-dominated dynamic. Kotkin (1999:12–15) argues that on some level, the relationship was beneficial to both. The Soviet Union brought Mongolia modernization in exchange for its resources and shielded the country from China, but in return it dominated Mongolia politically and closed it off from the rest of the world.

30. Kaplonski (2011) distinguishes three stages of "technologies of exception" in overthrowing the Buddhist clergy and in establishing the new socialist government. The first was nonviolent modernization and restructuring of the country and reeducation of the lamas through schooling, work, and intensive propaganda. The second, class-based approach included criticism, accusation, and censorship. The third stage was physical violence—resorted to, according to Kaplonski (2011), because the first two stages had failed.

CHAPTER TWO

1. During my research there was widespread suspicion about the credibility of existing knowledge, the discrediting of one's own knowledge, and the fear that additional knowledge would emerge and override one's memory. Even when recalling some details of a family or community past, people devalued their memories and insisted to me that they had been cut off from their past, that they were a generation of non-knowledge. Many people tend to imagine that their truthful past was somewhere else obscure and unobtainable, whereas whatever knowledge remained with them was unimportant.

2. Halbwachs ([1950] 1980) observes that individuals sustain their memories through social interactions and networks as members of a group. As a provisional collective process, memory is updated through social frameworks, and its expression varies with the social setting and the social forces that shape the present circumstances. Connerton (1989), followed by Stoller (1995), among others, points out that commemorative rituals and physical habits are some of the most prominent techniques through which societies sustain and transmit memories. Cole (2001), an anthropologist, critiques Halbwachs for limiting his attention to individual memories at the expense of the social. Cole finds that the Betsimisaraka community she lived with appeared when she first arrived to have forgotten its colonial past. But during the election campaigns, which reminded the people about colonial violence, memories of colonialism erupted.

3. This became apparent during my research, when individuals who claimed not to remember much about a certain issue were in fact able to recall extensive details in further conversation. People told me that they were giving voice to some of these narratives for the first time—they had been too afraid, and too cautious, ever to share their memories before then. Some were not even aware of the existence of certain memories until they articulated them to me. The case of the Buryats of Mongolia suggests that individual memories can sometimes be preserved in silence without becoming a part of social memory.

4. Unlike works that stress the repressive nature of the totalitarian regime, recent scholarship reveals the irregularity of state power. They show that subtle forms of subversion and resistance, creative forms of "weapons of the weak," cynicism, spaces

outside of the state, the underground economy, and "evocative transcripts" were everywhere (Watson 1994; Humphrey 1994).

5. According to the MPRP newspaper *Ünen*, 28,523 people were rehabilitated and 15,750 compensated as of September 9, 2003. Kaplonski comments that some of those who were persecuted will not be rehabilitated because they also had criminal records, but the number for whom no records exist at all is larger: "There are also at least several hundred who cannot be rehabilitated because no records exist for them, but this is a different group of people. And this is where there may well be many more that we will never really know about for certain" (personal communication, 2006).

6. In the scholarly literature that was published during socialism, state violence against the clergy was framed as a fight against the enemies of the state. In Minis (1963, 1972), Sambuu (1961), and Purevjav and Dashj'amts (1965), for example, the state's destruction of monastic libraries and cultural artifacts and its confiscation of the monasteries' property were seen as completely justified and morally right. Owing to the state's strict censorship of all printed material, it is impossible to filter out the individual positions of the scholars working during socialism. After socialism a wide range of scholarly works, memoirs, archival material, and journalistic accounts were published on violence against clergy, Buryats, intellectuals, elites, lords, and feudal, including Myagmarjav and Navagchamba (2000), Tserendulam (2000), Ichinnorov (2003), Dashdavaa (2004), Ölziibaatar (2004), Rinchin (2000), Baatar (2007), and Sanj and Bold (2006). For English-language sources see Kaplonski (2002, 2008a, 2008b, 2011, 2012, in press), Sandag and Kendall (2000), and Pedersen (2011).

7. On the violence against the Buryats see Dashdavaa (2004), Baatar (2007), and Tseren (2008).

8. Kaplonski's (2008b) research reveals that the state's role in the violence was not incidental. Under pressure from the Soviets in the late 1920s, the state began preparing the public for the upcoming violence by holding Soviet-style show trials of Buddhist clergy in a state theater called the Green Round (2008b:326).

9. These rehabilitations and persecutions have not been clearly presented and discussed in public. The details of these cycles have been researched and written about by historians in the aftermath of socialism (see, e.g., Rinchin 2000, Ölziibaatar 2004, and Kaplonski 2008b), but otherwise knowledge about them remains patchy.

10. Mongolian films that illustrate the socialist revolution and life at the turn of the twentieth century include *Temtsel* (Struggle), *Öglöö* (Morning), *Sukhbaatar* (Sukhbaatar), *Ardin Elch* (The People's Messenger), and *Tungalag Tamir* (And Quiet Flows the Tamir).

11. The leaders killed by Stalin before Choibalsan assumed power were Balingiin Tserendorj, Navaandorjiin Jadamba, Tseren-Ochiryn Dambadorj, Anandyn Amar, Peljidiin Genden, and Gelegdorjiin Demid (Baabar 1999:372). On Choibalsan and his life, see Roshin (2005).

12. Although most ordinary Mongols, especially those born during the socialist era, recognize Soviet domination, they do not feel unequivocal hatred toward the Soviets. Nowadays there is some nostalgia about socialist times, but there is also strong awareness of the need to maintain global connections. Many people with whom I spoke were grateful to the Soviets for their help in bringing the country from its tattered post-Qing state to its present condition. However, many also questioned the nature of that assistance, the pricing of goods, and the currency exchange rates that

the Soviets used for transactions, much of which was kept hidden from the Mongols. Punsalmaagiin Ochirbat, the former president of Mongolia and a minister of energy during the 1980s, once during a television interview acknowledged that he had become aware that in the name of economic assistance, the Soviet Union was exploiting its satellite countries.

13. Bira and Natsagdorj (1984).

14. Some scholars encountered forgetting based on their intimate knowledge from previous fieldwork and were able to "diagnose" omissions and gaps. For instance, decades of research in Congo caused Fabian (2003) to notice not only remembering but also forgetting in the narrative of a local historian. The interviewee's acts of "not recalling" (2003:493), the "typification" of his life as an "abstract colonial subject" (2003:499), "disinterest" in recalling certain events (2003: 499), and "leap[s]" through decades (2003:498) were, in Fabian's interpretation, deliberate forgetting that distanced the speaker from an unpleasant past. Steedly (2000) observed the omission of details from memory at the juncture of the social and the individual. Performances that were meant to move large audiences tended to fit a grand story about the "common experiences of terror, uncertainty, and heartache" (2000:838) while omitting unique personal details. This allowed all individuals to identify themselves in the performance.

15. Many of the forgotten spirits used to be origin spirits but became estranged from their descendants during the socialist suppression of religion. Some of them are the souls of shamans who died during that time and did not receive the rituals necessary for them to become origin spirits. There are also spirits who were abandoned prior to socialism, during Mongolia's Buddhist conversion, or in the Buryats' often haphazard migrations between Russia and Mongolia to escape exploitation, violence, and poverty.

16. It is worthwhile speculating why uheer were represented as female, given certain aspects of Buddhism and traditional Mongolian concepts of gender. First, in Gelugpa Buddhism, female bodies are seen as inherently polluted and lower in karma than male bodies (Gutschow 2004). Therefore, the souls of the dead, either male or female, become reanimated only in female corpses, never in male bodies. Second, since women are seen as inherently more sinful than men, women are more likely than men to become uheer after their deaths. And finally, in a male-dominated patrilocal society where women were often mistreated by their in-laws and husbands, the premature deaths of unhappy women could logically have added to a higher female uheer population.

17. In Klein (1997:318–319).

18. According to a Mongolian newspaper, *Zuunii Medee* (September 10, 2003, p. 2), 28,523 people were rehabilitated and 15,750 compensated as of September 9, 2003. Kaplonski comments that some of those who were persecuted will not be rehabilitated because they also had criminal records, but the number for whom no records exist at all is larger: "There are also at least several hundred who cannot be rehabilitated because no records exist for them, but this is a different group of people. And this is where there may well be many more that we will never really know about for certain" (personal communication, 2006).

CHAPTER THREE

1. Much of the literature on Mongolia's postsocialist economic crisis concerned decollectivization, land use, changing pasturelands, the environment, and the tradi-

tions, such as *khot ail* (reciprocity-based pastoral communities), that have remained throughout socialism and collectives (Broon and Odgaard 1996; Humphrey and Sneath 1996; Sneath 1999, 2004; Humphrey 2002). But little research has been done on the experiences of communities over an extended period of time on the repercussions of the collapse of socialism and arrival of capitalism.

2. Weber argues that there are three major doctrines that gave "rationally satisfactory answers to the questioning for the basis of the incongruity between destiny and merit [i.e., unequal suffering]: the Indian doctrine of Kharma, Zoroastrian dualism, and the predestination decree of the *deus abscondidus*" (1946, 1958:275).

3. See Buyandelgeriyn (2007) on the assumption of ill-intention on the part of others.

4. Humphrey (1983) explores in detail the complicated state-centralized system of managing the collective farms and preventing the bankruptcy of individual farms.

5. Heaton (1980, 1986, 1992) and Weidlich (1981).

6. The switch from a CF to an SF was a complex affair that involved changing the location of the enterprises and merging several CFs into a single SF (Galsan 1994).

7. There was also some disbelief on the part of the citizens. After decades of socialist propaganda against private property and a threat of punishment, the state's immediate propaganda about private property in the 1990s was confusing and difficult to take in.

8. Most of the livestock transported from Bayan-Uul (and other regions) was sold to families in the city of Ulaanbaatar.

9. According to *China and Mongolia Country Report 1993*, that year the Mongolian government sought and received a loan of three hundred million yen from international donors to purchase flour from China. The *China and Mongolia Country Report 1996* states that in January and February 1996 Mongolia imported 3,600 tons of flour and 251 tons of rice. On February 18, 1997, the *E-mail Daily News* noted that by February of that year Mongolia was so dependent on these sources that it reduced the tax on imported flour by 50 percent; once customs duties were eliminated, on May 1, 1997, imports of Chinese flour increased, according to the September 5, 1997, *E-mail Daily News*. And by the end of the year, as reported in the *Montsame News Agency* in 1998, 40 to 60 percent of Mongolia's rice, flour, and sugar were being imported from China (Rossabi 2001).

10. Also see Sneath (2002), Atwood (2003), Wheeler (2004).

11. Trade with Russian border towns was also more or less monopolized by a few families in Bayan-Uul. These traders imported evaporated milk, dried fruit, grain, candy, sugar, and tea, as well as gasoline, machinery, and tools. The Buryats, like other Mongols, had gotten used to Russian goods during socialism and trusted their quality over that of comparable Chinese manufactures.

12. On the Barga Mongols, see Bira and Natsagdorj (1984), Humphrey (1979), Batuev (1996), Baabar (1999), and Tsibiktarov (2001).

13. Also called Manchurian or spotted deer, they are found in Mongolia, northeastern China, and Siberia.

14. Batchelder (2000), http://www.wapiti.net/news/default2.cfm?articleID=37, accessed July 29, 2006. Also see Ludt, Schroeder, Rottmann, and Kuehn (2004).

15. For works on witchcraft in African countries see Geschier (1997), Comaroff and Comaroff (1999), Moore and Sanders (2004), and Ashforth (2005); witchcraft in Indonesia is discussed in Siegel (2006). Ashforth (2005) notes that spiritual insecurity is different from other forms of insecurity such as poverty, political oppression, and disease, since it does not disappear with enlightenment or modernization.

CHAPTER FOUR

1. It is likely that there are stories of other shamans who practiced in secret during socialism. I caught some glimpses of them but ended up pursuing mostly the stories about Genen and Khorlo because, during the time I stayed in Bayan-Uul, these two women dominated local memories.

2. With such a position I could be expected to join the well-established critics of Foucault. Hall (1996) discusses the contributions and limits characterizing Foucault's position on the question of identity formation; his observations are especially relevant to the present inquiry. As Hall noted, in his earlier, "archaeological" works Foucault showed that his subjects were being produced "as an effect" within specific discursive formations. In his later, "genealogical" works the overestimation of disciplinary power leads to an impoverished understanding that individuals are restricted to their "docile bodies." Hall then argues that in his third shift, to "the subject," Foucault came close to the realization that the constitution and recognition of a subject belongs to the realm of "identity." He speculates that Foucault almost inadvertently approached what has since been realized as a "specific mode of conduct" (Hall 1996:13), or a performativity. But Foucault did not articulate clearly why and how subjects are summoned to particular positions and how they perform those positions. I agree with the critiques of Foucault by Hall and others, but it seems to me that Foucault's omissions—he did not deal with resistance or with the variety of possible subject positions—do not prove that he was unaware of their complexity. His aimed to show the full capacity of institutional power, with all its possible effects. This is why he writes exhaustively about power, without stopping to attend to its limits. In such a study, focusing on resistance would leave less conceptual space in which to see the outreach of power. Instead of taking Foucault's work literally or looking for something that was clearly secondary to his project, it is more fruitful to read his works as a speculation on the gaps that are left for the sake of furthering certain arguments, but not others.

3. The Internal Ministry kept a file on every citizen.

4. Mueggler (2001) discusses these techniques of domination as used by the Chinese state. They apply to Mongolia and other socialist countries as well.

5. The state invested in the health of its citizens in order to maintain a productive labor force and increase reproduction.

6. There was another female shaman who was unrelated to Genen and who led Luvsan's next few shanars. After she died, Luvsan led his last few himself, completing all thirteen stages of the shanar to become a zaarin.

7. The phrase "everything goes if it is not harmful for others and is beneficial for you" was not a joke; rather, it was almost a way of life for everyone regardless of rank and position.

8. Among the Mongols, including the Buryats, it is commonly held that excess goods, respect, or luck brings misfortunes rather than happiness. Each person is said to be born with a designated amount of resources for his or her use. Exceeding these limits results in scarcity later on.

9. Although they underwent systematic ideological training from a young age in socialist propaganda, I never heard of Mongolian children turning against their parents. The state did not necessarily promote generational conflicts. Khorlo's case was unique, not only in my experience, but also for the people of Bayan-Uul.

CHAPTER FIVE

1. Years later, however, I learned that the argument during the ritual was due to Chimeg's refusal to follow Tömör's instructions. She noted that the way Tömör wanted her to perform was much too flamboyant and that she did not want to be a clown or the center of attention.

2. Tedlock (2005), who is both a scholar of shamanism and a practitioner, also holds a view that women are more talented as shamans than men owing to their psychological and biological makeup, and thus they need less training than men to become full-fledged shamans.

3. As Thomas and Humphrey (1996) argue, throughout history the power and role of shamanism fluctuated a great deal: when the state was weak, shamanism proliferated and even contributed to the empowerment of some leaders, but at times of political and religious consolidation, shamanism was neglected in favor of a more organized religion and pushed to the margins, and its practitioners were persecuted. The authors provide an example of ascent to power by Chinggis (Genghis) Khan in the thirteenth century. At the beginning of his mission to consolidate the warring tribes, young Temujin relied on shamanic services and charisma in convincing the tribes of the legitimacy of his political power. But once the shamans' prophecies no longer supported his absolute power, he eliminated the shamans. Thomas and Humphrey's (1996) theory can be applied to later periods as well. Both in Qing-dominated Mongolia and in czarist Russia, prior to socialism the political rulers preferred the organized religions of Buddhism and Christianity, respectively, to legitimate their powers.

4. Abortions were allowed only in two instances: if a woman already had more than four children, and if pregnancy caused a significant threat to a woman's life.

5. In addition, there was very little makeup or fashionable clothing available in stores.

6. See Wolf (1985), Buckley (1989), Clements (1997), Einhorn (1993), and Gal and Kligman (2000).

7. In a 1998 interview with Tsendin Dashdondov, head of the Mongolian Free Democratic Journalists Association in Ulaanbaatar, he underlined the importance of the campaign for the eradication of sexually transmitted diseases that was carried out all over the country in the 1960s. He took part in the program and traveled throughout the country with Soviet doctors as a translator and a coordinator. Children who were born in the 1960s were informally labeled "red injection children" for the injections that were used to cure syphilis.

8. The Human Development Report, Mongolia (2000), states that Mongolia made impressive gains in the sphere of education during the Soviet era. Ninety-six percent of the population became literate during socialism. Women made up more than 40 percent of higher-education graduates, and around 85 percent of women worked outside the home. Even if these numbers suggest relative equality between men and women, the percentage of women in jobs does not show the position of women in the society or their status and power in relation to men.

9. See Bulag (1998:30). He indicates that the population number is correct but misleading. It includes 100,000 Chinese and 5,000 Russians. The actual population of Mongols is 542,504, according to Maiskii (1959).

10. There were, however, additional reasons to remain in a marriages. The stigma attached to divorce had different but equally negative effects on both men and women. Divorced men were officially denounced in their work meetings as having

"no family stability"—an official and a more "civilized" term for promiscuity. They would be demoted at work to lower-paying positions for a certain length of time. Most important (depending on the case), men would often lose their membership in the MPRP, which was necessary for being considered for any kind of promotion and career advancement. Most men refused to divorce in order to protect their reputation and career opportunities. Child support for one child was up to 30 percent of a man's salary, and even more for additional children.

11. After the end of the pro-natal policy in the late 1980s, the average number of children in rural households dropped from six to two.

12. Gal and Kligman (2000) argue that during socialism in Eastern and Central Europe, women depended on the state more than on individual men. Such an argument might hold true for the elite urban Mongol women who had access to illegal contraception, to doctors willing to take the risk of performing illegal abortions, and to foreign-language medical knowledge to control their childbearing, and who could limit their children to two at the most. Only a select number of highly educated urban women with prestigious jobs and fewer children were able to claim independence from their husbands and have the courage to raise their children on their own.

13. After socialism, with the arrival of democratic freedom, the divorce rate soared to 50 percent.

14. See Burn and Oyuntsetseg (2001).

15. Gal and Kligman (2000:4) argue that the socialist states "can be imagined as male, even though both men and women are involved in their operation."

16. According to the Family Law of Mongolia, spouses have equal rights in owning their property. However, according to the report by UNIFEM (Burn and Oyuntsetseg 2001), men, as the heads of the household, had more chances than women to obtain and own property during the campaigns of privatization of livestock, state factories, housing, cash, bonds, and other means.

17. For modern-day Greek women in Athens, this means meeting conflicting goals: becoming mothers and subordinating their interests to those of others, but also being proper modern women, which entails achieving independence, well-being, and control over their lives.

18. For a detailed list and descriptions of paraphernalia and the ways in which each item corresponds to the number of shanars, see Buyandelgeriyn (2004).

19. Similarly, Meilassoux (1975) shows how, in a self-sustaining agricultural community, "women's subordination makes them susceptible . . . in the exploitation of their labor in that they lose their claim to their produce . . . and the exploitation of their reproductive capacities" (1975:77).

20. Shamanic paraphernalia consists of white (healer) objects and black (hard) objects. The white objects are made mostly by seamstresses; only a few small objects are crafted by blacksmiths. The materials used for white objects are not as expensive as those for black ones. A relatively poor shaman can obtain the white objects (coral bracelet, prayer beads, mirror, bell, cane, gown, headdress, and cap) and even start-up black objects (mirror, drum, drumstick, heart pendant, "shielding stick," gown, and cloth headdress) and become a beginner. Black objects, especially the antelope-skin gown and metal headdress, are time-consuming and labor-intensive to make because they are made from expensive and rare materials such as steel, rare woods, animal skins, and deer antlers. More important, only blacksmiths

who possess the ancestral deity of metallurgy, Dorlik, are certified to make black paraphernalia.

21. Among the Wana in Indonesia, men travel to sacred places for power (Atkinson 1989), and Meratus male shamans (Tsing 1993) travel to take leadership positions, but women's everyday activities preclude travel and access to the same power.

22. Nimaev (1983).

23. Humphrey (1992:174) argues that throughout history, women in Mongolian hierarchical empires had more power and a greater voice in the household than their counterparts in China. Mongol women were never secluded, nor were their feet bound: "They were expected to be quiet and competent. They maintained authority by actions rather than by words."

24. Parry and Bloch (1989).

25. Ibid.

CHAPTER SIX

1. Kendall (2009) explores the new type of urban shaman serving the new Korean bourgeoisie and addressing their anxieties through the Asian financial crisis and the uncertainty of capitalism.

2. Shirendyv and Natsagdorj (1956–1969), 3:366–376.

3. The Soviet Union's participation in the Battle of Khalkhin Gol in 1939 was interpreted as friendly assistance to Mongolia on the part of the Soviets. The Soviets' involvement, the goal of which was to protect its eastern borders from Japan, has been understated in Mongolian history textbooks. The Mongols are depicted as grateful recipients of Soviet help; no explanation of the complex geopolitics of the region is offered.

4. The situation in Mongolia is not completely consistent; among the Darkhads, for example, scholars have interviewed and filmed many female shamans (Dulam 1992). See also the website for the Mongolian Shamans' Association at http://www .buryatmongol.com/msa.html (accessed 2010).

5. Eliade (1964) canonized the North Asian shaman as the "true" shaman.

6. Although Luvsan's shamanic endeavors constitute the marketing of tradition and commodification of culture, he was the only one in the area who did this. Other shamans did not join him in his marketing. It did not become a group identity or movement, like those discussed by Comaroff and Comaroff (2009).

7. Atkinson (1989), Tsing (1993), and Steedly (1993).

8. As evidence of Luvsan's appeal and influence, I met a Japanese anthropologist, Ippey Shimamura, and a Swiss anthropologist, Amélie Schenk, at his camp.

9. The American scriptwriter and stage director Virlana Tkacz went to Buryat sites in Russia and Mongolia and commented on the powerful performances of female shamans (personal communication). In Russian Buryatia, women have more privilege, power, and respect than do their Mongolian counterparts.

10. In her study of zar (women's spirit possession) in northern Sudan, Boddy (1989) shows the ethnic community's subordination to be metaphorically represented through the bodies of women that are inscribed with their history of oppression through the medium of the zar cult. In contrast, among the Buryats of Mongolia, the female spirits possess both male and female shamans, thus making oppression an experience that goes beyond gender. Comaroff (1985) has also emphasized the importance of the body and bodily practices such as spirit possession as resistance.

11. See chapter 1 for the historical contexts of the white and black structures of the sha-manic deities.

12. Many shamans told me that Burhan Garval is actually a "shamanified" version of Burhan, the supreme Buddhist deity. But others argue that there is no connection between the two and that Burhan Garval is an original shamanic deity.

13. There are many more tengris in Buryat shamanism, such as Güjir Tengri (god of cattle), Higan Tengri, and Ataa Ulaan Tengri (god of revenge).

14. The list of the Buryats' Thirteen Lords of the Island of Oikhon was almost the same as that documented by Rinchen (1959).

15. Unless otherwise specified, the gods and deities are assumed to be male.

CHAPTER SEVEN

1. Some shamans claim no moral responsibility for any information uttered while they are possessed by spirits. As Morris puts it, the predicament of a shaman is "to speak and not be the subject of their speech, to know and not be the subject of knowledge" (2000:102). Although that is true to some extent among the Buryats, audiences and clients often criticize this stance. They argue that shamans must take responsibility because they should be able to control their origin spirits and not let them maneuver the shaman.

2. Shamans differ greatly in how much of the knowledge received from spirits they re-member and retell—and in their willingness to show how much of that knowledge they actually remember after the ritual.

3. One reason the shanar ritual takes three days is that the shaman-teacher is supposed to make sure that each person's soul is intact in his or her body by checking each one through individual ritual or divination.

4. The Mongolian education system under socialism was similar to that of the Sovi-ets, which was directly imported from the German system. There was no system of liberal arts colleges like the United States has. Instead, a university degree was con-sidered to be a professional degree, roughly equivalent to a master's degree in the United States. It is earned in five years and provides professional training.

5. A blue goat is actually black. The color terms that Mongols use for animals do not necessarily correspond to the actual physical color.

6. Baasan was well aware that I was acquainted with all the shamans in the area, in-cluding Tömör, Tsend, and many others, and that I had spent many months fre-quenting Chimeg's house and traveling with her. She also knew that I did not take sides and that I studied shamans "objectively, like a scientist," as she put it. She told me these stories for didactic purposes so that I would become aware of the different kinds of shamans—"business versus genuine," as she put it.

7. Did the state really expect its citizens naively and voluntarily to report their negative backgrounds? Many knew only too well that the state would persecute them if they revealed unfavorable backgrounds. These three-generation biographies were made part of the registrations and applications for housing, schools, jobs, and pensions. Extensive research is needed on this topic; several individuals with whom I spoke had carefully crafted their biographies in order to downplay the middle-class ele-ments of their backgrounds and emphasize the "poor herdsmen" ones—satisfying the state's fictions as they schemed to survive.

GLOSSARY

albin. lowland spirits

böö. shaman

Burhshuul. term of endearment for a spirit or deity

Burkhan Garval. originator deity, a supreme deity in the Celestial Court

buuz. steamed dumplings

Darhan Dorlik. *see* Dorlik

degel. traditional robe worn both by men and women ("deel" in Khalkha dialect)

dharani. magic Buddhist spells

Dorlik. deity of blacksmithing

duurisah. fully accomplished female shaman

ger. round felt dwelling of Mongols

khadag. Tibetan ceremonial silk scarf

Higan Tengri. deity of warfare

Hoimorin Högshin. lit., "house mother"; a female protective deity of the home and children

huudal buudal. the places of origin spirits' habitation and visitation

ih amitai. antelope-skin gown; part of a shaman's paraphernalia

lus. lords of the water

ovoo. sacred cairns built atop hills and mountains, made of piles of rocks and topped with offerings

sahius. "sacra"; also refers to shamanic paraphernalia, a deity, or god

sanah. to remember; to miss

savdag. lords of the forest, plains, and ditches

shanar. degree-elevating ceremony

sutra. Buddhist prayer book written in Tibetan

tengri. celestial gods or deities

tögrög. unit of Mongolian currency

tulmaashi. "white" shaman; healer

tuukhe. history

udgan. fully accomplished female shaman

ug garval. origin spirits or genealogical roots

uheer. malevolent spirits of the dead or demons

zaarin. fully accomplished male shaman

zud. disastrous snow condition characterized by the formation of an ice crust over snow; livestock cannot reach the winter grass and consequently starve to death

REFERENCES

Agamben, Giorgio
    1998   Homo Sacer: Sovereign Power and Bare Life. Stanford, CA: Stanford University Press.

Ahern, Laura
    2000   Agency. Journal of Linguistic Anthropology 9(1–2):12–15.

Alexander, Catherine
    2004   Value, Relations, and Changing Bodies: Privatization and Property Rights in Kahzakhstan. *In* Property in Question: Value Transformation in the Global Economy. Katherine Verdery and Caroline Humphrey, eds. Pp. 251–275. Oxford: Berg.

Appadurai, Arjun
    1996   Modernity at Large: Cultural Dimensions of Globalization. Minneapolis: University of Minnesota Press.

Ardener, Edwin
    1972   Belief and the Problem of Women. *In* The Interpretation of Ritual: Essays in Honour of A. I. Richards. J. S. La Fontaine, ed. Pp. 135–159. London: Routledge.
    1975   Belief and the Problem of Women. *In* Perceiving Women. Shirley Ardener, ed. Pp. 1–17. London: Malaby Press.

Ardener, Shirley
    1975   The "Problem" Revisited. *In* Perceiving Women. Shirley Ardener, ed. Pp. 17–19. London: Malaby Press.
    1978   Defining Females: The Nature of Women in Society. New York: John Wiley & Sons.

Ashforth, Adam
    2000   Madumo: A Man Bewitched. Chicago: University of Chicago Press.
    2001   On Living in a World with Witches: Everyday Epistemology and Spiritual Insecurity in a Modern African City (Soweto). *In* Magical Interpretations, Material Realities: Modernity, Witchcraft and the Occult in Postcolonial Africa. Henrietta L. Moore and Todd Sanders, eds. Pp. 206–226. London: Routledge.
    2005   Witchcraft, Violence, and Democracy in South Africa. Chicago: University of Chicago Press.

Atkinson, Jane Monning
    1989   The Art and Politics of Wanna Shamanship. Berkeley and Los Angeles: University of California Press.
    1992   Shamanisms Today. Annual Review of Anthropology 21:307–330.
Atwood, Christopher P.
    2003   The Mutual-Aid Co-Operatives and the Animal Products Trade in Mongolia, 1913–1928. Inner Asia 5(1):65–91.
    2006   Mongolia. In World Encyclopedia of Political Systems and Parties, 4th edition. Neil Schlager and Jayne Weisblatt, eds. 3 vols. Pp. 906–911. New York: Facts on File.
Baabar (Bat-Erdene Batbayar)
    1999   Twentieth Century Mongolia. Knapwell, UK: White Horse.
Baatar, Sovdin
    2007   The Prosecution of Buryats [Buryad zonig zalhaan tseerluulsen ni]. Ulaanbaatar: Admon Printing.
Badamnyam, Mootgon
    2000   Are the Buryats Really the Remnants from the "Whites" . . . [Buryaduud Tsagaani orgodol gej uu . . .]. Dashbalbar, Dornod, Mongolia: Interpress.
Ballinger, Pamela
    2002   History in Exile: Memory and Identity at the Borders of the Balkans. Princeton, NJ: Princeton University Press.
Balzer, Marjorie Mandelstam
    1981   Rituals of Gender Identity: Markers of Siberian Khanty Ethnicity, Status and Belief. American Anthropologist 83(4): 850–867.
    2002   Shamans across Space, Time and Language Barriers. Shaman 10(1–2):7–20.
    2012   Shamans, Spirituality, and Cultural Revitalization: Explorations in Siberia and Beyond. New York: Palgrave-Macmillan, 2012.
Banzarov, Dorj
    1891   Black Belief or Shamanism among the Mongols and Other Articles [Chernaya vera ili shamanstvo u Mongolov i drugie stat'i]. St. Petersburg: Printing House of the Imperial Academy of Sciences.
Bataille, Georges
    1985   The Notion of Expenditure. In Visions of Excess: Selected Writings, 1927–39. Allan Steokl, trans. and ed. Pp. 116–130. Minneapolis: University of Minnesota Press.
    1989   The Accursed Share: An Essay on General Economy. Vol. 1. Consumption. Robert Hurley, trans. New York: Zone Books.
Battogtoh, S.
    1991   From the Secret Plot to the Deviation [Nuuts huivaldaanaas nugalaa zavhrald]. Ulaanbaatar: State Publishing House.
Baudrillard, Jean
    1975   The Mirror of Production. Mark Poster, trans. St. Louis: Telos Press.
Batbayar, T.
    1993   Mongolia in 1992: Back to One Party Rule. Asian Survey 33(1):61–66.
Batchelder, Helen J.
    2000   "Velvet Antler: A Literature Review." http://www.wapiti.net/news/default2.cfm?articleID=37.
Batuev, B. B.
    1977   The Struggle for the Power of the Soviets in Buryatia [Bor'ba za vlast' Sovetov v Buriatii]. Ulan-Ude: Buriat Book Printing.

1996 The Buryats in the 17th–18th Centuries [Buriaty v XVII–LVIII vv.]. Ulan-Ude: Sibir'.

Bawden, Charles
1968 The Modern History of Mongolia. New York: Praeger.
1985 Shamans, Lamas and Evangelicals: The English Missionaries in Siberia. London: Routledge & Kegan Paul.

Benjamin, Walter
1968 Thesis on the Philosophy of History. *In* Illuminations. Pp. 253–264. New York: Schocken Books.

Bernstein, Anya
2006 Performing Shamanism: From Wild Men to Businessmen. N.p.
2011 The Post-Soviet Treasure Hunt: Time, Space, and Necropolitics in Siberian Buddhism. Comparative Studies in Society and History 53(3):623–653.
2012 More Alive than All the Living: Sovereign Bodies and Cosmic Politics in Buddhist Siberia. Cultural Anthropology 27(2): 261–285.
In press Religious Bodies Politic: Rituals of Sovereignty in Buryat Buddhism. Chicago: University of Chicago Press.

Bira, Sh.
1969 History of the Mongolian People's Republic [Bugd Nairamdah Mongol Ard Ulsin tuukh], volume 3 [Gutgaar boti]. Ulaanbaatar: State Printing House.

Bira, Sh., and Sh. Natsagdorj
1984 History of the Mongolian People's Republic [Bugd Nairamdah Mongol Ard Ulsin tuukh]. 3rd edition. Ulaanbaatar. State Printing House.

Bloch, Maurice
1996 Internal and External Memory: Different Ways of Being in History. *In* Tense Past: Cultural Essays in Trauma and Memory. Paul Antze and Michael Lambek, eds. Pp. 215–232. New York: Routledge.

Boddy, Janice
1989 Wombs and Alien Spirits: Women, Men, and the Zar Cult in Northern Sudan. Madison: University of Wisconsin Press.
1994 Spirit Possession Revisited: Beyond Instrumentality. Annual Review of Anthropology 23:407–434.

Boekhoven, Jeroen W.
2011 Genealogies of Shamanism: Struggles for Power, Charisma, and Authority. Eelde, Netherlands: Barkhuis.

Broon, Ole, and Ole Odgaard, eds.
1996 Mongolia in Transition: Old Patterns, New Challenges. Richmond, Surrey, UK: Curzon Press.

Brundage, W. Fitzhugh
2000 Where The Memories Grow: History, Memory, and Southern Identity. Chapel Hill: University of North Carolina Press.

Buckley, Mary
1989 Women and Ideology in Soviet Union. Ann Arbor: University of Michigan Press.

Bulag, Uradyn E.
1998 Nationalism and Hybridity in Mongolia. New York: Clarendon Press.

Bum-Ochir, Dulam
2002 Mongol Shamanic Rituals [Mongol böögin zan uil]. Ulaanbaatar: Mönkhin useg.

Burawoy, Michael, and Katherine Verdery, eds.
  1999   Uncertain Transition: Ethnographies of Change in the Postsocialist World. Lanham, MD; Rowman and Littlefield.
Burn, Nalini, and Oidovin Oyuntsetseg
  2001   UN Development Fund for Women (UNIFEM). Women in Mongolia: Mapping Progress under Transition, 2001. http://www.unhcr.org/refworld/docid/46cadabb0.html (accessed February 18, 2013).
Butler, Judith
  1997   The Psychic Life of Power: Theories of Subjection. Stanford: Stanford University Press.
Buyandelgeriyn, Manduhai
  2004   Between Hearth and Celestial Court: Gender and the Politics of Shamanic Practices among the Buriats of Mongolia. Ph.D. dissertation, Department of Anthropology, Harvard University.
  2007   Dealing with Uncertainty: Shamans, Marginal Capitalism, and the Remaking of History in Post-Socialist Mongolia. American Ethnologist 34(1):127–147.
  2008   Post-Post-Transition Theories: Walking on Multiple Paths. Annual Review of Anthropology 37:235–250.
Chakrabarty, Dipesh
  2000   Provincializing Europe: Postcolonial Thought and Historical Difference. Princeton, NJ: Princeton University Press.
Chimitdorji'ev, Sh. B., ed.
  1992   Chronicle of Buryat History [Buriadai tuuhe besheguud]. Ulan-Ude: Press of the Buryat Books.
China and Mongolia Country Report
  1993   Economist Intelligence Unit, China and Mongolia Country Report. 3rd quarter:47.
  1996   Economist Intelligence Unit, China and Mongolia Country Report. 2nd quarter:56.
Cleaves, Francis Woodman, ed. and trans.
  1982   The Secret History of the Mongols. Cambridge, MA: Harvard University Press.
Clements, Barbara Evan
  1997   Bolshevik Women. New York: Cambridge University Press.
Cole, Jennifer
  2001   Forget Colonialism? Sacrifice and the Art of Memory in Madagascar. Berkeley and Los Angeles: University of California Press.
  2003   Narratives and Moral Projects: Generational Memories of the Malagasy 1947 Rebellion. Ethos 31(1):95–126.
  2004   Memory and Modernity: Overcoming the Social/Individual Divide in Memory Studies. In A Companion to Psychological Anthropology. Conerly Casey and Robert B. Edgerton, eds. Pp. 103–120. London: Blackwell. Reprinted in Russian, 2009.
Collier, Jane, and Michelle Rosaldo
  1981   Politics and Gender in Simple Societies. In Sexual Meanings: The Cultural Construction of Gender and Sexuality. Sherry Ortner and Harriet Whitehead, eds. Pp. 275–330. Cambridge: Cambridge University Press.
Comaroff, Jean
  1985   Body of Power, Spirit of Resistance: The Culture and History of a South African People. Chicago: University of Chicago Press.

Comaroff, Jean, and John Comaroff
  1999 Occult Economies and the Violence of Abstraction: Notes from the South African Postcolony. American Ethnologist 26(3): 279–302.
  2000 Millennial Capitalism: First Thoughts on a Second Coming. Public Culture 12(2):291–343.
  2009 Ethnicity, Inc. Chicago and London: University of Chicago Press.
Comay, Rebecca
  2000 Benjamin's Endgame. In Walter Benjamin's Philosophy: Destruction and Experience. Andrew Benjamin and Peter Osborne, eds. Pp. 246–286. Manchester: Clinamen Press.
Connerton, Paul
  1989 How Societies Remember. Cambridge: Cambridge University Press.
  2009 How Modernity Forgets. Cambridge: Cambridge University Press.
Crapanzano, Vincent
  1977 Introduction. In Case Studies in Spirit Possession. Vincent Crapanzano and Vivian Garrison, eds. Pp. 1–40. New York: John Wiley & Sons.
Curtin, Jeremiah
  1909 A Journey in Southern Siberia: The Mongols, Their Religion and Their Myths. Boston: Little, Brown.
Dalai, Chuluni
  1991 Do Not Forget We Have Two Big Neighbors! [Hoyor ih horshtei gedgee buu mart!] Unen, June 25.
Das, Veena
  1995 Critical Events: An Anthropological Perspective on Contemporary India. Delhi and New York: Oxford University Press.
Dashdavaa, Damdini
  2004 The Sufferings of the Families and Children of Our Victims of Political Violence [Manai ulstörin helmegdegsdin ür sadinhni hohirol]/ Ulaanbaatar: Urlah Erdem Publishing House.
de Lauretis, Teresa
  1984 Alice Doesn't: Feminism, Semiotics, Cinema. Indiana University Press.
Diment, Galya, and Yuri Slezkine, eds.
  1993 Between Heaven and Hell: The Myth of Siberia in Russian Culture. New York: St. Martin's Press.
Dondog, Ch.
  1988 The Echoes of the Ulz River [Ulz golin tsuurai]. Ulaanbaatar: State Publishing House.
Dulam, S.
  1992 The Tradition of Darhad Shamans [Darhad boogiin ulamjlal]. Ulaanbaatar: Mongolian National University Press.
  2000 Ceremony for the Deity of House Mother among the Khori Buryats [Aga, Khorin Buryat zoni huuhiin naiji "Khoimorin Hoimorin Högshini tailga"]. In Buryad-Mongolchuudin ugsaa-tuukhin zarim asuudal. G. Gantogtokh and G. Tserenkhand, eds. Pp. 168–173. Ulaanbaatar.
Durkheim, Émile
  2001 [1912] Elementary Forms of Religious Life. Oxford: Oxford University Press.
Düttman, Alexander Garcia
  1993 Tradition and Destruction: Walter Benjamin's Politics of Language. In Walter

Benjamin's Philosophy: Destruction and Experience. Pp. 31–57. Manchester: Clinamen Press.

Egunov, N. P.
  1984   The Baikal Region in the Past and the Problem of the Origin of the Buriat People [Pribaikal'e v drevnosti i problema proiskhozhdeniia buriatskogo naroda]. Ulan-Ude: Buryat Book Publishers.

Einhorn, Barbara
  1993   Cinderella Goes to Market: Citizenship, Gender, and Women's Movements in East Central Europe. London: Verso.

Eliade, Mircea
  1964   Shamanism: Archaic Techniques of Ecstasy. Princeton, NJ: Princeton University Press.

Elleman, Bruce A.
  1994   Soviet Policy on Outer Mongolia and the Chinese Communist Party. Journal of Asian History 28(2):108–123.

Enkhbat, Badarchyn, and Ole Odgaard
  1996   Decentralization and Local Governance. In Mongolia in Transition: Old Patterns, New Challenges. Ole Broon and Ole Odgaard, eds. Pp. 165–189. Richmond, Surrey, UK: Curzon.

Evans-Pritchard, E. E.
  1969 [1940]   Nuer: A Description of the Modes of Livelihood and Political Institutions of a Nilotic People. New York and Oxford: Oxford University Press.
  1976   Witchcraft, Oracles, and Magic among the Azande. Oxford: Clarendon Press.

Ewing, Thomas E.
  1978   Revolution on the Chinese Frontier: Outer Mongolia in 1911. Journal of Asian History 12:101–119.
  1980   Between the Hammer and the Anvil? Chinese and Russian Policies in Outer Mongolia, 1911–1921. Indiana University Uralic and Altaic Series 138. Bloomington: Research Institute for Inner Asian Studies, Indiana University.

Fabian, Johannes
  2003   Forgetful Remembering: A Colonial Life in the Congo. Africa: Journal of the International African Institute 73(4):489–504.

Feeley-Harnik, Gillian
  1991   A Green Estate: Restoring Independence in Madagascar. Washington, DC: Smithsonian Institution Press.

Flaherty, Gloria
  1992   Shamanism and the Eighteenth Century. Princeton, NJ: Princeton University Press.

Forsyth, James
  1992   History of the Peoples of Siberia: Russia's North Asian Colony. Cambridge: Cambridge University Press.

Foucault, Michel
  1977   Discipline and Punish: The Birth of the Prison. New York. Pantheon Books.
  1994   Power. James D. Faubion, ed. Vol. 3. New York: New Press.

Gal, Susan, and Gail Kligman, eds.
  2000   Reproducing Gender: Politics, Publics, and Everyday Life after Socialism. Princeton, NJ: Princeton University Press.

Galdanova, G. R., and V. V. Mantatov, eds.
  1983   Lamaism in Buryatia in the XVIIIth–Beginning of the XXth century: Structure

and Social Significance of the Ritual System [Lamaism v Buryatii v XVIII–nachalo XX veka: Struktura i sotsial'naya rol' kul'tovoi sistemy]. Novosibirsk: Izdatel'stvo Nauka.

Galsan, Toisomin
1994 The Recent History of Bayan-Uul [Bayan-Uul sumin oirin tuuhiin toim]. Choibalsan, Mongolia: Möngön Bar Printing.

Galsan, T., and Zh. Chuluunbaatar
2004 The Bayan-Uul District of Dornod Province: A History [Dornod Aimgin Bayan-Uul sum: tuukhen toim]. Ulaanbaatar, Bembi San Printing House.

Garrison, Vivian, and Vincent Crapanzano
1978 Comment on Leacock's Review of Case Studies in Spirit Possession. Annual Review of Anthropology 5:420–425.

Geertz, Clifford
1973 The Interpretation of Cultures. New York: Basic Books.

Gerasimova, K. M.
1981 Lamaism in Buriatia [Lamaism v Buriatii]. In Buddhism and Traditional Beleifs of Central Asian Peoples. K. M. Gerasimova with R. E Pubayev and N. D. Bolsokoeva, eds. Pp. 116–154. Novosibirsk: Izd-vo Nauka, Sibirskoe Otd-nie.

Geschier, Peter
1997 The Modernity of Witchcraft: Politics and the Occult in Postcolonial Africa. Charlottesville: University of Virginia Press.

Ginsburg, Tom
1997 Mongolia in 1996: Fighting Fire and Ice. Asian Survey 37(1): 60–65.
1999 Nationalism, Elites, and Mongolia's Rapid Transformation. In Landlocked Cosmopolitan: Mongolia in the Twentieth Century. Stephen Kotkin and Bruce A. Elleman, eds. Pp. 247–277. Armonk, NY: M. E. Sharpe.

Godelier, Maurice
1999 The Enigma of the Gift. University of Chicago Press.

Government of Mongolia
1997 Mongolia in the 21st Century: New Economic and Social Policy [Mongol uls XXI zuund: ediin zasag, niigmiin shine bodlogo]. Ulaanbaatar: Admon.

Government of Mongolia and UNDP
2000 Human Development Report, Mongolia: Reorienting the State. Ulaanbaatar: Admon Printing Company.

Grant, Bruce
1995 In the Soviet House of Culture: A Century of Perestroikas. Princeton: Princeton University Press.

Green, Elizabeth E.
1986 China and Mongolia: Recurring Trends and Prospects for Change. Asian Survey 26(12):1137–1162.

Griffin, Keith, ed.
1995 Poverty and Transition to a Market Economy in Mongolia. London: Macmillan.

Gutschow, Kim
2004 Being a Buddhist Nun: The Struggle for Enlightenment in the Himalayas. Cambridge, MA: Harvard University Press.

Halbwachs, Maurice
1980 [1950] The Collective Memory. Francis J. Ditter Jr. and Vida Yazdi Ditter, trans. New York: Harper & Row.

1992 [1925] On Collective Memory. Lewis A. Coser, ed.and trans. Chicago: University of Chicago Press.

Hall, Stuart

1977 Culture, the Media and the "Ideological Effect." *In* Mass Communication and Society. J.Curran, M. Gurevitch, and J. Woollacott, eds. Pp. 315–348. London: Edward Arnold.

1990 Cultural Identity and Diaspora. *In* Identity: Community, Culture, Difference. J. Rutherford, ed. Pp. 222–237. London: Lawrence & Wishart.

1996 Introduction: Who Needs "Identity"? *In* Questions of Cultural Identity. Stuart Hall and Paul Du Gay, eds. Pp. 1–17. London and Thousand Oaks, CA: Sage.

Hamayon, Roberte

1994 Shamanism in Siberia: From Partnership in Supernature to Counter-Power in Society. *In* Shamanism, History, and the State. Nicholas Thomas and Caroline Humphrey, eds. Pp. 76–90. Ann Arbor: University of Michigan Press.

Heaton, William

1980 Mongolia 1979: Learning from "Leading Experiences." Asian Survey 20(1): 77–83.

1986 Mongolia in 1985: From Plan to Plan. Asian Survey 26(1):86–93.

1992 Mongolia in 1991: The Uneasy Transition. Asian Survey 32(1):50–55.

Heissig, Walter

1980 The Religions of the Mongols. London: Routledge & Kegan Paul.

Herzfeld, Michael

1985 The Poetics of Manhood: Contest and Identity in a Cretan Mountain Village. Princeton, NJ: Princeton University Press.

1991 Silence, Submission, and Subversion: Toward a Poetics of Womanhood. *In* Contested Identities: Gender and Kinship in Modern Greece. Peter Loizos and Akis Papataxiarchis, eds. Pp. 79–97. Princeton: Princeton University Press.

Ho, Engseng

2004 The Graves of Tarim: Genealogy and Mobility across the Indian Ocean. Berkeley and Los Angeles: University of California Press.

Hodgkin, Katharine, and Susanna Radstone, eds.

2003 Contested Pasts: The Politics of Memory. London: Routledge.

Højer, Lars

2009 Absent Powers: Magic and Loss in Postsocialist Mongolia. Journal of the Royal Anthropological Institute, n.s., 15(3):575–591.

Humphrey, Caroline

1979 The Uses of Genealogy: A Historical Study of the Nomadic and Sedentarized Buriats. *In* Pastoral Production and Society/Production pastorale et société. L'Équipe écologie et anthropologie des sociétés pastorales, ed. Pp. 235–260. Cambridge: Cambridge University Press; Paris: Maison des Sciences de l'Homme.

1983 Karl Marx Collective: Economy, Society and Religion in a Siberian Collective Farm. Cambridge: Cambridge University Press.

1992 Women and Ideology in Hierarchical Societies in East Asia. *In* Persons and Powers of Women in Diverse Cultures. Shirley Ardener, ed. Pp. 173–192. New York: Berg.

1994 Remembering an "Enemy": The Bogd Khaan in Twentieth-Century Mongolia. *In* Memory, History, and Opposition under State Socialism. Rubie S. Watson, ed. Pp. 21–44. Santa Fe, NM: School of American Research Press.

1995 Chiefly and Shamanist Landscapes in Mongolia. *In* The Anthropology of Landscape: Perspectives on Place and Spaces. Eric Hirsch and Michael O'Hanlon, eds. Pp. 135–163. Oxford: Clarendon Press.

1996 Shamanic Practices and the State in Northern Asia: Views from the Center and Periphery. *In* Shamanism, History, and the State. Nicholas Thomas and Caroline Humphrey, eds. Pp. 135–162. Ann Arbor: University of Michigan Press.

1998 Marx Went Away—but Karl Stayed Behind. Ann Arbor: University of Michigan Press.

2000 An Anthropological View of Barter in Russia. *In* The Vanishing Rouble: Barter Networks and Non-Monetary Transactions in Post-Soviet Societies. Paul Seabright, ed. Pp. 71– 90. Cambridge: Cambridge University Press.

2002 Unmaking of Soviet Life: Everyday Economics after Socialism. Ithaca, NY: Cornell University Press.

Humphrey, Caroline, with Urgunge Onon
1996 Shamans and Elders: Experience, Knowledge, and Power among the Daur Mongols. Oxford: Clarendon Press.

Humphrey, Caroline, and David Sneath
1999 The End of Nomadism? Society, State and the Environment in Inner Asia. Durham, NC: Duke University Press.

Humphrey, Caroline, and David Sneath, eds.
1996 Culture and Environment in Inner Asia. 2 vols. Volume 1: The Pastoral Economy and Environment. Volume II: Society and Culture. Cambridge: White Horse Press.

Humphrey, Caroline, and Ruth Mandel
2002 The Market in Everyday Life. *In* Markets and Moralities: Ethnographies of Postsocialism. Ruth Mandel and Caroline Humphrey, eds. Pp. 1–18. Oxford: Berg.

Hutton, Ronald
2001 Shamans: Siberian Spirituality and the Western Imagination. London: Hambledon and London.

Ichinnorov, S.
2003 The Shadow-Stricken Years [Suuder dairsan jiluud]. Ulaanbaatar: State Standard Publishing House.

Jing, Jun
1996 The Temple of Memories: History, Power, and Morality in a Chinese Village. Stanford, CA: Stanford University Press.

Kaplonski, Christopher
1999 Blame, Guilt and Avoidance: The Struggle to Control the Past in Post-Socialist Mongolia. History and Memory 11(2):94–114.

2002 Thirty Thousand Bullets: Remembering Political Repression in Mongolia. *In* Historical Injustice and Democratic Transition in Eastern Asia and Northern Europe: Ghosts at the Table of Democracy. Kenneth Christie and Robert Cribb, eds. Pp. 155–168. London: Routledge Curzon.

2004 Truth, History and Politics in Mongolia: Memory of Heroes. London and New York: RoutledgeCurzon.

2008a Neither Truth nor Reconciliation: Political Violence and the Surfeit of Memory in Post-Socialist Mongolia. Totalitarian Movements and Political Religions 9(2):371–388.

2008b Prelude to Violence: Show Trials and State Power in 1930s Mongolia. *American Ethnologist* 35(2):321–337.

2011 Archived Relations: Repression, Rehabilitation and the Secret Life of Documents in Mongolia. The Political Life of Documents, special issue, History and Anthropology 22(4):431–444.

2012 Resorting to Violence: Technologies of Exception, Contingent states, and the Repression of Buddhist Lamas in 1930s Mongolia. Ethnos 77(1):72–92.

In press The Question of the Lamas: Violence, Sovereignty, and Exception in Early Socialist Mongolia. University of Hawaii Press.

Kendall, Laurel

1985 Korean Shamans and the Spirit of Capitalism. American Anthropologist 98(3):517–527.

1988 Life and Hard Times of a Korean Shaman: Of Tales and the Telling of Tales. University of Hawaii Press.

2003 Gods, Markets, and the IMF in the Korean Spirit World. *In* Transparency and Conspiracy: Ethnographies of Suspicion in the New World Order. Harry G. West and Todd Sanders, eds. Pp. 38–65. Durham, NC: Duke University Press.

2009 Shamans, Nostalgias, and the IMF: South Korean Popular Religion in Motion. Honolulu: University of Hawai'i Press.

Klein, Norman M.

1997 The History of Forgetting: Los Angeles and the Erasure of Memory. New York: Verso.

Kleinman, Arthur

1988 The Illness Narratives: Suffering, Healing, and the Human Condition. Basic Books.

Kleinman, Arthur, ed.

1996 Social Suffering, special issue, Daedalus 125(1).

Kligman, Gail

1998 The Politics of Duplicity: Controlling Reproduction in Ceausescu's Romania. Berkeley and Los Angeles: University of California Press.

Kojima, Yukiko

1995 Women in Development: Mongolia. Country Briefing Paper, Asian Development Bank, Programs Department (East). Printed by the Asian Development Bank.

Konagaya, Yuki

2002 A People Divided: Buryat Mongols in Russia, Mongolia and China. Mongolian Culture Studies 4. Cologne: International Society for the Study of the Culture and Economy of the Ordos Mongols.

Kotkin, Stephen

1995 Magnetic Mountain: Stalinism as a Civilization. Berkeley and Los Angeles: University of California Press.

1999 Introduction: In Search of the Mongols and Mongolia; A Multinational Odyssey. *In* Mongolia and the Mongols: Landlocked Cosmopolitan. Stephen Kotkin and Bruce A. Elleman, eds. Pp. 3–27. Armonk. NY: M. E. Sharpe.

Kotkin, Stephen, and David Wolff, eds.

1995 Rediscovering Russia in Asia: Siberia and the Russian Far East. Armonk, NY: M. E. Sharpe.

Kramarae, Cheris
   1981   Women and Men Speaking: Frameworks for Analysis. Rowley, MA: Newbury House.
Krausse, Alexis Sidney
   1899   Russia in Asia: A Record and a Study, 1558–1899. New York: Henry Holt.
Lambek, Michael
   1988   Spirit Possession/Spirit Succession: Aspects of Social Continuity among Malagasy Speakers in Mayoette. American Ethnologist 15(4):710–731.
   1998   The Sakalava Poiesis of History: Realizing the Past through Spirit Possession in Madagascar. American Ethnologist 25(2):106–127.
   2002   The Weight of the Past: Living with History in Mahajanga, Madagascar. New York: Palgrave Macmillan.
Lan, David
   1985   Guns and Rain: Guerrillas and Spirit Mediums in Zimbabwe. Berkeley and Los Angeles: University of California Press.
Lewis, I. M.
   1971   Ecstatic Religion: An Anthropological Study of Spirit Possession and Shamanism. Harmondsworth, UK: Penguin.
   1986   Religion in Context: Cults and Charisma. Cambridge: Cambridge University Press.
   1989   Ecstatic Religion: A Study of Spirit Possession and Shamanism. 2nd edition. London: Routledge.
Lindquist, Galina
   2002   Spirits and Souls of Business: New Russians, Magic and the Esthetics of Kitsch. Journal of Material Culture 7(3):329–343.
Ludt, Christian J., Wolf Schroeder, Oswald Rottmann, and Ralph Kuehn
   2004   Mitochondrial DNA Phylogeography of Red Deer (Cervus elaphus). Molecular Phylogenetics and Evolution 31(3): 1064–1083.
Lutz, Catherine
   1990   Erasure of Women's Writing in Sociocultural Anthropology. American Ethnologist 17(4):611–624.
Maiskii, I. M.
   1959   Mongolia before the Revolution [Mongolia nakanune revolutsii]. Moscow: Izdatel'stvo Vostochnoi Literatury.
Malkki, Luisa
   1995   Purity and Exile: Violence, Memory, and National Cosmology among Hutu Refugees in Tanzania. Chicago and London: University of Chicago Press.
Mauss, Marcel
   1967   Gift: Forms and Functions of Exchange in Archaic Societies. New York: Norton.
Mbembe, Achille
   1992   On the Postcolony. Berkeley and Los Angeles. University of California Press.
McGranahan, Carole
   2010   Arrested Histories: Tibet, the CIA, and Memories of a Forgotten War. Durham, NC: Duke University Press.
Mead, Rebecca
   1999   Letter from Mongolia: The Crisis in Cashmere—How a Very Soft Wool Reflects a Revolution in the Global Economy. New Yorker, 1 February: 56–63.

Meilassoux, Claude
   1975   Maidens, Meal and Money: Capitalism and the Domestic Community. Cambridge: Cambridge University Press.
Meyers, Bridgit, and Peter Pels
   2003   Magic and Modernity: Interfaces of Revelation and Concealment. Stanford: Stanford University Press.
Mikhailov, T. M.
   1980   Some History of the Buryat Shamanism: From the Distant Past to the 18th Century [Iz istorii buriatskogo shamanizma: s drevneishikh vremen po XVIII v]. Novosibirsk: Izd-vo Nauka, Sibirskoe Otd-nie.
   1987   Buryat Shamanism: History, Structure, and Social Functions [Buriatskii shamanizm: istoriia, struktura i sotsial'nye funktsii]. Novosibirsk: Izd-vo Nauka, Sibirskoe Otd-nie.
Minis, A.
   1963   The Struggle of the Mongolian People's Revolutionary Party to Destroy the Political and Economic Domination of the Feudal Class [MAHN-aas feodal angiin uls tor, ediin zasgiin noyorholiig ustgahin toloo yavuulsan temtsel]. Ulaanbaatar: Institute of MPRP History of the Central Committee of MPRP.
   1972   The Struggle of the Mongolian People's Revolutionary Party to Destroy and Abolish the Economic Power of the Buddhist Clergy [MAHN-aas sym hiid, lam narin ediin zasgiin huchin chadliig evdej ustgahin toloo yavuulsan temtsel]. Ulaanbaatar: State Printing House.
Misztal, Barbara A.
   2003   Theories of Social Remembering. Maidenhead, Berkshire, UK: Open University Press.
   2005   Memory and Democracy. Sociology of Memory, special issue, American Behavioral Scientist 48(10):1320–1338.
   2009   Collective Memory in a Global Age: Learning How and What to Remember. Current Sociology 58(1):2–22.
Mongolian People's Revolutionary Party
   1985   A Short History of the Mongolian People's Revolutionary Party [MAHN tovch tuukh]. Ulaanbaatar: Institute of History of the MPRP.
Morgan, David
   1987   The Mongols. New York: Basil Blackwell.
Moore, Henrietta, and Todd Sanders, eds.
   2004   Magical Interpretations, Material Realities: Modernity, Witchcraft and the Occult in Postcolonial Africa. New York: Routledge.
Morris, Rosalind C.
   2000   In the Place of Origins: Modernity and Its Mediums in Northern Thailand. Durham, NC: Duke University Press.
Mote, Victor L.
   1998   Siberia: Worlds Apart. Boulder, CO: Westview Press.
Mueggler, Erik
   2001   The Age of Wild Ghosts: Memory, Violence, and Place in Southwest China. Berkeley and Los Angeles: University of California Press.
Murphy, George
   1966   Soviet Mongolia: A Study of the Oldest Political Satellite. Berkeley and Los Angeles: University of California Press.

Myagmarjav, B., and Ts. Navagchamba
   2000   Prosecuted Destiny, volume 17 [Helmegdsen zaya.17]. Ulaanbaatar. Union of
          the Victims of Political Repression.
Nash, June
   1993   We Eat the Mines and the Mines Eat Us: Dependency and Exploitation in Bo-
          livian Tin Mines. Rev. edition. New York: Columbia University Press.
Natsagdorj, Sh.
   1963   The History of Khalkha under the Manchus (1691–1911) [Manjiin erkhsheeld
          baisan üyeiin Khalkhyn khurangui tüükh (1691–1911)]. Ulaanbaatar: State
          Publishing House.
Natsov, G.-D.
   1995   Materials on Buryat History [Materialy po istorii i kul'ture Buriat]. Ulan-Ude:
          BNTSSO RAN.
Nietzsche, Friedrich
   1983   .Untimely Meditations. Cambridge: Cambridge University Press.
Nimaev, D. D.
   1983   Ethnic, Historical, and Cultural Connections among Mongol Groups [Eth-
          nicheskier i istoriiko-kul'turnye svi'a'zi Mongol'skikh narodov]. Ulan-Ude:
          Buriatskii Filial.
   1988   Problems in Ethnogenesis of the Buriats [Problemy etnogeneza Buriat]. No-
          vosibirsk: Izd-vo Nauka, Sibirskoe Otd-nie.
Nora, Pierre
   1989   Between Memory and History: Les Lieux de Memoire. Representations 26
          (Spring):7–25.
Okladnikov, A. P.
   1937   Historical Narratives of Barguzin Buriat Mongols in the 17th–18th Centuries
          [Ocherki iz istorii Barguzinskikh Buriat-Mongolov v 17–18 vekakh]. Lenin-
          grad: Sotsekgiz.
   1976   History and Culture of Buriatia [Istoriia i kul'tura Buriatii]. Sbornik statei.
          Ulan-Ude: Izdvo Buriatskoye knizj.
   1979   The Discovery of Siberia [Otkrytie Sibiri]. Moscow: Molodaia Gvardiia.
Okladnikov, A. P., and Sh. Bira, eds.
   1983   History of the Mongolian People's Republic [Istoriia Mongolskoi Narodnoi
          Respubliki]. Moscow: Izdatel'stvo Nauka.
Ölziibaatar, Dembereliin
   2004   Why 1937? [Yagaad 1937 on?]. Ulaanbaatar: Undesni Arkhivin Khevleh Kheseg.
Ong, Aihwa
   1987   Spirits of Resistance and Capitalist Discipline: Factory Women in Malaysia.
          Albany: State University of New York Press.
Ortner, Sherry
   1984   Theory in Anthropology since the Sixties. Comparative Studies in Society and
          History 26(1):126–166.
   1989–90   Gender Hegemonies. Cultural Critique 14 (Winter): 35–80.
   1995   Resistance and the Problem of Ethnographic Refusal. Comparative Studies in
          Society and History 37(1):173–193.
Osborn, Peter, and Andrew Benjamin, eds.
   2000   Walter Benjamin's Philosophy: Destruction and Experience. 2nd edition.
          Manchester: Clinamen Press.

Parry, Jonathan, and Maurice Bloch, eds.
    1989   Money and the Morality of Exchange. Cambridge: Cambridge University Press.

Passerini, Luisa
    2003   Memories between Silence and Oblivion. *In* Contested Pasts: The Politics of Memory. Pp. 238–255. London: Routledge.

Paxson, Heather
    2004   Making Modern Mothers: Ethics and Family Planning in Urban Greece. Berkeley and Los Angeles: University of California Press.

Pedersen, Morten Axel
    2011   Not Quite Shamans: Spirit Worlds and Political Lives in Northern Mongolia. Ithaca and London: Cornell University Press.

Perdue, Peter C.
    2005   China Marches West: The Qing Conquest of Central Eurasia. Cambridge, MA: The Belknap Press of Harvard University Press.

Pigg, Stacey Leigh
    1996   Credible and the Credulous: The Question of "Villagers' Beliefs" in Nepal. Cultural Anthropology 11(2):160–201.

Pincheon, Bill Standford
    2000   An Ethnography of Silences: Race, (Homo)sexualities, and a Discourse of Africa. African Studies Review 43(3):39–58.

Pomfret, John
    2000   Mongolia Beset by Cashmere Crisis: Herders, Mills Struggle in New Economy. Washington Post, 17 July: A1.

Potapov, L. P.
    1978   The Beliefs of the Buriats Prior to Lamaism [Do-lamaistskie verovaniia Buriat]. Novosibirsk: Izdatel'stvo Nauka.

Purevjav, S., and D. Dashj'amts
    1965   The Resolution Regarding Buddhist Clergy in the Mongolian People's Republic in 1921–1940 [BNMAU-d sum khiid lam nariin asuudliig shiidverlesen ni 1921–1940]. Ulaanbaatar: State Printing House.

Reed, John
    2002   Ten Days that Shook the World. Toronto: Penguin Group (Canada). Rehabilitation of 28,523 Citizens [Helmegdsen 28523 irgeniig tsagaatgajee]
    2003   Zuunii Medee, September 10, p. 2.

Ricoeur, Paul
    2004   Memory, History, Forgetting. Chicago: University of Chicago Press.

Rinchen Byambin
    1959   Les matériaux pour l'étude du chamanisme mongol. Wiesbaden: O. Harrassowitz.

Rinchin, Munhdalain
    2000   Political Accusations and Rehabilitation [Uls torin helmegdeluulelt ba tsagaatgal]. Ulaanbaatar: Center for Political Rehabilitation.

Roshin, S. K.
    2005   Choibalsan Kh., The Marshal of Mongolia: Biographical Remarks [Marshal Mongolii Kh. Choibalsan: shtrihi biographii]. Moscow: Institute Vostokovedenia.

Rossabi, Morris
    2001   Sino-Mongol Relations, 1986–2000: A Mongol Perspective. Unpublished MS, Queens College and Columbia University.

2005   Modern Mongolia: From Khans to Commissars to Capitalists. Berkeley and Los Angeles: University of California Press.

Rumyantsev, G. N.

1962   The Emergence of the Khori Buriats [Proiskhozhdenie Khorinskikh Buriat]. Ulan-Ude: Buriatskoe knizhnoe izd-vo.

Rupen, Robert

1964   Mongols of the Twentieth Century. Bloomington: Indiana University Press.

1979   How Mongolia Is Really Ruled: A Political History of the Mongolian People's Republic, 1900–1978. Stanford, CA: Hoover Institution Press.

Sachs, Jeffrey

1994   Shock Therapy in Poland: Perspectives of Five Years. The Tanner Lectures on Human Values. Paper given at the University of Utah. http://tannerlectures. utah.edu/lectures/documents/sachs95.pdf (accessed January 30, 2013).

2000   "Commanding Heights," PBS interview. http://www.pbs.org/wgbh/commanding heights/shared/minitextlo/ufd_shocktherapy_full.html (accessed January 30, 2013).

Sahlins, Marshall

1972   Stone Age Economics. New York: Aldine

Sambuu, J.

1961   Religion and the Issues of Lamas [Shashin ba lam narin asuudal]. Ulaanbaatar: State Publishing House.

Sandag, Shagdariin, and Harry H. Kendall

2000   Poisoned Arrows: The Stalin-Choibalsan Mongolian Massacres, 1921–1941. Boulder, CO: Westview Press.

Sanders, Alan

1974   Mongolia: From Sambuu to Tsedenbal. Asian Survey 16(11):971–984.

1987   Mongolia: Politics, Economics and Society. London: Frances Printer.

1991   Restructuring and "Openness." In Mongolia Today. Shirin Akiner, ed. Pp. 57–58. London: Kegan Paul.

1992   Mongolia's New Constitution: Blueprint for Democracy. Asian Survey 32(6): 506–520.

Sanj Purevin, and Bold Budin

2006   The Tsunami of Persecutions [Khelmegduuleltin tsunami]. Ulaanbaatar: Admon Printing.

Schudson, Michael

1992   Watergate in American Memory: How We Remember, Forget, and Reconstruct the Past. New York: Basic Books.

Scott, James

1985   Weapons of the Weak: Everyday Forms of Peasant Resistance. New Haven, CT: Yale University Press.

1990   Domination and the Arts of Resistance: Hidden Transcripts. New Haven, CT: Yale University Press.

Scott, James M., ed.

1998   After the End: Making U.S. Foreign Policy in the Post–Cold War World. Durham, NC: Duke University Press.

Shirendyv, B.

1968   By-Passing Capitalism. Ulaanbaatar: State Publishing House.

Shirendyv, B., and Sh. Natsagdorj, eds.
  1956–1969   History of the Mongolian People's Republic [Bugd Nairamdah Mongol
      Ard Ulsin tuukh]. 3 vols. Ulaanbaatar: State Printing House.
Siegel, James
  2006   Naming the Witch. Stanford, CA: Stanford University Press.
Smith, Robert
  1970   Mongolia: In the Soviet Camp. Asian Survey 10(1):25–29.
Sneath, David
  1993   Social Relations, Networks and Social Organization in Post-Socialist Rural
      Mongolia. Nomadic Peoples 33:193–207.
  1999   Mobility, Technology and Decollectivisation of Pastoralism in Mongolia. In
      Mongolia in the Twentieth Century: Landlocked Cosmopolitan. S. Kotkin
      and B. Elleman, eds. Pp. 223–23. Armonk, NY: M. E. Sharpe.
  2001   Notions of Rights over Land and the History of Mongolian Pastoralism. Inner
      Asia 3(1):41–59.
  2002   Mongolia in the "Age of the Market": Pastoral Land-Use and the Develop-
      ment Discourse. In Markets and Moralities: Ethnographies of Postsocialism.
      Ruth Mandel and Caroline Humphrey, eds. Pp. 191–210. London: Routledge.
  2004   Proprietary Regimes and Sociotechnical Systems: Rights over Land in Mon-
      golia's "Age of the Market." In Property in Question: Value Transformation
      in the Global Economy. Katherine Verdery and Caroline Humphrey, eds.
      Pp. 161–182. Oxford: Berg.
Ssorin-Chaikov, Nikolai V.
  2003   The Social Life of the State in Subarctic Siberia. Stanford, CA: Stanford Uni-
      versity Press.
Steedly, Mary Margaret
  1993   Hanging without a Rope: Narrative Experience in Colonial and Post-Colonial
      Karoland. Princeton, NJ: Princeton University Press.
  2000   Modernity and the Memory Artist: The Work of Memory in Highland Suma-
      tra, 1947–1995. Comparative Studies in Society and History 43(4):811–846.
Stoller, Paul
  1989   Fusion of the Worlds: An Ethnography of Possession among the Songhay of
      Niger. Chicago: University of Chicago Press.
  1995   Embodying Colonial Memories: Spirit Possession, Power, and the Hauka in
      West Africa. New York: Routledge.
Stoller, Paul, and Cheryl Olkes
  1987   In Sorcery's Shadow: A Memoir of Apprenticeship among the Songhay of Ni-
      ger. Chicago: University of Chicago Press.
Sumyabaatar
  1966   From the Genealogical Records of the Buriats [Buriadin ugin bichgees]. Ulaan-
      baatar: Academy of Science Press.
Swancutt, Katherine
  2008   The Undead Genealogy: Omnipresence, Spirit Perspectives, and a Case of
      Mongolian Vampirism. Journal of the Royal Anthropological Institute, n.s.,
      14:843–864.
Tambiah, Stanley
  1977   World Conqueror and World Renouncer: A Study of Buddhism and Polity in
      Thailand against a Historical Background. Cambridge: Cambridge University
      Press.

1984   The Buddhist Saint of the Forest and the Cult of Amulets: A Study in Cha-
       risma, Hagiography, Sectarianism, and Millennial Buddhism. Cambridge:
       Cambridge University Press.
1985   A Performative Approach to Ritual. London: British Academy.
1990   Magic, Science, Religion, and the Scope of Rationality. New York: Cambridge
       University Press.
1991   The Charisma of Saints and the Cults of Relics, Amulets and Shrines. Daryll T.
       Forde Memorial Lecture, University College London, November 14.
2007 [1977]   Buddhism and Spirit Cults in North-East Thailand. Cambridge: Cam-
       bridge University Press.

Taussig, Michael
1980   The Devil and Commodity Fetishism in South America. Chapel Hill: Univer-
       sity of North Carolina Press
1987   Shamanism, Colonialism, and the Wild Man: A Study in Terror and Healing.
       Chicago: University of Chicago Press.
1992   The Magic of the State. Public Culture 5(1):63–66.
1993   Mimesis and Alterity: A Particular History of the Senses. New York: Routledge.
1997   The Magic of the State. New York and London: Routledge.

Taylor, Charles
1989   Sources of the Self: The Making of the Modern Identity. New York: Cambridge
       University Press.

Tedlock, Barbara
2005   The Woman in the Shaman's Body: Reclaiming the Feminine in Religion and
       Medicine. New York: Bantam Books.

Thomas, Nicolas, and Caroline Humphrey
1996   Introduction. In Shamanism, History, and the State. Nicolas Thomas and Car-
       oline Humphrey, eds. Pp. 1–13. Ann Arbor: University of Michigan Press.

Tilly, Charles
1975   Reflections on the History of European State-Making. In The Formation of
       National States in Western Europe. Pp. 601–638. Princeton, NJ: Princeton
       Univeristy Press.

Trouillot, Michel-Rolph
1995   Silencing the Past: Power and the Production of History. Boston, MA: Beacon
       Press.

Tseren, Tsedevin
2008   The Buryat Displacement: How They Were Associated with the So-Called
       Lhumbe Affiar and Persecuted [Buryaduudin durvelt: "Lhumbin hereg"
       gegchid tedniig holbogdduulan helmegduulsen ni]. Ulaanbaatar: OB Press.

Tserendulam, Genden
2000   P. Genden: To the Memory of My Father. Ulaanbaatar: Admon Printing
       Company.

Tsibiktarov, A. D.
2001   Buriatia in the Past: The History from the Ancient Period to the 17th Century
       [Buriatiia v drevnosti: istoriia s drevneishikh vremen do XVII veka]. Ulan-
       Ude: Izdatel'stvo Buryatskogo Gosuniversisteta.

Tsing, Anna Lowenhaupt
1990   Gender and Performance in Meratus Dispute Settlement. In Power and Dif-
       ference: Gender in Island Southeast Asia. Jane Monnig Atkinson and Shelly
       Errington, eds. Pp. 95–125. Stanford: Stanford University Press.

1993   In the Realm of the Diamond Queen. Princeton, NJ: Princeton University Press.

1994   From the Margins. Cultural Anthropology 9(3):279–297.

Urbana'eva, Irina, ed.

1996   Central-Asian Shamanism: Philosophical, Religious, Ecological Aspects. Ulan-Ude: Russian Academy of Sciences, Siberian Division.

Vansina, Jan

1985   Oral Tradition and History. Madison: University of Wisconsin Press.

Verdery, Katherine

1991   Theorizing Socialism: A Prologue to the "Transition." American Ethnology 18(3):419–439.

1993   Ethnic Relations, Economics of Shortage, and the Transition in Eastern Europe. In Socialism: Ideals, Ideologies, and Local Practice. C. M. Hann, ed. Pp. 172–86. London: Routledge.

1996   What Was Socialism and What Comes Next? Princeton, NJ: Princeton University Press.

1999   Fuzzy Property: Rights, Power, and Identity in Transylvania's Decollectivization. In Uncertain Transition: Ethnographies of Change in the Postsocialist World. Michael Burawoy and Katherine Verdery, eds. Pp. 53–81. Lanham, MD: Rowman & Littlefield.

2004   The Obligations of Ownership: Restoring Rights to Land in Postsocialist Transylvania. In Property in Question: Value Transformation in the Global Economy. Katherine Verdery and Caroline Humphrey, eds. Pp. 139–161. Oxford: Berg.

Verdery, Katherine, and Caroline Humphrey, eds.

2004   Property in Question: Value Transformation in the Global Economy. Oxford: Berg.

Vivian, Bradford

2010   Public Forgetting: The Rhetoric and Politics of Beginning Again. University Park: Penn State University Press.

Vidal-Naquet, Pierre

1992   Assassins of Memory: Essays on the Denial of the Holocaust. New York: Columbia University Press.

Vitebsky, Piers

1995   From Cosmology to Environmentalism: Shamanism as Local Knowledge in a Global Setting. In Counterworks: Managing the Diversity of Knowledge. Richard Fardon, ed. Pp. 172–192. London: Routledge.

2001 [1995]   Shamanism. Norman: University of Oklahoma Press.

2005   The Reindeer People: Living with Animals and Spirits in Siberia. London: HarperCollins.

Watson, Rubie

1986   The Named and Nameless: Gender and Person in Chinese Society. American Ethnologist 13(4):619–631.

Watson, Rubie, ed.

1994   Memory, History, and Opposition under State Socialism. Santa Fe, NM: School of American Research Press.

Weber, Max

1946   From Max Weber: Essays in Sociology. Oxford: Oxford University Press.

1958   The Protestant Ethic and the Spirit of Capitalism. New York: Charles Scribner's Sons.

Weidlich, Mary
  1981   Mongolia in 1980: A Year of Adjustments and Resolves. Asian Survey 21(1):
          63–69.
Weller, Robert
  1994   Capitalism, Community, and the Rise of Moral Cults in Taiwan. *In* Asian Vi-
          sions of Authority: Religion and Modern States of East and South-East Asia.
          Charles Keyes, Laurel Kendall, and Helen Hardcare, eds. Pp. 141–164. Hono-
          lulu: University of Hawai'i Press.
West, Harry G., and Todd Sanders, eds.
  2003   Transparency and Conspiracy: Ethnographies of Suspicion in the New World
          Order. Durham, NC: Duke University Press.
Wheeler, Alan
  2004   Moralities of the Mongolian "Market": A Genealogy of Trade Relations and
          the Zah Zeel. Inner Asia 6(2):215–238.
Wolf, Margery
  1985   Revolution Postponed: Women in Contemporary China. Stanford: Stanford
          University Press.
Wood, Alan, ed.
  1991   The History of Siberia: From Russian Conquest to Revolution. London:
          Routledge.
Yanagisako, Sylvia, and Jane Collier
  1987   Toward a Unified Analysis of Gender and Kinship. *In* Gender and Kinship:
          Essays toward a Unified Analysis. Sylvia Yanagisako and Jane Collier, eds.
          Pp. 14–53. Stanford, CA: Stanford University Press.
Yang, Meifair Mei-hui
  2000   Putting Global Capitalism in Its Place: Economic Hybridity, Bataille, and Rit-
          ual Expenditure. Current Anthropology 41(4):477–509.
Young, James Edward
  1992   The Texture of Memory: Holocaust Memorials and Meaning. New Haven, CT:
          Yale University Press.
Yurchak, Alexei
  2006   Everything Was Forever, Until It Was No More: The Last Soviet Generation.
          Princeton, NJ: Princeton University Press.
Zhukovskaya, Natalia L.
  1991   Buddhism in the History of Mongols and Buriads: Political and Cultural As-
          pects. *In* Rulers from the Steppe: State Formation on the Eurasian Periphery.
          Gary Seaman and Daniel Marks, eds. Pp. 242–254. Los Angeles: Ethnograph-
          ics Press.
  1995   Religion and Ethnicity in Eastern Russia, Republic of Buryatia: A Panorama of
          the 1990s. Central Asian Survey 14(1):25–42.
Znamenski, Andrei A.
  1999   Shamanism and Christianity: Native Encounters with Russian Orthodox Mis-
          sions in Siberia and Alaska, 1820–1917. Westport, CT: Greenwood Press.

INDEX

Page references followed by f denote figures. References to endnotes give the endnote page number followed by n, the note number, and the text page of endnote citation in parentheses.

abortions, 177, 181, 277n4 (177)
Agamben, Giorgio, 47
agency, 69; political, 136; of shamanic
    clients, 204; shaman's, 182; of spirits,
    13, 14; of the state, 74, 95
agriculture, 54, 106–7, 109, 113
albin (spirits), 232, 238
Altan Khan, 42
Amar (grandfather of Baasan), 253–60, 261f
Amgalan, Dagdangiin, 89–90
ancestor, 1, 4, 20, 21, 41, 46
ancestral death pollution, 247, 250
Appadurai, Arjun, 70
Arin Arvan Gurvan Noyod (the Thirteen
    Lords of the North), 45
arrow, 43, 55
Ashforth, Adam, 7–8, 125
Asian Development Bank, 7, 10
assimilation, cultural, 47
Association of Political Victims, 95
assumption, 125, 275; of gender, 136, 229;
    of malice, 127, 129
Atkinson, Jane, 16, 27, 31, 170
Atwood, Christopher P., 271, 275
audience(s) (shamanic), 7, 8, 16–19, 23,
    26–32, 36, 41, 46, 62–65, 77, 125,
    132–35, 142, 147, 154–61, 167,
    188–89, 191, 200–201, 203–7, 213,
    219, 221, 223, 225, 227, 229, 254,
    274, 280

Baasan (physics teacher), 233–66;
    Baigal and, 160; brother (Bat), 233,
    235–46; death of brother, 233,
    235–36, 240–45, 250; finding sha-
    manic errors, 240–44; genealogy of,
    233–35, 238, 256–62, 261f; health
    of, 237, 265; Ichin Choinhor temple
    divinations, 247–48, 250; memory
    of her father and grandmother,
    252–54; old female spirit and, 245;
    Otgon and Amar (ancestors/*uheer*),
    253–64, 261f; state institutions and,
    264–65; on Tömör, 208; *uheer* and,
    253–55
Baigal (shaman; granddaughter of
    Khorlo), 132, 151–53, 155–61,
    164–66, 264
Baikal (lake), 22, 23, 32, 42–43, 48, 221,
    230, 268
Baljima (origin spirit), 212–13
Banzarov, Dorji (Buryat scholar), 28
Barga Mongols, 117
barter and exchange, 108
Bat (brother of Baasan), 235–46; death of,
    233, 235–36, 240–45, 250; employ-
    ment of, 237; Golden Box, 236, 242,
    246–47; initiation as shaman, 236,
    242–44; visions by, 238, 239
Bataille, Georges, 12
Baudrillard, Jean, 12